"With Constant Light"

The Collected Essays and Reviews,
with Selections from the Diaries, Letters,
and Other Prose of John Martin Finlay
(1941–1991)

Edited by David Middleton & John P. Doucet

Wiseblood Books

Printed in the United States of America

Set in Baskerville Typesetting

Cover Illustration by Sharon Doucet

Book Design by L. Maltese

ISBN-13: 978-0-9915832-2-5

Essay / Literary

Wiseblood Books
Belmont, North Carolina
www.wisebloodbooks.com

John Finlay, in his late thirties or early forties, with Scotch and cigarette, in conversation, at a friend's home in Baton Rouge, Louisiana.

Acknowledgments

Some of the works by John Finlay included in this book first appeared in the following journals and on the following presses: Blue Heron Press; Cengage; *Comment*; *The Dictionary of Literary Biography*; *Explorations* (Maurice DuQuesnay, editor); *Hellas: A Journal of Poetry and the Humanities* (Gerald Harnett, editor); *The Hudson Review*; John Daniel and Company; *The Louisiana English Journal*; Louisiana State University Press; *PN Review* (Manchester, England); and *The Southern Review*.

Every effort has been made to identify and contact all possible copyright holders. For additional bibliographical data, the reader should consult the bibliography at the end of this volume.

Special Thanks

The John Finlay Literary Estate and the Finlay family, especially Finlay's surviving sisters, Betty Finlay Phillips and JoAnn Finlay Hall; Louisiana State University Libraries, Lower Mississippi Valley Special Collections, The John Finlay Papers; Special Collections, W.S. Hoole Special Collections Library, University of Alabama at Tuscaloosa; Stephen Utz; David Simpson, for the essay by his father, Lewis P. Simpson; Stella Nesanovich; Glenn Bergeron; Cathy Edmonston; Madison Kiger, student research assistant; and especially Angela Cybulski, Managing Editor, Wiseblood Books.

in memory of John Finlay's grandmothers

Mattie Coston Finlay

and

Toxey Ard Sorrell

as well as

great-grandmother Granny Coston

and

Annie Laurie Cullens, loving family friend of the Finlays

To live in the world of creation—to get into it and stay in it—to frequent it and haunt it—to think intensely and fruitfully—to woo combinations and inspirations into being by a depth and continuity of attention and meditation—this is the only thing.[1]

—Henry James

In Advent

You know the flesh and soul's profoundest night
Marked out by that Thomistic intellect
Whose terms, now as ever, lead you to expect
To find in utter darkness utmost light.

—David Middleton, epigraph poem
in *A Garland for John Finlay* (1990)

On Rembrandt's Portrait of an Old Man Reading the Scriptures

Exposure salted his grave Northern face.
An unerasable sadness tinged that grace
Of sourceless light glowing on solid form.
Hard winter nights—the isolating storm—
His oil burned out onto the living word.
A man matured in loss, in griefs incurred
By love outside himself, he would expend
His mind on God, still opened to the end.

—John Finlay

CONTENTS

BOOK REVIEWS

SHORT STORY

OTHER PROSE

APPENDICES

NOTES

BIBLIOGRAPHY

THE JOHN FINLAY PAPERS

A RECOLLECTION

Preface

This edition of works in prose by Alabama poet, scholar, and critic John Martin Finlay (1941–1991) brings together for the first time all of Finlay's essays and book reviews, a short story, statements about poetics, and other prose writings including selections from Finlay's letters and diaries. Two of the four appendices—one by Lewis P. Simpson and one by David Middleton—put into historical context, and the context of Finlay's own life, the essays that make up his posthumously published book on Gnosticism and Modernity. For this Wiseblood Books edition, these essays have been re-edited and the original title of the book has been restored: *Flaubert in Egypt and Other Essays*. An updated bibliography of works by and about Finlay will be found at the end of this volume.[1]

Following the line of argument in the essay "Mere Literature and the Lost Traveller" by Allen Tate (1899–1979)—fellow southerner, poet-critic, and convert to Roman Catholicism—Finlay searched for, detected, and then subjected to an analysis both passionate and dispassionate certain Gnostic beliefs concerning the relationship between God (as the detached and absent *Deus absconditus*), the human mind, and the natural world. Finlay discovered this sometimes-hidden presence of Gnosticism not only in self-consciously modern writers such as Flaubert, Valéry, Nietzsche, Freud, and Kafka, but even in some of the theological writings of Cardinal John Henry Newman and in the poetry of the poet-priest Gerard Manley Hopkins. At the same time, Finlay, was confronting such Gnostic demons in his own life and mind.

That life and mind were deeply divided. The title that Finlay chose for his posthumously published collected poems—*Mind and Blood*—indicates the nature of this division. Finlay could be irrationally drawn toward Gnostic beliefs and acts in his personal life (blood) while at the same time being able, rationally (mind), and by way of his Christian faith, to condemn these same beliefs and acts. On some level, almost all of Finlay's writings, however seemingly objective, are autobiographical. Taken together, they tell the story of an heroic spiritual struggle that was won in Finlay's writings and in his Roman Catholic faith but that may be said to have cost him his life at just barely fifty.

John Finlay was raised in the Southern Baptist church in southern Alabama. However, of all of the members of his immediate family, only Finlay would not consent to be baptized into that denomination, of which he did not feel a part.

During his junior year at the University of Alabama, Tuscaloosa (c. 1961–62), Finlay became a member of the Episcopal Church. Finlay remained an Episcopalian until 1980 when he converted to Roman Catholicism during his graduate school years at Louisiana State University in Baton Rouge. Finlay was formally received into the Catholic Church at Easter of 1980. (With characteristic dramatic flare, Finlay told some of his friends that he had had a dream in which St. Thomas More appeared to him, holding his own decapitated head at arm's length, the head telling Finlay that he should convert to Roman Catholicism.)

As best can be recalled by family members after all these years, Finlay left the Episcopal Church following the introduction of the 1979 *Book of Common Prayer* with its contemporary language and theology, including its changing the words "visible" and "invisible" to "seen" and "unseen" in a translation of The Nicene Creed. Finlay felt strongly that the new wording opened the door to false understanding because what may be "unseen"—the Cathedral of Notre-Dame in Paris from a farm in Enterprise, Alabama, for example—is not "invisible."

Finlay stated that his major reasons for converting to Rome were his commitment to the Aristotelian-Thomistic understanding of the ordered, loving relationship between God, the human mind, and the created world; the force of the Petrine argument; and the complete assurance of the forgiveness of sins and the promise of salvation that Finlay had come to believe was to be found in its fullness only in the Catholic Church. As Finlay wrote in a diary entry in 1980 about attending Mass, "The health of the body, or rather the acceptance of the body, is an essential part of the moral life. Soul, body, and mind have to be in harmony with each other and with themselves, apart from the others. Benediction after Mass moved me profoundly—the element of adoration, almost of an impersonal or supra-rational nature, is so absent today and yet still such a need of human nature, that when it does happen, such relief is experienced."[2]

Yet Finlay was still self-divided. Even during the time of instruction prior to conversion, he complained that the old priest who served as his spiritual director had told him that his intellectual assent to the arguments and proofs of Aquinas (mind) was not enough. He also had to feel in his heart (blood) that conversion was the right thing for him to do. Finlay was initially outraged by the old priest's wise counsel.

This mind-blood division can be seen in Finlay's prose. In his essay on Newman, Finlay expresses his Aristotelian-Thomistic beliefs with precision: "He [Newman] converted to a church that adhered to the philosophical doctrine that the intellect possesses certain dogmatic powers given to it by God at its creation. The higher mysteries, according to Catholic doctrine, are provided the mind by revelation, but the lower ones, such as the bare fact that God exists, are held to be comprehensible by the unaided intellect. Catholic doctrine also maintained that our reason is capable of arriving at the telos of human beings and so can work out a morality on its own. An enormous philosophical dignity is thus given the human mind by the Thomistic-Aristotelian system."[3]

Yet in his essay on Flaubert, Finlay imaginatively enters into, and terrifyingly evokes, a pre-Christian goddess as an expression of an ever-present tendency in our fallen human nature toward the Gnostic: "The same sky appears in *Salammbô*, presided over by the Carthaginian goddess Tanit, and the world under her lunar intensity is the same as the Egypt of [Flaubert's] *Letters*. . . . Her influence extends beyond fertility and growth to embrace insanity and death, all of which indifferently mean the same to her. Her eyes eat up the stones of buildings and animals go mad under her dark side. Nothing touches her in her remoteness and purity. Her detachment is beyond good and evil, and the peace she dispenses is obtained only after the nerves have been deadened and the mind washed out."[4]

Even more disturbingly, in his essay on Valéry, Finlay describes the final fate of the modern mind cut off in the end even from itself: "Descartes was the first systematically to isolate the mind and to use it as an instrument of absolute authority. He did so hoping to demolish the medieval synthesis that recognized various natural and supernatural authorities beyond the human intellect, and on the basis of the mind's own internal evidence he sought to prove the existence of God and to give a perfectly logical explanation of the world. Given the human craving for experiment, it was inevitable that someone like Valéry should eventually prolong the Cartesian retreat within the mind, to stay there, in fact, forgetting God and the world, and to set up intellectual consciousness as a God in itself. But he discovered the destruction of the mind locked into itself, its futility in attempting to know itself without the reflecting medium of an object that engages it. The mind feeds on itself, or abandons itself, in the philosophical loss of the world and of the body connecting it to the world. At the end of its inhuman abstraction it turns demonic inside its purity and commits intellectual suicide."[5]

Finlay described his analysis of the Gnostic spirit in modern writers as a "journey through hell" and said that he was going to clear his mind by reading poets like Chaucer and Dryden.[6] In fact, Finlay began instead what was to have been a second book of essays, on the fate of the pre-Christian Western mind, in this case using not Aquinas but Plato's Socrates as his measuring-rod. Finlay lived to complete two of these Greek essays and part of a third before illness forced him to stop writing.

Gathered together here for the first time, "The Night of Alcibiades," "The Socratics and the Flight from This World," and the unfinished (and previously unpublished) essay on Plato's *Crito*, show Finlay finding among the ancient Greeks problems similar to those he found in modern writers.[7] The complicated story of the relationship between Socrates and Alcibiades—another example of the tension between "mind" and "blood" in Finlay's own being—is so powerfully and dramatically told that when the essay appeared posthumously in *The Hudson Review* in 1994, the review's founding editor, Frederick Morgan, stated that he had gotten praise for this essay from readers "coast to coast" and added that in all his years as editor of the *Hudson* he had never had such a strong, positive, widespread reaction to an essay.[8]

Other writings by Finlay in this edition of his prose include an essay on English poet Elizabeth Daryush, book reviews, statements on poetics, a short story, and miscellaneous prose, letters, and diaries.

Finlay wrote seven book reviews, all of them on books either by or about modern British and American poets who wrote traditional metrical verse, as did Finlay. Finlay's comments on the poetry of English poet Dick Davis could be applied to Finlay's own verse: "Style and content are compatible in his mind; aesthetics and moral wisdom mutually enrich each other, as do the personal and the traditional. And the objectivity of his vision always presupposes the presence of the discrete human being, with his own complicating and peculiar history to be reckoned with, without whom such an objectivity would be impossible."[9]

To these comments may be added Finlay's Mary Roberts Rinehart Foundation application and "Notes for the Perfect Poem"—both included here—which, taken together, are a comprehensive statement of Finlay's poetics. As Jeffrey Goodman has said, the "'Notes for the Perfect Poem' stand as one of the genuinely revealing and fascinating documents of the Modern or Post-modern period."[10]

Finlay's single known short story, "The Up-There," a story of good and evil and the difficulty human beings have with leaving the final administration of justice to God, appeared in the University of Alabama literary magazine *Comment* in 1962 when Finlay was only 21. Given the age of the author, the story is remarkably mature.[11]

Finlay's letters to fellow writers, letters most often written from his family's farm in Alabama, reveal the life of a writer and thinker feeling isolated yet fulfilled—having time to write in rustic seclusion, but craving intellectual conversation with absent friends.[12] Growing up to be a poet on a farm in the South, Finlay, especially as a younger man, felt a deep affinity with the southern Fugitive poets and the broader group of southern Agrarian writers, some of whom—including Andrew Lytle and Allen Tate—he met and sometimes visited, as his earlier diaries indicate.

The diaries themselves—kept in Enterprise, in London, on Corfu, in Paris, in Tuscaloosa, and in Baton Rouge—are a record of Finlay's literary, intellectual, and spiritual concerns and struggles. Many of these entries have the polish of a well-crafted miniature essay or piece of poetic prose, like the entry on Finlay's reaction to the Impressionists in a museum in Paris: "The surrounding pattern of thick, bright blue-green colors, that remind me of liquid flames (whatever they would be), seems to be locking in and engulfing the face. A kind of total subjectivity is being suggested. And the frightened, quietly desperate quality in his eyes, the sense of neurotic inability to grasp and feed on tangible reality, or to make contact with another person, all this is a result of those thick swarms of paint that enclose the head. One way to get at what these painters were after is to notice what is not in any (or most) of their work: religion, man as a social being with certain obligations and responsibilities, human love, the human face, 'normally' represented and illuminated by character, knowledge, moral virtues or vices."[13]

In contrast, Finlay, in other diaries, describes the solid facts of rural life on an Alabama farm, including the nature of a beloved milk cow: "Her name was Red and of the many animals I knew in my childhood on the farm it is she that I still remember most vividly. We kept her for over ten years, during which time my brother and I took turns milking and feeding her in a barn my father had built especially for her. She had good blood in her and at the height of summer could give up to three or four gallons of milk a day. I can still feel the weight of the milk pail between my knees and see the thick foam of her milk falling sluggishly in the early morning light over its brim. But her most impressive feature was her horns. They were long and magnificent and the upward thrust of their sharp points made her majestic, primitive, and unapproachable, especially after she had sleeked and honed them on the bark of pine trees."[14]

Other diary entries on farm life may be taken as implied commentaries on modernity and on the general postlapsarian human condition: "We cut oats and wheat in June. I used to ride the combine and sack up the grain as it came through the chute. The combine shook, grumbled, [ground], roared in the scorching heat. It looked grotesque with all its complicated wheels and wheels within wheels turning with a rapidity that only increased its incredible complication. I remember how it cut evenly into the tall golden wheat, a thousand grasshoppers jumping out of its path. The chaff of the oats. The rattlesnakes that desperately jumped out of the oats and stood for one moment upright as they struck at the terrifying machine. They glittered in the sunlight. To ride the combine in the heat. The narcotic effect of it, the trance."[15]

In some of the later diary entries, Finlay strives to understand and confront what he calls (perhaps the two were one) his "demon" and a demanding, condemning, unforgiving, remote "father" figure reminiscent of the Gnostic *Deus absconditus*.[16] But against these beings Finlay, quoting St. Augustine, posits a loving God the Father who says, "I want you to be." This prolonged conflict was finally resolved only at the very end of Finlay's life when Finlay said to his mother, "Mama, God has finally taken my demon away from me."[17]

And at the close of his poem "The Black Earth," about the killing of a father in a dream—the father screaming as he dies—, Finlay strikingly presents the final triumph of goodness and the rational. The poem ends with the rational and the good (the sun) triumphant over evil and the irrational (the moon):

> The moon has risen white. The mirror clears
> Of darker fire. His voice now fades like pain
> A human takes, absorbs, and then survives.
> This moon itself will fade, whose cobalt glow
> The dawn soon strikes to almost nothingness.
> Throughout morning it will but faintly gleam
> There in the west, a disc of thin white bone,
> The center eaten through with constant light.[18]

And, at the point of death in Flowers Hospital in Dothan, Alabama, Finlay, by then blinded by disease, looked far off, as though seeing beyond this world, and, interrogatively, uttered in his last breath, "Plato?"[19] Some of those who knew Finlay best believe that he spoke this word to some guiding figure whom Finlay surely saw and thought possibly to be the spirit of Plato—perhaps a Christianized Plato—coming to receive and guide him, but who may well have been one greater than Plato, a divine being whom Finlay would have fully recognized only in passing through and beyond death.

In a letter to me of March 25, 2002, John's eldest sister, Betty, speaking on behalf of herself and John's mother, Jean Finlay, wrote the following:

"John asked that 1 Corinthians 13 be read at his funeral. He also asked that the song 'Humbly, Humbly, I Adore Thee' be sung. In fact, I was surprised that he considered having the song 'Just As I Am' sung. That's a Baptist song usually sung at the end of the service, when they ask for people to come forward and make a profession of faith. John had considered it because the words are beautiful, but decided against it because it was a 'Baptist' song.

"John was very quiet about his religious life and beliefs. He would answer a question if asked, but rarely said anything unless asked. When I decided to convert to Catholicism, again, he would only answer questions that I asked, or offer a book for me to read.

"John faced death with courage and faith. Father Meyer was the priest at the Catholic Church in Enterprise who came out to see John weekly, to hear his confession and give him the Holy Eucharist when John could no longer go to church. John told Father that he wanted to offer all his suffering to God in reparation for his sins, and John did suffer with such courage. His last poem, 'A Prayer to the Father,' was written after John could no longer see or write. He quoted it to me from his heart."[20]

In the spring of 1990, when Finlay knew that death was near, he composed in his head and then dictated that final poem, his death poem, "A Prayer to the Father," in which mind (thought) and blood (body) are finally reconciled, though also sundered, as the poet passes from this life to the life everlasting:

> Death is not far from me. At times I crave
> The peace I think that it will bring. Be brave,
> I tell myself, for soon your pain will cease.
> But terror still obtains when our long lease
> On life ends at last. Body and soul,
> Which fused together should make up one whole,
> Suffer deprived as they are wrenched apart.
> O God of love and power, hold still my heart
> When death, that ancient, awful fact appears;
> Preserve my mind from all deranging fears,
> And let me offer up my reason free
> And where I thought, there see Thee perfectly.[21]

In a letter to Lewis P. Simpson written several months after Finlay's passing, Jean Finlay spoke of her son's courage in facing death.

Dear Lewis Simpson,

I am at a loss for words to tell you how much your friendship and support of John during his terrible illness meant to John and us . . . The nurses in the hospital all loved him so . . . and that helped. They said in all their profession . . . they had never seen anybody accept death so calmly and die with such dignity. I never heard him complain although I saw him very frustrated at times. We all miss him so much, and I know I always will but he lives in my heart.

With best wishes and God Bless,

Jean Finlay[22]

David Middleton
January 2019

ESSAYS

The author's introduction and the six essays that make up *Flaubert in Egypt and Other Essays* were all written by Finlay during the 1980s, the final full decade of his life, most of which he spent in some degree of intellectual isolation on his family's farm in Enterprise, Alabama. Finlay died on February 17, 1991 with his book of essays completed but unpublished. The essays address the problem of the persistence of ancient Gnosticism in modern western culture and the threat of this Gnostic spirit to the classical-Christian tradition, especially the Aristotelian-Thomistic worldview. Two essays included here as Appendix A, "The Dark Rooms of John Finlay" by Lewis P. Simpson, and as Appendix B, "'The Deathless Word': John Finlay and the Triumph over Gnosticism" by David Middleton, put *Flaubert in Egypt and Other Essays* into the context of Finlay's life and thought. What is said in those two essays need not be repeated here.

Finlay's essays on the Gnostic spirit in modernity are published in the order in which Finlay assembled them, as a book, at some point in the late 1980s, and, for the first time, they are being presented under Finlay's original title for the collection: *Flaubert in Egypt and Other Essays*. In 1994, the essays were published as *Hermetic Light: Essays on the Gnostic Spirit in Modern Literature and Thought* (Santa Barbara, CA: John Daniel & Company). At the publisher's request, the main title was changed because of the announced, forthcoming publication of an edition of Flaubert's letters under the same original title: *Flaubert in Egypt: A Sensibility on Tour* (Gustave Flaubert and Francis Steegmuller, Penguin Books, released on March 1, 1996). The new main title for Finlay's book, *Hermetic Light*, chosen by the editor, David Middleton, was taken from a short poem by Finlay entitled "The *Illumination* of Arthur Rimbaud":

African sunlight seared the grimy walls,
The windows opened to the furnace noon.
He gazed into its objectless pure style,
Hermetic light destroying common earth,
Until he saw the fated animal reach night,
This century of holocaust and suicide.

This poem seems, at least in part, to be about the same Gnostic spirit found in the writings of the authors discussed in Finlay's book, so the new title of Finlay's book, *Hermetic Light*, remained in words that Finlay himself had written, words that also link the essays and the poems. The poems are collected in *"Dense Poems and Socratic Light": The Poetry of John Martin Finlay (1941–1991)*, a companion volume, also published by Wiseblood Books. Like the poems, Finlay's essays, including these essays on the Gnostic spirit in the modern world, have been thoroughly reedited for this Wiseblood Books edition of Finlay's collected prose. And, like the poems, they have—for the first time—been annotated.

In the later 1980s, after he had completed the essays in *Flaubert in Egypt*, Finlay turned his attention to writing a new book of essays, this time on a spirit similar to, perhaps even identical with, the Gnostic spirit, a spirit he found in the works of certain ancient Greek philosophers. Finlay lived to complete two of these essays—"The Night of Alcibiades" and "The Socratics and the Flight from This World." He left behind a partial draft of a third essay, untitled, on Plato's *Crito*. These Greek essays are brought together in this Wiseblood Books edition for the first time, and the *Crito* essay is also published here, in its entirety, for the first time. Further comments on the Greek essays may be found in the Preface to this volume and in Appendix B.

Finlay's essay on English poet Elizabeth Daryush (1887–1977) stands apart from the essays in *Flaubert in Egypt* and the essays on the Greeks. Published in 1983 in Volume 20 of the *Dictionary of Literary Biography (DLB)–British Poets, 1914–1945*,—it follows the prescribed format for a *DLB* entry, including the two bibliographies, which are constructed and placed in accordance with the *DLB* style. This opportunity to write on Daryush was offered to Finlay by Donald E. Stanford, editor of this *DLB* volume and Finlay's major professor and dissertation director at Louisiana State University. Finlay's dissertation was on the American poet and critic, Yvor Winters (1900–1968), with whom Stanford had studied in the 1930s at Stanford University. Both Winters and Stanford admired Daryush's poetry, as did Finlay.

In fact, a story circulated for years after his death that Finlay, on an impulse, had flown to London and then taken a train to Oxford, just to meet Daryush in her home outside of Oxford. After the visit, so the story goes, Finlay returned to London and immediately flew back home to America. Reportedly, Finlay's reason for going to England was simply to tell Daryush face to face how much he admired her poem "Still-Life." This story was thought to be highly unlikely, if not apocryphal, because many stories—some true, some not, some exaggerated in the retelling—had gathered around Finlay for years. Recently, however, an old yellowed sheet of stationery from the Royal London Hotel was discovered inside Finlay's edition of Daryush's *Collected Poems* (Manchester, England: Carcanet New Press, 1976). On this sheet are notes made by Finlay on September 7, 1969, upon his return to London from Oxford after a visit—whether prearranged or not—with Daryush. So there is some truth to this story, however much the story may have been embellished by later storytellers. Finlay's notes on the visit with Daryush are published here for the first time.

Finally, a word needs to be said about the editorial practice followed in annotating Finlay's essays. Except for the dictionary-style entry on Elizabeth Daryush, Finlay's essays were all written and published, or were intended to be published, as "literary quarterly" style essays—which, by nature, very rarely have endnotes and are often meant to be read more as works of literary art, like a poem or a story, than as heavily footnoted essays such as are found in purely scholarly journals.

This is especially true for Finlay's essays, which, as noted in Appendix B, and as Finlay himself admitted, are deeply autobiographical, even though, on the surface, they are picked clean of any details from Finlay's personal life. However, when passages in the essays can be clearly linked to events in Finlay's life or to the poems, such connections are indicated in the endnotes.

Finlay's essays appeared, either before or after his death, in two quarterlies, *The Hudson Review* and *The Southern Review*, in the biannual journal *Hellas: A Journal of Poetry and the Humanities*, and in the annual journal *Explorations*. So, as stated above, and in keeping with the nature of a quarterly essay, editorial notes to these essays by Finlay are, whenever possible, kept short and simple and do not venture far beyond the very few notes that Finlay wrote himself. For the general reader, additional information in the form of an encyclopedia article or literary dictionary style entry on the authors and works that Finlay deals with is readily available both in book form and on the web. Nonetheless, a few such articles are cited in the endnotes when deemed necessary by the editors. For the scholar, Finlay provides sufficient information in the text of the essay itself. In any case, Finlay expected the essays to be read just as they are. Furthermore, Finlay's personal library has long since been dispersed and very few records remain in his papers noting the editions, including the sources of the translations, of the works of the writers he discusses and from whose writings he quotes. Finlay seems to have destroyed most, if not all, notes for, and drafts of, the essays. Tracking down these sources, where possible, will be a worthy project for later scholars of Finlay's works.

FLAUBERT IN EGYPT

&

OTHER ESSAYS

My art, like the God of the Jews, feasts on holocausts.

—Flaubert, *The Letters*

To worship God does not mean that we must first destroy our nature.

—St. Thomas Aquinas, *The Summa*

Leaning through silence to a dead man's mind

—Dick Davis, "Edward FitzGerald"

Introduction

Toward the end of his life Allen Tate delivered a lecture at Vanderbilt University, "Mere Literature and the Lost Traveller," which was later published in the November 1979 issue of *Poetry*. Tate's subject in the lecture was the Gnostic spirit of modern poetry. He did not mean by this phrase that modern poetry had attempted to recover the historical and theological specificity of a religious system that had flourished around twenty centuries ago. Tate wasn't interested in systems, but in the human experience to which all systems are attempted answers. I would imagine that Tate himself would have believed that Gnosticism is a recurrent temptation of fallen humanity and that the first Gnostic was Satan. But such a spirit is not so unhistorical that it cannot be talked about, and Tate gives us a full-bodied explanation of what exactly he means by the Gnostic spirit. As he acknowledges, he does so with the help of the historical reconstruction of Gnosticism in Hans Jonas' *The Gnostic Religion*:

> In these schemes [i.e., the Gnostic and Manichaean] we are to be saved by "knowledge," not by faith, or by hope, or by charity; for only through *gnosis*, through intellectual mastery of the relation of the natural work to a divine order can we be saved. The natural world is beyond redemption, for it was created by the powers of evil, the Archons, the lower Angels, or whatever beings at war with the remote and alien God the particular Gnostic school of thought might invent. It seems that the Gnostic heresy and its variant, the Manichaean, rise spontaneously at certain historical moments of crisis and strain, when the world of man and his natural setting seem beyond his control and are therefore looked upon as evil. The Gnostic version of Christ gives us the central mythical figure for this alienation of man from God and nature. Was

not the *human* nature of the Gnostic Christ a deception of the senses? This human nature of Christ was not natural, for the Godhead (such was the abstraction used to refer to God then as now) would not so degrade *It*self as to enter into human flesh. To *know* this, to achieve insight into this delusion . . . was to achieve the first step toward salvation. The adept must know that God was remote and alien and could do nothing for us in a natural order of corruption and evil.[1]

Tate's vision is most fixed on the Gnostic spirit in modern poetry. He cites a poem of his own, "The Eagle," which he said was written apart from conscious religious belief and which consequently must have come to him out of the "atmospheric effluvium"[2] that contains the Gnostic spirit. I quote the second and third stanzas of the poem and then part of Tate's explication that follows:

> Look! whirring on the rind
> Of aether a white eagle
> Shot out of the mind,
> The windy apple, burning,
>
> Hears no more, past compass
> In his topless flight,
> The apple wormed, blown up
> By shells of light.[3]

"The Eagle is the Gnostic intellect which by means of gnosis will save itself by flying upwards away from the rotten apple, the earth. This intellectual pride is partly motivated by fear. In the union with God man saves God and becomes God himself."[4]

I should like to use Tate's words as a text for this book, which also is concerned with the Gnostic spirit of modern literature. Like Tate, at least in this one respect, I am not interested in Gnostic systems as such that would involve particular theological commitment on the part of the writers I study and whom I see as illustrating the Gnostic spirit. Of all the various tenets of Gnosticism—I am basically concentrating on just one, though I incidentally deal with others. What I see as unifying certain modern writers and historical Gnosticism is the idea of an ontological alienation of God from both the natural and human world. The desire to escape from this world, which Tate and the historians view as essential to all Gnosticisms, only results from the belief that God has abandoned the world to darkness, evil, and meaninglessness, and that there is no analogy between His pure essence and the gross matter of this world.

It is the alienation of God from the mind, which we can see in even such a writer as Cardinal Newman, that I find most disturbing. Both modern literature and historical Gnosticism are profoundly anti-intellectual, even if the latter confessedly offers *gnosis* to its initiates and prides itself on its rejection of blind faith. Too frequently in both is the intellect dismissed as an inadequate instrument for apprehending spiritual realities, while other irrational areas of the human composite are valued instead as appropriate means to an ineffable grace. The Gnostics believed that the "foreign god" was beyond any of the categories of our intellect, even the most generalized one of existence. We see nearly the same thing in Rimbaud's *derangement of the senses*[5] and in other non-rational practices of other modern writers, all undertaken for the sake of some unearthly illumination that cannot rationally be even talked about. Newman himself believed that the operations of God's grace are best conducted in the subterranean depths of the psyche, which are forever sealed off from the conscious mind, though Newman himself at times could be the most Thomistic of writers.

I should say a few words about the method I have used in writing this book. It is not a systematic or historical study of the *Deus absconditus*[6] in modern literature. There is, in fact, a deliberate randomness in my approach to the subject. I thought that such an approach might stand a better chance than others of capturing the elusive Gnostic spirit, which, after all, frequently exists only in the indirections and implications of what the writer "publicly" says. My method was to choose writers for study who possess little or nothing in common with each other. Three of them are poets, two fiction writers, one a Catholic apologist; the remaining are philosophers, with a psychologist included for good measure. They variously come from Great Britain, France, Germany, and the United States, the countries that collectively created the Proteus of modernity. As far as time goes, the writers I selected extend from the middle of the nineteenth century to the middle of the twentieth. And I wrote each part of the book as if I started out anew, so that its chapters can be read and understood separately as essays, though altogether they compose, I hope, variations on a single theme. I did not approach these writers looking for Gnosticism. I concentrated on the totality of their lives and the Gnostic spirit and let that spirit emerge on its own.

Of the writers I deal with, Flaubert and Kafka are the most undiluted examples of Gnosticism in spite of the disbelief in religion we find in their lives. A vision of an impure world abandoned by a pure God—with Flaubert an inhuman ideal of pure art frequently standing for God—influenced nearly everything they felt and thought. And so I begin and end with them. The other writers do not approach the extremity of Flaubert and Kafka. They cannot be called Gnostics with any strict justice at all; instead, they would be more accurately designated as puritans, purists, ascetics, or Jansenists[7] of both the religious and the aesthetic variety. But I am concerned in this book not with Gnosticism, but with the Gnostic spirit, and in important areas of each one of these writers' minds the Gnostic idea of an absent God does enter in and decisively influence their thought. In Newman, God is absent from and opposed to the rational scientific intellect as it operates in fallen man. I go into the Enlightenment with Newman primarily because its philosophers worked out an anti-intellectual view of the mind that can be taken from its philosophical context and applied to mysticism, including Gnosticism. In Hopkins, God is absent from a human will vitiated by original sin, from the ordinary instincts and desires of human beings, from our nature in general, though He is for Hopkins almost heretically present and active in the inhuman world of pure nature. Finally, in Valéry and Yvor Winters, God is absent from the *otherness* of phenomenal existence, the difference between the two poets being that, whereas Valéry saw the mind as a possible God, Winters, on the other hand, saw an actual God as just pure mind. In any event, the divine and the natural split apart in their thought. I should add that Nietzsche and Freud are largely dealt with as providing background to Kafka, though the themes of the death of God and parricide, which are prominent in both, and which I deal with, are not unrelated even to historical Gnosticism, which insisted on the destruction in the mind of any idea of God the Father.

Flaubert in Egypt[1]

I.

The Egypt of Flaubert which we are concerned with here is not the geographical one that Flaubert visited with his friend, Maxime DuCamp, in 1849 and 1850, and about which he wrote in some of the most memorable letters ever written. It is rather the Egypt that Flaubert made in his own mind and then found reflected in the one he visited. All artists have landscapes of their own, governed by a particular kind of weather and influenced by seasons all their own. Flaubert knew himself a northerner, infected with all the sadness and nervousness that prolonged darkness and ice can breed in the human soul. He felt himself drawn to the south just as he said his barbaric ancestors had been drawn to the occupation and pillage of the whole Mediterranean world centuries before. He wanted and found there warmth and color, and clarity of vision, the insistence on which seems innate in French artists. But at the heart of the matter he also wanted a particular atmosphere purged of miasmas so that he could breathe in its cleanness and be rid of a sickness that existed, I think, at the deepest level of his being.

Flaubert's Egypt in essence is the land of the dead where intense sunlight quickly burns up putrefied flesh and leaves only the skeleton behind. Its poetic image is the monumental charnel house of *The Temptation of St. Antony*, where the dead, soaked in perfumes and rendered indestructible, sleep out thousands of years, while above them the desert stretches endlessly away and the statues of "unmoving gods," with their massive shoulders stained white by the excrement of birds, stare off blindly into space. It resembles the Egypt of the Gnostic mythologies that used the country as a symbol for the prison-house of the whole cosmos and for the corruption and death dealt out by the archons governing it. And Flaubert reveals himself infected here with the same *Egyptianism* that Nietzsche found all past philosophers guilty of. They violated actual existence, Nietzsche argues in *The Twilight of the*

Idols, to the extent that they placed any value at all in things changeless and eternal, the nothingness of death being a greater violation than the Platonic Forms or the Christian afterlife.

Of course, the *Letters* swarm with those carefully observed details that attest to Flaubert's famous attention to the immediate world around him, which the novels also are filled with. A sense of frenetic activity, a youthful exuberance, apparent in the sexual freedom Flaubert enjoyed in Egypt, characterize the *Letters* and make them different from the sober and more labored visions of *Salammbô* and *The Temptation of St. Antony.* But even in the *Letters,* what gives the details their color and vividness is the Egyptian blackness just under their surfaces, and Flaubert, we suspect, is interested in them because they occasion this starkly defining contrast.

What rivets him at all times is the Egypt of vacancy populated on its surface with things beautiful because they are either exhausted or rotten inside. The old Coptic bishop in Cairo is soon worn out by the theological conversation which Flaubert has with him as he sits mumbling half-intelligibly in his white beard. Vultures and eagles circle above the Nile as naked monks race down the cliffs lining the shore and swim out to the passing boats to beg for alms. It is not the pearls themselves Flaubert is interested in, but the blood coming out of both ears and eyes of the pearl-fishers as they emerge out of tons of pressure on their skulls. The numerous prostitutes whom Flaubert has dealings with all seem both bruised and metallic; their stomachs are cold to the touch and one senses disease and sores under the painted coins and jewels with which they decorate their bodies. "Splendid things gleam in the filth," he says in the *Letters.* And there is the night he spent with the famous courtesan Kuchuk Hanem: "I sucked her furiously, her body was covered with sweat, she was tired after dancing, she was cold." The nauseating odor of bedbugs mingled with the scent of her skin, which was dripping with sandalwood oil—the "bitter undertaste" that Flaubert said he wanted in everything.[2] Later, he gets up to urinate in the street outside her house, and looks up into the luminous depths of the Egyptian night-sky and sees it "clear and immensely distant."

The same sky appears in *Salammbô,* presided over by the Carthaginian goddess Tanit, and the world under her lunar intensity is the same as the Egypt of the *Letters.* With its peculiar combination of the precise and the grotesque, only Flaubert could have written the catalogue of the goddess's activities that appears in the third chapter: "As you wax and wane, so cats' eyes and panthers' spots expand and shrink. Mothers cry your name in the pangs of childhood. You swell the seashells. You make wines ferment. You make corpses rot. You form pearls at the bottom of the sea." But she is terrifying for the human being not completely devoted to her worship. Her influence extends beyond fertility and growth to embrace insanity and death, all of which indifferently mean the same to her. Her eyes eat up the stones of buildings and animals go mad under her dark side. Nothing touches her in her remoteness and purity. Her detachment is beyond good and evil, and the peace she dispenses is obtained only after the nerves have been deadened and the mind washed out.

The desert and the void are never far away for Flaubert in Egypt. "I shall show you," the personified Death tells St. Antony in the *Temptation*, "what you tried to glean, by the light of tapers, from the faces of the dead—or when you vagabonded beyond the Pyramids, in those great sands composed of human remains. From time to time a fragment of skull turned beneath your sandal. You grasped some dust, you let it sift through your fingers; and your mind, mixing with it, vanished into the void."

Flaubert himself had had opportunities to discover what one can from the faces of the dead. His father and sister died within a few months of each other in the early part of 1846. In April of 1848 he suffered the greatest loss of his life, the death by tuberculosis of his friend Alfred LePoittevin, to whom he later dedicated *The Temptation of St. Antony*. Flaubert's accounts in the *Letters* of the nightlong vigils he kept beside the coffins of his sister and LePoittevin contain the secret of his response to Egypt:

> I was reading Montaigne, my eyes kept turning from my book to the corpse; her husband and the priest were snoring; and I kept telling myself, as I saw all this, that forms disappear, that the idea alone remains; and I kept feeling thrills at turns of phrase in the Montaigne, and reflected that he too would be forgotten. It was freezing, the window was open because of the odor, and from time to time I got up to look at the stars, calm, radiant, eternal.

> *

> At daybreak, about four o'clock, the attendant and I began our task. I lifted him, turned him, covered him. The feeling of the coldness and rigidity of his limbs stayed in my fingertips all the next day. He was horribly decomposed; the sheets were stained through. We wrapped him in two shrouds. When it was done he looked like an Egyptian mummy in its bandages, and I was filled with an indescribable sense of joy and relief on his account. There was a whitish mist, the trees

37

were beginning to be visible through it. The two tapers shone in the dawning whiteness; two or three birds sang, and I recited to myself this sequence from his *Bélial: Il ira, joyeux oiseau, saluer dans les pins le soleil levant.*

Some quintessential quality of Flaubert, and of Europe after the Enlightenment and the Revolution, is clearly and completely expressed in these passages. They are as static and emblematic in this respect as illuminations in a medieval manuscript. A fatalistic sadness permeates the clarity and succinctness of their style, and through them we realize the full extent of what the loss of Christendom cost the European mind. No real consolation exists for Flaubert as he suffers through these nights. His philosophical skepticism and secularism, his overt commitment to the scientific attitude of his father do not allow him the passion and purgation of grief. There is only the night sky outside, the infinite stretches of space, and the calmness and radiance of eternal stars. The annihilation of the human being deprives life of permanent substance and finally renders it as meaningless as the black tunnel and the locked door of Emma Bovary. And in the loss of substance and the absence of religion, what is left the mind to save itself from a terrifying boredom but the strategy of detachment and an obsession with style?

We wrapped him in two shrouds. Grief goes underground in this modern *Pietà*, or else finds muffled expression in the sense of relief and joy Flaubert says he felt when the death-stench was taken care of and his friend lay shrouded in the white dawn like an Egyptian mummy. One thinks of Emma Bovary's agonizing last hours and the black liquid that pours out of her mouth after she has died and that stains the wedding dress. The childhood experience of observing the cadavers laid out on slabs in the dissecting room of his father's hospital, with the sunlight pouring in on them, must have seared itself into Flaubert's mind as the vision of what human life actually is. He took care of the disgust and horror death surely inspired in him only by staring straight into its face and accustoming himself by degrees to its hideousness, after which he then could afford to be cool and realistic. Since it is only because of existence that death has any terror at all, he could free himself of that terror only by disengaging himself, as far as he could, from existence itself. According to the strange logic of the situation, existence then is shunned as a contaminated falseness and death is seen as release. The very thing that provokes the horror becomes the thing desired.

Flaubert responded to Egypt because he thought he saw there an indifference to pain and disease, and a familiarization with the grotesque and the repulsive so complete they no longer disturbed or offended. The depths and luminous precision of the eastern nights, the hodgepodge of cults one found in Egypt, the persistence of primitive forms of worship, the whole scattered and promiscuous evidence of corruption and mortality that met one everywhere—all this suggested to Flaubert's mind an acceptance of death at those ancient levels that mysteriously combine the mystical and the animalistic. "But after pillaging temples," the narrator says of the mercenaries in *Salammbô,* "seeing numerous nations and massacres, many finished by believing only in fate and death; and every evening they fell asleep with the same placidity as wild beasts." Here was none of the smudge of Christianity, for which death is the consequence of sin, nor any of the vagueness of those substitute religions that nineteenth-century Europe hoped somehow would take the place of Christianity, the dogma of progress and perfectibility of man, the spiritualization of nature, political and economic utopianism, even bourgeois respectability, for all of which the fact of death presented insoluble problems and caused profound embarrassment. Egypt also eliminated the sexual neurosis of the nineteenth century. The moral abandonment, to which the "vermilion depths of Africa" invited Flaubert, and after him Rimbaud and countless others, released sex from all restrictions so that it too could regress to its primitive association with death and become part of the whole Egyptian matrix.

In a certain sense, the whole nineteenth century was drawn into the depths of Africa. The numerous voyages into unexplored wildernesses undertaken then, the invasions and pillage of Africa and Asia, the artistic cult of the irrational and the instinctual, the descent through layer upon layer of biological and geological strata in search of what Nietzsche called *Homo naturus,* the naked X—all this indicates the extent to which primitivism gripped the Western mind. God was either dead or remote in their minds. Philosophical absolutes, even the idea of objective truth itself, were medieval cobwebs to them. Nothing prevented these intrepid explorers from an increasingly deeper investigation of the only reality they recognized, naked and pure naturalism. Progress gave them the idea of a primitive origin, the first crude basis for all further progressions and improvements. If they could discover that, they then would have in hand the basic stuff of their own identities. In other words, they were searching for themselves and a death's-head. Many of them found a great deal of the former; all of them discovered the latter.

Flaubert, of course, went home, disentangled himself from his mistress, lived with his mother, and, as everyone knows, devoted himself ascetically to his art. He felt nothing but bored disgust with nearly all the prevailing passions and preoccupations of the century he lived and died in. He thought its optimism naïve and its ambitions unrealizable, and he prided himself on the fact that he had no illusions. In the *Temptation*, after St. Antony has listened to the incantatory dialogue of Lust and Death, in which Death says his irony exceeds all other, the fragmented saint is shown the biological origin of life and sees nothing but vague deformity and monstrous pullulations. He then cries out in fearless and suicidal frenzy that he wants to be reduced back to matter, his last statement in the book. Flaubert knew that the problem facing modern man after the death of God was not only the horror of death, but the desire for it. No wonder Sigmund Freud admired *The Temptation of St. Antony,* saying that it "confirms the awareness of our perplexity in the mysteriousness that reigns everywhere." *Beyond the Pleasure Principle* is nothing but a systematic abstraction of St. Antony's last cry. Flaubert's Egyptianism is now drained of its color and presented with a chilling scientific rigor. The death instinct is placed inside the mind itself as its most primitive and fundamental element. This conservative instinct abides for its time the tensions and complications of eros and then, following its own inaccessible laws, it asserts its own domination and sucks the human being back into the silence and purity of matter.

II.

Existence itself becomes intolerable for Emma Bovary and she ends by committing suicide. The French Revolution destroyed the medieval concept of the state in the person of a king as the reflector of divine order. It created instead the totally secular state expressing itself through bureaucracy and committed to the satisfaction of mundane processes. The masses came out of their dark places, felt their whole existence a deprivation, and demanded that they be filled. Emma Bovary is a psychological child of these masses, with something still left in her of the callousness of her rustic forefathers. Unlike them, she has nothing to do. We feel at times we barely know her and become impatient with the externality of Flaubert's vision. Then we realize there is not *one* person in her to know. Given neither solidity nor graininess by a specific station or task, she can only dream of successive identities and become none of them. She is always waiting for something to transform her or provide her with an object adequate to her immeasurable passion. She too wants to be filled, or consumed, but in the winter light she sees at Tostes, the light that looks as if it were filtered through ground glass, she is convulsed with nausea.

"We are beginning the history of man," Comte de Mirabeau once asserted during the early days of the Revolution. Perhaps Flaubert had Mirabeau's confident statement in mind when he gave the name *Homais* to his bourgeois pharmacist. In any event, Homais's type dominates that history and his egotistic materialism creates the world in which Emma Bovary finally becomes tragic. His coadjutor is the shopkeeper and moneylender Lheureux, Plato's economic man, who lives parasitically on Emma's compulsive desire for inessential goods. He instigates the crisis which she resolves by suicide and Homais unwittingly furnishes her the poison.

Their foil is the priest Bournisien, a man committed to his vocation, but one whose simple piety renders him pathetically unequal to the desperateness of Emma's condition. The plaster priest in the Bovary back garden at Tostes, with white scruff breaking out on his face, more accurately reflects the invalidity of the Catholic Church, which Flaubert assumes as a historical fact in *Madame Bovary*. Only on Emma's deathbed does the Church for a moment claim his serious attention; yet the intrusion of the blind beggar, appearing suddenly at the window, shatters the tentative peace induced by extreme unction and the woman dies in uncontrolled terror.

Existence becomes intolerable because she asks that passion be consummated in a world where nothing coheres, where everything deceives and dissolves. Her two lovers, Léon and Rodolphe, play their roles for a time to gratify their lust, then desert her for bourgeois duties in "the molds and mildews of the nineteenth century." Both men, understandably perhaps, refuse to destroy themselves for Emma's spiritual impossibilities. But her passion gives her no quarter. A romanticism of illusion and escape informs its surface, but underneath it resembles some primitive force, much like the moon she sees rising straight out of the earth, and forming headless serpents on the river's surface. Its undischarged energy makes her mad and depraved, but her stubborn devotion to it drives her to the extreme vision, where suffering illuminates error. The reality of human existence is not the image of the earthly Rodolphe or the poetic Léon; neither is it discoverable in the fiction and journalism she devours in her vacant hours at Yonville. It is rather the blind beggar with bloody sockets for eyelids and flesh dissolving from his hideous face. Emma turns away from him in disgusted horror throughout the novel, but at the end she is forced to see him as life stripped bare, as the truth behind deceptive appearance, which passion mistook for reality. As with all thinkers and artists who live out the death of God, the great error in Flaubert's universe is not disobedience but delusion.

And yet, if he dramatizes the tragic consequences of passion, he nowhere celebrates the world that destroyed that passion. "Spongy fetuses in the pharmacy window continue to disintegrate in their cloudy alcohol," he says of time since Homais won his Legion of Honor. Mirabeau's "history of man" disgusts him more than Emma's passion attracts *and* terrifies him. The first modern novel offers only the vision of the four walls closing in and the soul anguished by the sense that it belongs somewhere else. After Léon leaves Emma for his studies in Paris, the bad days of Tostes start all over again, the days when the future loomed before her as a "pitch-black tunnel, ending in a locked door." She watches the night close in upon Yonville and feels herself "left alone in a horrible void of piercing cold." Flaubert's detachment in rendering this hopeless vision of the modern world would be unbearable were it not for the strange sadness one finds everywhere in this novel, and with reason since he said Emma Bovary was himself.

"You lack sufficient hatred of life," he wrote his mistress Louise Colet, wishing she would realize once and for all that existing and suffering are horribly bound together. Disillusionment is not enough, but must be animated by hate if one wants to escape the agonies of Emma Bovary. Since it is eros that binds us to life and causes its instinctive repetition, he defeated that force in himself, devised an aesthetic that made him immune to passion, and so eluded the fate of the heroine he resembled. He wished not only to achieve stoical sufficiency in this strange warfare, but, more compellingly, to sterilize the Manichaean germ that he believed polluted existence at its core. The horror of causing another human life riveted him to celibacy. In his youth he thought once of castrating himself. He released art from all dependency, purified it of emotional contamination, and gave it an aseity that most people would think attributable only to a god. Art need be nothing, he kept saying, but its own dispassionate and isolated self; in fact, it should be concerned with nothing just as God Himself is *about* nothing, only because He *is* everything. The obligations inherent in communal language, the moral responsibilities of the artist, even the very idea of an audience, are all surgically removed from the artistic process so that nothing need blemish the compulsive self-reflection of the Flaubertian aesthetic. No theory of art appears so monolithically impersonal and no theory is so rooted in a psychological obsession with cleaning oneself of the defilement of human existence.

How did it come about that Flaubert sickened of existence and responded so avidly to Egypt? Part of the answer must lie in his earliest years; evidence indicates some internal scar that he received then, and which affected him for the rest of his life. Its exact nature eludes us completely, as most likely it did Flaubert himself, for we are here talking about an impenetrable obscurity, something, in fact, demonic in its unverifiability and immediacy. The epileptic seizures to which he was subjected also form part of this dark picture. A psychological sense of *being maimed* must have permanently lodged itself in Flaubert's mind after the disease's other debris had dissolved away. There is another cause. The one strange fact about himself that he returns to over and over again in the *Letters* is that at bottom he is religious. Of course, he uses religion to explain his art, but something is left over unappropriated by pure aestheticism, that reveals an unsatisfied longing to believe and be done with it. *A Simple Heart* is animated by this longing from the beginning to the end. He felt most at home not in his own time, but in those first centuries of the Christian era, whose religions and mysticism he studied and knew so well. How strongly he reminds us at times of a combination of St. Jerome and Marcus Aurelius! But even though he said he hated it, he knew he belonged to the nineteenth century, to "the molds and mildews" of its bleak scientific systems, which claimed him and coerced his intellectual assent. The religious longing so frustrated could turn only into a strange form of mysticism allied in its denigration of human life to the very science that drove religion underground. As Nietzsche alone rightly saw, nineteenth-century science, so insisted upon as enlightenment itself, did not liberate modern Europe from its gnostic nightmare, from its "ascetical sickness." It continued it under new guises only by ruthlessly stripping man bare of moral and metaphysical dignity and by flinging him into a meaningless universe in which his life is as vain indeed as any of Nietzsche's maddest monks could have hoped for.

III.

And yet there is a God concealed in Flaubert's life and work, one who alone escapes unharmed all the acid tests of skepticism and who invites, conveniently enough for Flaubert, an imaginative, instead of a dogmatic, assent. This God is the Unknown Father, the *Deus absconditus* of dogmatic mysticism, whose presence is revealed only in negations and annihilations. He has always reappeared whenever the Western world sickens of itself and begins to crave mystical and totalitarian solutions to its problems. "But as I have revolved," the Gymnosophist says in a passage from the *Temptation*, which the *Letters* continually re-echo, "through an infinite quantity of existence in the guise of gods, men, and animals, I renounce the journey, I want no more of this exhaustion! I am abandoning the dirty inn of my body walled with flesh, red with blood, covered with hideous skin, full of filth—and as my reward I shall sleep in the depth of the absolute, in Annihilation."

With the succinctness of the most compressed philosophical formula, this same mask of a character states the central paradox of such mysticism: *By the very fact that I know a thing, that thing ceases to exist.* According to Gnostic theodicy, inferior gods created this world. The material they used was nothing in its essence but unreal dregs vomited out of other gods who had tried through passion to know the unknowable Father. This world, consequently, embodies no reality but is only mattered ignorance instead. When one knows *this thing*, one then brings it back to its original state of nothingness and thus annihilates it. In the same way one must kill any god the idea of whom might exist in the human mind. Nothing can express the unknowable God, who does not exist according to any category of being the mind can apprehend. This God requires then, most strangely enough, a form of atheism, and one approaches him by nullifying the created world and by committing intellectual suicide.

After Rodolphe betrays and deserts Emma, she returns to religious devotions and briefly experiences the ecstatic union with such a divinity, whom some readers might innocently think Christian: "Emma felt something powerful pass over her that rid her of all pain, all perception, all feeling. Her flesh had been relieved of its burdens, even the burden of thought; another life was beginning; it seemed to her that her spirit, ascending to God, was about to find annihilation in this love, like burning incense dissolving in smoke." Still gripped by this vision, she later "turned her eyes inward and watched the destruction of her will." St. Antony goes further: "On the contrary! Man, being spirit, must withdraw from mortal things. All action degrades him. I could wish not to be attached to the earth—not even by the soles of my feet." Hilarion, the former disciple of St. Antony, knows his master's heretical yearning, not for the God of Genesis Who says flesh is good, nor for the God of the New Testament Who assumed flesh, but rather for the Unknown God to whom flesh is an obscuring defilement. He lives in a far country, but Hilarion offers to show the inhumanly allegorical way: "The secret you would like to hold is guarded by sages. They live in a far country, seated under gigantic trees, dressed in white and calm as gods. The air that nourishes them is hot. Leopards stalk about them on the grass. Murmuring springs and the whinnying of unicorns mix with their voices. You shall listen to them: and the face of the Unknown will be unveiled!" At the very end of the book, after the succession of *Götterdämmerungen*[3] has fragmented and dispersed the saint's mind, an enigmatic image of Christ inside the very disc of the sun suddenly appears and shines out over the expanses of nothingness. Through its silence and inscrutability the image confesses to the Gnostic transformation of Christ into an emissary from the Unknown God, to whom St. Antony then returns in his prayers.

The Jehovah of the Hebrews works in history which He would redeem for His chosen people; the Incarnation of the Christian God is history and promises through grace the redemption and restoration of a fallen nature, which in its radicalness is untainted by evil—through that act, as St. Augustine says with classical brevity, God tells the creature He created, "I want you to be." But the ahistorical and acosmic *Deus absconditus*[4] causes such conflict between the divine and the natural that only one of the two survives the vicious warfare they carry on in the human soul. "There comes a moment when one needs to make oneself suffer," Flaubert emphasizes in a horrifying moment of self-hate, "needs to loathe one's flesh, to fling mud in its face, so hideous does it seem." Such warfare has destroyed whatever humanity St. Antony might once have had; at Flaubert's hands he is now nothing but a hollowness cut off from the world, an un-man who no longer can endure himself. St. Julian kills his parents; Mâtho's desire for the mystical Salammbô consumes his life, just as Salammbô herself cries out that the god Moloch burns her through. Emma greedily eats her poison. Spiritual blindness made her accept this world as something other than a rotting shell with nothing but its own thin beauty of putrescence. She could not know it in her mind, and she suffered accordingly.

"I'm a mystic at bottom," Flaubert once said, "and I believe in nothing." How profoundly revealing is Flaubert's "and"! Nothingness and mysticism embrace each other in his mind. "Art, like the God of the Jews," he also said, "feasts on holocausts." Here Flaubert justifies those thinkers who consider him the father of modernity. Sigmund Freud some years later knew the revolutionary discoveries he made about the human mind, the buried secrets and impulses he unearthed and brought to scientific light, merely continued a destructive process that had been going on for some time. In his own words, the Copernican and Darwinian revolutions destroyed the illusions of earth's centrality and man's possession of a transcendent mind; accepting the Darwinian animality of man, Freud further showed only that this animal is not even the master of his own house, but a slave, instead, driven by unspeakable forces. None of Freud's theories would have surprised Flaubert had he lived to study them. He saw no escape from the abasement of man that modern scientific thought seemed inevitably to entail, and he accepted with intellectual equanimity the meaninglessness to which that science reduced all human values. At the same time, and with equal conviction, he revered the religious spirit as expressing the deepest, most instinctual part of man. But institutionalized religion was gutted for him, and philosophical or theological systems were dismissed by him as historical curiosities. What else could such a person say but that at bottom he was a mystic and that he believed in nothing? Scientific reductionism and mystical renunciation reinforced each other in his mind—both undermine the ground of man's earth, the shelter of his existence, and both strip man to that degree of nakedness and insignificance that their differing ends demand. Both involve, as we in this atomic and apocalyptic age should know, the prospect of horrifying waste and destruction. And what other God can so conveniently move into this skeptical void and instigate his mindless, even unconscious, worship but the Hidden God of Gnostic mysticism, whose "divine nothingness" is proof against thought itself?

Even Flaubert's apparently nihilistic moments, when all gods were done with, still resonated with the consequences, if not the cause, of mystical intensity. "I believe in nothing," he once more simply said. "I doubt everything, and why shouldn't I? I am quite resigned to working all my life like a nigger with no hope of reward. It is a sore that I keep scratching, that's all." But Flaubert betrays himself here—he cannot believe in nothing when he believes so passionately that life is some disease and work a futility. Only from the point of view of some still-persisting standard of mystical perfection, absent though it seemed, could he have arrived at such a judgment and stated it with such bitter but dogmatic assurance. True nihilists keep silent, or put bullets in their brains; they don't labor for years over a *Madame Bovary* or point to a *Temptation of St. Antony* as *l'oeuvre de taute ma vie*.

When Flaubert does have these moments of apparent nihilism, he then becomes completely modern. "If society continues on its present path," he wrote Louise Colet in 1852, "I think we shall once again see mystics, such as existed in all dark ages. Unable to expand, the soul will concentrate on itself." Theological frameworks fall away; subjective internalizations engorge the objective world; one never speaks or thinks of final causes; irrational fervors abuse the intellect; one goes deeper and deeper into the processes of self but discovers nothing that holds. In this dark night the modern mind does not see its Foreign God for the very nothingness that only that God caused to be.

The Dark Rooms of the Enlightenment:
The Case of Cardinal Newman[1]

I.

Toward the end of Cardinal Newman's *Apologia Pro Vita Sua* there occurs a passage that I should like to use as an occasion to say something about the relation, or the lack of relation, between the religious and the intellectual in modern times. Newman has just finished his account of the process of his conversion to the Catholic Church. The argument of that account has been *ad hominem*. He has involved himself not in providing publicly applicable reasons for his conversion, but in a frequently myopic concentration on the subtle and mysterious transitions of the process itself. A legalistic fussiness as to dates, letters, memoranda, and diaries has often possessed him. And underneath the graceful and lucid prose there is always a sense of the pain that the exposure of his private life has cost him, as well as a silent and baffled recognition on his part that he will never understand how God effected such a profound change in him. It is with some relief, consequently, that Newman leaves the psychological twisting of his apology behind him and mounts to a position where he is allowed more extensive and impersonal views. What he then sees is a vision of the whole human world vitiated by sin from its beginning in "some terrible aboriginal calamity" and continuing on to the present hour. But the peculiar source of spiritual anguish for modern times is the human intellect, which Newman believed is "actually and historically" hostile to the operations of God's grace. And it is on that intellect that his vision is most riveted. What power, he asks himself, could combat and destroy this evil serpent of the mind? He further explains himself:

> I am rather asking what must be the face-to-face

antagonist, by which to withstand and baffle the fierce energy of passion and the all-corroding skepticism of the intellect in religious inquiries? I have no intention at all of denying, that truth is the real object of our reason, and that, if it does not attain to truth, either the premise or the process is in fault; but I am not speaking here of right reason, but of reason as it acts in fact and concretely in fallen man. I know that even the unaided reason, when correctly exercised, leads to a belief in God, in the immortality of the soul, and in a future retribution; but I am considering the faculty of reason actually and historically; and in this point of view, I do not think I am wrong in saying that its tendency is towards a simple unbelief in matters of religion. No truth, however sacred, can stand against it, in the long run; and hence it is that in the pagan world, when our Lord came, the last traces of the religious knowledge of former times were all but disappearing from those portions of the world in which the intellect had been active and had had a career.

And in these latter days, in like manner, outside the Catholic Church things are tending,—with far greater rapidity than in that old time from the circumstance of the age,—to atheism in one shape or other. What a scene, what a prospect, does the whole of Europe present at this day! And not only Europe, but every government and every civilization through the world, which is under the influence of the European mind! Especially, for it most concerns us, how sorrowful, in the view of religion, even taken in its most elementary, most attenuated form, is the spectacle presented to us by the educated intellect of England, France, and Germany!

I am not concerned here with Newman's answer to the problem, which is that only a dogmatic church armed with infallibility can counteract and defeat the evil influence of the intellect. Neither do I care to question Newman's basic assumption, the idea, namely, that the mind of what we can loosely but accurately call the Enlightenment has been and continues to be inimical to any form of religious certitude. *Écrasez l'infâmie*[2] is one of the central imperatives of the Enlightenment, and frequently it is still strongly urged in those cases where it is not publicly avowed. Little or nothing of the religious as a matter of fact is left in the modern philosophical mind. What I would question, on the other hand, is Newman's characterization of the intellect as it appears in the Enlightenment tradition. He thinks of it as exuding that self-confidence that comes from the possession of unlimited power. It knows so certainly that it invades all areas of human life, sets up a reckless dictatorship, and suppresses all objections to its own dogmatism. He is emphatic on the point. Immediately after the passage just quoted he refers to it as "the wild living intellect," and then again to "the immense energy of the aggressive, capricious, untrustworthy intellect," just as if the intellect contained the core of sin itself, and the irrationalisms of the will and the blindness of psychological compulsion were nowhere involved. But is Newman historically accurate in this characterization? Do we indeed find such a powerful and vigorous intellect informing and being displayed in the thought of the Enlightenment? Newman saw his friend John Keble as the embodiment of those conservative values opposed to the insubordinate arrogance of the intellect. According to Newman's appendix on liberalism in the *Apologia*, Keble had "the purity and simplicity of a child." He never arrived at judgments by "processes of reason." If he should happen to employ reason, he did so only as "a means of recommending or explaining what had claims on his reception prior to proof." The principle of his life was not the mind; it was instead the rich sediment of unanalyzable "sentiments, presages, and prepossessions" that elude intellectual justification. Yet it was modern philosophy that discovered and placed highest value on these non-rational claims that exist "prior to proof." David Hume, for one, thought that reason should be the slave of passion, and, consequently, with him no completely intellectual explanation is possible for a single act of the mind. Can it be that finally Keble's mind and the mind of the Enlightenment, apart from political and religious differences, are more similar than Newman would have cared to admit? And exactly what powers did such thinkers, for instance, as Locke, Condillac, or even Mill, give the intellect to make it the terrifying force of destruction that it was for Newman?

To answer this question I should like to make a survey of the Enlightenment and to collect what its representative philosophers thought about the powers of the human mind. By Enlightenment I mean that philosophy that began with Francis Bacon, but that received its first systematic articulation with John Locke. Certain doctrines as to the extent of human knowledge expounded by Locke in his *Essay* stimulated philosophic discussion for a long time afterward. British empiricism and utilitarianism, the main part, that is, of British philosophy in the eighteenth and nineteenth centuries, as well as what is more narrowly called the French Enlightenment, were various developments, modifications, revisions, or criticisms of certain positions held by Locke. It was this philosophic tradition that formed that "European mind" that Newman so passionately objects to in his *Apologia Pro Vita Sua*. Its chief motivation was to purify the science of human nature of all extraneous authorities, to discover some simple, indivisible unit or thing generated by that nature itself, and to explain the human being in the terms of that ultimate building block. It began by glorifying the scientific light of observation and experience, but increasingly, and ironically enough, it found itself retreating into the subjective interiors of the mind, even descending into the underworld of the psyche, in search of these basic, primitive units, with what consequences for its theories of the mind we shall soon be able to see.[3]

But before our summary we must first make an important distinction, or else we shall entangle ourselves in confusion. There are actually two intellects in the Enlightenment. One is the intellect as the object of scientific inquiry, the one whose faculties and powers are being dissected, described, and limited through the process of reductive analysis so that its own primitive core can be located and seized. The other is the intellect that is doing the dissecting and describing, *but which leaves its own self out of the account,* exactly as if its different nature were not liable to those laws that might happen to bind the first intellect. The two minds are frequently at odds with each other, and we ourselves must keep them separate if we wish to evaluate accurately the philosophy of the Enlightenment.[4] For example, David Hume reduces even the most rational act of the mind to a kind of instinctual habit of our individual psychologies. We see a relation between a cause and its effect—or rather we *imagine* such a relation—not because it actually exists, but because there is in us a certain quirk to think it does exist. An intellectual act is a *satisfaction* of our psyches, not an understanding of some reality external to our minds. Hume dissects the mind to discover a mysterious emotionalism, not objective logic which aims at truth. But for such a conclusion to make any sense at all as a philosophical assertion, we must posit the existence of another mind, one undetermined and unaffected by the instinctualism in question, or else that conclusion, like the Gnostic snake being swallowed by itself, will be consumed by that same instinctualism; it will consist of nothing more philosophically real than a piece of reflexive psychologism, which the philosopher Hume says is the only act the mind can perform. The judgment on the mind made by the mind and the empirical reality contained in the judgment mutually destroy one another if we do not posit separate minds, and we are then left nowhere.

I am going to take the philosophers at their word. When I speak of the mind of the Enlightenment, I will be referring to the dissected intellect, the obvious one that we read about in the epistemologies of Locke and Hume and in such works as Condillac's *A Treatise of the Sensations,* Helvetius's *On the Mind,* and John Stuart Mill's *An Examination of Sir William Hamilton's Philosophy.* Since Newman himself makes no distinction and always refers to only one modern mind, I am assuming that he also means the same mind and is not referring to the other one, the elusive, disassociated intellect, which is dissecting the first and which has been called "angelic." In fact, without making this distinction no one can even know of the latter intellect's existence—it is only detectable in the very process of its dissecting the first and the obvious mind. If Newman had seen the difference between the two intellects and had directed his hostile remarks against the angelic intellect in his *Apologia*, I would have no argument with him. The angelic intellect, as we shall see, is indeed a destructive force. It would deserve Newman's, or anyone's, condemnation. But the particular object of its most focused wrath is not at all religious belief, as perhaps it would have surprised Newman to have discovered, but, instead, the human intellect itself, the one that is dissected. All this though is another subject entirely.

II.

John Locke's philosophy, and so the systematic origin of the Enlightenment, contains in it a myth of justification. There was once a time, the myth so runs, when the human mind lived in the Garden of Experience.[5] The happiness it enjoyed there was caused by its submission to the plain truth that experience gave it. Its direction was outward to things, not inward to ideas. Of course, the mind reflected upon itself, but such reflection was concerned with those processes stimulated in it by external, sensible things. The mind itself was happily ignorant of any powers it might have in its own right. It had what we would call today a low opinion of itself. There were angels superior with whom it could compare itself, those beings whose intellectual vision was far more acute and penetrating than the composed, and hence muddled, vision of human beings. But low opinion or not, the mind was content with the mean position in which God had placed it between the beasts and angels. Things would have proceeded smoothly in this happy anti-intellectualism had not the mind eventually discovered and become infatuated with its own powers of invention. It then disdained the corrective discipline of the sensible world and retreated inside its own darkness, which it pathetically decked out with artificial lights. Instead of plain truth, it now valued fictions, the chief of which were the notions of "essences" and "innate ideas." It thereby inflated its self-importance to the point of hubris, and would have set itself up in atheistic independence had not God banished it to the sterility of language. Its sorriest time was the medieval age. Then it all but withered away on the unreality of endless verbal distinctions. Logical disputations, all motivated by a desire to overcome the opponent and not to discover truth, embittered its days and distracted its nights. But redemption was at hand in the modern philosophy, which would break the tyranny of words and return the mind to the reality of sensible things.

At times the more Promethean or Satanic aspects of the myth got the upper hand. Locke then came close to the view that the intellect has in itself, and apart from the will, the seed of the greatest and most reckless of sins. Instead of saying simply that no God exists, the intellect would now desire to become God itself and to mock the divine creation with systems and fabrications of its own. In the fragment entitled *De Arte Medica* and dated 1668—the very time when the idea for *An Essay Concerning Human Understanding* must have been forming itself in Locke's mind—he speaks of this dangerous intellectual tendency:

> Man, still affecting something of Deity, laboured by his imagination to supply what his observation and experience failed him in; and when he could not discover (by experience) the principles, causes and methods of nature's workmanship, he would needs fashion all these out of his own thought, and make a world to himself, framed and governed by his own intelligence.

Locke's metaphor for the dogmatic intellect was that of a ship boldly launched upon "the vast ocean of Being, as if that boundless extent were the natural and undoubted possession of our understandings." He would discipline such intellectual arrogance by showing how little indeed it is that the mind possesses, how limited are its powers, how uncertainly it arrives at any truth at all. He shrunk the proportions of the mind. The image he considered appropriate for its modern range was that of "a closet wholly shut from light." The sources of its knowledge were not located in some metaphysical dreamland of innate ideas, but in the experience of sensory sensation and mental reflection on how that sensation fills out the intellect's blank page. "These alone," he asserted, "as far as I can discover, are the windows by which light is led into this *dark room*."[6] The mind is a candle, he wrote elsewhere in the *Essay*, requiring the match of outside sensation to set its own small light going. The area of its illumination concerned practical conduct in this world. Anyone who sought to reach beyond that area into the metaphysical would only subtilize his mind into unreality and eventually become blinded by a philosophical form of either superstition or enthusiasm, the two horrors of the Enlightenment mind. The *dark room* and its restricted movement assured one at least of having to behave properly, even if one felt claustrophobic at odd moments and metaphysically saw next to nothing in the narrow dimness.

Of all the Enlightenment philosophers, it is Berkeley alone who seems at first impression to have expanded the mind and given it extraordinary powers. After all, the mind sensing and the idea being sensed are the only realities of his universe. To exist for him was only to perceive or be perceived—the famous *esse est percipi* of the *Principles of Human Knowledge*—and he carried out the dictum to its logical nullification of the world outside the mind and composed of inconceivable matter. The deepest abyss and the most extended space exist nowhere but in the spiritual substance of the percipient mind. Furthermore, the mind possesses the capacity in Berkeley's system to withstand direct contact with God Himself Who alone in the absence of secondary natural causes impresses those ideas on the mind that make up the universe. It is difficult indeed to think of another philosopher in whose system the mind plays a more important role—even the brain, as Berkeley said in the *Three Dialogues Between Hylas and Philonous*, "being a sensible thing, exists only in the mind." But we are looking at the situation from just one angle as we make such a judgment. When we shift our position, when we specifically consider the relationship between any one individual mind and other minds that might or might not exist, we begin to see a poverty and loneliness in this powerful mind which contains the world.

For Berkeley, the perception or idea of the mind was a unique sensory event that could never be repeated; in fact, it was so unique that none of the senses could combine together and present the same object at the same time to the mind. If I see a rose, for example, and touch it as I see it, the object of my sight and the object of my touch are philosophically unrelatable. Each comprises two different things even though for the sake of convenience we think of them as the same thing and refer to them with the same name. If this is true of one object apprehended at once by two or more of the senses, it is that much truer of the same object apprehended by either one or more of the senses at different times and different places. Nothing remains the same so that the perceptions can have an identity.[7] What then can the mind know of them when they mutually exclude each other and are isolated each in discrete existences? And deprived of the act of knowing, which so often, as Locke stated in his *Essay*, is only the recognition of similitude, what can the mind be but an arena for the meaningless succession of ideas? At one point in the *Philosophical Commentaries*, Berkeley even embraced an extreme phenomenalistic position; the mind then collapsed into the perceptions. "Take away perceptions and you take away the mind," he said with brutal simplicity.

When we turn to the question of the existence of other minds, we find similar problems. Berkeley stated his doctrine in the *Principles*:

From what hath been said, it is plain that we cannot know

the existence of other spirits otherwise than by their operations, or the ideas by them excited in us. I perceive several motions, changes, and combinations of ideas that inform me there are certain particular agents, like myself, which accompany them and concur in their production. Hence, the knowledge I have of other spirits is not immediate, as is the knowledge of my ideas, but depending on the intervention of ideas...

But Berkeley's ideas are inert and passive, with no causal efficiency in them at all. How can they inform him of anything? It requires, besides, considerable boldness to argue from the effects of one particular nature to the existence of a cause of an entirely different nature. No aggregate of disorganized sensible qualities can logically add up to an insensible unity of pure spirit. Are we not left with the conclusion that in the final stages of its logic Berkeley's mind knows only itself and its non-referential perceptions? His mind then is like some mirror endowed mysteriously with unreflected objects that emerge and disappear out of its own extended and solitary being.

Locke kept a great deal of the classical-medieval synthesis. Ideas or perceptions correspond in his mind with outside things; those things make up a coherent world that the mind can somewhat understand with patience and humility. He recognized existent relations among the perceptions and so provided a basis in reality for the similitude that the mind requires for the possibility of knowledge. And St. Thomas Aquinas had also rejected innate ideas and had posited sensory experience as the origin of human knowledge. But Berkeley saw the internal image representing the external thing as giving ground for skepticism. How can we be sure, he asked, the two correspond when *we experience and know the image alone?* His solution was the drastic one of eliminating the external world and saving only the mind and its perceptions. But his question introduced a centrifugal force in philosophy; given the spirit of restless criticism and experimentation that was everywhere in the intellectual air, it was inevitable that someone should go beyond Berkeley to protect the perceptions but eliminate the mind. That more radical person was David Hume, who proceeded according to this "principle with regard to the mind, *that we have no notion of it distinct from the particular perceptions.*" It was all, as Thomas Reid would later observe with great irony, "the triumph of ideas."

Hume's two crucial descriptions of the mind—we cannot call them definitions—occur in the *Treatise of Human Nature* and in the *Dialogue Concerning Natural Religion.* The first one I quote here, from the Treatise, presents the problem in the terms of the philosophical difference between mind and perception. The last one, from the

Dialogues, is unembarrassed in its psychologism; the unanalyzable sense of personality now dominates the mental scene, and in the resulting subjectivity little or nothing of the intellect is left. We are in the age of Rousseau and the Revolution:

> The mind is a kind of theatre, where several perceptions successively make their appearance; pass, re-pass, glide away, and mingle in an infinite variety of postures and situations. There is properly no *simplicity* in it at one time, nor identity in different; whatever natural propension we may have to imagine that simplicity and identity. The comparison of the theatre must not mislead us. They are the successive perceptions only, that constitute the mind; nor have we the most distant notion of the place, where these scenes are represented, or of the materials, of which it is compos'd.

*

> What is the soul of man? A composition of various faculties, passions, sentiments, ideas; united, indeed, into one self or person, but still distinct from each other. When it reasons, the ideas, which are part of its discourse, arrange themselves in a certain form or order; which is not preserved entire for a moment, but immediately gives place to another arrangement. New opinions, new passions, new affections, new feelings arise, which continually diversify the mental scene, and produce in it the greatest variety, and most rapid succession imaginable.

Our impression of the first passage is one of unreality. An unintelligible drama is being enacted on the mind. The mind can do nothing by way of selection or interpretation; it must suffer whatever comes to it from the outside. Our impression of the second passage is one of neurotic instability and compulsive change. The mind is being compelled down certain courses at a bewildering speed and acted on by forces it cannot understand. It is always a victim. If one wishes to know a good life, one cannot derive the principles of morality from the passivity and the derangement of Hume's mind. Reason is just as much an impossibility as exploded religious authority. There is, besides, no permanent human nature, the laws of which can be ascertained by the mind and lived out by the whole person. What remains is only an inexplicable instinctualism. We automatically approve or disapprove of things that affect us. Such approval or disapproval can, of course, be further derived from the physiological sensations of pleasure or pain, but beyond that Hume says he dares not go for all the mystery that surrounds him. It is not, though, a matter of just morality—life itself would be intolerable according to Hume's doctrine. The mind requires the illusion of stability if no stability actually exists, and if the human being attempted to live out the unbearable attrition described in these two passages, he would go insane. Philosophy and human nature, consequently, part company in David Hume's mind, the first ever deliberate case of schizophrenia in modern thought. Philosophy dictates an unlivable doctrine of the mind, which human nature must reject if it wishes to survive. Outside his philosophical study he lived according to principles that inside that study he rejected as nonexistent. "I am . . . affrighted and confounded," he once said in a momentary loss of his usual serenity, "with that forlorn solitude in which I am placed in my philosophy." But he saw no resolution to the conflict. He wrote in the *Treatise* of his *double existence*:[8]

> Nature is obstinate, and will not quit the field, however strongly attack'd by reason; and at the same time reason is so clear in the point that there is no possibility of disguising her. Not being able to reconcile these two enemies, we endeavor to set ourselves at ease as much as possible, by successively, granting to each whatever it demands and by feigning a double existence where each may find something, that has all the conditions it desires.

When we turn to the French Enlightenment, we discover the same insistence on passion and sensation that we find in Hume, the same hard application of the empirical maxim that nothing exists in the intellect that did not first enter it through either the senses or our instinctive emotional reaction to the senses. Passion, not reason, is again the specific difference that distinguishes the human being as such. Ernst Cassirer states in *The Philosophy of the Enlightenment*:

> It sounds like a violent revolution when Vauvenargues, in his *Introduction to the Knowledge of the Human Mind* (1746), says that the true nature of man does not lie in reason, but in the passions. The Stoic demand for control of the passions by reason is and always will be a mere dream. Reason is not the dominating force in man; reason is comparable only to the hand that tells the time on the face of a clock. The mechanism that moves this hand lies within; the motivating force and ultimate cause of knowledge lie in those primary and original impulses which we continually receive from another, a

completely irrational realm.

Voltaire, in his *Treatise on Metaphysics*, extended the dominance of passion from the human world to the totality of nature: "It is with this motivating force [i.e., of passion] that God, whom Plato called the eternal geometer, and whom I call the eternal machinist, has animated and embellished nature: the passions are the wheels which make all these machines go." Helvetius's *On the Mind* and Diderot's *Philosophical Thoughts* adopted the same belief. The cruder materialism of La Mettrie, d'Holbach, and Cabanis destroyed the intellectual identity of the mind. It reduced its unity to an accidental, temporary cohesion of matter that has been inexplicably endowed with consciousness. When Condillac, on the other hand, said he believed in an internally unified soul, he conceived of it merely as a mechanized passivity. All the faculties and powers that the mind possesses have been occasioned by the sensations, without which the mind could not exist. Condillac's image of our intellectual life is that of a series of vortices driven by physical need and psychological passion:

> Those vortices gain ascendancy by turns over one another according as their needs become more urgent. They accomplish their revolutions with amazing variations. They crowd one another, destroy one another, or come into being again according as the feelings to which they owe their power weaken, are eclipsed, or appear in a form hitherto unknown. From one instant to the next the vortex, which now drew others into its orbit, can itself be consumed; and as soon as the need vanishes, all vortices are fused into one. Chaos alone remains. Ideas come and go without order, forming only moving tableaux which offer bizarre and imperfect images.

John Stuart Mill said in his *Autobiography* that he never participated in the nineteenth century's rebellion against the eighteenth century. A continuity exists between his own mind and the minds of his father and of Jeremy Bentham, notwithstanding the fact that Mill the son subjected his two fathers to considerable modification and expansion. The mind for Bentham was a rather cold-blooded calculator for which the most important categories were the "quantifiable" ones of pleasure and pain. The mind for James Mill was reducible to the primitive units of sensations and images. Anything that it might consider as some spiritual or intellectual property was ultimately derived from this phenomenal base. He stated in his *Analysis of the Phenomena of the Human Mind* that "reflection is nothing but consciousness." Since consciousness in his system is nothing but the experiencing of a sensation or of the reproduced version of the sensation that he called its idea, then reflection is nothing but more of the same. As a historian of philosophy has explained his position, for James Mill "to reflect on an idea is the same thing as to have it. There is no room for any additional factor." The mind can never detach itself from experience and intellectually understand experience. James Mill makes the mind impossible in his very theory of the mind, so much was he insistent, and dogmatically so, that its identity be subsumed by actual or reproduced sensation.

As I have said, John Stuart Mill modified and expanded his two intellectual fathers. He is the most cosmopolitan and most catholic of the British empirical philosophers. He opened himself to varied, extensive philosophical and artistic influences; consequently, he saved himself from the reductive extremism and the prideful insularity that marked many of his predecessors and contemporaries. At all times was he animated by *amor mentis*. It is better to be a dissatisfied Socrates, he says passionately in *Utilitarianism*, than a satisfied fool. But when Mill states in scientific terms exactly what his doctrine was as to the nature of the mind, we see the crudities of his fathers claiming him. He gives his definition of the intellect in *An Examination of Sir William Hamilton's Philosophy*, and it is the same as his father's and Hume's. The mind is nothing but a "series of feelings," a "thread of consciousness," one constituted exclusively by present sense data. The data do not furnish evidence for an external world; at most they can be said to refer to some "permanent possibility of sensation"—Mill's term for objective matter. Neither do they furnish evidence for any causal efficacy outside or inside themselves, any causal efficacy, that is, more than a certain "invariable sequence" that Mill allows to adhere between what he still continues to designate as causes and effects. Such a definition cannot even account for memory; according to it, the intellect contains nothing but the one sensory experience that it happens to be having. The past, consequently, is annihilated. The mind is stripped to its moments; its sensory exclusiveness will not admit the phenomenologically dead, immaterial past. Mill himself makes this criticism. In a remarkable instance of intellectual candor he faces the difficulties that memory, as well as expectation, presents his definition of the mind. Toward the conclusion of chapter 12 of the *Examination* he asks how a series of feelings, all of which by definition occur in the present tense, can become aware of either past or future events, all of which by definition are temporally nonexistent, without at the same time becoming more than just a present series of feelings. One would think that the easiest and most logical solution to Mill's problem would be a modification of his definition to accommodate this more than just a present series of feelings. Memory is apparent in every act the mind performs; it is a common and obvious power of the mind, and one, I might add, that we share with animals. But Mill adamantly refuses this alternative. He sticks to his definition, and in a, for him, singular act of philosophical abandonment, he is left invoking the unlogical ghost of "final inexplicability," which he says surrounds all ultimate facts. And he *must* invoke this bit of supra-rationalism because the only alternative to it is the admission of an element of immateriality—which memory presupposes—into his definition of the mind, the presence of which his entire empiricist tradition had forbidden him to allow in a scientific definition. To avoid an unquantifiable inconvenience, then, Mill in this instance has to eat the whole hog of pure mystery itself.[9]

But more than the loss of memory is involved in Mill's definition. When he discusses logic in the *Examination* and *System of Logic*, he sounds like a passionate Aristotle or Aquinas. "And what is," he asks in the *Examination*, "peculiarly and emphatically, the end of Thinking? Surely it is the attainment of Truth." It is apparent, furthermore, that he does not conceive of truth as an internal agreement between ideas in the mind, as John Locke frequently did, but as an agreement between the idea *inside* the mind and its corresponding reality *outside* the mind. "If thought be anything more than a sportive exercise of the mind," he asserts, "its purpose is to enable us to know what can be known respecting the facts of the universe." But what "facts of the universe" can the mind-as-states-of-feelings know? Physical sensations and intellectual conceptions belong to different orders. The latter can never be made by the former without contradicting its very identity as a sensation. Mill's definition frustrates the mind's attainment of truth, the very reason for the mind's existence, as he elsewhere conceives it. If we press too Mill's doctrine that the objective world of matter external to the perceiving ego is only just a "permanent possibility of sensation" for that ego, we see the specter of solipsism arising as it finally must out of any form of phenomenalism. We never immediately perceive another person in his or her very mind. We know other human beings through their bodies and the actions those bodies perform. But if body is merely a possibility for sensation that exists only in my own mind, I can never certainly know that anybody besides myself exists in a world we both share. I only know myself experiencing sensation. That sort of philosophical loneliness that we saw possessing Berkeley's mind moves also to possess Mill's.

It was precisely the relation between mind and matter that, among other things, finally brought the Enlightenment tradition in nineteenth-century Britain to what we may quite plainly call the Altar of the Unknowable. Given Darwinian evolution and the materialism that modern science seemed to necessitate, the intellectuals could not explain how immaterial mind could have arisen in a universe that was everywhere and totally extended matter. Various theories were put forth, but they turned out to be makeshifts—actually the statements of the problem to be solved, not solutions to it. They all beg the question. T.H. Huxley considered consciousness to be an epiphenomenon of certain biological and chemical actions of the brain. The mind appears, according to him, when the matter of an organism has evolved into a particular structural complication and chemical complexity. John Tyndall, in *The Scope and Limit of Scientific Materialism*, asserted that "thought, as exercised by us, has its correlative in the physics of the brain." W.K. Clifford proposed a theory of "mind-stuff," which similarly attempted to solve the problem by positing a correlation between mental and physical processes. But the question at issue is not the observed fact of the co-existence of consciousness and matter. The question, instead, is the origin and continuing presence of the intellect, admittedly immaterial, in a world in which the only cause allowed to have any scientific validity is the material one. What eventually occurred in the presence of this insoluble problem was the abandonment of the philosophical mind to mystery. The unknowable acquired the air of religious belief, and the Enlightenment tradition ended in darkness. In reference to his correlation between the material object and the thinking object, Tyndall finally said that "man the *object* is separated by an impassable gulf from man the *subject*. There is no motor energy in the human intellect to carry it, without logical rupture, from the one to the other." The universe followed the fate of the mind and became mysterious. "We cannot get behind the curtain, which is reality," Leslie Stephen asserted. "The real mystery of the universe," Tyndall said, "lies unsolved and, as far as we are concerned, is incapable of solution." And the scientific Herbert Spencer turned the unknowable into an ultimate, and hence unprovable, metaphysical fact. The ideas of science and the ideas of religion to him are the same in that even scientific ideas are at the end bare symbols, as he designates them in *The First Principles*, of realities that can never be comprehended by the human mind.

All the wits whom Francis Bacon's bell had called together in the early seventeenth century would have been shocked and saddened by their progeny in the nineteenth century. The universe that had been spread before the first moderns' confident vision and was ripe for their exploration and analysis, that universe for their nineteenth-century descendants became finally an ungraspable enigma. Everywhere they met darkness and the unknowable. In the interval the mind also of the later moderns had been completely gutted by a successively greater and more dogmatic insistence that everything be taken from the mind but its sensory content. They had nothing to guide them as they went deeper into the agnostic obscurity.

III.

Cardinal Newman was wrong. There is no "wild living intellect" forming or being formed in the Enlightenment. When we study carefully the evidence we have collected, Newman's error is apparent. Locke's "closet shut wholly from light," Hume's surrealistic theater of impressions, Condillac's vortices, Mill's thin thread of consciousness—these are the controlling images of what the modern philosophers thought about the human mind; what do they reveal but an intellect scanted, limited, confined, without even the stuff of an identity and so eviscerated? We do discover, to be sure, a wild living instinctualism or emotionalism or psychologism, even a wild living sensibility, to use the word in its eighteenth-century sense, but there is no trace of a wild living intellect in what these philosophers actually said the human mind is. If anyone wishes to oppose the destructiveness of such intellectualism in inquiries religious or otherwise, he would have short shrift of work to do. He would have only to repeat the philosophers against themselves. The epistemologically impoverished state to which they had reduced the mind could not enable it to utter one word of valid judgment on any subject at all. The only thing the Enlightenment mind actually claims it can do in what Locke called its "twilight of probability" is to venture guesses and to make soliloquies.

If indeed the Enlightenment is destructive of religious certitude, just as Newman and everybody else accurately asserts it historically to be, and if in fact one form or other of anti-intellectualism is at the core of the Enlightenment, as I hope I have just shown, must we not then conclude that the mind alone is not the automatic agent of spiritual corruption that Newman assumes it to be in his tirade? And must we not further conclude that those various types of anti-intellectualism that we find in the Enlightenment are all of them far more apt to be subversive of absolute theism than other philosophical positions based on dogmatic powers of the mind?

A great deal of both historical and theoretical evidence exists to support such a conclusion. All philosophers who hold to the doctrine that the human mind is capable of apprehending degrees of absolute truth also hold to the doctrine that absolute truth, supernaturally conceived, must exist as the cause of the mind. Plato and Aristotle maintained such a position in the classical world. St. Augustine always went internally to the mind for his most immediate analogy to the divine architect. All the medieval philosophers, it goes without saying, saw a logical inevitability between intellectualism and theism. The rationalists of the seventeenth century, though with varying degrees of authentic religious feeling, adhered to the necessity of God's existence as the only possible explanation of the fact that the human being possesses a mind. Locke and Berkeley, to be sure, were empiricists who were also theists, but they appear at the inchoate stage of the Enlightenment and it is precisely the still lingering presence of the mind in their systems that enables them to offer their proofs for the existence of God. Nietzsche saw all this so clearly that he said he feared we will never destroy God until we first destroy grammar, destroy, that is, the human ability to express truth in ordered discourse. When we approach the matter from a theoretical point of view, we find more evidence for the superiority of intellectualism over, say, instinctualism as a support for religious values. All arguments for the existence of God proceed from an effect to a cause, and they presuppose some element of similarity between the two, which must be enough alike that it is not logically inconceivable that the one should come from the other. When we place the mind next to the instincts, we discover that instincts are biological and psychological compulsions that are inevitabilities and necessities of our very nature; the mind, in contrast, possesses a will that enables it to begin a possible action or to desist from a possible action as it best judges in what light of knowledge it has. The mind then possesses an internal principle of action and so has freedom. Since it is impossible by definition that God should suffer a compulsion from any source, internal or external, we see it is the mind's freedom but not the instincts' compulsion that suggests itself at once as the effect, the cause of which must be a more perfect will and a more perfect mind. The intellect also experiences a sort of finality. It rests in a conclusion and enjoys its own moment of eternity, the *nunc stans*, the *standing-and-holding-now* of medieval philosophy and mysticism, which "it served," as Hannah Arendt wrote in *The Life of the Mind*, "as model and metaphor for divine eternity." The instincts, on the other hand, when considered alone, cause an *endlessness* in the human being. The processes of the body are forever restlessly repeated and without the mind they would have no end in meaning or purpose. They offer, therefore, no similitude to the perfect motionlessness of God.

But the most conclusive evidence against instinctualism as a support to religious values comes from the logical tendency of any form of phenomenalism eventually to fall into solipsism. We have seen this tendency at work in Berkeley and Mill, both of whom defined the intellect exclusively in the terms of its own non-referential perceptions. The tendency is just as compelling with instincts in place of perceptions. Nearly all the instincts, of course, have an external object for their satisfaction. But without an interpreting mind they do not know that object; they feel only the process of their satisfaction in appropriating that object or their frustration in being deprived of it. Assuming that belief in God presupposes some degree of at least negative knowledge of God as a being different from the believer, we cannot even say that the solipsist is an atheist. He does not know of a God to deny His existence. Thus with the instincts eliminated, it is the mind or nothing.

All this, we may be assured, is heresy for most moderns, who automatically assume that the possession of an intellect means disbelief in God. If God is allowed an existence, it is one believed to be apprehended or verified only in the instinctual, the emotional, above all the subconscious depths of the psyche, but not in or through the operations of an intellect fully awake and conscious. Of the innumerable examples of this attitude, we may use here William James's *The Varieties of Religious Experience*. Coming a few decades after Newman's *Apologia*, these Gifford Lectures on Natural Religion for 1901-02 attempt at the end to give religion a scientific basis. He thinks he is able to do so by placing its source in a *subconscious self*, which he says "is nowadays a well-accredited psychological entity." He presents his position as a hypothesis:

> Let me then propose, as a hypothesis, that whatever it may be on its *farther* side, the "more" with which in religious experience we feel ourselves connected is on its *hither* side the subconscious continuation of our conscious life. Starting thus with a recognized psychological fact as our basis, we seem to preserve a contact with "science" which the ordinary theologian lacks. At the same time the theologian's contention that the religious man is moved by an external power is vindicated, for it is one of the peculiarities of invasions from the subconscious region to take on objective appearances, and to suggest to the Subject an external control. In the religious life the control is felt as "higher"; but since in our hypothesis it is primarily the higher faculties of our own hidden mind which are controlling, the sense of union with the power beyond us is a sense of something, not merely apparently, but literally true.

Was James taking some sort of philosophical holiday from his pragmatism and from his radical empiricism in this passage, or did he actually mean it? He is also the expounder of the "will to believe," and I think we must conclude that he did indeed mean it. In any event, the very year before James was delivering these lectures in Edinburgh, Sigmund Freud was publishing his *The Interpretations of Dreams* in

Vienna. Where James hoped it might be possible to discover God, Freud in reality was discovering a lot of ugly stuff quite remote from religious certitude of any kind. But for one Freud there is a host of Jungs and, besides, Freud's work, most of it valid indeed, has been sucked back into its own psychologism. Now that the sexual secrets of his own private life have been exposed to light, the work itself is read as a dream, and the modern assurances about the subconscious continue to exert themselves undisturbed.

I have said that Newman himself helped to prepare for the receptiveness to the subconscious and to the consequent undervaluation of the intellect. I should now explain myself. We have seen that Newman committed an error in assuming a strong intellectualism in that modern tradition to which he had to have been referring in his *Apologia*. That tradition developed non-rational instead of rational systems and it stripped the intellect of nearly all the powers it possesses in the older philosophies. But Newman was correct in assuming, on the other hand, that the Enlightenment was hostile to religious values, intensely so to those of orthodoxy. On the basis of this historical fact we concluded that the anti-intellectualism of modern philosophy and that philosophy's irreligiousness are connected, that irrationalism is destructive of religion, and that positively the presence of a strong mind is of unquestionable value in the religious life in that it provides a philosophic support to absolute theism not found in any of the irrational systems of the Enlightenment. But Newman was there the victim of error. He thought he saw an excessive intellectualism in modern philosophy, and of course causes existed to make his error understandable—the surface-cool reasonableness of the philosophers' discourses, their detached style and reserves of irony, above all the corrosive critical spirit with which they approached all received opinions and traditions. But what the philosophers themselves said about the mind itself was an entirely different matter. Because of this mistake, Newman saw the intellect by its very nature in fallen man as an agent for spiritual decadence. With the intellect so eliminated, the less rational areas of the human composite—especially those in which, as James stated, the human being feels subject to an external control, including of course the subconscious—these areas become the more appropriate sphere for divine grace. And so the argument of *Apologia Pro Vita Sua* is *ad hominem*. The elusive and ungraspable personality of Newman the man, with that legalistic mania for chronological precisions contrasting so starkly with the obscure depths, that personality dominates its pages and its God works through "sentiments, presages, and prepossessions," which are actually entrances for the *subconscious self* of William James.

Throughout all his life Newman was suspicious of the intellect. In the *University Sermons* he preached at Oxford as an Anglican, he warned his congregation of "the nothingness of natural Reason." As to the immoral effects of the intellect, he pointed out that criminals are most often those men "who have received more than the ordinary share of intellectual gifts." "Reason can but ascertain," he said in the same *Sermons*, "the profound difficulties of our condition, it cannot remove them." The only intellectual process that *The Development of Christian Doctrine* allows as spiritually valuable is that organic one "carried on silently and spontaneously in the mind" by which a body of thought forms itself in a person's life "without his recognizing what is going on within him." In *The Present Position of Catholics in England* he incidentally imputes the suicidal violence of the French Revolution to excessive and wild "praises of the rights of reason." And later on he characterizes the *First Principles* of human thought as if they were tyrannical prejudices and not those ultimate principles of logic that are presupposed in every rational act the mind performs; he describes their enslavement of our minds as "sovereign, irresponsible, and secret;—what an awful form of government the human mind is under from its very constitution." The whole theme reaches its psychologically most subtle form in *The Idea of a University*, the very book where one would least expect to find it. Two contrary tendencies exist in this work. One consists of Newman's desire to baptize the intellect and to make it a servant of faith and dogma. The other consists of Newman's fear that "even within the pale of the Church," the intellect will act, "if left to itself, as an element of corruption and debility." The attractions of the intellect cause a frisson in us, he feared, not unlike that caused by "the sight of beasts of prey" whose strangeness "throws us out of ourselves" and makes us think they were created by another God. In his portrait of Julian the Apostate in *Discourse VIII*, Newman delineated one of the most repellent forms human existence could assume for him, the cold "gentleman" who has made a religion out of his reason. He uses the dying hours of Julian as illustrating the utter "helplessness of philosophy under the stern realities of our being" and he concludes:

> Such, Gentlemen, is the final exhibition of the Religion of Reason: in the insensibility of conscience, in the ignorance of the very idea of sin, in the contemplation of his own moral consistency, in the simple absence of fear, in the cloudless self-confidence, in the serene self-possession, in the cold self-satisfaction, we recognize the mere Philosopher.

It turns out that Newman was a romantic who thought, for instance, that the work of art is not deliberately made but subconsciously *evolved* out of the personality of the artist. Its greatness depends according to his view on the degree to which it reflects that personality. Where are the *personal letters* of Aquinas, he once asked in exasperation at scholastic objectivities. He was, more importantly, a Catholic apologist who at times committed himself overtly to that quite ancient tradition of mystics who see faith as being augmented by the impoverishment, even the extinction, of the intellect. In "The Christian Mysteries" of *Parochial and Plain Sermons*, he stated the central paradox of that tradition: the idea, namely, that "our religious light is intellectual darkness"—the more we are blinded in the intellect, that is, the more we see by faith. Beneath his Oxonian civilities and his rhetorical grace he responded more to Pascal than to Aquinas, more to the Primitive Fathers than to the Medieval Doctors. His Deity is the God of obscurities and resembles the *Deus absconditus* of Gnosticism.

But there is no important difference between an intellect blinded by God and one impoverished by the philosophers, that is, as far as the intellect itself goes. When we compare the minds of Newman and of the Enlightenment, *we must conclude that practically they are the same.*[10] Both have had the rational intellect taken out of them so that non-rational principles may dominate the person's life. The intellect that Newman characterized as some vigorous, wild beast possessed in reality a reason that was, as David Hume described it, "so minute, so weak, so bounded a principle," and it is just the same mind as Newman himself had and that through its intellectual emptiness he saw as most exposed to divine grace. Hume is the pivotal figure. He continued the anti-intellectual epistemology of the Enlightenment out to its conclusion and so cleared the way for the non-rational subjectivism of the nineteenth and twentieth centuries, of which Newman is one of the principal representatives. Hume's anti-intellectualism is radical. He demolished causality and the unified mind; he attacked thought itself, calling it "this little agitation of the brain." It took him alone to destroy the idols of the intellect and to state that the human mind could *know* nothing but could *believe* anything. Newman should have acknowledged one of his fathers in the mind of Hume instead of indulging in rhetorical invective against the imagined tyranny of intellectualism in the modern mind. He could have done so and still have disassociated himself from the particular religious position of Hume. The mind of Hume, if not his reason, is unbounded. It is just as open to fideism as it is to atheism.

The most notorious sentence in Hume, as N.K. Smith called it, occurs at the end of the section on "miracles" in the *Enquiry Concerning Human Understanding*. It is Hume's sop to the mystics and fideists, and they devoured it in varying degrees of realizing that the price they paid for their kind of faith was the inanition of their minds. We now interpret the passage as being ironic from the beginning to the end; Hume is concealing, we believe, his real atheism in a texture of irony and ambiguity. But Newman believed every word of it, and F.W. Maurice must have had the passage in mind when he said that the doctrines of Hume led men to blessed mysteries. Hume intended in the section on miracles "to confound those dangerous friends or disguised enemies to the *Christian Religion*, who have undertaken to defend it by the principles of human reason." "Our most holy religion," the bold ironist went on to pontificate, "is founded on faith, not reason." He concluded the section with his "notorious" statement, which can accommodate with equal facility the mystics and the atheists of modernity:

> So that, upon the whole, we may conclude, that the *Christian Religion* not only was at first attended with miracles, but even at this day cannot be believed by any reasonable person without one. Mere reason is insufficient to convince us of its veracity: and whoever is moved by *Faith* to assent to it, is conscious of a continued miracle in his own person, which subverts all the principles of his understanding, and gives him a determination to believe what is most contrary to custom and experience.

And so we come to the last irony: the mind of Newman and the mind of the Enlightenment are the same in what the philosophers themselves would surely consider as their darkest room, the secret link, that is, between the anti-intellectual epistemology of modern philosophy and the non-rational subjectivism of modern religion. Might we not now suggest a psychological explanation for Newman's attack on the intellect in the *Apologia*? He converted to a church that adhered to the philosophical doctrine that the intellect possesses certain dogmatic powers given to it by God at its creation. The higher mysteries, according to Catholic doctrine, are provided the mind by revelation, but the lower ones, such as the bare fact that God exists, are held to be comprehensible by the unaided intellect. Catholic doctrine also maintained that our reason is capable of arriving at the telos of human beings and so can work out a morality on its own. An enormous philosophical dignity is thus given the human mind by the Thomistic-Aristotelian system.[11] But Newman was long a Protestant before he was a Catholic, and as a Protestant he was permanently influenced by the Calvinist doctrine that the intellect has been radically contaminated by original sin and that its freed exercise can blind the human being to his utter depravity and so nullify in him the operations of grace.

(It was this Calvinistic doctrine, along with similar ones of Jansenism and late medieval nominalism, that Alasdair MacIntyre argues formed the core of the Enlightenment, the origin of which he says was Protestant Britain, Catholic France being just its articulate popularizer. MacIntyre also sees a direct influence of Pascal on Hume in the latter's view of the incapacities of human reason.) Newman brought into the Catholic Church this strain of Protestant anti-intellectualism, and I do not think his northern eyes ever accustomed themselves to the rational clarities of Aristotle and Aquinas. Assenting completely and sincerely to its theological dogma, he nevertheless fretted under the philosophical tradition of his adoptive church. And so in the psychological disclosures of his *Apologia*, disclosures that coexist, I might add, with some incredible Victorian modesties and repressions, Newman gave vent to the old Protestant distrust of the intellect. He could safely do so since he located the disdained intellectualism in a philosophical movement that included libertines and atheists, thus evading the Catholic censor inside himself, but all the while I think he was also protesting against the intellectualism of his own church. In any event, Newman's autobiographical account of his conversion to the Catholic Church does not oppose in actual practice the ways of the mind as they are described by modern philosophers, but it follows them. The mind that he ostensibly attacked was in reality his own. And there is little or no relation between the religious and the intellectual in modern times precisely because there was little or nothing left of the intellect when the philosophers of the Enlightenment got finished with the human mind.

The Slaughter of the Innocents:
The Case of Gerard Manley Hopkins[1]

I.

Gerard Manley Hopkins thought the selfhood of any created nature was so explosively charged with uniqueness that it could never be defined by those common properties it might happen to share with others in its class, if indeed we can speak of "class" as having for him any philosophical validity at all. He valued the music of Purcell, as he said in his sonnet on the English composer, not for any meaning he could find in it—such a mental construction would have had to abstract *one* truth out of the multiple experiences of the artist, his music, and the listener, and in so doing violated the individuality of each. He valued the music instead for the indications in it of the unique personality of Purcell the man, those rehearsals of "abrupt self" that in its unrepeatable singularity possessed his mind. Every natural thing, he declared in "As kingfishers catch fire," exists for only one end: *What I do is me: for that I came.* And in order to catch the idiomatic movement of this egoism, unamenable as it is to intellectual treatment, he got rid of logical structure in his poetry, concentrated myopically on imagistic minutia, and extracted the most idiosyncratic music he could from surely the most violent meter[2] ever devised for English poetry. He didn't leave us, either, to guess from his poems just how extreme his view actually was. He spelled it out in prose with all the rigor and intensity one would expect from a man who was both a Jesuit and a romantic:

> . . . when I consider my selfbeing, my consciousness and feeling of myself, that taste of myself, of *I* and *me* above and in all things, which is more distinctive than the taste of ale or alum, more distinctive than the smell of walnutleaf or camphor, and is incommunicable by any means to another man (as when I

was a child I used to ask myself; What must it be to be someone else?). Nothing else in nature comes near this unspeakable stress of pitch, distinctiveness, and selving, this selfbeing of my own. Nothing explains it or resembles it. . . .

But just at its most "unspeakable stress of pitch" Hopkins turned against this "selfbeing," derived from Duns Scotus's theory of *haecceitas*,[3] and sacrificed it to God. It was then reinterpreted in the divine oneness to the destruction of its original life. We can see the one moment being turned into its opposite in a poem from which I have already quoted, the "As kingfishers catch fire":

> As kingfishers catch fire, dragonflies draw flame;
>> As tumbled over rim in roundy wells
>> Stones ring; like each tucked string tells, each hung bell's
> Bow swung finds tongue to fling out broad its name;
> Each mortal thing does one thing and the same;
>> Deals out that being indoors each one dwells;
>> Selves—goes itself; *myself* it speaks and spells,
> Crying *What I do is me: for that I came.*
>
> I say more: the just man justices;
>> Keeps grace: that keeps all his goings graces;
> Acts in God's eye what in God's eye he is—
>> Christ. For Christ plays in ten thousand places,
> Lovely in limbs, and lovely in eyes not his
>> To the Father through the features of men's faces.

The divine nature of Christ cannot be broken up and assimilated piecemeal by creatures who keep intact their separate existences. We must assume, as Hopkins makes quite clear in the sestet of this poem, that when God the Father intuits God the Son in human beings, He can only be apprehending the one infrangible nature of Christ, and also that the fate of the human self, limited in *haecceitas* to its unique identity, is subsumption in the divine oneness. We have to because Hopkins refused here to use the traditional metaphors of *adoption* and *kinship* to describe the union of the human with the divine, metaphors that insist on the continuation of the human self in its final beautification.[4] He did not say the human being becomes like unto Christ; he said he is Christ in God's eye, and that Christ uses the human being as a medium through which He displays Himself to God the Father, almost as if Christ were indulging in theatrics and needed the human properties for His solitary performance. In any event, the movement in Hopkins's thought toward the uniqueness of the human self is nullified in the theoretical mysticism of this poem. The mortal individuality of its octave is met and necessarily destroyed by that one Christ of its sestet. "He annihilated himself," as he bafflingly wrote of how even Christ renounced His divine self when He assumed the flesh. "He emptied or exhausted himself as far as that was possible, of godhead and behaved as God's slave," exactly as if the absolute requirement of holiness was to have no identity at all.

It was the elective will that for Hopkins effected this sacrifice of the self. He never conceived of the human will as undivided against itself; the Thomist idea that it is a unity grounded in the very animality of man was repugnant to him since he believed original sin reached and completely corrupted that nature to its core. The sole end of his moral life, already culturally stiffened by the puritan and Victorian insistence on psychological repression, consisted not in the discipline and completion of natural appetite but in its total subjugation. The idea of a natural desire for God, of an appetitive movement toward Him even in just the normal activity of adult human beings, such an idea was inconceivable to Hopkins. The elective will, as he saw it, was the most spiritualized element in human intention exactly because it was separated from natural appetites, all of which collectively taken together and informed, or uninformed, by consciousness comprise the lower will, the one polluted by original sin, which Hopkins called the affective. God *stresses* the elective will with a vision of that one perfect self among the infinitely possible selves that each human being has in the mind of God. Since its essence is in the being of God and not in phenomenal existence, this self is dis-natural and only reflects the divine Christ outside His temporal incarnation. Existence itself was considered an accident of the self. Only the one perfect idea of ourselves in God's mind is our absolute essence; it alone can participate in divine being. The entire discipline of the religious life, therefore, centered for Hopkins on the extirpation of his natural self and the painful acquisition through grace of a different self who repeats the Christ. He split himself apart and waged systematic warfare in a divided will.

But Hopkins discovered his helplessness in the presence of his own nature. The more he turned the screws of discipline, the more the pressure released the irrational raw powers of a nature that fought back like a cunning beast and drove him into states of madness. The Scotist doctrine of *haecceitas* then became cruelly reversed. The whole stuff of the self, which he had once so celebrated, was turned into an instrument of torture. His curse was his own individuality, the taste of his bitter self. *Bones built in me,* he said in one of the "terrible sonnets," *flesh filled, blood brimmed the curse.* He found no solution for the dilemma he had created for himself in pitting his will so against his nature. If he moved decisively toward spiritual perfection, the contrast he inevitably saw between himself and the ideal he strained to achieve generated in him a self-hatred which ate at his insides like acid. "I was continuing this train of thought this evening," he noted during a retreat at the very end of his life, "when I began to enter on that course of loathing and hopelessness which I have so often felt before, which made me fear madness and led me to give up the practice of meditation except, as now, in retreat and here it is again." On the other hand, if he returned to his common nature, his "Jackself" as he called it, he only paralyzed himself in despair at the mutilated self he had become in those spiritual struggles, which after years of disciplines had gone nowhere. "I am like a straining eunuch," he wrote at the end. "Nature in all her parcels and faculties," he had written earlier, "gaped and fell apart. . . like a clod cleaving and holding only by strings of root."

In such a crisis Hopkins came to see his nature as containing unknowable and ungovernable forces inside itself. During his bleakest moments he felt not just the absence of God but, more terribly, the defeat of God at the hands of something within him he could neither understand nor control. His mind in its depths was no longer just a mystery; it was a lawless tyranny that in the psychological crisis of 1884–85 brought him to the point of clinical madness. One more least turn of the screw and his psyche would have exploded. He had no philosophical principles that would have enabled him to see the subjectivity of his anguish through its contrast with an objective world not vitiated by romantic sublimations. The only thing that held him together was dogma, which addressed itself only to his blind instinct for obedience. And it was not a matter at all of specific sins he might have committed. If it were, his anguish would have been contained in objective acts or intentions he could have discovered, confessed, and been absolved from. It was his whole life, the man himself at some unlocatable source of personal contamination, which was involved in nameless, pervasive guilt. It would have been impossible for him to have specified his sense of pure shame. The result, which he recorded in the "terrible sonnets," was a vision of the mind lost in depths foreign to itself but still of itself, and so victimized by its own subjective terror:

> No worst, there is none. Pitched past pitch of grief,
> More pangs will, schooled at forepangs, wilder wring.
> Comforter, where, where is your comforting?
> Mary, mother of us, where is your relief?

My cries heave, herds-long; huddle in a main, a chief-
woe, world-sorrow; on an age-old anvil wince and sing—
Then lull, then leave off. Fury had shrieked 'No lingering! Let me be fell: force I must be brief'.

O the mind, mind has mountains; cliffs of fall
Frightful, sheer, no-man-fathomed. Hold them cheap
May who ne'er hung there. Nor does long our small
Durance deal with that steep or deep. Here! creep,
Wretch, under a comfort serves in a whirlwind: all
Life death does end and each day dies with sleep.

This poem shows that the end of Hopkins's conflict was either
in death-like sleep or in death itself. So much for the attempt of his
elective will to subjugate his affective will.[5] It turned out that the animal
nature of the affective will possesses a resistance of its own, a palpable
toughness in its texture, which would not so easily allow itself to be
deconstructed at the theological behest of the elective will. It must,
consequently, have some religious sanctions of its own, or else religion
necessarily causes schizophrenia in the human being and a Manichaean
principle rules the spiritual world. Church dogma prevented him from
holding this latter position. He could have then concluded that any
extreme opposition between the two wills is as dangerous religiously
as it is psychologically, that the God of grace is also the God of nature,
and that original sin by itself does not create realms where the divine
omnipotence is nullified by uncontrollable human perversity. Evidence
indeed exists that indicates that Hopkins came to a kind of psychological
realization of such a conclusion. "Pray not to be tormented," he finally
said just to himself, leaving God out of the account. Instead of treating
the appetites of the affective will as slaves, he was moving to the notion
of them as members of a whole commonwealth, to use the Thomistic
metaphor, with rights of their own, which God respects and blesses.
"My own heart let me more have pity on," he asked in one of his last
poems. But it was tragically too late for him and, besides, Hopkins had
a great fear of systematic logical thought, believing it to be spiritually
dangerous and subversive. He died at forty-five without coming to a
completely intellectual awareness of the exact harm that his two wills
had done his religious life and his psychological integrity as a man. Our
final impression of him is that of a nature close to insanity in its struggle
against both divine injunctions and human desire.

Hopkins's mind was the battleground of three separate religious
traditions, each one of them at the others' intellectual throats. His
puritanism[6], derived from his Protestant Victorian past, emphasized

original sin, divided the human being into opposing wills, and saw the end of morality as the deconstruction of his existent self. Human agency was eliminated from the fulfillment of this end. Only the grace of God was adequate to the rehabilitation of depraved human nature. His puritanism also disparaged the intellect as an instrument incapable of understanding the extent of man's iniquity or of realizing the inexplicable grace of God's salvation. It valued instead subjective, emotional states as more appropriate to a God who reveals Himself through the will and not the mind. Opposed to the puritanism was his romanticism. Notwithstanding their differences, the two are alike at least in one respect: if his theologism had not already done the job for him, his enthusiasm for the radical individuality of natural things would have itself dispersed the world to nominalistic fragments and rendered it meaningless to the mind. The romanticism also caused Hopkins, as we shall see, to make theologically questionable claims for the spiritual purity of childhood. We might say that for him original sin began at puberty and left the Wordsworthian child alone. At the same time, Hopkins converted to Roman Catholicism and joined an order whose philosophical tradition was Thomistic and intellectualist, and diametrically opposed to both puritanism and romanticism. Of the manifold oppositions between Thomism and the other two traditions, we should here emphasize the respect Thomism pays the creative powers of God. It gives an unassailable integrity to the nature God created, protects it from all forms of mystical or Gnostic annihilations, and sees the end of morality as the fulfillment, not the deconstruction, of the natural self. The intellect is considered an essential part of the fulfillment: it apprehends the good that the will completely and inevitably desires. Of the three traditions it was the puritanism that won out in Hopkins—it had been dominant from the beginning—and created the "terrible pathos" that his friend Richard Watson Dixon singled out as the overwhelming effect of his poetry.

II.

We turn now to the effect that Hopkins's divided will had on his conception of God. One fundamental principle governing a religious person's belief is that God's moral perfection is absolute. If Hopkins saw original sin creating an area of contagious moral pollution, it was inevitable then that he should move toward separating God from that area and insisting on an ontological partition between the divine purity and human evil. God's absolutism, he must have felt with not altogether complete theological propriety, would be invalidated by contact with unredeemed human nature. To the extent that Hopkins saw himself as trapped in this realm on account of his own rebellious nature, then God became for him the God of absence, the one who has deserted the human world because of its moral repulsiveness and Who leaves it a spiritual void. But to the extent, on the other hand, that he saw the Deity as providentially intervening in human affairs to save the soul, then God became for him the God of violence, the one who uses catastrophe, crisis, and tragedy to extricate the soul from its corrupted nature in order to restore it to spiritual health. Absence and violence, consequently, were the two poles between which Hopkins's thought about God moved, and all through the excessive hold that the idea of the divided will had over his mind.

The early poem *Nondum* dramatized the theme of the *Deus absconditus*[7] in its most extreme form. God is so absent from us, it states, that we cannot even imagine what He is like; in place of a certain knowledge of Him, either revealed or unrevealed, we set up futile shadows on His throne and worship in reality the pure silence. The nocturnal stars are like lamps burning in an empty house. Being itself has been drained of meaning and lies extended in a "dread and vacant maze." "My heaven is brass and iron my earth," he had written a year before. The whole force of "Spelt from Sibyl's Leaves" lies in its image of the primordial night, not in its reference to God's final judgment with which the poem ends. The night is seen as the "womb-of-all, home-of-all, hearse-of-all," which breeds, then destroys life meaninglessly, exactly as if the power of evil had created a separate atheistic world where it now works its will undisturbed. God is the *someone else* of its Manichaean universe. In "I wake and feel the fell of dark," Hopkins is caught within the nightmare of a self from whom God has removed Himself because of sin, and he writes in his desolation:

> And my lament
> Is cries countless, cries like dead letters sent
> To dearest him that lives alas! away.

Hopkins's encounter with modern industrialism and with the poverty and squalor it spawned in cities reinforced the division of his mind between the withdrawn God and abandoned humanity. He is the first of the modern poets to register the full impact of the industrial transformation of England. Nothing at Oxford had prepared him for what he saw on the streets and heard in the confessional at Liverpool. The exploited urban masses, with their addictions and violence, caused revulsion in the sensitive Hopkins. He became physically sick at times. He had none of the religious toughness in him that would have enabled him to seek out and discover the image of God even in the filthiest and

75

most degraded of human beings.[8] The visions he saw in the sulfurous atmosphere of the industrial cities drove him at times instead to a misanthropic sense of man's being forsaken by God and given over to passion and vice. "The drunkards go on drinking," he once wrote about Liverpool, "the filthy . . . are filthy still; human nature is so inveterate. Would I have seen the last of it."

It was the God of violence, though, that most held Hopkins's attention. It had to have been so since he believed, finally, in a providential God Who intervened in human affairs to save the imperiled soul. What He intervened against was an intractable human nature, and He resorted to violence in Hopkins's mind to abolish the barrier. The *Deus absconditus*[9] consequently was for his times of despair, the God of violence for his times of belief. God the Son would return as a soldier, he stated in one poem, because He "knows war." Christ is the "sword and strife" of "To seem the stranger lies my lot." As Perseus in "Andromeda," He hovers above His endangered church, "barebill" in hand, prepared for mortal combat with the "wilder beast." At Oxford, in "My prayers must meet a brazen heaven," Hopkins described his existence as "battling with God"; at Dublin, in "Thou are indeed just," near the end, he would "contend" with God Who though a friend was acting like an enemy. The embers of "The Windhover" as they disintegrate under the intrusion of grace "fall, gall themselves, and gash gold-vermilion." The theme reaches its intensest pitch in "Carrion Comfort." God inflicts extreme suffering, the poet asserts, so the human being will be cleansed and his grain lie "sheer and clear." The suffering was extreme, as it had to have been if God were to break through and save a man whose "memory, understanding, and affective will," as Hopkins stated the dilemma in *The Spiritual Writings*, "are incapable themselves of an infinite object and do not tend towards it." What else indeed but extreme suffering could an "infinite object" inflict on a creature not able by nature to sustain it? But we forget these theological distinctions in the presence of the actual violence of the angry God:

> But ah, but O thou terrible, why wouldst thou rude on me
> Thy wring-world right foot rock? lay a lionlimb against me? Scan
> With darksome devouring eyes my bruisèd bones? and fan,
> O in turns of tempest, me heaped there; me frantic to avoid thee
>   and flee?

"Breathe, body of lovely death," Hopkins utters at one point in *The Wreck of the Deutschland*, the one poem of his that treats most extensively the theme of the violent God. The line is admittedly excessively rhetorical, but it is one of the most thematically important statements

Hopkins ever made. In it the idea of divine violence fuses with the obsession of romantic love. An ecstatic Isolde sings herself to death over the body of her dead lover and in doing so protests against what she sees as the tragic limitations of ordinary human existence. That existence not only cannot realize the intensities of her love, she implies in her suicide, but it actually thwarts and defeats it. If life is its enemy, then death must be its friend, and so in its extremest form romantic love becomes suicidal. There is, of course, nothing of the suicidal in Hopkins's poem. But its five nuns symbolically are the lovers of Christ, and the basic meaning of the poem is that God causes the shipwreck in which they are drowned so that their love may be consummated in death. They are "sealed in wild waters," just as Hopkins, undergoing a similar but far less physically destructive experience, was sealed in the terror of God's lightning, as he states in the poem, and consented to His "lashed rod." God's salvific love of human beings, *The Wreck of the Deutschland* states, rejects the *order* of created nature for its expression. It drives them out into a winter storm on some symbolical sea and drowns them, giving them in their last moments of anguish a glimpse of that mystical union that is achieved through the destruction of their natures.

Hopkins belonged to that modern tradition that feels it must renounce nature as either inadequate for being an instrument of divinity or incapable of providing evidence for the existence of divinity. The tradition was first most fully expressed in David Hume's *Dialogues Concerning Natural Religion*. Bishop Butler in the first half of the eighteenth century assumed as a given fact in *The Analogy of Religion* that the natural world possessed such order and was regulated with such precision that by itself it argued successfully for the existence of a designing God. He assumed this fact and he went on to play the dangerous game of pointing out those areas of ambiguity and irregularity—the darker undersides to the lighted surfaces—which exist in the normal uniformity of the natural world. He did so in hopes that his audience would thereby become either reconciled or resigned to the irrationalities and the contradictions that the "man of reason" was beginning to discover, and be disgusted by, in the Christian Church, in her traditions and in her Scriptures. If you accept those problematical areas of nature, he argued, why not also accept the problematical areas of revelation, the latter being concerned, after all, more specifically with the transcendental, which natural evidence only suggests in the most general terms possible. And isn't some ambiguity inevitable in any communication of the infinite divine to the finite human? It was a dangerous game that Butler was playing because his argument left open the alternative of someone's rejecting both nature and revelation as containing too many obscurities for either of them to be used in any kind of rational argument at all. Hume embraced the alternative and developed it with all his destructive logical skills in the *Dialogues Concerning Natural Religion*; he demolished the argument from design for the existence of God, and the natural world, unconnected with divinity, was denuded of sacramental and analogical values. It furnished no evidence for anything but its own disorder. But the realm of the secular for Hopkins was human nature, not physical nature in general. Where that latter was concerned, he came close to pantheism in the degree to which he thought God was present in the inhuman world of pure nature. The stuff of our common humanity was that problematical area where he joined Hume in seeing a complete severance of the divine from the natural. There the absence and violence of Hopkins's God were bred. He further joined Hume in believing that "the most perfect worship" of this deity, so terrifyingly remote from us, was, as Hume said in the *Dialogues*, "a certain mysterious self-annihilation or total extinction of all our faculties." And Hopkins would have concurred with the reason Hume gave for this worship: "the infirmities of our nature do not permit us to reach any ideas, which in the least correspond to the ineffable sublimity of the divine attributes." With Hopkins then we have a reversal of the Catholic intellectual tradition, which has as its source the Augustinian doctrine that man most resembles God in the powers of his mind. But in the psychological chaos of the "terrible sonnets," as in the emotionalism and death-wish of *The Wreck of the Deutschland*, that mind has been lost and nothing left in human nature resembles God at all.

III.

From the beginning of his life as a Roman Catholic, Hopkins determined to see a moral opposition between poetry and religion. One of his first acts upon conversion was to burn all manuscripts of his poems—"the slaughter of the innocents," as he not unambiguously called the immolation—and throughout the remainder of his life he often expressed the conviction that poetry was unbecoming to those particular devotions that he professed as a member of the Society of Jesus. What reasons did he give for this belief? He did not treat immoral subjects in his poetry; neither was poetry proscribed by the Jesuits who, after all, had an illustrious history of intellectual and artistic achievements in avowedly non-religious areas. The only reason he could then fall back on, and the one he consistently used, was the dangers of poetic fame, ludicrously as if the few publications his friends offered him had any chance of transforming him overnight into some famous poet and one too besieged by downright pernicious temptations. The rationalization is transparent. He besides contradicted his conviction by the secret decision he made not to write poems, as he told Dixon, unless commanded to do so by his superiors, knowing as he did they would command nothing immoral. Yet he tied their hands by keeping them ignorant of his poetic genius, and when he did break his silence and write his first poem as a Jesuit, it was not at the command of anyone but at some vague hint dropped by his rector, which Hopkins took as a command. The bulk of his poems he never showed to a superior at all.

Poetry for Hopkins was something intensely private.[10] He was unwilling, I think, to expose it to a public world, one either secular or religious, for fear that the possibly hostile criticism of that world would stifle the peculiar spontaneities he wished to release in a poetic medium he had made up for himself. In obscurity and isolation he could more freely indulge that psychological rawness he at other times kept under a tight control. Like a private code he used poetry to say things to himself that all internal and external censors would not understand. He was even theoretically prepared for this procedure. Anticipating our own times' preoccupation with irony, Hopkins worked out a critical theory, which he expressed in his *Letters*, of what we might call thematic ambiguity whereby he explained some obscure passages in certain choruses of Greek tragedies. He saw a double level of meaning in the choruses, a public one overtly concerned with the historical plot, and a private one covertly concerned with the intended or unintended self-expression of the poet himself. Through this counterpoint, consequently, a mysterious underworld was created in the tragedy; in the allusive irony of his language the poet could say a host of things remote indeed from the actual plot at hand, things perhaps even contradictory to the basic "public" structure of the drama. But Hopkins's other aesthetic theories, especially those to be found in "Henry Purcell" and "On a Piece of Music," determined the nature of what it was in his case the poet said. He did not believe the poet exercised freedom over the poem. He saw the work as inevitably evolving out of certain forces in the personality of the artist, which the work expressed frequently even against the conscious will of the artist. Since he held no control over these forces, and since furthermore his concept of the beautiful was beyond the categories of good and evil, Hopkins did not think the poet should be morally judged, at least in the poem. The end of it all was that poetry became fixed in Hopkins's mind as an ironic and amoral revelation of his personality at those obscure levels no human being can control or understand. He surrendered the craft of poetry to psychological compulsion. It became for him a kind of neurotic symptom.

The essential note of the neurotic symptom is ambivalence. It is formed as a compromise between two mental forces in conflict with each other, the one the conscience, the other some instinctual impulse or desire that the conscience has condemned. In a trapped effort to recover balance the mind seeks contradictorily to combine the opposites together and to obtain a satisfaction for each through symbolic substitutes. Lady Macbeth realizes again her desire to have Duncan murdered through the blood on her hands and at the same time attempts to appease her horrified conscience by imagining herself washing those hands clean of defilement. Guilt has split her mind in two; she is simultaneously in one person the impulsive criminal and that criminal's most pitiless judge. Her conscience has been perverted from its legitimate function of protecting her nature and in her tragic confusion it has been transformed into a suicidal self-condemnation. Hopkins split his own mind in two and emphasized the dogma of original sin because of a conflict he suffered between what he called the elective and the affective wills, a division that corresponds exactly with conscience and impulse. What that specific desire was that provoked repression, the repression in turn leading to conflict and psychological crisis, we do not know. The evidence we have suggests homosexuality, which he could not accept in himself and about which he felt the greatest shame. In any event, some forbidden impulse did exist in him; otherwise, there would not have been the crisis we know as a fact. And neurotic symptoms must have inevitably emerged by which he tried to express the desire—the pressure to do so would have been overwhelming—and at the same time to condemn it in order to prevent his conscience from demanding suicide.

Another note of the neurotic symptom, that is, in its final form, is its ubiquity. The more the repressed impulse must content itself with a half-existence through substitution and transference, the more it moves, impelled by fierce necessities, to invade all areas of the mind and to dominate all the faculties. Its powers of self-transformation, its protean deceits, are enormous. Through the principle of the *association of ideas* run wild, it finally forces its victim to see everything as either enemies to, or embodiments of, its unrealized desire. It acquires ubiquity and symptoms are everywhere in the mind, often disguised as the most impersonal of facts. And so even without his romantic principle of self-expression, without his aesthetic egoism, there would still have been in Hopkins a strong tendency to subvert the object of poetry and to turn it into a vehicle for whatever forbidden impulse it was that caused him such anguish. But with that principle he gave himself absolutely no choice, and the tendency became for him something like hard fate.

A great deal of Hopkins's poetic energy was spent on translating the impulse into such acceptable forms as his culture had made available to him. Two of the more important of these forms were the romantic concepts of nature and childhood. As he stretched himself on the rack of scrupulosity, he constructed poetic dreams about the spontaneity and moral purity of the natural world and of the sexually inchoate boy. He eluded his conscience because for him both the boy and the wilderness were immune to impulsive moral corruption; yet psychologically they were nothing but impulse itself and could satisfy all the requirements for Hopkins's vicarious drama of emotional abandonment. Nearly every one of his nature poems contains contradictory participation in a moralized wilderness, and "The Bugler's First Communion" best illustrates Hopkins's psychological involvement with the uncorrupted child. He encountered, though, some uneasiness in the latter poem: the boy was too close to manhood and in a moment of pastoral dereliction Hopkins expressed the wish never to have to see him again for fear the boy would soon fall into adult sin. The screen of projected moralism would then be torn away and reality would call the man's hand. Another translation his culture made available to him was through the Victorian notion of a certain kind of masculinity, one in which physical strength, constant labor, and life related to the earth were all thought to combine and to create moral solidity in the man, just as if that solidity could best form itself in poverty and exhaustion. Felix Randal, Tom Navvy, and Harry Ploughman are characters in Hopkins's poems who are instances of such masculinity. It is the violence of the diction in these poems, the clotted thickness and unrelieved excitability of their style, the abrupt hard meter, that indicate more than theme itself a psychological exploitation on the poet's part. He appears only to be expressing and exhausting some unfaced impulse in the romanticized strength of the men involved, protected as he was by their moral solidity, and at the same time to be blocking the impulse by creating an impenetrable medium through which it must pass. No one can even read the latter two poems coherently aloud.

At other moments in his poetry he makes a nearer approach to the impulse now more narrowly and realistically embodied. In "The Lantern out of Doors" he refers to an experience that for him was charged with ungraspable meaning: the accidental but arresting encounter with male physical beauty that is either accompanied or unaccompanied by a corresponding moral beauty:

> Men go by me whom either beauty bright
> In mould or mind or what not else makes rare:
> They rain against our much-thick and marsh air
> Rich beams, till death or distance buys them quite.

In "To what serves Mortal Beauty?" Gregory the Great sees some Angle slave boys in the Roman Forum, "those lovely lads once, wet-fresh," and moved by their beauty he sends Augustine to evangelize the Britons. Hopkins seemed at ease in this poem with a moral purpose for beauty. But when the poem is carefully read, a contradiction is discovered. If beauty so confidently and so unambiguously serves such a moral purpose, why is it called "dangerous" in the first line? Why is it admitted to agitate the blood? There is no moral purpose alleged at all in the unfinished "Epithalamion." A stranger accidentally comes upon a "bevy" of boys swimming in a river. Stimulated by the whole abandonment of their bodies to sunlight and water, he strips off his clothes and dives naked in a "pool neighbouring." There is no connection between this totally masculine swimming party and the wedding for which Hopkins wrote the poem. In another poem, the finished "The Loss of the Eurydice," it is the sight of the drowned sailor, his body "strained to beauty" and washed ashore to be exposed there, that provokes the most haunting and powerful lines of the poem:

> They say who saw one sea-corpse cold
> He was all of lovely manly mould,
>> Every inch a tar,
> Of the best we boast our sailors are.

> Look, foot to forelock, how all things suit! He
> Is strung by duty, is strained to beauty,
>> And brown-as-dawning-skinned
> With brine and shine and whirling wind.

It is as if the sailor had first to be made a corpse before Hopkins could admit and observe his beauty. But even as a corpse his beauty reanimates the drowned man and brings him back to life for Hopkins's fascinated gaze.[11]

But such explicit abandonments are infrequent in Hopkins's poetry. More recurrently it is his poetic medium itself, as I have suggested above, the strangeness and violence of his diction, the ambiguity and displaceableness of his "sprung meter"[12] as the multiple candidates for accent crowd together and present their blunt, loud claims—it is all this in which the impulse finds its substituted and its vicarious existence. And the subject matter of his most compelling poetry deals more with the other side of the neurotic symptom, that is, with the condemning conscience, which has lost rational control of itself and is driven by sadistic and suicidal intentions. These poems, I would maintain, are not religious no matter what theological language they might employ.

They belong more to the claustrophobic psychologism of Sigmund Freud's *Civilization and Its Discontents* than they do to the spiritual severities of St. Ignatius. A father of some nature has been attacked or killed in the nightmare world of these poems;[13] his condemnation has been internalized by the guilty son—the grave, as Allen Tate would later say, has been set up in the house—and the son's very life becomes the material of a death sentence, "this tormented mind," as Hopkins says, "tormenting yet." The "terrible sonnets" inform us exactly what kinds of death the sentence took: isolation from family and country in "To seem the stranger"; the spiritual desolation of "I wake and feel the fell of dark"; a poetic sterility that he thought of as a castration in "Thou are indeed just, Lord." If we go beyond the record of the poems, we discover in his biography only further painful details of vocational failure, sickness, crisis, and early death. It turns out that Hopkins's whole existence executed against itself a death sentence issued by a judge disgusted at the moral ugliness and pathos of his instinctual rebellion, a judge Hopkins must have both murdered and assimilated in his dream world. His tragedy was that he couldn't see that the judge was an idol he had himself made out of his own prideful refusal to forgive himself and to accept what Aquinas calls the *burden of nature*. The idol for him was no one less than God the Father Himself:

> Wert thou my enemy, O thou my friend,
> How wouldst thou worse, I wonder, than thou dost
> Defeat, thwart me?

> *

> But ah, but O thou terrible, why wouldst thou rude on me
> Thy wring-world right foot rock? lay a lionlimb against me?

> *

> I am gall, I am heartburn. God's most deep decree
> Bitter would have me taste: my taste was me.

We are back with the violent God of the second part of this essay. But we are now able, I think, to see Him more clearly. He contradicts the God of Hopkins's own order, the God Whose purpose, according to Aquinas, is *not to destroy but to cherish the nature of things*. The ubiquity of the neurotic symptom reached, it would seem, and infiltrated even Hopkins's religious belief. His violent God finally was the perverted conscience of Hopkins himself—the disownable agent of suicide—and His reality was restricted to, and exhausted in, Hopkins's own isolated mind.

I.

For the Satan of Paul Valéry's *Ébauche d'un serpent*—a poem that takes us at once to Valéry's intellectual and spiritual position—the original sin occurred when God inexplicably turned aside from the contemplation of His own perfection to utter that Word whereby the universe itself came violently into existence. In that one metaphysically obscene decision to create *otherness*, God renounced the freedom of His internality and locked Himself, according to the merciless reasoning of Satan, into the logical impossibility of creating anything other than a realm of death and error. By definition, creation means the coming into existence of something different from the agent who causes it to be. If the two enjoyed an identity with each other, if the made and the maker were the same, there would be no emerging new thing, but merely an extended duplication of the maker. And what comprises the *otherness* of God's perfect unity but fragmented multiplicity, of His underived plenitude but deprived contingency, of his pure mind but sensual animality and death? But Valéry's angel goes further. He carries the argument to deicide. If perfection chooses to create, and if by the nature of the case it can create only imperfection, then it must cease to be. It cannot survive the pollution it necessarily incurs in the presence of what it has imperfectly created. God thus destroys Himself, and the universe becomes His open tomb:

> Ô Vanité! Cause Première!
> Celui qui règne dans les Cieux,
> D'une voix qui fut la lumière
> Ouvrit l'univers spacieux.
> Comme las de son pur spectacle,
> Dieu lui-même a rompu l'obstacle
> De sa parfaite éternité;

Il se fit Celui qui dissipe
En conséquences, son Principe,
En étoiles, son Unité.

Cieux, son erreur! Temps, sa ruine!
Et l'abîme animal, béant! . . .
Queue chute dans l'origine
    Étincelle au lieu de néant! . . .

*

O Vanity! First Cause! The one who reigns in heaven,
with a voice that was the light opened the spacious universe.
As if He were bored with the pure spectacle of Himself, God
shattered the obstacle of His perfect eternity; He became one
who dissipates His Principle into consequences, His Unity into
stars.

    The firmament, His error! Time, His ruin! And the
animal abyss, gaping wide! . . . What a fall into origin now
shines in place of nothingness! . . .

Satan is pure intellect. He cannot believe God incurred any
impurity in creating his angelic self, which does not suffer the duality of
body and soul. Since the purity of such an uncompounded state alone
confers reality in his order of things, he sees himself as the sole being
now left and, consequently, the only one able to do justice to what God
had been before He dissipated Himself in the debris of a meaningless
universe. Intellectual as he inescapably is, he is possessed by the vision
of God's extractable essence—the idea, that is, of what He should have
been, which can survive His existential death in the memory of anyone
remaining and capable of conceiving it. Satan wishes to restore the
concept of being through a mimesis of Godhead within his own intellect.
To do so he must attempt to annihilate, according to the rigors of purity,
everything different from that intellect. To deconstruct and destroy can
then be his only motive as long as the pollution of phenomenal creation
obtains. An egoistic mysticism dictates every move he makes.

    Valéry's poem deals with Satan's seduction of Eve. The combination
of an animal body and an intellectual soul, found only in human
beings, would indeed exasperate the Satanic purity. God Himself could
only sigh over the pathos of their abortive birth. Satan in his gnostic
hatred of their ambiguous complexity cannot endure the steatopygia
of their brutal state, the awkwardness that their innocence presents in
the electrical presence of pure spirit. But they are embarrassingly kin

to him. They possess his intellect, obscured though it is by flesh. The absurd composite begs in his eyes for the knife of the Cartesian analysis whereby intellect can become cleanly severed, if only in mind alone, from its contaminating opposite.[2] In isolation the intellect will then see itself as having been degraded by the God who had compounded it with an animal, and it will be at one with Satan in a revaluation and radical revision of the creative Godhead.

He does not intend, though, to seduce Eve into any kind of intellectual life as it is normally conceived. The theology of the Satanic intellect destroys the basis of knowledge—the existence, that is, of the thing to be known, different as it must be from the mind knowing it and formed in a resistant body or action of its own. Philosophically he cannot withstand the body of the world, and *something different* disfigures for him the purity he wishes to restore. Truth for Satan, therefore, is not what one discovers about the substance of the world, or even about one's own mind, objectively considered; it is rather what the self invents or dreams inside the mind that reveals the mind only to itself. He can intend only to deconstruct Eve's separate identity and to transform her into a pure similitude with himself so that his intellect will have no foreign thing to contaminate its experiment in Godhead. "Nothing more remains of thought," Valéry said elsewhere of the final act of the mind, "but its pure acts, by which, in its own presence, it changes and transforms itself into itself." God turned aside from such self-involved perfection to ruin Himself in those levels of different beings to whom He had mistakenly wished to communicate degrees of His own goodness. In seducing the origin of the human race, Satan sees himself as returning to that perfection through the transmutation of those different beings into the ego of his own mind.

Such an ego then is a symbolist poem, a "monster of silence and lucidity" cunningly created from the Word, which, as Valéry said in his essay on Mallarmé, "neither demonstrates, nor describes, nor represents anything at all." Mallarmé submitted language, as Satan would Eve, to a "Jansenist"[3] purification whereby *use* and *end* are separated from purity of form. The symbolist poet sought to subsume the rational content of language under the self-absorbing processes of pure art so that poetry should be about nothing but itself.[4] He frustrates the conscious mind, which craves meaning, and, in the name of purely verbal form, he appeals to sub-rational states that are themselves formless and inscrutable. Satan also acts to free the intellect from the constraints of objective meaning and, for the sake of deifying the intellect, to set it up as an end in itself. He consistently employs the rhetoric of symbolist inscrutability. He tells Eve *ne pense pas* and asks the sun to warm his iciness that he may daydream of evil; his meditation murmurs in the coils of his tail; he seeks lodgments for dreams in the toughest souls; when he seduces Eve, he exploits the allusions and connotations of "fables" and "systems of gossamer," and he knows his most potent weapon is not the substance of intellectual argument but, instead, the scent arising from his "insidious depths," which he says nothing can elucidate. He is pure self-awareness, not self-knowledge.

Such an intellect cannot be penetrated by experience. It suffers no scars such as Odysseus received from the boar or St. Francis in the stigmata. At the end of the poem he fails in his attempt at transformation of human nature. Surrounded by the chaos and madness that have fallen out of the convulsed Tree of Knowledge— the "new science" he has introduced to the human mind—he realizes he has only infected human beings with a hatred for their contingent existence and for the God who created it; he also realizes he can only *imagine* his intellect as a substitute for God. Yet he is unaffected by the experience, even by the pain he has caused himself. The male sadness he feels after his "infertile copulation" with human nature is ironic; it detaches him from the woman he seduces and abandons. His mistake, as Valéry said of Bergson, was to think human beings are worth saving. He chooses to live in the operations of only two faculties of the mind, the analytical and the imaginative: the one to tear the world apart, the other to dream in its debris of some perfect Self. Neither of the faculties requires experience in a stable objective world; both, in fact, can best perform their operations when the very existence of the world is questioned. Isolated inside the pride of its cool internality, the Satanic intellect determines purely to know itself unsubmitted and uncompared to another thing or being.

Satan's position, and Valéry's, in its final reaches becomes what I have called egoistic mysticism. Thought being pure thought or mind knowing pure mind is unthinkable. The mind can no more directly know itself than the eyes can see themselves. It can only indirectly infer itself through the operations it performs in the presence of an object it seeks to know.[5] It sees itself in the mirror of *the other*, which has stimulated it to its proper life so that it can become aware of itself. Only then occurs that mysterious and often chilling moment of self-vision. But without the mediation of the object the mind cannot know itself any more than, again, the eyes can see themselves in a world without reflection. Valéry knew this futility just as he had known that Mallarmé's conflict with objective reality, and with the denotative element in language representing that reality, was "a match that is lost in advance." But he did not renounce the ideal he dramatized in *Ébauche d'un serpent*; it remained central for him to the end. There is always that moment in the poem and in scientific thought when the mind intoxicates itself with its naked strength; the very crust of the earth seems to melt in its fires.[6] It was the sensation of the power the mind experiences in such moments of supreme self-confidence that mesmerized Valéry and justified for him those sacrifices he made to his impossible intellectual ideal. He felt, but did not think, that the mind needed nothing, that the only object adequate to its power was its own Self abstracted from reality and opposed to truth, even to thought itself. Writing in a late essay on Descartes, he says:

> The effect of the *Cogito*, to me, is like a clarion sounded by Descartes to summon up the powers of his ego. He repeats it as the watchword of the Self in a number of different places in his work, sounding the reveille to pride and intellectual courage. That is the secret of the charm—in the magical sense of the term—of this formula which has been so much discussed, when it ought, I think, to be enough to feel it. At the sound of the words the entities vanish; the will to power invades the man, pulls the hero to his feet, reminds him of his utterly personal mission, his own destiny; even of his difference, his individual injustice. For it is possible, after all, that the man born to achieve greatness must become deaf, blind, impervious to everything, even truths and realities, which is liable to cut across his aims, his impulses, his destiny, his way of growth, his inward light, his own world-line.
>
> And lastly, if the sense of Self achieves such consciousness and central control of our powers, if it deliberately turns itself into a system of world reference, a source of creative reforms which it sets up against the incoherence, the multiplicity, and the complexity of the world as well as against the inadequacy of conventional explanations, it feels itself nourished by an inexpressible sensation, in face of which the resources of language wither, similitudes cease to be valid, the will to know, directed toward it, is absorbed by it and no longer returns to its point of origin because there is no longer any object which can reflect it. It is no longer a case of thinking. . . .

But this Satanic intellect of *Ébauche d'un serpent*—a baffling combination of Nietzsche and Descartes—is only one part of Valéry the whole man. Another part of him, as we shall now see, registered what happens to the human being possessed by an intellect that wishes to deify itself through the destruction of *otherness*.

II.

Valéry saw the modern mind as pathologically tolerant of disparate phenomena, its vision as "scorched" in "the insane displays of light in the capitals of those days" before the war, none more intense than Paris. He dreamed, as we discover in *Introduction to the Method of Leonardo da Vinci*, of a scientific artist, or rather an artistic scientist, whose mind through self-observing its own synthesizing powers could bring order to the heterogeneous and apparently indigestible data, which the modern mind had accumulated for itself in its critical, scientific phase. But he had too strong a sense of the fatalistic in his Mediterranean sensibility, and he was, besides, too much "the skeptic, the detached Parisian," as he called Manet, for such an innocent vision to possess his mind. The Great War disclosed the metamorphosis of da Vinci's *grand swan* into aerial bombers, and at the end of that hell of scientific slaughter no mind could hope too much for the reintegrations of *l'homme universel.*[7] In "The Crisis of the Mind" (1919), the most helpless and shocked of his essays, he wrote what amounts to a death notice for a civilization destroyed by its own mind:

> . . . the facts are clear and pitiless: thousands of young writers and young artists have died; the illusion of a European culture has been lost, and knowledge has been proved impotent to save anything whatever; science is mortally wounded in its moral ambitions and, as it were, put to shame by the cruelty of its applications; idealism is barely surviving, deeply stricken, and called to account for its dreams; realism is hopeless, beaten, routed by its own crimes and errors; greed and abstinence are equally flouted; faiths are confused in their aim—cross against cross. . . ; and even the skeptics, confounded by the sudden, violent, and moving events that play with our minds as a cat with a mouse . . . even the skeptics lose their doubts, recover, and lose them again, no longer the master of the motions of their thought.
>
> The swaying of the ship has been so violent that the best-hung lamps have finally overturned. . . .

To measure Valéry's shock we must understand the profound dislocation he felt in external influence of any sort. Like Descartes, he wanted to surprise the mind in a vision of its original, historically unencrusted state, and owe nothing to other minds, dead or alive, who constitute a tradition. Two world wars forced Valéry out of that mind into the common agony of history. "A kind of angel was seated on the rim of a well," he said in "L'Ange," his very last poem, finished two months before he died and immediately after the Second World War: "He looked for his reflection and found he was a Man, and in tears, and he was dumbfounded at the appearance in the naked water of this prey to an infinite sorrow." The angelic intellect[8] faces here for once, though at the very end, the fact that its roots lie in a piece of creaturehood, which it had only either ignored or exploited in the past. After a war, in the presence of the corpse, if you will, as the not-dreaming dead are being counted, the body is tragically thickened with an unassailable reality. The whole human person, mind and body fused and both alive,[9] is then the only conceivable good.

The European mind, by which Valéry meant the scientific instrument of the Enlightenment, had severed itself from any accountability to a theistic absolute. It pursued its investigations as if it had decided beforehand that the moral and metaphysical claims for human nature were all pieces of conceit. The wars unleashed a savagery that it did nothing to contain. Its "new science" perfected those weapons that can kill on a scale only imaginable before this century. The inapprehensible impulse of this mind *in its purest state* is toward the disintegration of that relationship between subject and object, which had been at the heart of nearly all previous philosophy. A subject had then stood in the presence of objective Being and disinterestedly studied and admired its forms; he sought to see, not to make or imagine. In the act of observing subatomic processes, an historian of modern science has stated, the separability of the observed and observer becomes meaningless. No *otherness* can exist in those omnipresent and releasable fields of formless pure energy. What else indeed but anguish can the human being experience in such a mind in which he and his world are obliterated?[10]

Valéry had his own moments of anguish throughout all his life, a sense that possessed him at times of *not belonging anywhere*. "I would walk and walk," the autobiographical persona of *Idée Fixe* says, "well aware that being driven on by the exasperated mind in no way deterred the atrocious insect whose sting in my spiritual body kept up a scalding pain inseparable from my very existence. This inner burning destroyed the values of the visible world." He wanted to believe in a luminous, Homeric objectivity for that world, and once said in bitter opposition to psychology that "nothing is deeper in man than his skin," but there were depths inside himself he could not ignore, out of which he involuntarily protested against his own mind. "I have to ask him to repeat one out of every four sentences," Gide once confided to his journal about the nervous, unintelligible rapidity of his speech. Just as his eyes appeared to his friends as either too remote or too immediate, so a languid despair succeeded those intense states of self-analysis that he found perverse and absurd in their uncontrollability and uselessness. He then felt a nothingness at the end of the mind, a fear that "all our intellectual efforts . . . have served only to raise to a savage and crushing power the means of bringing the human race to an end." And he describes the nocturnal rooms[11] of Monsieur Teste, Valéry's fictional embodiment of the deracinated intellect: "I was terrified at the infinite dreariness possible in that abstract and banal place. I have lived in such rooms—I could never believe, without a shudder, that they were my final destination."

But Valéry had nowhere else to go but to such rooms. If he recoiled at the inhuman excesses of this intellect, he still remained committed to it. Increasingly, in fact, he tried to create another mind to the mind he already had, one bitterly precise and fatal to all ambiguity, with which he could correct the habitual vagueness of the first mind's uncritical impulsiveness. In this respect he is as cleanly severed as the most realized creature Descartes could have dreamed. But he saw that in the absence of an absolute measurement provided by a transcendent mind he could not rest there. A third mind would be necessary to watch over the second mind, and a fourth over the third, and so on to an infinite regression of mind watching mind, as in some epistemological police state of constant surveillance.[12]

Valéry knew in *Monsieur Teste* that he was dealing with a form of intellectual madness. He could never make up his mind about his emblematic character, and his ambivalence is expressed in entries he made in his notebooks to the end of his life. Teste represented the extreme possibility of the mind. What would the mind be like if the human composite were subjected to a kind of chemical decomposition whereby the mind was separated from the body and left clinically unaffected by emotion? At times Valéry unambiguously thought of Teste as a lonely hero whose intellectual clarity and disinterested precision deprived him of human satisfactions. At other times he turned and saw him as a monster of intellectual excess, the sterile last son of Descartes, a Jansenist or a Stoic, an angel or an idol, of inhuman sacrifice. To his greatness, there were even times when he judged him out of those human, and almost religious, depths of his, which the other Valéry, the intellectual one, consistently ignored as the reservoirs of indecipherable trash. Then he quite simply saw Teste the man as a moral tragedy and his intellect as an agent of evil.

Those depths are represented by Madame Teste and the priest who is her friend and confessor. The priest knows that evil most strangely can exist only in the nonexistence of something essential to any given nature's fulfillment of itself. Knowledge is the fulfillment of the mind.

Knowledge of necessity involves the duality of *known* and *knower*—the existence, that is, of something different from the mind knowing it, which the mind fuses with in the similitude of form. Evil, therefore, cannot enter the human being through any exercise itself of the intellect, but rather through the intellect's refusal to accept its dependence on other things and other beings, the knowledge of whom constitutes its only fulfillment.[13] Such a refusal proceeds out of a corrupted will, which despises natural limits and wishes its nature to be what it can never be. In the isolation of pride, even that self-torment of pride turned against itself, the intellect must suffer an endlessness. It is immaterial and cannot undergo the decomposition of flesh; a total self-absorption leaves it then to stagnate like a hydra head of perpetual suicide, the greater the evil, paradoxically enough, showing the even greater power of the mind to withstand the internal onslaught. The priest consequently rejects Madame Teste's explanation that her husband is a "mystic without God." He cannot believe, he says, that "any movement is conceivable without direction and aim, without going somewhere in the end." And yet he still sees ground for some hope. He tells Madame Teste:

> He has in him a sort of frightening purity, a detachment, an undeniable strength and clarity. I have never observed such an absence of uncertainty and doubt in a mind so profoundly tormented! No uneasiness of spirit can be attributed to him, no inner darkness—and nothing, moreover, derived from the instincts of fear or desire. . . . Yet nothing that tends toward Charity.
>
> His heart is a desert island. . . . The whole scope, the whole energy of his mind surround and protect him; his depths isolate him and guard him against the truth. He flatters himself that he is entirely alone there. . . . Patience, dear lady. Perhaps one day he will discover some footprint on the sand. . . . What holy and happy terror, what salutary fright, once he recognizes in that pure sign of grace that his island is mysteriously inhabited!

Though Madame Teste loves her husband, she yet entertains no hope that another being can penetrate his mind and command respect there on its own terms. He would translate such respect as compulsion, the mind's movement outward as servility to a tyrannical externality, its love of form as the exhaustion of process. It is always dawn or late afternoon with him, both times when he can most easily be alone; in the crepuscular vagueness she feels a terrifying certainty in his eyes, a sense that what is left of his human self is undergoing some silent, invisible explosion in the confinement of his mind, that nothing can reach him there without being killed in that acid of analysis, which is himself. She ends her letter in this, Valéry's only "novel," with what actually is a vision of hell, but one appropriately painless for the purity of her husband's mind:

> But I must stop. It is time now for our daily walk. I am going to put on my hat. We shall walk slowly through the stony and tortuous little streets of this old city, which you know somewhat. In the end, we go down where you would like to go if you were there, to that ancient garden where all those who think, or worry, or talk to themselves, go down towards evening as water goes to the river, and gather necessarily together. They are scholars, lovers, old men, priests, and the disillusioned; all *dreamers*, of every possible kind. They seem to be seeking their distances from each other. They must like to see but not know one another, and their separate sorts of bitterness are accustomed to encountering each other. One drags his illness, another is driven by his anguish; they are shadows fleeing from each other; but there is no other place to escape the others but this, where the same idea of solitude invincibly draws each of all those absorbed souls. In a few minutes we shall be in that place worthy of the dead. It is a botanical ruin. We shall be there a little before sunset. Imagine us walking slowly, exposed to the sun, the cypresses, the cries of birds. The wind is cool in the sun; the sky, too beautiful at times, grips my heart. The unseen cathedral tolls. Here and there are round basins, banked and standing waist-high. They are filled to the brim with dark impenetrable water, on which the enormous leaves of the Nymphaea Nelumbo lie flat; and the drops that venture upon those leaves roll and glitter like mercury.

But how can the human being suffer "that place worthy of the dead" without at some time rebelling against it, and continuing to do so even if the rebellion should eventually become suicidal?

III.

A fact often either ignored or repressed in all the critical preoccupation with his intellectualism is that Valéry in certain works does not at all break with the romanticism he so despised, but continues it in one of its theoretically most extreme forms of mindlessness, just as if the intellectual Valéry were indeed another person. Like everything Valéry did, the structure and style of these works are of course severely classical; their surfaces remind us of the cool mathematics of Poussin; but, underneath, their content is of ecstasy and mindlessness.

"What is the dance?" the Socrates of the dialogue *Dance and the Soul* asks his friends. It is, he answers himself, a diversion from a life poisoned by thought. Reality is unbearable; the mind's perception of it congeals desire and "ruins all the gods present in our blood." An antidote of illusion is required against the mind's murderous lucidity. The tortuous preparation, the sustained discipline, the final act itself of the dance, the aloof, hardened body as it prolongs and complicates the tension that builds up to the unthinkable climax, the cathartic release of both the dancer and her beholder, the sense of the very annihilation of the world in the finished act—all this, according to Valéry's Socrates, intoxicates the mind out of those ruthless perceptions it must of necessity make and frees it from truth.

The two shepherds in another dialogue, the *Dialogue of the Tree*, envision a night under whose innumerable stars their human identities are overwhelmed and extinguished. They have become a single voice, though using the different modes of myth and science, for that one entity, mystically conceived, which they believe unifies the total natural world. The Tree is their symbol for that entity. The first shepherd explains the Tree as the embodiment of Love—the force, that is, by which Being attracts all apparently different things, abolishes their individuality, and maintains itself through them in extended sameness. Combining Parmenides with Nietzsche, he says the sameness is ceaseless growth. The other shepherd conceives the Tree as the Idea of an uncreated and indestructible whole. Nothing, therefore, exists outside the world, or prior to it, that could give meaning, order, or purpose to its eternal cycle of death and rebirth. It comes from nowhere and it goes nowhere in its totalitarian present, which defies the *before* and *after* of logic. The mind cannot know it; it can only blindly be it.

The First Cause of *Le Cimetière marin* is inaccessibly unique; it agrees so purely and completely only with itself that it becomes the same as death as far as the human intellect is concerned. *That* it exists the mind thinks it knows through its effects in the phenomenal world, which it has composed out of fire; but *what* it is that exists the mind can never attain. The human being furthermore feels that he is a kind of scapegoat, as it were, on whom the First Cause has discharged all the pollution of its own logically inconceivable contact with the phenomenal world. The insoluble contradictions and paradoxes arising from a unity's generation of multiplicity are all packed and concentrated in the human intellect, which alone conceives of the one as it suffers the fragmentation of change. The speaker, as the human representative, informs the First Cause at its perfect noon: "You only have my soul to hold your fears." The poet turns away from such an unthinkable absolute. He abandons the mind in the Dionysian waves that at the end of the poem "burst pulverized on rock":

> Oui! Grande mer de délires douée,
> Peau de panthère et chlamyde trouée
> De mille et mille idoles du soleil,
> Hydre absolue, ivre de ta chair bleue,
> Qui te remords l'étincelante queue
> Dans un tumulte au silence pareil,
>
> Le vent se lève! . . . Il faut tenter de vivre!
> L'air immense ouvre et referme mon livre,
> La vague en poudre ose jaillir des rocs!
> Envolez-vous, pages tout éblouies!
> Rompez, vagues! Rompez d'eaux réjouies
> Ce toit tranquille où picoraient des focs!

*

> Yes! Giant sea endowed with ecstasies,
> Hide of Bacchic panther, chlamys slit
> By thousands of those icons of the sun,
> Hydra absolute, drunk in your blue flesh,
> Biting endlessly your glittering tail
> In noise as deep as silence is its like,
>
> The wind is rising! . . . We must try to live!
> Immense air riffles through my taken book;
> A reckless wave bursts pulverized on rock.
> Let brilliant pages scatter in the flaws!
> And crash, waves, crush this tranquil vault
> Where crying taut sails plunged, predators![14]

How do we exactly explain these abandonments of the mind in the intellectual Valéry? I have said Valéry had nowhere else to go but to the abstract rooms of Monsieur Teste. I should have qualified the statement by adding if *he wished to stay in his mind*. The tensions and sacrifices caused and required by the pure intellect as we have seen it dramatized in Monsieur Teste and in the Satan of *Ébauche d'un serpent* threaten to destroy the actual or possible wholeness of the man. They derive from actualities that can blight the soul. Human nature inevitably will protect itself. In its movement to adjust imbalances, *but with no mean held as viable,* all extreme states that cause an imbalance must necessarily provoke their opposites into existence as each other's only corrective. They then successively undo each other. Pure mind begets mindlessness, which destroys mind; mindlessness brings back alive pure mind; the human being caught between the poles, deprived of compromise—such as Valéry in fact was in his bent to purity—will be pulled back and forth between contradictions and never find rest in any truth. A principle of intellectual psychology explains then the alternation in Valéry of the extreme intellectualism of Monsieur Teste and the kind of ecstatic mindlessness we are able to see in the two dialogues and *Le Cimetière marin,* different as the philosophical vehicles of these latter works otherwise are.

But Valéry went further. After all, these acts or entities that deny the mind—Nature, the dance, the Dionysian sea—can be considered, at least from one point of view, as nothing in the end but deceptive masks of that very intellect intolerant of anything different from itself. And the mind still plays a limited role in the ecstasy they illogically induce in the human beholder. It prepares for an effect that annuls it. But the extent to which the "severed head" had sterilized his world caused in Valéry a repulsion that finally could not tolerate even the least presence of the mind. An impulse toward mystical nihilism, that last alternative of modern thought, would then eliminate the mind altogether. It would keep it alive, though, long enough to vilify it in one of the bitterest pieces of anti-intellectualism in the whole literature of irrationalism. I mean here Valéry's *Le Solitaire,* a closet drama written under the Nazi occupation[15] and part of a cycle on Faust that Valéry never lived to complete. The eponymous hero of *Le Solitaire,* the one who is to show Faust the futility of the mind, lives in Arctically cold regions up above "that strange chaos of being that persists in living on the frail crust of slag and debris that coats the earth." He sees perfection as ineffably mindless, and he excoriates the intellect as an instrument that deforms incommunicable reality; in his words, it is a barren whore who copulates with everyone, a pathetic thing of excretion that can cause only anguish. In lines that resonate with Valéry's own spiritual autobiography, he informs the Faust who has ventured up to his inhuman heights:

> Yes, I used to be very intelligent, too. More than was needed to be an idolater of the Mind. My own (good as it was) offered me nothing but the wearisome ferment of its own malignant restlessness. The endless travail of an activity inventing, dividing, revising itself, exploring the narrow bounds of each single moment, only begets senseless longings, futile

hypotheses, ridiculous problems, vain regrets, imaginary fears.
. . . What else do you suppose it can do?

The "Solitary" believes the intellect is driven by a fear of death. It desperately constructs its theories and systems, its poems and sciences to divert itself from the prospect of its annihilation. These constructions attempt to transform a corrupted universe but have reference to nothing beyond the mind's own processes. They are futile noise the mind makes to itself and possess the effectiveness of dreams. The only truth as he now sees it is annihilation, an *is-not* that purifies the defective *is*. And the intellect becomes as much a thing of pollution in his final vision as the material universe. Even if the mind should obliterate the universe, stay within itself and study only itself, it still must meet at every turn of its purest process the same constricting *is* that it shares with the contaminating universe at large. As the intellect formulates the idea of nothingness, it drags the presence of language into the void, uses *is* to speak of nothingness, and destroys the void's unutterable peace. But no desire to experience the powers of the deracinated intellect, such as restrained the egoistic Satan, now operates to prevent Valéry's infinitely disgusted hero from consistently applying the Satanic critique of *otherness* to the whole of himself, mind included. He takes the indeterminate chaos of modern science, that "oven fired to the point of incandescence," and translates its undifferentiated purity into the Arctic terms of mystical nihilism: all existence, mind and matter, is the scarring of what never should have been disturbed by the convulsions of creation; it is a crime expiated in the death of the mind.

Descartes was the first systematically to isolate the mind and to use it as an instrument of absolute authority. He did so hoping to demolish the medieval synthesis that recognized various natural and supernatural authorities beyond the human intellect, and on the basis of the mind's own internal evidence he sought to prove the existence of God and to give a perfectly logical explanation of the world. Given the human craving for experiment, it was inevitable that someone like Valéry should eventually prolong the Cartesian retreat within the mind, to stay there, in fact, forgetting God and the world, and to set up intellectual consciousness as a God in itself. But he discovered the destruction of the mind locked into itself, its futility in attempting to know itself without the reflecting medium of an object that engages it.[16] The mind feeds on itself, or abandons itself, in the philosophical loss of the world and of the body connecting it to the world. At the end of its inhuman abstraction it turns demonic inside its purity and commits intellectual suicide.

The Unfleshed Eye:
The Unfleshed Eye:
A Reading of Yvor Winters' "To the Holy Spirit"[1]

I.

First published in *Poetry* magazine in 1946, "To the Holy Spirit" is the most complete statement Yvor Winters ever made on a particular philosophical problem he had been facing for some time. The problem concerned the existence of God. It had arisen for him in the late 1920s when he rejected the relativism and solipsism of his youth and embraced certain critical principles that were ultimately based on the mind's capacity to apprehend degrees of truth and then to express that truth in poetic language. He had read too much Thomas Aquinas not to realize that once he had admitted the existence of even limited degrees of truth, the rigor of the argument would eventually force him to posit the objective existence of absolute truth. Otherwise, in the absence of such an absolute standard, the *more* and *less* implied in degrees and gradations would be rendered illogical and meaningless, something Winters was not prepared to follow. He also knew that "absolute truth" was merely another name, as Aquinas would have said, for God.[2]

But a deeply ingrained distrust of the supernatural made him most uncomfortable with the idea. He wanted the realm of *humanitas*[3] protected at all costs, so that the two great human acts, moral choice and intellectual insight, would be guarded against any presence that might enslave them and nullify their operations. Whether rightly or wrongly, Winters saw the supernatural precisely as such a presence. At the same time, he realized that without God that same realm would be invaded by enemies far more insidious to him than the idea of God, namely, the solipsism and relativism that in his youth had brought him close to actual madness and that he had since totally rejected.[4] He clearly faced a problem. His commitment to the intellect made him suspicious of God, and yet without God that intellect and the objects of its perception would not even exist. And how can the creator of a thing reasonably be viewed as a threat to its existence?

If one is intellectually ill at ease with theism, as Winters was, but is forced by the logic of one's argument to embrace it, one will tend to refashion the theism in the most intellectually respectable terms at one's disposal. One such refashioning consists of extracting the divine essence out of God and setting it up as a separate concept. This concept then operates as a theoretical norm by which the moral and intellectual activity of an individual man can be measured and evaluated. Such a procedure is undertaken by Winters in a number of poems, most of which were written in his thirties, the decade, in fact, where most of his mature poetry is concentrated. Such conceptualism, if you will, must have struck Winters more and more as an unsatisfactory compromise. In any case, during his middle forties something seemed to be pushing him to out-and-out theistic absolutism, with the result that he published "To the Holy Spirit" in 1946 and made his theistic "confession" in the 1947 introduction to *In Defense of Reason*.[5] But the qualified theism is still intellectual to the core. Instead of extracting the divine essence out of God and setting it up as concept, Winters now leaves that divine essence within God, but eliminates everything else from Him, so that he becomes whatever that essence is defined as being, which, in Winters' case, is "pure mind." The importance of "To the Holy Spirit" lies in the completeness with which this particular form of theism is presented and realized.

But the poem is not as single-mindedly focused on theism as this last statement might suggest. In fact, it summarizes other themes that preoccupied Winters from the beginning of his poetic career to its very conclusion. The ceaselessly shifting and indeterminate universe of modern science, which so haunts the early poems, is subtly implied in the first stanza of the poem. The dilemma of the human mind trying to perceive and know something about that universe is faced and dealt with by the poet's resigning himself to an irreducible element of illusion and error in human perception. And the central theme of the poem, the intellectual essence of God and the analogy that the human mind possesses to Him, leads the poet to consider the relationship between mind and body, between flesh and spirit, in man himself, and then the relationship of both the Holy Spirit and man to the natural world outside both of them.[6] Finally, "To the Holy Spirit" is a meditation on death such as one finds more frequently in the seventeenth century than in the twentieth. In it the soul is taken to what Kenneth Fields calls "the brink of the incomprehensible," where it recognizes and accepts what for Winters was the tragic fact of human annihilation. The only consolation it offers the reader, as Winters himself said of many poems he admired, is the severe control and moral dignity with which the poet faces the catastrophe.

II.

"To the Holy Spirit"[7] takes place in a deserted graveyard in the Salinas Valley in western California. The first of its four stanzas describes the landscape surrounding the graveyard and develops through that description one of the secondary themes of the poem, but one that seems alien and unrelated to the Holy Spirit of the title:

> Immeasurable haze:
> The desert valley spreads
> Up golden river-beds
> As if in other days.
> Trees rise and thin away,
> And past the trees, the hills,
> Pure line and shade of dust
> Bear witness to our wills:
> We see them, for we must;
> Calm in deceit, they stay.

Is it possible for the human mind accurately to perceive the external physical world through the senses and then on the basis of that perception to obtain valid knowledge about that world's nature and operations? The first stanza presupposes some such question and answers it in the negative. An "immeasurable haze" distorts the appearance of all things the poet perceives, and no objective vision of those things in themselves is possible for him. The haze itself is indeterminate and defies all attempts at measuring and understanding it. The "pure line" of the distant hills might suggest the contours of a definable object, but the line is an illusion that exists only in the mind of the poet and is "pure" of any contact with actual physicality. The hills stay the same; that is, they remain constantly subjected to the same ceaseless and imperceptible change that frustrates the human attempt at knowing them. The deceit with which they appear one thing while being or becoming something else extends from a merely scientific indefiniteness to a quiet, unspoken demonism.[8]

But the poet sees no alternative to trusting the evidence of the senses and imposing the ordering "pure line" on a world that otherwise would be chaotic. "We see them," he tells us, "for we must." A passage in the introduction to *Forms of Discovery* illuminates this line, I think, to a remarkable degree. Winters has just admitted the deceptive unreliability of our senses, and he goes on to say:

The realm which we perceive with our unaided senses, the realm which our ancestors took to be real, may be an illusion; but in that illusion we pass our daily lives, including our moral lives; the illusion is quite obviously governed by principles which it is dangerous, often fatal, to violate; this illusion is our reality.

To accept an illusion as a reality requires more of the will than of the intellect, especially since the intellect knows otherwise. Perhaps this is the "will" the hills bear witness to in the poem. An instinctive aversion to meaninglessness, working at the deepest levels of the human psyche, and an equally instinctive desire that the world not collapse into *senselessness*, make such an act of the will necessary for the human being caught in the dilemma. Too much is at stake for him, most crucially his moral existence.

A further aspect of these "bare hills" should be mentioned, though it exists on the periphery of the stanza and is alluded to only indirectly in its "shade of dust." In the early poems the hills are always starkly and unambiguously related to death. Such an association is still working in "To the Holy Spirit." Their inorganic purity and remoteness from human consciousness, the inaccessibility of their identity to both sensory and intellectual apprehension, their baffling "outsideness" to the categories of the intellect, all suggest a state that, as far as the human being is concerned, is analogous to death. The necessity of seeing the hills then becomes at one with the inevitability of facing death, something that the poet immediately does in the next stanza:

> High noon returns the mind
> Upon its local fact:
> Dry grass and sand; we find
> No vision to distract.
> Low in the summer heat,
> Naming old graves, are stones
> Pushed here and there, the seat
> Of nothing, and the bones
> Beneath are similar:
> Relics of lonely men,
> Brutal and aimless, then,
> As now, irregular.

The "local fact" to which the mind returns is the commonplace one of death and moral chaos in the human realm. The poet knows the fact at high noon, the shadowless point of clearest sight, and no deceptive vision, such as the "immeasurable haze" produces, distracts him from its immediacy and clarity. The confusion of the dislocated gravestones, "pushed here and there," recalls to the poet's mind the aimlessness and moral irregularity of the men buried somewhere beneath them. These men are the same as those who figure in "John Sutter" and "The Journey," and their historical background, to use Grosvenor Powell's phrase, is the raw towns and bleak Western landscape of the turn of the century and afterward. They were completely determined by body and gravity, and in the absence of any rational principle to regulate their lives they were spiritually and intellectually dead before they were physically so. That no hope of resurrection is offered them is indicated by the fact that the stones are now the "seat / Of nothing." Death is the annihilation of the human being. There is, consequently, an element of compassion in Winters' judgment of them. "Relics of lonely men," he calls their scattered bones, as if the loneliness of the men in both life and death were a mitigating factor in considering the brutality of their existence. As he says in "The Journey" about the towns that these men, or others like them, once inhabited:

> Nothing one can say
> Names the compassion they stir in the heart.
> Obscure men shift and cry. . . .

Their loneliness extended beyond the social to the philosophical and the theological. Because of their thoughtless absorption in the earth, the Holy Spirit, the God of Pure Mind, could not participate in their severely limited existence; consequently, they were as spiritually deserted by God in life as they now are in death. Between the mindlessness of their existence and the perfection of His Pure Mind there looms the absolute cleavage that Winters's vision dictates. The dry grass and summer heat are their inferno, where they suffer the final loss of being.

In the third stanza the poet turns abruptly and finally addresses the Deity Himself, at first as if in accusation:

> These are thy fallen sons,
> Thou whom I try to reach.
> Thou whom the quick eye shuns,
> Thou dost elude my speech.
> Yet when I go from sense
> And trace thee down in thought,
> I meet thee, then, intense,
> And know thee as I ought.

> But thou art mind alone,
> And I, alas, am bound
> Pure mind to flesh and bone,
> And flesh and bone to ground.

It is as if, in the first line of this stanza, God had failed the fallen sons, for whom He was morally responsible by the act of creating them, or else as if He had failed Himself and compromised the purity of His own unity and essence by creating such multiplicity and more irregularity. The line indicates, I believe, Winters' absorption in the "theology" of Valéry's *Ébauche d'un serpent*, though the Gnostic vision of Valéry's intellectual angel is much more extreme and uncompromising than the position of Winters in "To the Holy Spirit." That angel considers creation itself as a tragic folly that inevitably blemished and disfigured the purity of God's above-being. Creation by such a perfect agent, the angel argues, had to result in imperfections and "fallen sons," since creation in such a case was not extension of perfection, but the actual making of something other than that perfection, something, that is, necessarily imperfect and contaminated with error. By this rash act God then dissipated His first cause into irrelevant consequences and fragmented His unity into multiplicity. The universe became *Cieux, son erreur! Temps, sa ruine!*, and it bears within its very core *un soupir de désespoir*.

"These are thy fallen sons" comes nowhere near the extremity of Valéry's vision in *Ébauche d'un serpent*, but the influence of the French poem, nevertheless, is quite discernible. Valéry's gnostic angelism and Winters' view that ultimate being is essentially and totally intellectual in nature both share the quality in Étienne Gilson's phrase, of existential neutrality, in that each of them disregards existence itself as irrelevant in the definition of ultimate reality.[9] Besides, if being is intellectual, and if God is perfect intellect and perfect being, then it is philosophically appropriate to question His creating the "fallen sons" and to wonder how such thoughtlessness could come out of perfect thought.

The rest of the stanza is devoted to the nature of God's essence and the poet's relationship to that essence. We have here the second of the two approaches to theism we listed at the beginning of this essay. Instead of the essence taken out of God and set up as concept, we have here God defined exclusively in terms of His essence, which in this case is pure intellect. "But thou art mind alone," the poet states quite simply and straightforwardly. Existence as such is disregarded as philosophically irrelevant to the "mind alone." As far as the poet's relationship with the Spirit goes, Winters describes Him as bafflingly remote, even almost inaccessible, for the human intellect, which painstakingly attempts to reach Him. There is no possibility that such a meeting can be accomplished through the senses, to which the intellectual essence of God is pure foreignness. There are no philosophical traces of Him left and still operating in the physical universe He created, which might reveal to the human mind studying them some limited, even negative, knowledge of His nature. In strict philosophical terms, none of the *cause* ~~is to be found through analogy in any of the *effects* of the created world,~~ even though these effects are admitted as coming out of that cause. The Thomistic position that man possesses a "natural" knowledge of God, and that it is rooted in his sensory experience, is thus rejected. The mind is the divine element in man, and it is only in that element, as like in like, that the Pure Mind can be traced down, met, and known as He ought to be known. The implication, if I am not mistaken, is that in this union the two minds become equated with each other, though Winters leaves undiscussed the exact nature of the equation.

How such a meeting is possible, if the Holy Spirit is to keep the obvious transcendence that Winters gives Him in the poem, is not clear; nor any clearer is how the Pure Mind can both elude the "speech" of the poet and yet be effectively traced down in his "thought." One might ask, if He is ineffably beyond any of the categories of language, how then can He be apprehended by the very intellect that produced those categories and that apparently operates only in them? Perhaps Winters means no more than that the subject is the most difficult of all subjects and that language becomes inadequate in attempting to express its complexity. For once, though, Winters does not treat divinity as undermining the human realm, but as supporting it and grounding it in truth in a manner that defies human analysis. As Howard Kaye says, "The poem acknowledges mystery."

But the union of the divine and the human is brief and uncertain. God as Pure Mind enjoys a simplicity and self-sufficiency that the poet finds tragically missing in his own complex and deprived existence. His mind is entangled in flesh, the breeding ground of error and imperception; the body is the impediment that interferes with and eventually frustrates the attempt of the human mind to reach and apprehend God.[10] The no uncertain terms with which Winters at this point laments the possession of a body are almost Gnostic, certainly Platonic, in their quiet intensity. Furthermore, it is the body's allegiance to the ground, its leaning toward nothingness, as St. Augustine somewhere expresses it, that drags the mind back to time and causes its annihilation in death. The only alternative to an indeterminate universe rotten with change and death is a transcendent intelligence to whom man is mysteriously related but from whom he is at the same time excluded because of his being "bound" in that universe. Man is literally caught between two infinities, one below him, one above him, and he experiences all the contradictions of Pascal's *grandeur et misère de l'homme.*

The final stanza summarizes the previous themes and draws the conclusions that, given the poet's position, are inevitable:

> These had no thought: at most
> Dark faith and blinding earth.
> Where is the trammeled ghost?
> Was there another birth?
> Only one certainty
> Beside thine unfleshed eye,
> Beside the spectral tree,
> Can I discern: these die.
> All of this stir of age,
> Though it elude my sense
> Into what heritage
> I know not, seems to fall,
> Quiet beyond recall,
> Into irrelevance.

Winters returns to the men buried in the graveyard, considers their separation from the Pure Mind in "blinding earth," and concludes against immortality for them. Their ghosts, enlightened at best only by "dark faith," are trammeled inextricably in matter. The poet does not say exactly that his fate will be the same as theirs, but the implication of the last part is that it is: *all* this stir of age falls into the irrelevance and meaninglessness of death. His mind, pushed to the "brink of the incomprehensible," returns with three certainties: the perfect intellectual vision of God's "unfleshed eye," the fact of moral choice between good and evil for man, and the concluding fact of death as annihilation. (I take the "spectral tree"[11] to refer to Genesis's Tree of the Knowledge of Good and Evil, whose "mortal taste" ended man's innocence and awakened his consciousness to moral and intellectual activity, death being somehow the price of such consciousness. Winters is following here, I think, Valéry's version of the Fall in *Ébauche d'un serpent.*) But the first two certainties are beside the last one in its overwhelming emotional effect on the human being facing it. To know that God exists as Pure Mind, to desire to reach Him and partake of His perfection, to be able to do so, even if briefly and uncertainly, but finally to be forced by the body back from that vision to where annihilation awaits the mind—all this explains the sense of tragedy working beneath Winters' tight lines. As he says in "At the San Francisco Airport,"

The rain of matter upon sense
Destroys me momently. The score:
There comes what will come. The expense
Is what one thought, and something more—
One's being and intelligence.

The terms of the tragedy are stated just as unrelentingly as his analysis of *Ébauche d'un serpent* in *The Function of Criticism*. As Winters interprets the poem, Satan is the embodiment of the human intellect. Of him he says, "He is so created that he desires infinite knowledge, and he is so created that he cannot have it. The desire is his nature, his greatness, his sin, and his torture, and it is inescapable."

III.

"To the Holy Spirit" is a summary of Winters' entire poetic career, one which began in free verse, imagism, and atheistic relativism and which ended in traditional meter, classicism, and theistic absolutism. The universe of the early poems, seething with constant change and intellectually ungraspable by the human mind, is the same as the one that appears in the "immeasurable haze" of "To the Holy Spirit." The "bare hills" of the free verse are transformed into the later "pure line and shade of dust," but both refer to the same reality for Winters, the presence of what we might call a death-principle in the physical world, which is either indifferent or hostile to the human attempt to create and maintain intellectual and moral cohesion. The aimless and brutal men buried somewhere beneath the irregular stones of "To the Holy Spirit" embody a theme that remains constant in all of Winters' criticism and poetry, the sense that human life is threatened inside itself by what he calls in *The Bare Hills* some horror "spined with rigid age," and that life will end in tragedy and the annihilation of the human being.

The difference between "To the Holy Spirit" and Winters' earlier experimental poetry is not subject matter as such, but the poetic treatment and intellectual understanding he was able to give that subject matter after his conversion in the late 1920s to a peculiarly modern version of classicism. As we have noted, the substance of that classicism is finally based on the power of the human mind to apprehend some degree of truth in a metrical form that permits "extraction from every unit of language of its maximum content, both of connotation and denotation." As a result, Winters' understanding of his subject became rational, and his treatment of it governed by the principles of traditional meter, which he saw as exerting a calming discipline on the emotional explosiveness often found in material for poetry.[12] He thus achieved some degree of intellectual balance and spiritual control, the moral and psychological benefits of which were inestimable when the subject was as tragic as that of "To the Holy Spirit."

This rational control ultimately rests on a theistic base. The whole theory that governs Winters' traditional poetry depends on the objective existence of truth. Philosophical necessity drove him to admit the existence of God in order first of all to account for and then to safeguard the existence of that truth. But he admitted the theism most reluctantly. A suspicion, even at times a fear, of the transcendent was very deeply rooted in him; for reasons of his own, he saw it as necessarily blurring moral distinctions and generating intellectual confusion.[13] Consequently, when he was forced by his "hard argument" to deal with God, he defined Him in those terms that would be least irrational in tone and substance and that would reflect his belief that ultimate reality is intellectual in nature.

Only thought assimilated as wisdom had *real* meaning for Winters. He continually conceived of wisdom in its perfected form as residing in a motionless and silent realm, which he most frequently characterizes as "eternal." Heracles is one of his symbols of the poet "in hand-to-hand or semi-intuitive combat with experience." That hero achieves victory over that experience only through intellectual mastery of it in a timeless sphere where he raids "eternal silence to eternal ends" and where he grows into the absolute only after slaying his flesh and bone. If we give *life* a definition denoting the phenomenological change of ordinary existence, and then contrast it to the conceptual essence that Heracles realizes in "eternal silence," we find that Valéry's remark in *Monsieur Teste* relates directly to Winters: "The essential is against life." As is the case with so many thinkers, a tension exists at the deepest levels of Winters' thought between the existence of a changing thing and the essence of that same thing as formulated by the intellect and given in definition. And so God is eventually defined by Winters as "pure mind," and existence as opposed to essence nowhere enters the definition.

The Pure Mind of "To the Holy Spirit" is thus more like Aristotle's Unmoved Mover, or Averroës' Separate Intelligence, than like Saint Thomas Aquinas' God of Pure Existence. In fact, the difference between Winters and Aquinas on this point is so radical and it extends to so many areas of their thought that it is untenable to say, as Grosvenor Powell does in *Language as Being in the Poetry of Yvor Winters*, that Winters' conception of being is Thomistic.[14] One such difference concerns the natural world. On account of his definition of God, everything in Aquinas' universe, because it exists, participates in its own way in the

Pure Existence of God; the natural world then for Aquinas through its analogy to God is saturated with order and intelligibility. That same natural world for Winters, because in its mindlessness it cannot participate in Pure Mind, is tainted with a disorder and irrationalism that at times actually assume demonic proportions.

Not only does "To the Holy Spirit" contain Winters' definition of God in its fullest form, but it also realizes all the important consequences of that definition, all of which derive from the inability of anything but the intellectual to partake of ultimate reality. First of all, with "mind alone" as one's absolute standard, evil will be defined, not as deprivation of existence, as in Thomism, but as deprivation of mind.[15] Intellectually vacant as it necessarily is, the natural world will then often be looked upon, as we have just noted, as a realm instinctive with blind hostility to moral and intellectual order; while recognizing its beauties, even at times surrendering to a temporary immersion in its restorative wash, the intellect will on the whole separate itself as far as it can in order to realize its own ends. What has just been said of the natural world applies, but to a lesser degree, to man's own body; the thoughtless principle in flesh is capable of unbalancing moral control and causing spiritual blindness; therefore, the relationship between soul and body is one that for Winters is fraught with ambiguity and peril; in fact, it is the source of tragedy, since the body's death, as we have seen in "To the Holy Spirit," entails the annihilation of the mind. Finally, since the principle of evil in man will be located not in a corrupt will or deprived existence but in an imperfect mind, and since only few men achieve intellectual excellence, a form of intellectual isolation will be advocated and practiced by the man of intellect—a countermovement, for instance, away from the "giant movements" of irrational modernity and the aimlessness and brutality of the "fallen sons," so that "your solitude's defined."

I am aware that other factors exist in Winters' thought and complicate its texture. His attitude toward the natural world, for instance, is not as unambiguous as my remarks might suggest to one unfamiliar with his poetry. He was fascinated by that world, even if he often thought of it as temptation, and he possessed an eye for its details such as few modern poets have. His political involvement and his concern for social justice have to be taken into account in determining the exact nature of the intellectual isolation mentioned above. I am merely, here, isolating one strain of his thought, though it is one that I believe is deep and extensive in its influence and consequences.

Ultimately, Winters' vision of life is tragic. "The mind's immortal," he says in one poem, "but the man is dead." Winters must surely have been influenced by Averroës in distinguishing so sharply and tragically between the immortal mind and the perishing man. Gilson has given us an account of Averroes' position that reads as if it were an explication of this last line of "Time and the Garden," with "To the Holy Spirit" in the immediate background:

> . . . the intellectual operations observable in man are caused in him by a separate intellectual substance that is present in him only by its operations. As separate, this intellectual substance is, by the same token, incorruptible and immortal; but its own immortality does not entail our personal immortality. We ourselves have a soul, which is personal to each of us and is the form of our body; but for this very reason it perishes along with the body. To sum up, that which causes intellectual knowledge in us is separate and immortal, but it is separate and immortal for the very reason that it is *not* the form of our body; it is not our soul.

He thought at one time of mitigating the rigor of his thought by embracing Christianity, but he just as quickly decided against it. The experience is recorded in an epigram, "A Fragment," which appears immediately after "To the Holy Spirit" in the *Collected Poems*:

> I cannot find my way to Nazareth.
> I have had enough of this. Thy will is death,
> And this unholy quiet is thy peace.
> Thy will be done; and let discussion cease.

It was enough for Winters that he embraced his own particular form of philosophical theism. He would rather himself have done without God, so that nothing transcendent or supernatural would be a factor at all in any of his thought. But he found that this, strangely enough, was *rationally* impossible. His submission to the argument down to its final conclusion, his recognition of a Being that everything in his own psychology and temperament opposed and resisted, is an admirable instance of his reaction against a modernity that now deals in almost nothing but psychology and temperament. One is forced to admiration even if one disagrees with the theism involved. Nietzsche too would rather do without God, and he does, without saying that He does not exist, but with saying that He is dead, a totally meaningless statement. Nietzsche would also rather do without objective truth, even without the intellect apprehending that truth, so that nothing is left to exercise any constraint on the individual will making and doing whatever it will in its instinctual blindness. It is Winters' refusal to destroy objective truth that finally and irrevocably makes him a reactionary. "One does not make truth," Samuel Johnson once said; "one can only hope to find it."[16]

Three Variations on the Killing of the Father: Nietzsche, Freud, and Kafka[1]

I.

Like the Satan of Paul Valéry's *Ébauche d'un serpent*, Nietzsche found it extremely difficult to rid himself of God and to achieve that atheistic independence that he thought his own expansion required.[2] One could dogmatize and simply state that God does not exist, but if one is rid of God existentially, what we can call His conceptual residue still remains in the memory and is bound to influence the mind. To use a profane analogy, all rulers of states possessing the atomic and hydrogen bombs could agree on total disarmament, dismantle their arsenals, and defuse every bomb in existence, and yet the world would still not be free of nuclear holocaust.[3] The concept of the bomb is now part of the very substance of the collective human intellect, and there is no way to get rid of it in the mind. Nietzsche had this kind of potent conceptual residue in mind when he referred to God's shadow—"a tremendous, gruesome shadow"—still hanging in a cave for centuries after His death. "And we," he insisted, with apparent confidence in his own strength, "we still have to vanquish his shadow, too." Nietzsche thought and wrote, intensely so during the hectic last year of his sanity, as if he had vanquished God's shadow and had ended the sacrificial mutilation of human nature, which he endlessly said any worship of God demanded. But he did so through means of a concept that confesses to the very God Nietzsche thought he was rid of. The concept is the one of the *Übermensch*.

The *Übermensch*—the "overman" as Kaufmann translates it—is Nietzsche's projected idea of what an individual man can be once he has de-deified his world and assumed his own self-possession. The attributes Nietzsche gives him are an Olympian aloofness from common humanity, an internal wholeness that never suffers mental division, and a freedom from all moral restrictions. Above all, it is the strength of the *Übermensch* that most impresses us, the strength, that is, that comes from a full expansion of one's powers and a shameless joy in their exercise. Such powers enable him to be completely self-sufficient. The most immediate explanation of the *Übermensch* is a psychological one. This apotheosis of man, we are apt to think, is nothing but a wish-embodiment of Nietzsche's own psychic and physical sickness, a projection of that health and strength he craved but never enjoyed in his life. As such the *Übermensch* has nothing to do with the actualities or even the possibilities of the real world. But the *Übermensch* is also the god Dionysus, or even that "strong" Christ who appears in certain schools of Renaissance art. No mere mortal can achieve that self-sufficiency that is the essential quality of the *Übermensch*. If he did, he would have had to evolve out of humanity altogether. And so Nietzsche himself constructs with the *Übermensch* an inhuman ideal in opposition to the rest of his philosophy, which aimed at the destruction of all gods and a return to just the stuff of this untranscended world. If ever one wanted evidence of the persistence of the concept of divinity in the human mind, one could find none more compelling than his *Übermensch*. But we discover similar difficulties in freeing himself of God when we turn to Nietzsche's notions of truth.

Nietzsche took various and sometimes contradictory positions as to the question of truth. Two positions, though, stand out as central to his thought. According to one of these positions, he eliminates truth altogether, saying that its putative absoluteness is nowhere found in the chaos of natural existence, the only existence Nietzsche believed we have. According to the other, he keeps truth but redefines it pragmatically as anything that promotes or enhances life, that is, the will-to-power. No consideration is given to whether or not the idea corresponds to objective reality; in fact, deliberate lies and deceits, such as Odysseus practiced in his travels, can be turned into truths by this account since they aided him in asserting his power against hostile forces. But in both these cases, either that of elimination or that of redefinition, Nietzsche found it impossible completely to rid himself of God.

"We simply lack any organ for knowledge," Nietzsche emphasized at one point in *The Gay Science*. In one of the poems appended to the same book he said that truth was the "old hag" he left behind in the fog of Germanic religiosity and metaphysics. The death of God involves also the death of truth. No determinate world exists that has been created and endowed with objective validity by God for the scientist to investigate and know.[4] The indeterminacy of the world is repeated by the indeterminacy of the scientist's own mind, and truth, in the sense of something that holds and stays the same no matter what, disappears in the atheistic void. The will-to-power also necessitates the elimination of anything of an outside, objective nature that would constrict the uninhibited exercise of will. This applies to anything in the mind as well. The very idea of truth is thus undermined. The will cannot even be called truthful to itself. But the extremity of his position turns around and destroys the very atheism on which that position is based. If truth must be discarded along with God, then the statement that God does not exist cannot claim truth either. Is God's existence therefore negatively proved? But such a conclusion would also be invalid; no statement—neither one claiming nonexistence for God, nor the other claiming existence for Him—can truthfully follow from the premise of Nietzsche's nihilistic epistemology. But at least one thing is certain: Nietzsche himself cuts himself off from any dogmatic assurance about atheism. What he is left with is agnosticism, if he wants it, and an inability to rid himself completely and logically of God.

We see the same outcome in Nietzsche's pragmatic definition of truth. As I have said, such a view defines truth as whatever helps the human being in his struggle for existence and the assertions of his will, even if it happens to be simulation, deceit, or lies. The most pregnant term he gives the powerful individual is *polytropoi*, the untranslatable epithet by which Homer characterizes Odysseus in the very first line of his epic. The intended notion behind the word is that of a shiftingness and craft, of an elusive agility of imaginative wit, which the human being must possess if he wishes to survive any severe trial, much less to achieve power at the expense of others. But what if this trial becomes desperate? What if the human being cannot long endure the attrition of objective meaning and his whole mind becomes atomized as in a nightmare? Would not Nietzsche's pragmatism then have to allow the idea of God as a truthful one if that idea caused a reintegration of mind, a strengthening of will, and a resumption of the struggle for life?

But Nietzsche would have had nothing to do with these rational deductions. He had one of the acutest and most penetrating minds of the nineteenth century, but he despised logic as one of the subtleties of priestcraft, as the means by which "God" supplies the human mind with meaning, and thus continued His intellectual tyranny over it.[5] He believed that human consciousness itself was a disaster as to our animal survival, that thought was only a dry, unimportant surfacing of an unfathomable instinctualism, that each act of the mind finally was unknowable. He didn't rationally disprove the existence of God just because he had absolutely no desire to do so. The only thing mattering in Nietzsche is the autonomy of the will, which conceives what it wishes and dispenses with the requirements of rational thought.

Determined to give the will total freedom, Nietzsche released it from a noetic dependence on the mind; at the risk of incurring pure irrationalism, he not only asserted that the will can act in the absence of an object apprehended by the intellect but also in spite of the only conceivable object the intellect can possibly entertain, say, in a certain given situation. Nietzsche destroyed any outside stimulant of the will that possesses objective validity and can be rationally formulated. His will-to-power owes nothing to anything beyond itself—it is a power that has created itself. Nietzsche continues the deification of the will through the "eternal recurrency." In the infinity stretching before it the will-to-power eternally repeats itself without suffering the least diminution of its being. It is this god then in Nietzsche, cut off from truth and indulging in its own unbound imagination, that disdains even to attempt to disprove rationally the existence of God. It throws logic away and says it has killed Him instead.

But we should be careful indeed as to which Nietzsche this god is to be attributed. There are two Nietzsches.[6] One Nietzsche existed in his literal person. The biographical crudities of the man consisted, among other things, of prolonged periods of sickness, acute headaches followed by convulsive vomiting, failures of nerve, and finally a total collapse into insanity. It makes only for either pathos or cruel comedy to think of this Nietzsche as an embodiment of any kind of a deified will. As he confessed of himself, he had an unerring insight into *decadence* precisely because he had known and suffered it in his own life. But the other Nietzsche, the one we are left facing, exists only in his books, and in a philosophy whose superfetations of the will caused him to renounce reason and to enter at the last into states of clinical megalomania. He wrote his books, he said, so he could enjoy a posthumous existence, so he could become a state where he would die no more. And it is to this posthumous and deathless Nietzsche that the god of the will is to be attributed. It is not without meaning that he thought of Nietzsche the philosopher or, more accurately, Nietzsche the prophet, as a supernatural hammer or a stick of dynamite; neither is it without further meaning that at the end he became obsessed with the two deities, Dionysus and Christ, identifying himself alternately with them and signing his last letters as "the crucified," as if he were internalizing the God he believed he had destroyed.

We can now begin to see the real meaning behind Nietzsche's most famous sentence, "God is dead," a sentence that all the commentators agree upon as expressing the essential theme of modernity. Considered in itself, the statement is senseless. If a being who is called God does indeed die, then he was never God in the first place. Either God is or He is not and never has been or will be. The very definition of God excludes absolutely the notion and the fact of mortality just as angularity is excluded from the circle. But Nietzsche's sentence was never intended logically. Like the modernity of which it expresses the essence, its life does not reside in its overt meaning but lies concealed in its ironic indirection. The true meaning of Nietzsche's sentence is that he has killed God in his own mind so that *Nietzsche* or later the *Übermensch* can become God in His place. Nietzsche did not rationally disprove the existence of God then for the sole and terrifying reason that he needed God as a kind of supreme antagonist, the murder of whom would be infallible proof of his own new divinity. He believed in God to the extent that he had to in order to kill Him. Only a god can destroy another god. No mere mortal can enter that conflict and survive, even if the battlefield should be only the isolated interior of a lonely and rootless man. Nietzsche's "atheism" comes in actuality to supplanting the ancient God with a modern one, the man, that is, "who feels himself," as Nietzsche says in the third *Untimely Meditations*, "perfect and boundless in knowledge and love, perception and power, and who in his completeness is at one with nature, the judge and evaluator of things." Like Spinoza, Nietzsche was intoxicated with God; like Satan, he wanted to become one.

But we discover something we are not prepared for when we study carefully the account of the murder of God as it appears in *The Gay Science*:

> —Have you not heard of that madman who lit a lantern in the bright morning hours, ran to the market place, and cried incessantly: "I seek God! I seek God!"—As many of those who did not believe in God were standing around just then, he provoked much laughter. Has he got lost? asked one. Did he lose his way like a child? asked another. Or is he hiding? Is he afraid of us? Has he gone on a voyage? emigrated?—Thus they yelled and laughed.
>
> The madman jumped into their midst and pierced them with his eyes. "Whither is God?" he cried; "I will tell you. *We have killed him*—you and I. All of us are his murderers. But how did we do this? How could we drink up the sea? Who gave us the sponge to wipe away the entire horizon? What were we doing when we unchained this earth from its sun? Whither is it moving now? Whither are we moving? Away from all suns? Are we not plunging continually? Backward, sideward, forward, in all directions? Is there still any way up and down? Are we not straying as through an infinite nothing? Do we not feel the breath of empty space? Has it not become colder? Is not night continually closing in upon us? Do we not need to light lanterns in the morning? Do we hear nothing as yet of the noise of the gravediggers who are burying God? Do we

smell nothing as yet of the divine decomposition? Gods, too, decompose. God is dead. God remains dead. And we have killed him.

"How shall we comfort ourselves, the murderers of all murderers? What was holiest and mightiest of all that the world has yet owned has bled to death under our knives: who will wipe this blood off us? What water is there for us to clean ourselves? What festivals of atonement, what sacred games shall we have to invent? Is not the greatness of this deed too great for us? Must we ourselves not become gods simply to appear worthy of it?"

As we find elsewhere in his writings, the negative motive of this deicide concerns what Nietzsche thought was the greatest injustice. "And they did not know how to love their god," he says in *Zarathustra* of the devotees of the Christian God, "except by crucifying man." He wrote in other places of God as a siphon of human virtue and strengths, as a robber of powers that are by right man's. The "death of God" then was to correct this injustice so that the human being could reacquire his own powers. What could we not make and become, he said over and over, if we removed this barrier of the absolute?

But we find none of this in the passage I have just cited. There is no enlivening sense of release and freedom; instead, there is horror at the deed done and a deranging suspicion that the human being will never recover from the murder of the being who is the very source of his life. Strong undercurrents also exist in the passage of the denial and repression that Sigmund Freud would soon be wresting from the control of the guilty ego. The madman, for instance, says at first unambiguously that he is seeking God, and yet he believes all the time that God is dead and is nowhere to be found. Nietzsche's spokesman argues, and according to the logic of neurosis, that since the deed turned out to be too horrifying, it was impossible for it to be done at all, and so it was imagined only and never done. *But how did we do this?* he asked. *How could we drink up the sea?* But these strategies are not equal either to the reality of the murder or to the instinctual disgust that the human being feels in its continual presence in his memory. All actions cause certain consequences, which in turn cause other actions and so on and on into the nets and coils. The madman's final fear, and also Nietzsche's, is that the murder of God will be endlessly repeated in the disorder to which His death reduces the world, and that, instead of being made bold by the prospect of his own apotheosis, the human being will only be riveted that much tighter and closer to the God dead in his own mind.

Freud's most complete account of the murder of what he designates as "the primal father" occurs in *Totem and Taboo*. He also alludes to it near the end of *Civilization and Its Discontents*, but, as a component of the Oedipus complex, the murder dominates his entire psychology, and its spirit is felt everywhere in his work. His account argues from present empirically verified psychological data back to the causes the data must have. But these causes are past and are no longer susceptible to scientific investigation, even though they are logically to be presupposed in those effects. Hence, Freud resorts to myth, just as the far differently scientific intellect of Plato was also compelled to the same method when his dialectic reached a similar blockage. Freud's account, furthermore, makes two essential assumptions, never afterward proven, which we should mention before we look at the myth and its meaning. The first is that at the very beginning of its evolutionary development, the human race was loosely organized in hordes of individuals all dominated by one single strong male. Freud often speaks as if the organization was more for the purpose of this one man than as an adjustment to fierce physical necessities that must have then been absolutely coercive. The second assumption is of a much more comprehensive nature. Freud assumes as his hypothesis that the human being is so constituted that one traumatic event occurring in the prehistoric past and involving a limited number of men can afterward be transferred to each and every member of the race and be transmitted in our genes to the present day.

The myth itself can be briefly told. The individual strong male who was the leader was, to begin with, the father of the younger men included in the horde. He exercised a tyranny over these sons, subjecting their total lives to his control and denying them any outlet to their stunted sexuality. As to that attitude the sons had toward the father, their minds were a battlefield of contradictory emotions. They felt a respect for his strength, which their immature minds exaggerated to omnipotence. They loved him insofar as their own lives depended upon his provisions and protection. They simultaneously hated him insofar as his power painfully clarified their weakness and vulnerability. Above all, they were afraid that his Jehovah-like capriciousness would prompt him to desert them and leave them exposed to the gravest dangers or else simply to destroy them altogether as do certain males in the animal kingdom. This psychological maelstrom was resolved by their decision to kill their father. They did so and afterward, in the belief that a man's power resided in his blood, and with the desire to incorporate that detachable power into themselves, the sons made the first sacramental meal out of their dead father and consumed him bodily. The essence of the myth lies here: the sons want to become the man whom beforehand they had seen as a living condemnation of their lives. They will never live themselves out of this contradiction. How can *they* become *him?* Their initial sexual objects had been incestuous ones, and one of their more compelling reasons for killing their father had been to procure these objects for themselves. But in the horrifying silence following his death, they gave up this desire, created a sexual taboo against kin, and thus continued a submission to the man whom they had wished to supplant. And in place of the exhilarations of a new, independent life, the sons experienced a remorse that ate continually into their minds. But Freud was not concerned with their individual lives. As we have said, it was his conviction that their trauma was not exhausted in them individually, but that it spilled over into that humanity the sons originated and radically transfigured the basic psychological structure of the whole race. Exactly what were these basic transformations, which their trauma effected in our minds and made us there what we now are?

The consequence of the killing of the father was the formation of the super-ego in the minds of the guilty sons. Continuing with the mythical terms, Freud states that the sons internalized the condemning cries of the father as he was being murdered. Seared indelibly into the memory and deriving their strength from what the sons once perceived as the primal omnipotence of the father, these cries became a single, permanent part of the mind, namely, the conscience that ostensibly acts as an inhibitor of forbidden impulses. The son then finds it impossible to escape his savage father; the older man lives again in the son, but this time as an internal agent not just meting out criticism directed against specific mistakes or sins, but producing a pervasive sense of guilt affecting the son's whole life. I have said the ostensible purpose of the super-ego is to inhibit forbidden impulses, but its original and most fundamental purpose is to judge and to punish the son for the murder of the primal father. It accomplishes this by erecting an unrealizable standard of perfection in the son's mind, by goading him on to attempt this impossibility, and by finally condemning the totality of his life as a failure worthy of death. Freud's concept of the super-ego consequently is as severe as the Christian doctrine of original sin. For him, too, death is the wages of sin; for him, too, human nature is radically contaminated with fault. But Freud turns a further twist to the screw that is not found in the Christian dogma. One would think that since it is adventitious and not indigenous to the mind, the super-ego would not possess much energy in his system and so could be readily overcome by the conscious, rational mind. But Freud insisted the super-ego is mysteriously connected with, or rooted in, the fiercest energies of the id. Though it seems an alien and isolated part of the mind, yet it paradoxically attacks us as with the strength of our own impulse, as if it were native to the core of us. Its connection with the id explains too the irrationalities of the super-ego. Its judgments and criticisms possess often an element of reason, but the cold severity of its sentences, the intense emotion with which they are charged and delivered, more frequently exceeds reason and becomes uncontrollable in self-hate. The human being then becomes the executioner of himself, in so causing internal pain the super-ego contradicts that axiom of nearly all ethical philosophy that states that the human entity always acts, whether mistakenly or not, for what it sees as its good. But in defiance of that axiom and because of its baffling alliance with the id, the super-ego can goad the person to the madness of a psychologically unproductive self-torture and do so as if it were following the order of reason itself.

There is one more paradox. This faculty of the mind, which judges according to an impossible standard of perfection and frequently acts like an irrational tyrant, yet contains the origin of civilization. After the murder of the father each son punished himself, as we have seen, by denying himself his incestuous impulses and by also relinquishing his ambition to achieve dominance over his brothers through the spilling of their blood. A fraternal clan was thus formed, bound together by common guilt, by mutual fear, and most essentially, by common instinctual renunciation. The bonding of the sons that then occurred is the first example of civilized society and the prototype for all subsequent ones, based as they are, in Freud's view, on the forgoing of natural instincts. The male is consequently more moral than the female in the psychology of Freud, more adaptable to the restraint of civilization, precisely because he has more to repress. The female never murdered her mother and therefore doesn't suffer the compulsion for masochistic artifices that the male feels he must attempt in order to satisfy a conscience which apparently will never be satisfied.

Freud saw the compulsion to repeat as the fundamental law of human nature. Intellectually we do learn a new thing only after we see it as the same as something the mind already knows; biologically we conserve our physical identities; sexually we reproduce our own race; psychologically we revive a traumatic event, usually for the purpose of guarding ourselves against its recurrence. But in the sons this repetition has become a self-destructive punishment. They find that they cannot erase from their minds the killing of their father. The fear of castration enters through their fantasy that the father is not actually dead, but is still alive and seeking revenge. And thus this bonding of the sons is being constantly renewed. Civilization offers a continual sacrifice of the instincts through either sublimation or repression to the dead father who lives on in the minds of the sons. It removes a stain that always reappears.

In this theory of civilization, Freud turns away completely from that tradition of natural law, which is to be found in the Greeks and in Thomas Aquinas. The very first paragraph of Aristotle's *Politics* contains the basic principle of that tradition, namely the belief that a political community has as its end the unqualified good. Aristotle conceived of the state in the positive terms of providing those structures that are necessary so that all the good potentialities of human nature can be fully realized. Since he maintained that man is by nature a social being, he saw civilization as a natural expression of human nature and never set up any kind of radical opposition between the instinctual as such and the civilized. Aquinas compared reason's rule of the impulses to a commonwealth in order to emphasize the rights and dignities that he believed natural instincts to possess. Of course, both these philosophers recognized the fact that some of the impulses can be cut off from reason and so freed can wreck civilized order, but the opposition there is one between what has reason and what does not, not one between civilization on one hand and the instincts of human nature on the opposite other. But Freud saw civilization in tragic terms. It arose out of the killing of the father; its primal function was punishment for that act, and throughout its later transformations it exists as an inhibitor of natural instincts and as an outlet for the guilt of the sons. Human nature pays an enormous price for its benefits. Freud defined neurosis as a frustration of an impulse that so unreleased becomes a poison in the instinctual animal. Civilization then in its roles as an inhibitor of instinct produces poison, and the eruption of the uncivilized and the barbaric in the form of brutal antidotes is always imminent in the mind of Freud. The choice the human being must deal with in his psychology is one between barbarism and neurosis. The only escape that Freud allows is through the therapeutic process of psychoanalysis. But at the same time he realizes that such therapy is reserved for only a few of the mental disorders, that it is useless against the more frightening ones, and that the few rational victories it does enjoy are tentative and always threatened by fresh irrationalities of either the sadistic, civilized super-ego or the simple, savage id.

The last act of the sons' tragedy is narcissism, a reversion to the primal stage of infantile self-absorption when the things of this world do not exist for the unformed mind. The sons' dilemma drives them in the night-journey of the neurotic reversion back through what Freud designated as the transference neurosis, which he characterized as still maintaining connection with the objects of this world, all the way to the narcissistic neurosis, which he called objectless. The being of the sons has been traumatized in the world by the murder of their father. Their minds have been split in two, their conscience against their impulse, their god against their nature. In their desire to escape the pain of mental anguish they retreat inside themselves and imagine there a perfect self who is incapable of any pain and who thinks it needs nothing in the world. The guilt of the sons for murdering their father is thus eliminated through fantasy. Frequently this imagined self is a projection onto something different from the self that nevertheless stands for the self. Such a projection results from the uncontrolled criticism of the superego. If the self has been totally condemned by the super-ego, no part of the self can then become available as a refuge for the reversion. The super-ego blocks the identification. In that case another thing or person must be substituted for the invalidated self, one capable of an inhuman resistance to pain and who meets all the requirements of the super-ego's demand of perfection. This substitute, once it has been seized or fabricated, becomes a psychological host from which the neurotic mind hopes to draw out a kind of subjectivity in which it isn't possible to experience guilt or pain. But the experience is vicarious. The symbolic substitute is charged by the contradictory tensions of the neurotic symptom. Seen from one angle, it allows the neurotic to identify himself with it; that angle slightly altered, it mercilessly rejects him under the critical influence of the super-ego, the god-surrogate of the murdered father.

With this theory of a conflict between conscience and impulse Freud cannot see any unity in the human psyche. In his psychology we might well wonder who we indeed are. According to his famous archaeological metaphor in *Civilization and Its Discontents* we are Romes buried on top of other buried Romes. But there is this difference between our psyches and the buried Romes: *our mind gets rid of nothing.* It keeps intact its earliest Rome and preserves all its barbaric structures from decay. With such an inability to fuse the primitive impulse and the civilized conscience into one, the human being is radically and permanently fractured in Freud's psychology. Man cannot make one whole person of himself but must suffer continuous conflict between conscience and impulse, between civilization and barbarism, between God and nature. Freud thus continues the basic division of puritanism. He can see no wholeness possible in the warfare that one part of our nature wages against the other. The sons will never recover from parricide. Their guilt has now been made a part of the very structure of their minds.

III.

In Franz Kafka the neurosis reached a personal crisis, which he resolved, desperately and intuitively, in a form of Gnostic mysticism. The raw material of this mysticism was his own tortured existence as the son of a tyrannical father. He described that life in a letter that he never sent the man, the *Letter to My Father*, one of the most confessional and painful documents in all modern literature. Kafka internalized what he had reasons to see as his father's condemnation of his entire life. He suicidally set up his father as a destructive authority at the very center of his mind where it dominated every part of his life. As a student he existed in the fear that his teachers, embodying the ubiquitous father, at any time would form themselves into a tribunal, review his case under the influence of his father's condemnation, and expel him as a thing of worthlessness. The only example of Judaism that Kafka permitted himself to see was his father's. Because that Judaism appeared to the son as shallow and hypocritical, Kafka rejected it and so denied himself for most of his life the recognition of his own religious and racial inheritance. The Ark in the synagogue was nothing but a cupboard stuffed with "the same old dolls without heads." He chose his profession under the influence of his father. It allowed little or nothing to his art, but more tellingly didn't call for the assertion of himself in a world controlled in his mind by his father's ruthless power. And so there was no possibility of a conflict in which the son could only have been defeated. The failure of his attempt to marry Felice Bauer can be attributed to the emasculation that he judged himself to have suffered at the hands of his father. Even the tuberculosis from which he died at the age of forty-one he thought of as an execution of himself—"My head conspired with my lungs behind my back," he wrote. He was haunted all his life by the idea of a gratuitous yet justifiable execution, and the executioner and his guilty victim play a central role in his fiction. "It is as if someone is going to be hanged," he abruptly wrote in the course of *Letter to My Father* of his whole existence. Only in his life as an artist did he enjoy the freedom of being his own person. Yet that freedom was actually his illusion. "My writing was all about you," he told his father; "all I did there, after all, was to bemoan what I couldn't bemoan upon your breast."

Kafka was the artist of passivity. Without resistance, he incorporated the condemnation of his father. His perfect style, with its classical restraint and limpidity, has the air of an objective clinician probing a beautiful specimen of some strange cancer. He resisted to a degree, as we discover in his *Letter*, the psychological atrocities of his father, yet another and deeper part of him made no objection at all;

it loved the father on the reverse side of ambivalence and accepted his harshest verdicts; in fact, the only defense it saw as viable was total surrender, just as the captured animal collapses and pretends to be dead when there is no escape from the stronger predator. I know guilt better than anyone, he once stated. His belief in original sin possessed an instinctual power over him. The passive acceptance of an inhumanly cruel fate occurs repeatedly in his fiction. Gregor Samsa, in *The Metamorphosis*, never rages against the apparent injustice of his being turned into an insect. The K. of *The Castle* never once through his ordeal simply thinks of leaving the environs of the castle where his being is degraded. The officer of *In the Penal Colony*, the one drunk on original sin and justice, submits himself to his machine of torture and has a steel spike driven into his forehead.

All these persons are Kafka, just as their counterparts are his father. It is out of this raw material, the primal father whose brutalities have been reinterpreted as justice by his overwhelmed victim-son, that Kafka constructed his mysticism that is Gnostic in all its essential features. In all the Gnostic religions, salvation is interpreted as extrication from matter and annihilation of individuality. With salvation and annihilation thus equated in his mind, he could find an end to psychological warfare, and he could dream through the death-wish of the destruction of his contaminated individuality and so appease the father and at the same time escape from him. Kafka thus executed the orders of his father, and the father's brutalities could be felt as leading to the peace of nothingness.

Eric Heller offers us in his *The Disinherited Mind* an explanation of the Gnosticism as it appears in Kafka. Although he is speaking here of the situation of *The Castle*, what he says applies also to the whole of Kafka's work:

> This situation produces a theology very much after the model of Gnostic and Manichaean beliefs. The incarnation is implicitly denied in an unmitigated loathing of "determined" matter, and the powers which rule are perpetually suspected of an alliance with the Devil because they have consented to the creation of such a loathsome world. Heaven is at least at seven removes from the earth, and only begins where no more neighbourly relations are possible. There are no real points of contact between divinity and the earth, which is not even touched by divine emanation. Reality is the sovereign domain of strangely unangelic angels, made up of evil and hostility. The tedious task of the soul is, with much wisdom of initiation and often with cunning diplomacy, gradually to by-pass the

armies of angels and the strongpoints of evil, and finally to slip into the remote kingdom of light.

In one of the Gnostic cults that Hans Jonas explicates in his study, *The Gnostic Religion,* and which is applicable to Kafka, Hebraic elements are fused with Gnostic elements. The whole of these angels and strongpoints of evil that Heller refers to is collectively embodied in one god, the Jehovah of the Jews, who is the creator and ruler of the material cosmos. According to the Gnostic vision, the principle of evil is individuation, that is, the specificity and constriction involved in being a single thing cut off from the mystical one; the principle of individuation, to proceed on to the ultimate, is matter that limits the thing to the attrition of time and imprisons it in space. Since he created matter out of nothingness, the Jehovah is the cause of evil. He and his demonic angels actively seek to trap the human soul inside the universe and to starve it to spiritual death on what is seen as the poison of matter. Because the soul should be thus punished on account of its involvement with and its contamination by flesh, then the evil of Jehovah, at least as far as his treatment of the human soul is concerned, doesn't conflict at all with the most absolute concept of justice. Jehovah can be looked on as a strainer or filter, necessarily dirty himself, which prevents our human filth from reaching the remote deity of the *Deus absconditus,* the final and supreme god of all the Gnostic systems.

But the human soul is inexplicably kin to the *Deus absconditus.* It wants to return to the cosmic hidden god from whom it now suffers exile. There is consequently a conflict in Gnosticism between the soul's desire to return and those forces of Jehovah that would defeat the desire. The universe is a gigantic shell, with one sphere enclosed within another. A narrow corridor, like a hole, pierces the shell from its outermost sphere down to the earth, the center of the universe and that place where the dregs of matter are collected in all their concentrated poison. This constitutes the domain of Jehovah. To escape this prison-house of matter and justice and to reach the *Deus absconditus,* the human soul must make its way up the corridor and must fight off the host of demonic angels that block and guard the narrow passageway. In *The Great Wall of China,* Kafka gives us a parable of the enormous distance involved in the ascent. He writes though from the point of view of the *Deus absconditus,* symbolized by the dying Emperor of China, who tries to send a message to the human soul who lives far away from him:

> The Emperor . . . has sent a message to you, the humble subject, the insignificant shadow cowering in the remotest distance before the imperial sun; the Emperor from his deathbed has

sent a message to you alone. . . . The messenger immediately sets out on his journey; a powerful, an indefatigable man, now pushing with his right arm, now with his left, he cleaves a way for himself through the throng; if he encounters resistance he points to his breast, where the symbol of the sun glitters; the way is made easier for him than it would be for any other man. But the multitudes are so vast; their number has no end. If he could reach the open fields, how fast he would fly, and soon doubtless you would hear the welcome hammering of his fists on your door. But . . . how vainly does he wear out his strength; still he is only making his way through the chambers of the innermost palace; never will he get to the end of them; and if he succeeded in that nothing would be gained; he must fight his way next down the stair; and if he succeeded in that nothing would be gained; the courts would still have to be crossed; and after the courts the second outer palace; and once more stairs and courts; and once more another palace; and so on for thousands of years; and if at last he should burst through the outermost gate—but never, never can that happen—the imperial capital would lie before him, the center of the world, crammed with its own refuse.

The way by which the Gnostic seeks to find the hidden god is through spiritual minimalism, a systematic impoverishment of the self. The classic form of spiritual minimalism is fasting. The discipline as practiced by the Gnostics had both negative and positive aspects to it. The cruder, and negative, idea was that by fasting the initiate shrank the self to that thinness and emaciation that would enable him to slip by the demonic angels guarding the spiritual corridor of the cosmos. They would not detect the nonentity to which his severe discipline was capable of reducing him. The positive idea was that by fasting the initiate drained himself of the soul's poisons and thereby created that spiritual void the god could move into and fill. The two stories that reveal Kafka's preoccupation with the fast are *A Hunger Artist* and *Investigations of a Dog*. The hero of the first story is a professional faster who offers the martyrdom he suffers as a public exhibit. An average fast for him lasts the religiously significant forty days, though he always feels in himself an overwhelming desire to protract it out to what would be final inanition. He finds the discipline easy because he has never yet found that earthly food that he likes and that is not a poison for him. Kafka's description of him as he is being taken out of his cage once his fasting is over is a modern "descent from the cross." The body is still warm, but is lifeless:

The artist now submitted completely; his head lolled on his breast as if it had landed there by chance; his body was hollowed out; his legs in a spasm of self-preservation clung close to each other at the knees, yet scraped on the ground as if it were not really solid ground, as if they were only trying to find solid ground; and the whole weight of his body, a featherweight after all, relapsed onto one of the ladies. . . .

In the enigmatic *Investigations of a Dog* the protagonist is a theosophical dog. He is crushed by the earthen silence of a generation of dogs surrounding him that he says is lost. He is also haunted by his forefathers "who involved our dog life in guilt." They took the still open nature of the dog and locked it into a specific one that now has hardened and is spiritually unmalleable. He himself though is seeking "ultimate science." The goal of his quest is "to achieve truth and escape from this world of falsehood." And the method he has decided on as the way to arrive at this otherworldly truth is fasting, which he has discovered "to be the final and most potent weapon of research." "The way goes through fasting," he says. At the end of his autobiographical account, we find that he has not yet achieved the last illumination. *Ultimate science* eludes him and his existence is still religiously unconsummated. But he has been rewarded for his fasting by hearing a mysterious music, the source of which he cannot locate. In its angelic remoteness, its non-rational seizure of his mind, he feels the barriers of the self obliterated. What am I before this music, he asks himself, lying "in my pool of blood and filth?"

But the basic pattern of Kafka's art is not that of the attempt through fasting to find the hidden god. It is rather that of being trapped inside the shell of this cosmos, being given over to the cruelties of the Jehovah-father who, as Gregor Samsa realizes in *The Metamorphosis*, "was determined to bombard him," and then being frozen with the spirit's despair. Not Gnostic light, but the Manichaean darkness now seizes the soul. In the room where Gregor Samsa is imprisoned as an insect, the narrator describes how "the electric lights in the street cast a pale sheen here and there on the ceiling . . . but down below, where he lay, it was dark." We encounter this darkness or, what is the same thing, the emptiness of desolate light, throughout Kafka's fiction. We discover it in both the intense sunlight of *In the Penal Colony* and the boreal incandescence of snow and moon in *A Country Doctor*. The sense in all this imagery is that of the soul's being flung out in absolute foreignness and abandoned there. Even death does not release the soul and give it the painlessness of annihilation. It must still aimlessly wander in the same foreignness that it suffered in life. The "fundamental error of my onetime death grins at me as I lie in my cabin," the fated hunter states in one of Kafka's most haunting and beautiful of stories, *The Hunter Gracchus*. He bled to death and his ghost awoke aboard a ship that should have conveyed him to the other world, but through a mistake of its archonic boatman, he is tossed about instead on a mundane sea and is "always in motion." The longing though to enter the unknown kingdom of light still possesses him, but he now absolutely despairs of arriving there. He uses the ancient symbol of the stair as the connection between the two Manichaean kingdoms of light and darkness and says he is forever on it. When he exerts himself finally and, as he himself relates, makes out the distant "gate actually shining there before me I awake presently on my old ship, still stranded forlornly in some earthly sea or other." That ship has no rudder, Gracchus states in the last sentence of the story, "and it is driven by the wind that blows in the undermost regions of death."

The final truth though in Kafka is that this exile and the suffering it brings about are justified according to his vision of things. Human beings are implicated in sin by the very fact of their existence as human beings, and they deserve punishment. The matter doesn't concern at all particular crimes, errors, or sins, for which expiation can be obtained from some spiritual authority, which is neglected; it is rather the nature itself out of which these acts proceed that is felt to be a source of absolute contamination. Kafka states this belief bluntly and unequivocally in one of the aphorisms that comprise *Reflections on Sin, Pain, Hope, and the True Way*. "The state in which we find ourselves is sinful, quite independent of guilt," he says there of our loss of paradise. You are a devilish human being, the father emphasizes to the son in *The Judgment*, as he sentences him to a death by drowning. Guilt is never to be doubted, the officer of *In the Penal Colony* explains in his justification of the kind of justice instituted by the "old commandant" of the penal colony and still enforced there. When the protracted execution finally reaches the crucial transfiguration on the face of the culprit—"we bathed our cheeks," he asserts, "in the radiance of that justice."

"There is only a spiritual world," the Kafka of *The Reflections* states, explaining this mystical justice without mercy; "what we call the physical world is the evil in the spiritual one." It is a fierce light, he believes in the same place, that dissolves this world.

We can see the continuing, deranging influence of the father in all this. Through such fierce gnostic light, Kafka the son kills Kafka the father and annihilates the father's world. But the son stays trapped inside that world, and he too is destroyed in his own contaminated individuality. No fathers and no sons exist in the extremity of Kafka's vision. The tension of that duality has ceased, and there remains only the foreign god of nothingness.[7]

Three Essays on the Greeks

The Night of Alcibiades[1]

I.

Alcibiades was the child of the democracy.[2] I say this aware at the same time of the irony involved in the assertion. He belonged to one of the most aristocratic families in Athens. Through his father's side he traced his ancestors to Telamonian Ajax; through his mother's side he was connected to the Alcmaeonidae, perhaps the most influential of the Athenian tribes. He was brought up in the household of his cousin Pericles, who ruled Athens not as a democrat, but, so Thucydides implies, as an enlightened tyrant. Alcibiades himself insisted, often arrogantly and explosively, on all the privileges and immunities of his high station. He likewise possessed in his character that peculiar combination of forbidding insolence and ingratiating charm which we associate with the aristocratic temperament. But nevertheless underneath this solidly formed aristocratic exterior there swarmed all the fluidity and pluralism of democracy.[3] And isn't the last test of a true democracy, that is, in the final stages of its self-destructive purity, a toleration of anything, including an aristocratic egoist who once disdainfully told the oligarchic Spartans that of course he knew democracy was a "patent absurdity"?

It was Alcibiades whom Plato most likely had in mind as he delineated the democratic soul in Book VIII of *The Republic*. The philosopher defined democracy as that kind of constitution which has renounced the authoritative guidance of the intellect and embraced a hedonism which by definition is multiple and various—no one pleasure should dominate our soul and deny us the others. The basic animating principle of such a regime is that "all pleasures are equal and must be equally valued." The democratic soul is consequently characterized above all by its versatility, by the presence within it of many styles, attitudes, philosophies, and cults, each one of which frequently contradicts the others. To use the terminology of modern psychology, the democratic soul is ambivalent at its core. It is, though, when Plato turns from the more theoretical part of his definition to the details of descriptive psychology that we begin to feel the actual historical presence of Alcibiades:

> And does he not, said I, also live out his life in this fashion, day by day indulging the appetite of the day, now winebibbing and abandoning himself to the lascivious pleasing of the flute and again drinking only water and dieting, and at one time exercising his body, and sometimes idling and neglecting all things, and at another time seeming to occupy himself with philosophy. And frequently he goes in for politics and bounces up and says and does whatever enters his head. And if military men excite his emulation, thither he rushes, and if moneyed men, to that he turns, and there is no order or necessity to his existence, but he calls this life of his the life of pleasure and freedom and happiness and cleaves to it to the end.

All these illustrative marks of a democracy are derived from a decadent aristocracy. There is not a trace of vulgarity in the refined but corrupting list. Consequently, Plato's composite figure cannot be referred to any of those popular leaders, a Cleon or a Hyperbolus, for example, who rose to power from the lower ranks, all of whom had the reputation for a kind of crude violence. It would be quite hard to conceive of Cleon as applying himself, even superficially, to the study of philosophy, or to the lascivious charms of flute-music.[4] Alcibiades is the only one of the more important of the Athenian democratic leaders whom Plato's illustration fits in its details. Besides, since Plato believed that democracy originates out of a decaying aristocracy which has lost its mind, Alcibiades would have been for him the more appropriate example. In his biography of Alcibiades, Plutarch gives the most essential characteristics of his nature as being its open-endedness and diversity, the multiplicity and inconsistency of its passions, and, above all, its adaptability to different foreign cultures and influences. He could "submit himself," Plutarch says, "to more startling transformations than a chameleon." All of these features we see are prominent in Plato's portrait of the democratic soul in Book VIII of *The Republic*.

Alcibiades drank the black broth and ate the stale bread of the Spartan mess hall when he lived there in exile from an Athens which had sentenced him in absentia to death—"I'll show them I'm still alive," he is related to have then said. He wore his hair long and untrimmed in the Spartan way, took cold baths and then robed himself in the coarse, homespun cloak of a Spartan aristocrat. He sweated through all the manly exercises. For someone so much a victim of a multitude of passions this ascetical regimen must have been the last novelty. But he adapted himself with equal facility and abandonment to the manners of other cultures. In Thrace he out-drank them all in the drunk place. In "horse-breeding" Thessaly he was more of a centaur than the natives. While he lived in Asia Minor he was luxuriant and indulged in the pomps and the ostentations of an Eastern satrap. With cunning skill he moved through all the oily and vicious intricacies of the Oriental diplomatic game in which the least false step would have put a dagger in his back. His entire life seemed only a succession of brilliantly maintained but quickly discarded exteriors, a series of costumes and cosmetics such as figure in the haunting transvestite dream he had just before he died, which Plutarch relates and which is emblematic of the man's whole life:

> One night he had a dream that he was wearing his mistress's clothes while she was holding his head in her arms and painting his face with pigments and white lead like a woman's.

We see the same versatility in Alcibiades' political and his sexual lives. It seems that he was pathologically incapable of an impersonal loyalty; consequently, he could be whatever he wished under the impulse of the time and the place. He successively fitted into the democracy of Athens, the aristocracy of Sparta, and the despotism of Persia. He became a participant in whatever political philosophy he could use for his own machinations. He believed in anything that would further himself. As to his sexual life, he began in the homosexuality of his age, that is, one involving a youth and an older man. He was extraordinarily beautiful. The strange combination in him of a feline elusiveness and a masculine toughness many Greeks found overwhelming. He was effeminate in his dress at Athens, trailing long purple cloaks behind him as he paraded through the marketplace; he carried pet quail about his person; yet he could explode in a second and strike a man down for the least affront to his manly honor. But he had no respect for his admirers and treated them cruelly and contemptuously. He collected lovers as a part of a power game. Their flattery and importunity confirmed the irresistibility of his attraction and the finality of his hold over their minds. When he was older he shifted to heterosexuality. But the same ruthless egotism is seen in his heterosexuality as it is in his homosexuality. He married but was never long faithful to his wife, indulging in countless affairs with courtesans. When he was at Sparta he seduced the wife of King

Agis and so violated one of the most sacred bonds of the Greeks, that between host and guest. Plutarch cites ancient sources that attributed his death to his apparently uncontrollable sexuality:

> They say that he had seduced a girl belonging to a well-known family in Phrygia and had her living with him. It was this girl's brothers who were enraged at her dishonor, set fire by night to the house where Alcibiades was living, and shot him down, as has been described, when he dashed through the flames.

Some have explained this egotistic versatility in Alcibiades as an inevitability of the sophistic culture in which he lived. Moral law had lost its absoluteness in the minds of many of the intellectuals and their followers, among whom Alcibiades was included. It was revalued as custom, which changes from time to time and from place to place; its violations involve no supernatural visitation; it actually exists only on leave and for the convenience of powerful individuals who naturally manipulate, dominate, and exploit the weak and the helpless. In those demagogic circles of power that received Alcibiades, this philosophical relativism taught by the Sophists became translated into a brutal, amoral imperialism according to which Athens considered herself released from all morality in her treatment of the subject states composing her empire. She could be whatever she wished in the maintenance of her power. Her variousness extended through the entire political spectrum. In Sicily, she presented herself to the smaller cities as their maternalistic liberator from Syracusan and Dorian oppression; in Melos, a small island in the Cyclades which pathetically tried to maintain neutrality in the Peloponnesian War, she was the inhuman dictator who massacred the entire male population of the island in order to teach the would-be rebels in her own empire a lesson impressed in blood. A democracy at home, she elsewhere encouraged oligarchic tyrannies whenever it suited her self-interest and sought alliances of friendship with dictatorial rulers of the Persian Empire. Translate this relativistic imperialism into psychological terms and we have Alcibiades.

This public culture was re-enforced by private loss. Alcibiades was fatherless. During his earliest years his father, a famous general of the time, was killed in the battle of Coronea, and Alcibiades was raised as the ward of Pericles. The ancient Greeks placed the highest value on the father-son relationship. For a Greek boy to grow up deprived of it, as many a Greek doubtlessly did, must have made him a kind of freak in the eyes of other more fortunate boys. There is, as Nietzsche tells us, a streak of cruelty in the Greeks. Alcibiades as a child must have had his fatherlessness rubbed into his soul. Older boys must have made him the butt of their jokes. He would have been forced to feel his unnaturalness. Furthermore, what could have prevented the boy's unformed and irrational mind from interpreting his father's early death as abandonment and the abandonment as a verdict against his own existence? So attacked, all the forces of Alcibiades' proud and aristocratic nature would have aroused and mobilized themselves. But in his sophistic culture and without the rational discipline which a good father would have given him, he had nothing by which to assert himself but his naked ego. And in the unphilosophical depths of that ego to which he descended he released the compulsion and multiplicity that drove him through all the roles of his versatility.

If this last insight contains validity, we can now understand the nature of Alcibiades' attachment to Socrates. He was seeking his father. And I do not mean the word in a crudely specific sense but in a symbolic one which involves the *logos* of reason that brings an order to the soul, calms its passions, and feeds it on truth. How bafflingly opposite the two must have seemed, the glittering beautiful youth with his perfectly formed body and the ugly older man who had the wisest and most ordered soul any human being ever possessed. Instinctively Alcibiades desired the contagion of wisdom to affect him too and resolve his conflicts so that in the presence of his master he could achieve philosophical peace. We know, of course, that this vision was not realized and that Alcibiades ended in tragedy. No matter how beautiful his body, his soul was finally too infected, distorted, and maimed for it to acquire philosophical form. But while it lasted, in the years before the war— in the brilliant light of Athens, as Euripides says—the attachment of Alcibiades to Socrates is one of the most compelling examples we have of the human desire for wholeness.

Without such philosophical form Alcibiades never had peace. He was of the essence of those Athenians whom the Corinthian ambassador warned the Spartans of in the first part of Thucydides' *History of the Peloponnesian War.* The Athenians, the ambassador emphasized, are addicted to innovation. They are never at home. *They were born into the world to take no rest themselves and to give none to others.* It was Alcibiades, with the earlier help of the demagogue Cleon whom Thucydides terms "the most violent of men," who caused Athens to break with the Periclean policy of defensive containment, which had guided her during the first years of the Peloponnesian War, and to embark on the new one of expansion and aggression. The Sicilian expedition of 415 was the turning point. In the debate before the Athenian Assembly convened to decide on the expedition, the radical restlessness of Alcibiades was pitted against the conservative caution of Nicias. We should consolidate the empire we now enjoy, Nicias pleaded, not risk everything we have in uncertain and dangerous ventures in western waters. But Thucydides tells us that a madness for the exotic land of Sicily, its conquest and exploitation, possessed the Athenian soul, and reason was hopeless against the intensity of its passion. Alcibiades countered Nicias' argument with a policy of imperial limitlessness, a strategy of kill-or-be-killed which would make peace impossible. Under the influence of his brilliant rhetoric the Assembly voted for an expedition which resulted in the annihilation of the entire fleet sent out and the slaughter of thirty thousand men. We cannot fix the limits of our empire, Alcibiades argued; we must be constantly expanding it; and in the presence of our enemies we shall always be making, we must be continuously aggressive or we shall be destroyed. He told the Athenians:

> Remember, too, that the city, like everything else, will wear out of its own accord if it remains at rest, and its skill in everything will grow out of date; but in conflict it will constantly be gaining new experience and growing more used to defend itself not by speeches, but in action.

For the religious among the Greeks such a policy of pure process which has eliminated achievable purpose and which has refused the restraint of meaningful limits was not only impious, but also insane. According to legend, the *daemon*[5] of Socrates warned him against the evil recklessness of the Sicilian expedition. The whole of Nicias' speech was informed by his belief that the Athenians should leave Sicily within its own limits and that if the Athenians invaded the western island they would be transgressing divine sanctions. It would be an act of mindless hubris that would incur the wrath of the god. We should always remember, too, that the western part of the sea was associated with death in the Greek mind. It was on Sicily that Odysseus found the entrance to the Underworld in which he spoke with his bloodless ghosts. Monsters infected the Straits and devoured the ships that tried to navigate the narrow passageway. Without those countless islands which are found in the Aegean and which enabled Greek ships to hug to shores and always to keep land in view, the western sea was open, pure, and treacherous. Sicily to the untraveled Athenian was as strange as the moon. Thucydides' account, in fact, of one of the last night battles on Sicily, in which the minds of the Athenians were confused by the lunar light so that they often ended up turning against and killing themselves, imagistically summarizes the whole death and insanity of the Sicilian expedition. Alcibiades himself was relieved of his command during the very first part of the campaign because of his involvement in the profanation of the Mysteries, but the expedition was always tied to him by the Athenians. It was to his own mind. He was the one who fomented their passion for the tragic venture. We can then understand the justice of that one single attribution that the ancient writers all agree in giving to him: the *fatality* of his charm. His Egyptian soil, as Plutarch has it, produced some good drugs, to be sure, but intermingled with those drugs were found poisons. Aristophanes in *The Frogs* compared Alcibiades to a lion. You shouldn't raise up such a beast in the city, he warned the Athenians, but if you do, then humor every one of his moods. They love him and they hate him, he said in the same play about the Athenian people's ambivalent fixation on Alcibiades, and they cannot live without him. According to Plutarch, Timon the misanthrope told Alcibiades when he was young, and just after he had won a victory in the Assembly, "You are doing well, my boy! Keep it up and you will destroy them all."

The war dragged on for eight years or so after the defeat of Athens in Sicily. By the time it was finished Alcibiades had shifted to every position he could have. He betrayed Athenian strategy to the Spartans. In the mysterious shadow-theatre of the court of the satrap Tissaphernes, as F. E. Adcock[6] calls it, he sought the aid of the Persians for the Spartans against the Athenians and, finally, for the Athenians against the Spartans. He cared no more for oligarchy than he did for democracy. The one motive which united him through that shifting and elusive world was self-interest, for him a solipsistic pride and safety of the self in imposing his irrational will upon others. Ironically and tragically that self-interest caused the destruction of the self. He created so many enemies that he lost himself in a crepuscular world of assassins and paranoia. When he returned to Athens for the last time, after his recall and pardon, he waited some time on the deck of his ship, not trusting in the apparent friendliness of the people gathered to greet him, his eyes darting nervously through the crowd for murderers. Can it be that the ethic of self-interest is not at all motivated by an actual love of the self and the sources of the self's true power in the soul? Might it not instead be motivated by a fear of an impoverishment and inadequacy of the self, fear that then drives the self through all the self-destructive strategies of power politics and forces it continually and futilely to prove itself?

He must have exhausted himself. Plutarch tells of an incident involving Alcibiades during the last days of the war that contains a great deal of pathos. He was living at the time not far from where the Athenians massed their ships at Aegospotami. He had played every card in his hand and now lived in isolation, scorned and rejected by all three of the powers involved in the Asiatic theatre of the Peloponnesian

War. But he was a man obsessed by action to the end and so he observed the Athenian navy, knowing that the Spartans immediately across the narrow waters were preparing the deathblow. Alcibiades saw with alarm the general lack of discipline to which the Athenian fleet had degenerated, in contrast to the cool scientific precision and the deadly efficiency of former times. At some risk to his own safety, he was moved to warn his fellow countrymen of the dangers to which their carelessness was exposing them. But after riding over to the Athenian camp and giving his opinion, he was insulted and rudely dismissed by the Athenians. Every bit of his expert advice was disregarded as coming from an untrustworthy traitor. One of their generals superciliously informed him that "it is we who are in command now, not you."

How are we to explain this final public act of Alcibiades? We cannot do so by asserting it to be an example of his egotism. He gained nothing by it and actually exposed himself to considerable danger by going alone and defenseless to the camp of his enemies, even if they also were his fellow countrymen. We must then conclude that it was a disinterested act motivated by charity toward the Athenians, who had so far lost their minds as to become utterly vulnerable to their enemies. If so, Alcibiades must then have been groping his way out of the fluidity of egotism toward an objective and impersonal notion of the good such as Socrates would have approved of. But history can be brutal. It was too late for both the Athenians and for Alcibiades. The Athenians were destroyed at Aegospotami. Alcibiades himself was soon assassinated, not most likely by the brothers of the ravaged girl whom Plutarch cites, but more probably, as the same writer further states, by agents of the Persian satrap acting at the request of the Spartan King Agis, the man whose wife Alcibiades had earlier seduced and violated.

II.

Why did Socrates become intimate with Alcibiades? Why did the philosopher leave the cool serenity and comedy of his thought, descend into the cave which Plato would later describe, and contaminate himself with the man of tragic action? It is some such question as this that I would now like to try to answer.

We will begin with a fact about Socrates' body. He was physically an ugly man. With him it was as if the creative force had totally spent itself on the construction of his powerful intellect and had nothing left for his body, which then fell off as something unformed and gross. His huge nose was flattened against his face, the nostrils at the base abnormally distended. His eyes were set wide apart and they bulged out from their sockets. For that man caught under their spell, the effect would have been unnerving and frightening, especially if he were also being cut to pieces by the Socratic *elenchus*[7]. Socrates' mouth was thick and fleshy. His bodily ugliness was accented by the oddity of his dress and his habits. He wore the same ragged cloak throughout the year and went barefoot even in winter and, so Plato informs us, even during the Potidaean campaign in the freezing Chalcidice when he fought there as a soldier. Aristophanes tells us that when he walked he waddled like a waterfowl. He had the power to withdraw from his surroundings, to stand so motionless in a trance that his face suggested someone dead. But his ugliness wasn't the ugliness of sickness and emaciation. There was something in fact perennially green and tough about the man. His powers of brute endurance were enormous. He sired a child in his late sixties. It was, I think, his physical strength combined with his ugliness which made him grotesque in the eyes of some Greeks and which prompted Alcibiades once to compare him to a satyr. Seized by the intensities of the philosophical quest, he must have indeed seemed like a weird primal creature who had wandered into a disturbed Athens from some savage country of the naked mind. No wonder, some might be led to conclude, that the Athenians got rid of him.

Plato teaches us in the *Symposium* that when a man desires and loves, he is suffering from the absence and from the deprivation of whoever or whatever is being loved. Love then is that force by which the human being moves outside himself and seeks to acquire what he does not have, but what he needs for the completion and perfection of his being.[8] When this movement is consummated the emotion of love becomes transformed into the delight of actually possessing the desired object. Now if Socrates was grotesque in his ugliness, Alcibiades was pleasing in his beauty to a degree that the Greeks found astounding. Plutarch states that Alcibiades throughout all the seasons of his life, from his youth to his maturity, possessed in turn the beauties peculiar to each season, going from the vernal to the autumnal, so that he was a continual living embodiment of beauty in all its forms and aspects. Socrates then would have loved Alcibiades because both when young and when mature Alcibiades had what Socrates found that his own life was deprived of. In the presence of the younger man Socrates could enjoy that physical beauty which, added to the proportions of his own soul, would make him complete in all aspects. Since the human response to beauty is the least susceptible of all the emotions to rational analysis—we cannot readily see what beauty is good for and so lack a reason for its effect on us—we then have to say that there is an element of the irrational in Socrates' attachment to Alcibiades. Following the Greek habit of attributing anything in human nature for which no rational cause can be given to the operations of an intrusive deity, Socrates himself would have said that his love of Alcibiades was the work in him of the god Eros.

Allied to this is Socrates' bisexuality. I do not wish to be held to something binding in a clinical sense when I use this word. By it I only mean to express a fact which is clear in the historical testimony of Plato and Xenophon, namely, that while Socrates was a sexually adequate husband he also at the same time was peculiarly attracted to male beauty and that his attraction contained sexual elements that actually affected him in the physiology of his person. I do not mean to imply that Socrates indulged in homosexual acts. In fact, the evidence from Plato and Xenophon overwhelmingly suggests that he did not, that he instead channeled the admittedly fierce energy of his eroticism into non-sexual areas and subsumed it under his philosophical mission to educate the minds of the youths committed to him. We have here the origin of Platonic love, the doctrine which our Victorian grandparents emasculated in their great desire to spiritualize everything they could grasp. But neither Socrates nor Plato, no matter how far they sublimated the erotic, ever forgot or disregarded the fact that the basis of the sublimation was human blood. Consider this passage from the *Charmides*, one of the earliest of the dialogues, written when the memory of Socrates was still fresh in Plato's mind. Socrates has just been introduced to Charmides, a youth who, like Alcibiades, is noted for his extraordinary beauty. The boy is now suffering from a headache Socrates is said to be able to cure:

> And he came and sat down between Critias and me. But I, my friend, was beginning to feel awkward. My former bold belief in my powers of conversing naturally with him vanished. And when Critias told him that I was the person who had the cure, he looked at me in an indescribable manner and made as though to ask me a question. And all the people in the palaestra crowded about us, and at that moment, my good friend, I caught a sight of the inwards of his garment and took the flame[9]. . . I could no longer contain myself. I thought how well Cydias realized the nature of love, when, in speaking of a fair youth he warns someone "not to bring the fawn in the sight of the lion to be devoured by him," for I felt I had been overcome by a sort of wild-beast appetite.

It is inconceivable that Plato should have made this up to the extent that his contemporary readers, many of whom had known Socrates personally, would have been unable to recognize in it the historical reality of the older philosopher. Everything in Plato's own philosophical and moral temperament, which some have described as puritanical, would have caused him instead to suppress the scene. Its evidence of a strong sexuality barely held in check by Socrates we may then accept as truthful. We should also remember a fact which, as with another great moralist, Samuel Johnson, we habitually forget about Socrates, namely, that he was not always an old man.[10] He was only about twenty years older than Alcibiades. He was in his thirties when he first met the boy. Their friendship was carried on when Socrates was in his prime, not in his old age when the debilities of the blood weaken or extinguish the sexual drive. He would still have been susceptible physically to the sexual appeal of Alcibiades if, that is, such a tendency existed in him. Both Plato and Xenophon inform us that it did. We conclude that one reason Socrates became intimate with Alcibiades was the sexual attraction he must have felt for the younger man. Again we encounter an irrationalism in Socrates, one that exists in all other human beings as well. Human sexual identity is rooted in the dark region of instinct. While there is something inherent and automatic about it, the psychologists also tell us that the specific form it takes in us is derived from uncontrollable accidents of our earliest history. By the time our rational minds have formed themselves, these events have been either repressed or obliterated, so that in sexual matters we become governed by the unknowable in us.

But Socrates turned away from such obscurities. He was a philosopher, not a victim of his psychology. As we have noted, he sublimated the powerful erotic force he discovered in himself and disciplined it so that he was able to direct it to philosophical ends. The testimony of Plato and Xenophon unambiguously asserts this. But exactly what philosophical form did this sublimation take and how was Alcibiades related to it?

Socrates began his intellectual life as a student of that kind of non-experimental and excessively theoretical physical science which was what philosophy consisted of in the earliest stage of its development. Such philosophy sought to discover the one basic element that underneath the diversity and multiplicity apparent to the senses composed the stuff of the physical world.[11] But with neither the right instruments of investigation nor a properly thought-out scientific method to guide them, the philosophers lost themselves in what we can call systematic and theoretical unrealities. At some decisive but now indeterminable point in his life Socrates became dissatisfied with this kind of knowledge. He might have felt instinctively what Plato would later believe consciously, that no science in the real sense of the word is possible of anything so subjected to change as atomic matter. We do know that he thought the physicists neglected important and immediate realities for those Socrates considered remote, problematical, and practically useless. Why go off into fine-spun problems, he must have asked, and disregard essentials at hand and at home? But he meant no disparagement of such knowledge, as he said in the *Apology*, thus disassociating himself from anti-intellectualism and from the popular superstition which judged such science as subversive to religious authority. It was just finally irrelevant to what had become the main preoccupation of his life, the knowledge of what is necessary to live a good life here and now. In so placing this moral knowledge of the good as the central concern of his mind Socrates initiated a revolution in Greek systematic thought. He shifted it away from the detached, morally disengaged contemplation of what we would now call pure science and introduced it to the conduct of this life. As Cicero said, Socrates brought philosophy down from the sky and set it up in the streets and in the houses of men.

It is the nature of the good that it seeks to diffuse itself into all areas where it may possibly proceed. If it decided to hold itself aloof from those areas and so deprive them of its benefits, it would then be wishing them evil since evil is not some positive force of its own, but merely an absence of the good.[12] But this is impossible. It would defy the law of contradiction. Nothing can be both good and evil at the same time and under the same aspect. Therefore, the good seeks by its nature to diffuse itself. This doctrine receives its fullest articulation in the Christian doctrine of creation.[13] The divine goodness created a universe that contains all conceivable degrees of participation in the good, beginning with the angels closest to God, descending to the mediocrity of man, and plunging, if you will, into creatures which seem the slime of the universe but which yet, through at least the pure fact of their existence, are able to receive the last degree of the good. As we have seen, the controlling passion in Socrates' life was for the good. He thought of his philosophical mission as the attempt to define the good so that others of the city might understand it and live a good life according to the knowledge. If he had not been born and reared in Athens, the intellectual capital of his world, he would have had to go there as Jesus finally went up to Jerusalem where the benefits of his sacrifice would be most extensively felt. It is, in fact, inconceivable that Jesus or Socrates.[14] should have spent his life in some obscure village. Both required the great city, the capital of each man's world where the greatest concentration of power, the greatest diffusion of good were possible.

And what better agent of moral and intellectual diffusion could there have been for Socrates than Alcibiades, that is, the Alcibiades the boy promised to be, the one who existed in Socrates' hopeful mind before the poisons grew in Alcibiades and destroyed him? The Greeks never envisioned the moral life as being transacted by some isolated conscience in its privacy, the etymology of which in Greek means idiocy.[15] One's moral life and one's public life were for them the same. "We alone," Pericles said of the Athenians in the great funeral speech as related by Thucydides, "regard the man who takes no part in public affairs not as a harmless but as a useless person." Alcibiades as a youth must have struck all who could understand and who came into contact with him, not only Socrates, as being potentially the man who could acquire complete political control of the city—so that if he were good, the city would likewise be good. He came from one of the great families; he possessed the keenest of minds and was receiving the best education Athens provided; from his earliest years he instinctively knew the ways of power and, besides, exuded the magnetism that captivates, sways, and compels the intoxicated multitude. We are now in possession of the sublimated reason for Socrates' love of Alcibiades. He became intimate with the youth because he hoped, tragically it turned out, that through him ethics could be fused with politics, knowledge with power, so that the greatest degree of the good could be effected in the city. It was in the service of accomplishing this end that Socrates consigned the raw energy of his eroticism and so baptized it in philosophy. He did so undogmatically, not by virtue of some positive knowledge he enjoyed, but by the nature of the good he sought but always said he himself never possessed. But Alcibiades died even before his older friend, assassinated among barbarians in Asia. His whole life had turned out to be one violation after another of the good Socrates had lived for. The memory of what the boy could have been but the man never became must have given Socrates some of his bitterest moments in prison as he awaited his own execution.

III.

To understand Alcibiades' connection with the execution of Socrates, we must go back to the last stages of the Peloponnesian War and to two oligarchical revolutions which occurred in Athens, one in 411, the other in 404. The central purpose of the first of these, called the Revolution of the Four Hundred, was to procure the financial and military aid of the Persian satrap Tissaphernes, which the Athenians desperately needed in their war against Sparta. But they would never secure the aid, Alcibiades informed them, as long as democracy existed at Athens to offend the despotic sensibilities of the rich Easterners. Abolish the democracy, Alcibiades promised his alienated countrymen whose favor he wished to regain, and he would get for them the friendship of the Persians in their death-struggle with Sparta. The last of the two revolutions was brought about at the very end of the war by the so-called Thirty. Again, a small band of aristocrats seized power in the city, demolished the democratic constitution, ruled briefly as a self-destructive tyranny, and subjected the state to terror.

Though the two revolutions each lasted for only a short time, the memory of them persisted with full strength in the collective mind of Athens. The experience had been bitter. The revolutions had been infected with that systemic disease of all Greek political life. I mean the unwillingness, even the stubborn refusal, of the ancient Greeks to form impersonal political loyalties, and the consequent fragmentation of their polity into sects formed to gratify personal grudges and to carry out endless vendettas. Fratricide marked the revolutions, and judicial murders were a matter of course. The same paranoia of paralysis occurred in both. No one could trust his neighbor not to betray him to the government. Everyone lied for fear that the truth would have fatal consequences for him. The whole spirit of the people was extinguished in the silence and inactivity which the tyrants murderously imposed. And so it is understandable that after the fall of the Thirty the restored democracy would have wanted its revenge, especially after the city had also suffered the annihilation of her entire navy, the consequent surrender to Sparta, and the final humiliation of having the very walls of the proud city torn down by the victorious Spartans so that she now lay exposed to anyone.

It was the leadership of these two revolutions which related most directly to the execution of Socrates. Nearly all the plotters belonged to aristocratic and intellectual circles at the highest levels of Athenian society. These circles had always accepted Socrates as their own. Some of the revolutionaries had been his closest friends. He himself had been an unrelenting critic of the democracy. It is true that he also opposed the injustices of the oligarchical Thirty, but the popular mind chooses what it wishes to believe and emphasize, and the Socratic gibes against popular rule stuck in the sensitive democratic mind and festered. Above all Alcibiades cast the longest and deepest shadow. He wasn't involved in the last revolution—by then he had been assassinated—but it was his promise of Persian aid that had brought the first revolution to life and had given it its reason to exist. He did indeed later shift sides and embraced the very democracy he had earlier tried to subvert, but what was that but more evidence of his elusiveness and changeability? The democracy held Socrates responsible for the corruptions of Alcibiades. Xenophon in the *Memorabilia* refers to a contemporary writer named Polycrates who wrote a violent attack on Socrates. According to Xenophon, Polycrates in justifying the people's execution of Socrates pointed to the philosopher's "friendship" with the "unprincipled and licentious" Alcibiades and to the great injuries the latter had done the Athenian state under the influence of the philosopher. G. C. Field, in his *Plato and His Contemporaries*, summarizes the controversies which arose out of the attacks of Polycrates:

> For there is evidence that Socrates' relation to Alcibiades was a subject that excited great interest in the Socratic controversies of the time. It was an important element in the accusation of Polycrates that Socrates was responsible for Alcibiades and all the evil he had done. And it is quite likely that a similar accusation was also brought at the actual trial.[16]

The friends of Socrates who defended him after his death constantly and single-mindedly assert that the degeneration of Alcibiades occurred not because of but in spite of Socrates. A fragment of Antisthenes survives in which that minor Socratic philosopher, exculpating his friend, criticizes the character of Alcibiades as vitiated by such terrible passions that even the influence of Socrates was unable to subjugate them. And in a fragment of Aeschines, an orator who had been another friend of Socrates, we find the following dramatic passage in which Socrates himself speaks to defend himself against the implied accusation of corrupting the youth:

> For my part, the love I bore to Alcibiades brought me an experience just like that of the Bacchae. They, when they are inspired, draw honey and milk in places where others cannot even draw water from wells. Similarly I, though I have learned nothing that I could impart to a man to do him good, nevertheless thought that, because I loved him, my company could make him a better man.

That all these writers felt compelled to answer the same charge proves that Alcibiades was central in the Athenian mind as it tried and executed Socrates, then justified itself afterwards. The bill of complaint against Alcibiades would have indeed been a detailed one. It stretched back for more than fifteen years and included the profanation of the Mysteries immediately before the Sicilian expedition, an act which the mass of Athenians would have thought polluted the very existence of the state.[17] The rest of his betrayals and treasons we have already noted, as well as the mad passion he constantly fomented in the Athenian soul for a bitter war that finally ended in the tragedy of Aegospotami. The democracy had always both loved and hated the man, fatally drawn to him and repelled at the same time—he had been the spoiled child of the democracy—and in the irresolution of its contradictory emotions Alcibiades had eluded its justice and escaped punishment for his outrages. Besides, he was now dead. But who was that old man who had been ceaselessly at his side during all his youth, the one who had insultingly pitted aristocratic skill and knowledge against democratic incompetence and mere belief?

Others connected with Socrates were implicated. Critias, a first cousin of Plato's mother and a familiar of the Socratic circle, was a ringleader of the Thirty, as was also Charmides, Plato's uncle and that same beautiful youth whom we met earlier in the wrestling-school, the one in the insides of whose cloak Socrates spied the boy's cock and had thereby been inflamed. Xenophon quotes Polycrates as calling Critias "the most rapacious and violent figure of the oligarchy." Xenophon also tells us that "it was Socrates himself who first encouraged Charmides to overcome his bashfulness and take part in politics," without realizing the tragic consequences it would have for the youth, who with Critias was killed in the last battle of the Thirty. The popular mind which condemned Socrates would quite deliberately have deceived itself, misjudging Socrates' involvement with these men as all the evidence it needed for his own treason. The popular mind was not in any mood to distinguish fairly and justly between Socrates' mere friendship with the oligarchical revolutionaries and an actually criminal complicity with their thefts and murders. As we have noted, the people had just been defeated in a war that had lasted for more than a quarter of a century. They were exhausted, disillusioned, angry, and bitter. The Alcibiadeses of their politics had all but annihilated them. They needed a scapegoat, and what better candidate for the job was there than Socrates, the eternal babbler and questioner, the prying and irritating gadfly who had disturbed social peace for too long with his search after imaginary wisdom and imaginary virtue, the very one who loved, schooled and groomed those scintillating youths who had proved to be the bane of Athens? Let him collect on his ugly body the fears and sins of the people so they could be done with them and return to the proper business of this world. And so Socrates was put to death and the democracy got its revenge.

At the end of Plato's *Symposium* Alcibiades abruptly and unexpectedly intrudes on the party. It is one of the great scenes. He stands there framed intoxicated on the threshold, his head crowned with ivy and violets, among which brilliant ribbons are meandering over his hair. All eyes are directed to him. A flute-girl helps the drunk youth into the room. Later he gives a speech about Socrates to the guests, of whom Socrates is one. Socrates is the only man, he says, who can make him ashamed of himself. Socrates has wounded and stung him in his soul "by philosophical talk which clings more fiercely than a snake when it gets hold of a not ill-endowed young man." Socrates compels Alcibiades "to realize that I am still a mass of imperfections and yet persistently neglect my own true interests by meddling with the affairs of the state before my time." He further tells the guests of that night he once spent with the man. He was deliberately trying to seduce him sexually. He wished to tear through the philosophical facade and to discover in the hidden parts of Socrates the same blinding sensuality which would make the man just as compulsive and messy as everybody else. But Alcibiades discovered in the interior of Socrates' soul, instead, self-control and an imperturbable calm:

> But in spite of all my efforts he proved completely superior to my charms and triumphed over them and put them to scorn, insulting me in the very point on which I piqued myself. . . . I swear by all the gods in heaven that for anything that had happened between us when I got up after sleeping with Socrates, I might have been sleeping with my father or elder brother.
>
> What do you suppose to have been my state of mind after that? On the one hand I realized that I had been slighted, but on the other I felt reverence for Socrates' character, his self-control and courage; I had met a man whose like for wisdom and bravery I could *never* have expected to encounter. The result was that I could neither bring myself to be angry with him and tear myself away from his society, nor find a way of subduing him to my will. It was clear . . . that he was more completely proof against bribes than Ajax against sword-wounds, and in the one point in which I had expected him to be vulnerable he had eluded me. I was utterly disconcerted, and wandered about in a state of enslavement to the man the like of which has never been experienced.

I could not bring myself to be angry with him. So Alcibiades did feel some anger against Socrates, of the kind which disordered persons experience in the presence of those whose ordered lives are a standing reproof to their own. They love the ordered man since he has that which will save them from themselves and which they desire. They hate him to the extent that a despair has seized them that finally they cannot be saved, that the irrational principle in them has been fed like a beast with too much and is now too strong to resist and overcome. The pain of denying the beast is far greater than the pleasure of the incipient good only beginning to be formed. Disordered persons suffer a contradiction in their inner being. And their actions will reflect the contradiction. At the same time they will cleave to the ordered man and seek to destroy him, each impulse checked by the other. Some sort of resolution will eventually be found by the victim, but one not worked out by his conscious will. Our actions often contain consequences uncontrollable by us which oppose all our conscious intentions and act out some of our most buried and suppressed impulses and desires. It is this uncontrollability and compulsion which frequently make history a tragedy that can only be redeemed by the freedom of philosophic thought. It was the ghost of the dead Alcibiades, the one who existed as an inevitable historical consequence in the imagination of the democracy, who finally reached out of Hades and removed the disturbing philosopher by death from Athens. The political actions of Alcibiades, all proceeding from a ruthless egotism and a bewildering versatility and fluidity, indirectly seized and polluted Socrates and brought him down too. Thus Socrates paid an enormous price for that sexually uneventful night he spent with Alcibiades. Did he have something like this in mind when he made his last statement? As the mortal chill was spreading up from his legs to his waist, he pulled back from his face the sheet that he had placed there and told his friend Crito that he owed a cock to Asclepius.[18] Did he mean by this debt of gratitude to the god of health and medicine that he believed human existence was fundamentally diseased by passion and that death alone could heal us, as it was then about to heal him? And yet the mind of Socrates had remained unpolluted by Alcibiades, no matter what the restored democracy might think, and his whole life was a comedy in the old sense of the word, not a tragedy. The democracy had simply made a blind error. Its immorality, as Socrates himself would have said, was the result of ignorance alone. It was resolving its own ambivalent fixation on Alcibiades by executing the lover and teacher of the unforgettable young man.

I referred earlier to Socrates' ugliness, his unconventionality and uncouthness. But such is only one half of the truth. The other half is an amazing courtesy in the man, a fluidity of ease in human encounters, a mordant wit perfectly balanced with a natural kindness.[19] He has to be the most social of the philosophers. He could engage in the smoothest and most meaningless banter of the symposia, fight it out verbally with the thugs and bullies of the street, and philosophize with logical precision and emotional intensity on the graver problems of human life and death with closer friends. His severe intellectualism was furthermore balanced by religious faith. He revered the powers of the conscious intellect and saw in the clarities of the rational the natural source of virtue. "A man is good in so far as he is wise," he was reported to have once said, "evil in so far as he is stupid." At the same time he respected and obeyed the *daemon* that spoke to him out of his irrational unconsciousness. Above all, it is the courtesy of wholeness that most impresses us about this complex and endlessly fascinating man who holds us more than any other person except Jesus. "Be always to thy gathered self the same," Ben Jonson commands us in one of his epigrams. And Aristotle speaks of the internal friendship of the mind with itself in which no faculty of our mental being is in conflict with another, but all powers exist together in peace, the emotions and desires in subordination to their own good under the rule of reason— an aristocracy of the psyche. Multiple difference and variance at the very core of our being indicate a traumatic fragmentation of the mind against itself that soon will cause extreme anguish. Socrates possessed this wholeness and self-control to a pre-eminent degree, and without a trace of puritanical self-hatred or ascetical desolation—his morals are happily unembarrassed by pleasure. Through his wholeness he was able to withstand the seduction of Alcibiades and to face his executioners with a courtesy which must have infuriated them.

What is the ultimate source of Socrates' inner strength? It was his belief that he himself was not his body but his mind.[20] When he came to make the philosophically most exact definition of human identity, he turned away from the body with its multiple, different, and decomposing parts—that which we cannot *know* since it constantly suffers change in its sublunar vagueness—and went instead to the immaterial intellect. There in the mind he located who we really are. The body, Socrates believed, is merely the tool or vestment of the soul. He would not take the body for the self any more than he would take any instrument for its agent or user. The soul contains our essence; the body is its accident. He furthermore believed that since the intellect possesses unity and is immaterial, it also is deathless. Death means the dissolution of those material parts which just happen to have a temporary but unessential cohesion. But if something is not composed of material parts but instead is a unity, it cannot suffer their dispersion and will never die. And if the mind is deathless, it is also for Socrates divine, since the deathless and the divine mean the same for him, as they do in all of Greek thought and culture. From his belief in this immortal and god-like intellectual principle in him Socrates derived his inner strength, his self-control, his courtesy of wholeness. It explains the actual meaning of his pregnant sentence that no evil can happen to a good man in this life or in the next. For how could it if the man is such a soul? And so the inexpert and tragically blind and misguided democracy could poison and kill his body—Plato in scathing disgust would call his trial that of a doctor indicted and prosecuted by cookie-makers in front of a jury of children—but the executioners couldn't reach the man. Even as the hemlock was coursing through his blood, Socrates was already somewhere else in the indestructible cohesion of the undivided intellect. He maintained the enigmatic and baffling smile of the archaic Ionians, the refined and electric comedy of philosophy up until and beyond the very end.

The Socratics and the Flight from This World

Greek philosophy started in a search for one irreducible substratum which the philosophers believed composed the physical world. It ended with the philosophers condemning the physical world as philosophically worthless and turning from its stuff to the contemplation of a mystical oneness beyond the world. Greek philosophy, then, is of course preoccupied with oneness from its initiation to its end, but the thinkers' understanding of the One underwent this radical change. At first the One was perceived as located in nature, apparent to the senses, and knowable by the human mind; at the end it was believed to be unnatural, sensorily inapprehensible, and ineffable. The mind itself began with confidence in its epistemological and investigative powers, but it concluded by committing suicide in the presence of the One. I would now like to trace the beginnings of this mystical flight from the world in the work of those Greek philosophers whom we will conveniently call the Socratics through their association in one way or another, either as pupils or as pupils of pupils, with the first really great Athenian philosopher. They are, besides Socrates himself, Plato and Aristotle, and then the three most important of the minor Socratics, Euclides, Antisthenes, and Aristippus. The latter two are historically important as originators of, respectively, the Cynic and the Cyrenaic Schools which in turn developed into Stoicism and Epicureanism, the two dominant philosophies at the end of the classical world.

The ethical philosophy of Socrates has been called an example of the most uncompromising intellectualism possible. The philosopher believed that all the various virtues are one and that one virtue finally is the knowledge we have of ourselves and our world. The goodness of the good thing we do, according to Socratism, does not derive from the subjective motive we had in mind while performing the act so that even our practical failures become moral successes with the right intention. The goodness, instead, derives from our knowledge, not only of technically how the good thing should be done, but also of the act's final consequences and the degree of happiness it actually gives us in the long run. Look to the end, as Solon told the Lydian king, and following the spirit of Greek rationalism, Socrates always agreed.[1] It follows from Socratic intellectualism that no person ever knowingly and consciously performs an evil act. Ignorance alone causes evil in his vision of things. If the moral agent does do evil, it is either because he simply does not know what the good is in the particular situation he is faced with, or else because he is besotted out of his mind and suffers temporary intellectual and so moral blindness. If this assessment of the extent and force of Socrates' rationalism is true, and indeed it is, he does not belong in a discussion of the forerunners of irrational mysticism except insofar as he affords occasions of the starkest contrast. But another situation emerges as we turn our attention from his philosophy to his life, and his life is of far more consequence to us than his philosophy. We then discover possible connections of Socrates with the mystics.[2]

Throughout his life Socrates heard hallucinatory voices which he attributed to a demon which he believed protected him from harm.[3] As far as our historical record goes, he never once asked for a rational justification for any of the injunctions and inhibitions which the demon issued to him and which he painstakingly obeyed. In public religious matters Socrates was happily and easily conventional. He placed implicit trust in oracles, dreams, divination, charms, and incantations. He believed apparently in the worship of the dead and in other practices we today would have to consider superstitious. At the end of the *Phaedrus*, we discover Socrates quite unexpectedly falling into a prayer addressed to Pan and the other divinities who inhabit the haunted beautiful place where he and Phaedrus had their dialogue. In the beginning of the *Charmides*, we learn that during the campaign at Potidaea where he fought as a hoplite in the Athenian army the philosopher consulted with Thracian doctors who were followers of Zalmoxis, a god of the dead. Lest we be disarmed by the rationality of these doctors, we should note that they promised their patients immortality and that most likely they were shamans. We furthermore discover in the *Symposium* that Socrates consorted with the sorceress Diotima and that he learned from her his philosophy of the erotic. And how are we to explain the trances into which Socrates fell so that he stared motionless for hours as if he had died? The commentators usually assume that they were concerned with the solution of some specially resistant and complicated philosophical problem. But of the two related in the *Symposium*, one began abruptly as Socrates and Aristodemus were in the street on their way to the party and the other one at Potidaea lasted for nearly twenty hours and ended with a prayer to the sun. It is difficult to connect such seizures with anything intellectual. I myself would guess as their cause something instead of a religious nature.

Each one of these non-rationalisms, of course, can be dislodged from the broader context of Socratic intellectualism and used as an authority for whatever spiritualistic ambition one has. But it isn't the demonic Socrates or the religious one who comes closest to my main point. It is the ignorant Socrates. The one fact he continually insisted on was that he did not know what the good is. He spent his whole life searching for what at the end eludes him yet. He knew *that* the good exists, but *what* it is that exists remained beyond his mind. If we study the dialogues carefully, we catch glimpses at odd moments behind all the endless arguing of the pathos of incompleteness which overwhelms us about Socrates. I am not referring merely to the fact that so many of the definition-dialogues ended in verbal futilities; neither do I mean the perplexity and confusion in which the Socratic dialectic could involve issues. It is not during the dialogues themselves, but in the silence after the talking has stopped that we have a sense of Socrates as deprived of the one object, whatever it was, that could have completely satisfied his restless mind. He knew that his destructive logic was preliminary to something else of a positive kind. Socrates himself offered his ignorance as humility to the god Apollo. Explaining the Delphic oracle that had called him the wisest of men, he said in the *Apology* that "real wisdom is the property of God and this oracle in his way is telling us that human wisdom has little or no value." The god had only used Socrates as an example, as if he were to dictate, "The wisest of you men is he who has realized like Socrates that in respect of wisdom he is really worthless." It is this Socratic emptiness which the mystics later used for their own un-Socratic anti-intellectual ends. Yet the fact remains Socrates himself suffered through the philosophical dark night of the soul.

I shall not discuss here at any length the Socratic understanding of the soul. It has been much discussed elsewhere and is, in fact, one of the commonplaces of intellectual history. The sense of the soul as an immaterial and so deathless intellectual and moral entity in us is Socrates' greatest contribution to Western thought, though he worked from the matter, to be sure, of others who had preceded him. The discovery of such a soul—actually for Socrates the living out of the soul in the martyrdom of philosophical death—places Socrates at fount and center of the Western tradition. What relates to our subject is that attribute of separability from the body which Socrates gave the soul. When it came for him to a precise understanding of our identity, he did not explain our nature in terms of a fused composite of physical body and intellectual soul, as, say, Aristotle and Aquinas would later do. He detached instead the soul from the body and defined the man in terms of his soul alone. Such a self-sufficient, detachable entity made an overwhelming impression on subsequent thinkers, and when history reached crises and became too disturbing or too awful in its effect on human beings, as it so frequently can and does, the Socratic understanding of a separated soul was ready and at hand to furnish the victims with the wherewithal of escape from this world. Philosophy became for such the practice of death whereby an enslaved soul was liberated from the tomb of the body through special knowledge and unnatural enlightenment.[4] Why worry about summoning the necessary courage to face and to endure purging realities of this painful world, the Gnostics later asked, when the separable soul is already outside and beyond the wretchedness?

The most crucial event in Plato's life was the execution of Socrates. He tells us the effect on him of the judicial murder in the autobiographical Seventh Letter, which nearly all scholars today accept as authentic. He was a young man in his twenties when the event occurred. Everything in his social background, everything in his aristocratic nature naturally would have led him to an assumption of political power in the Athenian state. But because of the death of Socrates he realized he couldn't pay the moral price that he saw he would be forced to pay for political success in the states of this world. He renounced action for contemplation, politics for philosophy, and he placed his only hope for a redemption of human history in a transcendent justice beyond this life. After referring to the "wicked charges" brought against Socrates, the court's condemnation, and the execution of the old philosopher, Plato describes the momentous change that then occurred in his life:

> So when I saw this and the kind of men who were active in politics and the principles on which things were managed, I concluded that it was difficult to take part in public life and retain one's integrity, and this feeling became stronger the more I observed and the older I became. Nothing could be done without friends and loyal associates. Such men were not easy to find among one's existing acquaintance, for affairs were no longer conducted on the principles practiced by our ancestors, and new friends could not be acquired with any facility. Besides, the corruption of written law and established custom was proceeding at an astounding rate, so that I, who began by being full of enthusiasm for a political career, ended by growing dizzy at the spectacle of universal confusion. I did not cease to consider how an improvement might be

effected in this particular situation and in politics in general, and I remained on the watch for the right moment for action, but finally I came to the conclusion that the condition of all existing states is bad—nothing can cure their constitutions but a miraculous reform assisted by good luck—and I was driven to assert, in praise of true philosophy, that nothing else can enable one to see what is right for states and for individuals and that the troubles of mankind will never cease until either true and genuine philosophers attain political power or the rulers of states by some dispensation of providence become genuine philosophers.

The *Gorgias* is an early work. It possesses the unmellowed raw power of a moral young man's revulsion at human evil. In tone and substance recalling Aeschylean tragedy, it is, as Eric Voegelin characterizes the dialogue, the death-sentence Plato the philosopher issued on the Athenian state.[5] At its conclusion Plato presents us with a mythic vision of the ultimate justice awaiting the corrupt political realm in the spiritual world after death. The vision has something almost Hebraic in its moral intensity. All souls will be judged there stripped naked of the obscuring and disguising body. The judges are the sons of Zeus—Minos, Rhadamanthys, and Aeacus—whose vision is perfected by the true powers of philosophy. The soul corrupted by evil they consign either to punishment or torture, depending upon its capacity for correction. And of all the souls so corrupted with moral filth that they will never be made whole by cathartic discipline, the far greater part, Plato believed, was made up of politicians and tyrants, those whose possession of secular power enabled them to indulge with complete freedom the unintellectual principle of pure flesh and so led them to damnation. Plato's vision can be interpreted as resulting in an almost Manichaean division of things into an ultimate good and an ultimate evil. It is most certainly dualistic.

When we turn our attention from the tyrant to the citizen who is his victim, as the argument in the *Gorgias* at one point does, we see a painful dilemma emerging: what happens to the good man in an evil state? If he wishes to ensure his physical well-being, as naturally and inevitably he will do, he discovers he must accommodate himself to the existing evil and become like the tyrant in whatever intemperate desire or compulsion it is which has invaded the tyrant's soul and contaminated it. He must do so because the tyrant will destroy any good man whose rational happiness forces upon him too unsettling a contrast to the irrational turmoil of his own soul. But the good man realizes that such a compromise means the destruction of his own soul.

It would be to sacrifice the ultimate good of himself—assuming the deathlessness of the soul and a transcendent justice which judges it—for the immediate, but precarious, good of just the body alone. He chooses the greater good of the mind and so incurs the wrath of the tyrant. But though his choice involves a self-destruction in part, yet it is still an entirely rational one. The intellect calculates the difference in quality and lastingness between a physical good and a spiritual good, and it reasonably chooses the spiritual precisely on account of the nature and permanence of the happiness which a good soul is entitled to and enjoys at the hand of the god. All this is to stay within rational, even utilitarian, bounds. The Platonic argument assumes that the evil the tyrant inflicts is real, that it would be better to avoid it if one morally could, that the best of things would be if the tyrant converted to sound philosophy and helped to build the just city. But we see the dilemma of the good man in the evil state contains ground for an irrational mysticism. Others who came after Plato and who considered themselves as thinking under his inspirations would take the further step outside reason which Plato himself never took. They would come to conclude that the evil which the tyrant inflicts on his innocent victims is unreal, that the morally bad political state is not a corruption of something that could possibly be good, but is instead a pure illusion. They conclude in this manner influenced by the intensity with which Plato insisted on only limited degrees of reality for our mundane world. They got rid of even the limited degree. Nothing is real except the uncreative One, they would state, thus giving up human politics to a philosophical and religious oblivion. In taking this step they turned away from the rationalistic dualism of Plato which they started from and embraced a mystical monism which carried them totally out of this world.

We reverse slightly the chronological order and turn now to Aristotle. One of the vices to which philosophy is liable consists of so concentrating on the essence of a being or thing and so restricting its applicability that it finally becomes too good for this earth. Under the intensities of definition it loses its existential context, leaves ordinary mortals behind, and ascends to an impossible spirituality. We see such a process of inhumanization at work even in Aristotle, the one thinker of the Greeks most noted for his this-worldness, his respect for individualities and the concrete thing, his discomfort with what he saw as the excessively theoretical purity of Plato. But what actually happens to the virtues under Aristotle's treatment of them in *Nicomachean Ethics*? A good number of them leave the world and only a few remain to be realized by our common nature. Courage is mainly limited to the aristocratic soldier facing death on the battlefield. Liberality necessitates money and material goods. That excellence of character related to distinctions and honors is by nature only located, according to Aristotle, in aristocratic orders. The virtue of magnificence, which is the same as liberality but enlarged on the grand scale, required an extraordinary wealth and only one or two men in the entire populated city can achieve the virtue. Even a strain of puritanism enters Aristotle's discussion of temperateness. In deciding exactly what emotions or pleasures the temperate person is to inhibit and control, he eliminates the pleasures of the mind—would Aristotle refuse to see or admit the possibility of intellectual or spiritual vices?—and he decides on the pleasures of our animality. Because of what the philosopher calls their possibly destructive insatiability, such pleasures are to be disciplined by the temperate person. Few of us would disagree. It is when Aristotle further says that the temperate person *dislikes* these pleasures and considers them *odious*—and they are sex, food, and drink—that some of us might suspect that Aristotle, at least in this single case, is violating human wholeness and setting up one part of our nature in a puritanical warfare against the other. And what is one to make of Aristotle's famous portrait of the magnanimous man in Book IV, the one which all but by itself modeled the aristocratic ideal of Europe and which survives into modernity in Nietzsche's concept of the *Übermensch*?[6] Has anyone ever met such a man? Has even such a cold-blooded piece of insensibility actually ever existed? In his detached and imperturbable self-sufficiency he resembles a divinity. And when Aristotle says that nothing is great for the magnanimous man, that he is beyond both admiration and surprise, we are relieved that such an emotionless and egoistic purity is impossible for human beings ever to realize. But historically the magnanimous man is quite important. We see emerging through him the stoical standard of indifference. And if we strain our vision only slightly we also see the outline of some of those remote, inaccessible, and morally neutral gods that so thickly populated the irrational debris of the fall of the classical world. It was a time when purified virtue had gone clean from the world.

Another problem arises when we consider the range of knowledge which Aristotle makes available to the intellect. He states that its range is restricted to two kinds of form. The more basic of these, the one which we share with animals, is the sensible form that we perceive within matter in one or more of our five senses. The other is that intellectual form of the species into which the intellect divides and distributes the objects of the senses. It is only form of this kind or the other that Aristotle will allow the intellect in its purity to be able to apprehend. But what about the uniqueness of our uncomplicated personhood? Is such a piece of individuality, which by definition isn't assimilable to the requirements of form, to be thrown out of the mind as something philosophically contaminated and so not to be apprehended by the intellect? But this question, essentially Christian in origin, is totally absent from Aristotle's philosophical mind, just as the notion of self-consciousness is missing from the whole of his psychology. At the very most he will concede only an *incidental* perception of human individuality. In a parenthetical aside in the *De Anima*, his treatise on what it is to have a soul, he says that "we perceive the son of Cleon (*or any other individual*, I will add) not because he is the son of Cleon, but because he is white, and the white object happens to be the son of Cleon." The human identity of the white object is a sort of accident to the essential mental apprehension of the sensible form of whiteness to which the mind is innately and so naturally kin. And so if the desire for a mystical annihilation of our separate personal identity should emerge in an intellect, that intellect would find, if it looked into Aristotle, that his epistemology had already done some of the preparatory work of annihilation for it, at least insofar as Aristotle does not allow the perception of human individuality to be anything other than incidental to the intellect's more important perception of impersonal form, for which it leaves the individual behind it.

Aristotle in fact didn't believe that the more purely active part of the intellect had anything at all to do with our personal identity. In conformity with his tendency to explain all things in terms of actuality and potentiality, he divided the mind into two parts: the active intellect and the passive intellect. In its pure and uninterrupted actuality the former stimulates the latter into action and causes whatever intellectual movement is to be found in it. But the passive intellect is in a way not clearly defined by Aristotle as tied up with the body and its sensory processes; it consequently suffers the fate of mattered things and perishes. But the active intellect doesn't exist in flesh and in its immateriality and ceaseless activity it is divine. It survives the death of the individual, and it does so precisely because it is unindividuated by the numberless peculiarities of body and personhood. The eternalness of the active intellect can give us then no hope of personal immortality. It is an abstract and impersonal metaphysical principle that exists as a cause for whatever intellectual insight it is we just happen to achieve. Such insight is discrete from the dying individual. Persons don't think in Aristotle; intellects *in* persons do.[7] And so in view of the divine essence of the intellect, notwithstanding the costs in individual personhood, it isn't surprising that in the last book of the *Nicomachean Ethics* Aristotle should state that of the two lives, the one of action, the other of thought, the superior one is that of thought. True happiness is not to be found in the competitive culture of "agony"—that is, politics, arts, sports, or anything that requires the presence of spectators whose approval or disapproval bestows honor or dishonor on the now passive performer—but, instead, is to be found in the silence, even the breathlessness, of philosophical abstraction and retirement.[8] We have lived with this revaluation of Aristotle for so long now and still approve of it that we forget how revolutionary it must have seemed to the Greeks of Aristotle's day. They lived their lives in what we can call a blinding publicity. Pericles stated in his Funeral Oration in Thucydides, and most all Greeks would have concurred, that the man who refused to take part in public affairs wasn't harmless but was useless.[9] One's very humanity, they believed, was fulfilled in action, not in thought. The typical attitude toward the philosopher is expressed by Callicles in Plato's *Gorgias*. A sort of sexual obscenity attaches to the philosophical man according to this character who represents in the dialogue the most ruthless position possible of power politics, who would have cared not a fig for a divine essence of any part of the mind. The philosophic man deserves beating, Callicles says, for his womanly seclusion, avoiding the *agora* where real men win honor and distinction, sunk away as he says the philosopher is in some obscure corner, whispering to three or four boys.[10] We owe Aristotle an immense debt for counterattacking such repulsive boorishness by asserting in the *Nicomachean Ethics* the essential dignity of the mind. But a fatal compulsion to excess seems to exist in all things human, and it is not Aristotle's fault that thinkers after him, influenced by his revaluation, should explode in the most irresponsible of subjectivities and mysticisms. They did so once they overcame the shame of violating political objectivities and felt proud of the mind's isolation and purity. Then it was that the mind got revenge on such as Callicles by committing a boorishness of its own and consigning all political life to a kind of futile and sublunary madness, something that would have horrified the man who once said that the human being is by his very nature a political animal and who studied politics with the most serious philosophical attention he could command. If Aristotle had lived on to witness the spiritualistic excesses of, say, Alexandria in the first of the Christian era, he might well have reconsidered that pride of place which he had awarded the contemplative life in his *Ethics*. We can guess he would have felt disgust at the mystical wildness which his verdict in its own way helped to initiate but through no fault of his own, even indeed in spite of the fact that the revaluation was entirely rational and true.

Even though Plato anticipated the mystics far more than Aristotle, I have spent more time on the latter precisely because he represents the test case. If it can be shown that the smallest seedling of mysticism existed in the cooler and more scientific mind of Aristotle, that fact makes our case that much stronger. But with the rest of Greek thinkers whom we are here concerned with we may proceed in a more summary manner. Of none of them do we have anything at all like a complete corpus as we do with Plato and Aristotle. They exist like bloodless ghosts in fragments only. But we are trying to understand the forerunners of a very broad philosophical and religious movement, and detailed knowledge of a philosopher's worked-out system isn't required to determine the general outline of his position in reference to that movement. The historians can give us accurate information enough on that score. Besides, some of these philosophers founded schools of their own, all documented, and we can come to some cautious conclusions as to their doctrines by studying the more attested ones of their followers.

Euclides was one of the minor Socratics. He was present at the death of Socrates, and so must be counted among the more intimate of Socrates' followers and friends. As to his philosophical doctrine, he was an upholder of the monistic dogma of the Eleatics. He believed that nothing exists but the One. This present world of mattered differences and sensory diversity, a world in which ordinary experience also convinces most of us that elements of some evil and deficiency are to be found, such a world cannot exist, according to Euclides, insofar as evil or even any form of particularity can be said to be inevitable parts of it. It is apparent then that his Socratism caused him to qualify his monism by identifying the One with the Good. As Eduard Zeller expressed it, Euclides "ethicized" the Parmenidian unity of being and thereby "refused to admit the reality of an opposite to the One Good."[11] But modified or not, such a doctrine in its ethical fanaticism makes ethics itself a futility. As we human beings currently find ourselves, our moral life primarily consists of trying through reason to find the means which will enable us to achieve some limited good that we see we need for our being. It is the utilitarian good-for-the-sake-of-something-else we have to heed in what used to be called our fallen state. And if the complete truth were told, we are so beset with mortality we spend most of our moral energy just avoiding immediate evils instead of pursuing a remote positive good. But by identifying the One with the Good, Euclides renders such morality an impossibility; his logic destroys our manifold of multiple goods—goods for the sake of something else that is another good—and leaves us with the tyranny of one ethical absolute; such an entity has consumed in its unity the virtues which Aristotle tells us are states of character concerned with proportioned means determined by our reason and existing between an extreme of deficiency and an extreme of excess—a concept that logically requires the existence of three separate and different things. That Euclides' reduction of all three to the One prepares for mysticism, which then has nothing to do with morality, is apparent.

The disciples of Euclides, such men as Eubulides, Diodorus Cronus, and Stilpo, make up what the historians call the School of Megara. Although they are now no more than mere names in specialized histories, in their own day they were famous for their logical paradoxes and fallacies. The purpose of such ingenuities was to demonstrate the logical absurdity of motion and multiple things and thereby to deconstruct the phenomenal and composite world entirely under the category of the Eleatic One. Stilpo went so far in his monistic intensities as to assert that it is impermissible to apply to a subject a predicate *different from itself.* There is only the one subject, and knowledge of empirical facts, such as we might or might not discover about its existence in phenomenal otherness, is a logical impossibility. A great deal of intellectual energy was expended on these controversies. The Stoic Chrysippus wrote many books in a vain attempt to find their solution. But what do such riddles and conundrums do, besides stultifying our reason and dazzling us with the logician's too evident genius? They create in the minds of certain persons a disgust for intellectual matters which in turn inclines them to irrational enthusiasms, usually of a religious nature, as an antidote to the sterilities of pure logic. Or else in other minds, those, that is, who are quite eager to take logic out to its extremity no matter the insanities it might force on the mind, the logical puzzles establish a theoretical groundwork for the same enthusiasms. Mystical annihilation is then embraced as the only conceivable issue of logic itself. It is true that monistic systems do not by necessity lead to mysticism. Materialism is monistic in a certain sense, and no one surely would call a materialist a mystic. Parmenides' own concept of unified being can be read as applying just to the extended and material universe. But if all monisms are not mystical, yet all mysticisms are monistic. What we have called the tyranny of the One exerts such enormous intellectual pressure in any monistic system, as well as any mystical one, that since like calls to like a transition from the former to the latter is easily made in many minds.

The historian Theopompus stated that Antisthenes, the founder of Cynicism, was the most important of the Socratics. I should like here to emphasize a fact of his personal life which isn't directly related to philosophy as such. He was the bastard son of a Thracian slave-woman; and although his father was an Athenian, this did not entitle him to the citizenship of Athens. (Phaedo, another of the Socratics, was himself a slave whom Socrates had ransomed.) With Antisthenes we approach later classical times, the cosmopolitan world of empires' packed cities in which many different races and cultures conflicted to form strange fusions. It was a world in which the individual, deprived of the immediate political involvement of a small city-state, began to feel disenfranchised and lost in the abstraction of immense social and political structures and so suffered the need for religious consolation. It was, in short, the world of our own mongrel intellect, as Nietzsche calls it, the time of the rise of universal religion and the dominance of the Porch and the Garden.[12] Antisthenes himself advocated an international humaneness, an impartial love of mankind in general, a fact which would make him, if I am not mistaken, the first Greek thinker to treat the barbarians as full members of the human race. He too was alienated. His philosophy itself was severely ethical. What he sought above all else was freedom from desire. Zeller provides us with an excellent summary of Antisthenes in his discussion of cynical asceticism in his *Outlines of the History of Greek Philosophy* (1883, trans. 1886):

> Applying the opposition of nature and convention formulated by the Sophists they rejected completely the existing forms of communal life in favor of an extreme individualism. After this the Cynics led a life of formal mendicancy, without a house of their own, contenting themselves with the simplest food, and the scantiest clothing. They made a principle of inuring themselves to privation, hardships, and insults; they showed their complete indifference to life by making a voluntary departure from it. As a rule they renounced family life, Diogenes proposing to replace it by communities of women and children; they attached no value to the opposition of freedom and slavery; for the wise man was free even as a slave, and a born master; for the wise man they considered civic life dispensable; for he was everywhere at home, a citizen of the world; their conception of the ideal state was a natural existence in which the whole of mankind lived together like a herd.

The aim of Cynicism was indifference to pain and freedom from desire. It has many admirable qualities, but at its center it represented a contraction of the human being. Like Stoicism it insisted on a vicious opposition between the internal soul and the external world. Like mysticism it too left the world and sought to build up inside the soul an immunity against its philosophical diseases. In its failure of nerve, its profound disaffection with life, Cynicism caused man later to shift the responsibility for his life onto such abstract entities as the Fate of the Stoics or the deterministic Providence of some of the early Christians. We further see especially with the students of Diogenes the Dog, who was a pupil of Antisthenes, that cynical indifference urged them through rebellions against all established social norms on into out-and-out primitivism and barbarism. Though Diogenes, whom Plato was reputed to have once called "a Socratic gone mad," is like Falstaff in the inevitable attraction we feel toward him, we shouldn't forget that his paradoxes defended incest and cannibalism, the purest cases of atavism which we have. Finally, and to return to our subject at hand, Cynicism in attacking conventions, social order, traditions, and law undermined the human world and created that contempt for life which has always been a breeding ground for mysticism of an inhuman sort. As a consequence of Cynicism and the later Stoicism a tragic withdrawal occurred in Greek philosophy. The idea of ethics being concerned with what makes for right conduct in this world was abandoned. Similarly abandoned was the notion of the virtues as acquired powers that enable the human being to make something excellent of his existence and to present it to the world. The daydream of some impossibly unrealistic self-sufficiency possessed the mind. Behind the mask of theoretical apathy, especially behind the contemptuous brutality of Diogenes and his followers, one feels the desperate pathos of their desire never to be hurt again. Inside the hard shell of their philosophy they shrunk themselves out of the world.

There were three main schools which the minor Socratics formed among themselves. Euclides and his followers looked back to the Eleatics and continued their reduction of multiplicity to the One. Antisthenes and his pupil Diogenes originated the School of the Dog which developed into Stoicism. And there is finally Aristippus and his disciples who composed what has been called the Cyrenaic School or the School of Hedonism which developed into Epicureanism. I conclude with a discussion of the unexpected contribution which hedonism offered the mystical movements of the late world of antiquity.

The central doctrine of hedonism as it originated in the mind of Aristippus can be simply put. That which gives meaning to human existence is having enjoyment of the greatest amount of pleasure for the greatest length of time as is possible. Upon first encountering the doctrine we automatically assume that the pleasure canvassed by Aristippus inevitably presupposes an objective world in which the pleasure is experienced. Innocently we think of the effect of some object on our bodies or minds, ourselves knowing what the object is. But a closer study of Aristippus reveals a great irony. He based his hedonism on an epistemology that destroyed the world as we commonly think we know it. Like the empiricists of modernity, he didn't believe that our sensory perceptions can inform us of a world beyond our private sensations. He thought that *something* indeed was there external to our senses, but what exactly it was had to remain a complete mystery to him. He was certain of two facts, that our senses *are* modified, even if by some unknowable thing, and that certain rough movements in the modification occasion us pain and other certain smooth ones pleasure. Instinctively we prefer pleasure to pain and so it was on the modifications of a smooth nature that Aristippus based his philosophy of hedonism. But to do so he had to leave all objective reality behind him, retreat to the interiors of the soul and isolate himself in the non-referential processes of the body. Since a physiological event is both the origin and continuation of his highest good, not the knowledge of the object which caused the event, the hedonism of Aristippus is irrational. There had been systems before his that had centered their attention for the time being on the inside of soul or mind, but his is the first to stay there from the beginning to the end. And it is precisely the completeness of its interior journey and the permanence of its abode in a locked-in mind which enabled hedonism to offer the mystics the first perfected pattern of internality and subjectivity.[13] If the cynics and the stoics could teach the mystics an indifference to the world, the hedonists could better the lesson with the doctrine that, as far as the human mind goes, nothing exists but the sensations of the soul.

[On Plato's *Crito*][1]

I.

Before we examine the main argument of Plato's *Crito*, I should like to look at two points in the background of that argument.[2] Crito is attempting to persuade Socrates to escape from prison. He reminds Socrates of the shame he himself will suffer if it should be thought by the Athenian public that he was unwilling to save his friend because of the expense involved in effecting an escape. "And what could be more contemptible," he says, "than to get a name for thinking more of money than of your friends." To avoid such public humiliation Crito begs Socrates to allow him to engineer the escape. His argument is a direct appeal to the validity of public opinion. It is what people think of us, he believes, that should guide our moral actions. Socrates counters with two principles which he says have sustained him throughout his life. Of the advice offered him by his friends, he has always decided only to take that particular advice which he judged upon mature reflection to be in accord with reason. When the reason has been thus applied to opinions we then get the second principle: "some of the opinions which people entertain should be respected, and others should not." It is the presence of reason in the opinion, not the opinion's popularity, which according to Socrates should favorably determine our judgment toward it.

Socrates now makes a perhaps not completely logical shift. Up until this point in the explanation of his principles he has been considering the nature of the opinion itself, that is, whether or not the opinion is or is not rational no matter who holds it or how few or how many. He now shifts to the different consideration of the persons holding the opinion and their number, things that might, strictly speaking, be thought the accidents of the opinion. We discover that Socrates is automatically assuming—he never states the assumption explicitly—

that the good opinion to be respected belongs to just one person, the expert, and that the bad opinion to be rejected belongs to the many. Socrates seems to imply that this oneness and this multiplicity are infallible indicators of the rationality or the irrationality of the opinion. If the multitude entertain an opinion then that opinion is automatically suspect in Socrates' mind just for the reason that the multitude holds it. Doubtless a great deal of evidence could be found to justify Socrates in this belief. But still some questions bother us. Why the restriction to just one person? Is there something actually in the nature of expertise that renders it unable to tolerate more than one person possessing it? And isn't it logically conceivable that certain situations should emerge in which the many just happen to hold the correct opinion validated by reason, which after all ignores the question of the number of people holding the opinion and considers only its truth? It would have been better, we begin to think, if Socrates had left the standard by which an opinion is to be accepted or rejected just in its rationality abstractly considered and forgotten the one and the many.

But Socrates had the belief—I want to say the dream—that morality could be reduced to exact science. Virtue is knowledge, according to the famous Socratic paradox, by which is meant more practical skill than theoretical insight. The moralist is a calculator who knows the consequences of actions. He looks ahead and sees what actions do or do not make for his happiness in the long run, and behaves accordingly. The logical analogy for virtue is a craft such as medicine or architecture or ship-piloting. Each has its objective content that can be rationally formulated; each can be passed on through instruction to another person, and each has a final product or state of being which when arrived at completes the craft and gives it meaning. With medicine it is a healthy body, with architecture a building, with ship-piloting a safe voyage, and so with virtue the happiness peculiar to the rational mind. But the sad fact is that very few people become good craftsmen of any sort. The nature of such skill seems to exclude many people from possessing it. And so in discussing the moral craft, specifically here the question of whether or not he should escape from prison, Socrates is bound to refer to the division of the skillful few against the ignorant many, though in this case he goes to the extremity of the one instead of the few. He invokes "the expert in right and wrong, the one authority, who represents the actual truth." Such a one is to guide him and Crito in their deliberations.

But does such a man exist? In the *Apology* Socrates tells us that he spent most of his entire life searching for such a person but never found him. Year after year the search had gone on. Politicians, poets, and skilled craftsmen were all canvassed to discover if they had wisdom.

The craftsmen did indeed have knowledge, Socrates found out, but it was of an inferior kind and limited to the narrow requirements of their specific crafts. It could never satisfy the moral and intellectual intensity of Socrates. The rest thought they knew everything, but in actuality they did not even know that they knew nothing. At least Socrates knew the latter, but still his negative wisdom—the paradoxical wisdom of knowing one is not wise—could never enable him to become "the one authority" which he requires in the *Crito*. On the basis of the *Apology* then we have to conclude that the one expert in the moral craft did not exist for Socrates. It is a fact that such a one is no sooner invoked in the *Crito* than he is forgotten, and the subsequent argument proceeds without ever once deferring to his essential advice. Perhaps "the one authority" is meant to be no more than an allegorical embodiment of the wisdom human beings are capable of but never actually and concretely achieve in any one person. Such a conception is, of course, congenial to the mind of Plato, but it is foreign to the far more prosaic and realistic mind of Socrates, whose talk, as Callicles says so sarcastically in the *Gorgias*, was filled with nothing but "cobblers and fullers and cooks and doctors." In any event, the extraordinary anomaly of Socrates insisting on the one expert and believing at the same time that he himself has never located such a person and so cannot use him in the argument should cause us to treat that argument with some let us say respectful skepticism.

The second point can be more briefly stated. It concerns the apparent contradiction between the principle of the one expert and the historical reality behind the kind of statism which Socrates asserts in the *Crito*. He uncompromisingly argues for total obedience on the part of the subject to the state. He does allow the individual the right of attempting to persuade the state that a decision it has made and he objects to is wrong. But if he should fail then he must submit himself to the state and suffer whatever the state dictates in the matter. There is no contradiction between such obedience and the principle of the one expert. In fact, if the state should legitimately be the one expert, the two mesh together. The source of conflict involves Socrates' principle and the historical reality of the particular state which in the *Crito* Socrates is to be obedient to. That state is Athenian democracy which in legal, political, and moral matters renounced the one and gave an absolute and indisputable authority to the many instead. The democracy consulted professional experts for technical advice, to be sure, and a kind of aristocracy of talent still obtained in the military sphere where the very survival of the state was involved. But constitutionally it was nothing but the rule of the majority. For instance, there was not even a judge at Socrates' trial. No procedural or evidential laws governed or limited the jury, which could do what it wished and was too often swayed just by the raw emotions of the moment. Yet in the *Crito* it is precisely to this state of the multitude that Socrates attributes an authority such as no other philosopher, as far as I know, has ever given the state before or since. He says he must give the state implicit obedience, and as he does so, the one expert disappears.

Again, it might be objected that the state Socrates means to obey and to glorify isn't any specific state, least of all the Athenian democracy; it is rather the idea of the state, a kind of theoretical norm made up of and applicable to all the different, individual states. What these states philosophically have in common—the abstraction compounded of the particulars—is the real object of Socrates' mind. But the *Crito* isn't just a philosophical statement about the idea of the state; it is also a historical document dealing with specific legal and political acts done by the democracy of Athens at the end of the fifth century. Theoretical norms don't issue death sentences against individuals. The personified Laws do make use of themselves as such a norm at one point in the *Crito*. They console Socrates by telling him that he is "a victim of wrong done not by us, the Laws, but by your fellow men," as if they themselves in their theoretical purity were far away from the whole sordid mess. But there is something morally repulsive about the Laws' evading here any responsibility for the part they actually played in the tragedy. Socrates wasn't arrested, tried, and sentenced to death by a mob of stateless men. The whole affair was a series of perfectly legal acts, done exactly according to the constitution of Athens, based as that constitution was on the will and the rule of the many. The Laws were implicated in it from the beginning to the end.

II.

The main argument in the *Crito* for obedience can be divided into three parts. The first concerns the analogy Socrates sees existing between the child-parent relation and the subject-state relation; the second, the contractual obligation which Socrates has entered into with the state; the third, the destruction of the state which the philosopher believes will occur as a consequence of disobedience. Let us look at each of these arguments and determine what merit each has.

According to the first argument, the state gave Socrates his life. It was through the Laws that Socrates parents married and begat him in the first place. Continuing their protection over him, the Laws further required his parents to give him a proper education, to train and mold him in both his body and his mind. The Greeks didn't believe that virtue is natural in the same way as, say, the physical traits and capabilities of our bodies are. Virtue is acquired through discipline, culture, and instruction such as only the framework of the state can provide. Therefore, Socrates is the cultured child of the state who owes to it his moral and intellectual existence. A binding analogy holds then between a child and his parents on the one hand and on the other the subject and the state. What is true of one of the relations applies with logical rigor to the other. Just as a child has no right to retaliate against his parent if that parent should treat him unjustly, so the subject has no right to retaliate against the state, and even if, as in Socrates' case, the state should unjustly attempt to put him to death. The citizen has a limited right to try to persuade the state that it is wrong in a particular case, but if he should be unsuccessful, then he must submit himself to the awful power of the state. But if the analogy holds in kind, it doesn't in degree. The state has an absolute priority. In view of the enormous benefits that the state has conferred on the individual, he owes the state a far greater degree of devotion than he owes his parents. As the personified laws explain to Socrates:

> Do you expect to have such license against your country and its laws that if we try to put you to death in the belief that it is right to do so, you on your part will try your hardest to destroy your country and us its laws in return? And will you, the true devotee of goodness, claim that you are justified in doing so? Are you so wise as to have forgotten that compared with your mother and father and all the rest of your ancestors your country is something far more precious, more venerable, more sacred, and held in greater honor among gods and among all reasonable men? Do you not realize that you are even more bound to respect and placate the anger of your country than you are your father's anger? That if you cannot persuade your country you must do whatever it orders, and patiently submit to any punishment that it imposes, whether it be flogging or imprisonment?

The second argument contains the first statement we have of the social contract, which becomes so crucially important in the political thought of Locke and Rousseau. Its ultimate principle is that one should live up to the agreements one has willingly and knowingly entered into. By his residing in the city and by his receiving there the benefits of citizenship Socrates has bound himself to the state. The one essential condition of living in a civilized state is that its laws must be obeyed. If the state has so generously provided for Socrates, as we have seen he believes it has, then he must reciprocate and pay to the state the very thing that actually makes the state possible in the first place, which is obedience. Such obligation arising from agreement, the Laws state, is especially true of Socrates, who has consistently shown the greatest affection for the city and its life. Most rarely has he ever left Athens, so obviously he does find that state agreeable to him. The contract, furthermore, is binding for him in that not one of the circumstances which usually invalidate contracts is to be found in Socrates' case at all. No compulsion or fraud was practiced upon him. He was fully informed as to the terms of the contract. He wasn't pressured as to time. In fact, the whole seventy years of his life had been given him to make up his mind. During those years he had been free at any time to leave the city, to go somewhere else, and so to terminate the contract. But because he stayed he thus agreed to live according to the state he so evidently showed he wanted to be a part of. And because the claims of the whole transcend the claims of the part—otherwise, there would not even be a whole for there to be a part—Socrates must now do what the Laws of the whole require of him and drink the hemlock.

The third argument from destruction, which actually is the first to appear in the dialogue, isn't as developed as the other two and so has here been put after them. It is briefly given as an introduction to the first argument and is only incidentally referred to again, most tellingly at the conclusion when the Laws of the other world after death judge a disobedient Socrates as a "destroyer of laws." The earlier statement is as follows. Again, the Laws are addressing Socrates:

> Can you deny that by this act (i.e. of disobedience) which you are contemplating you intend, so far as you have the power, to destroy us, the Laws, and the whole state as well? Do you imagine that a city can continue to exist and not be turned upside down, if the legal judgments which are pronounced in it have no force but are nullified and destroyed by private persons?

How are we exactly to interpret this passage? Surely Socrates doesn't mean that a single act of disobedience on the part of just one person can and does destroy the state. It is a notorious fact that innumerable acts of disobedience occur all the time in every state and the government survives them all with no loss of power. It is true that such acts can be multiplied until a crisis is reached, and the state either explodes or just crumbles away. But this is revolution or disintegration, and it occurs most rarely. Perhaps Socrates means that a single piece of lawlessness committed by one individual who has extensive influence in the state can corrupt it through the contagion of example

172

and so eventually bring it to its destruction. But this surely isn't the case with Socrates, and Plato knows it in the qualification *so far as you have power*. Socrates furthermore makes no distinction at all between more important laws and those less so. Certainly the argument from destruction applies to just the former. But since Plato doesn't expand the argument we have no way of resolving these questions. But if we are not sure about its details, we are about the main drift of the argument, and if reformulated in positive terms it contains an undeniable fact: a state can only survive and enjoy well-being if a significant number of its citizens obey a significant number of its laws.

Of these three arguments, it is the second one from contractual agreement which is most rationally compelling, though we would wish indeed to mitigate its Socratic severity and to limit the absolute power it hands over to the state. But given the truth of its premises—and there are no logical or factual grounds for doubting them—then its conclusion inevitably follows. Both state and citizen are necessarily compacted together by their very identities. And Socrates, besides, had been almost defiant at his trial. He had scornfully rejected the alternative the state offered him of banishment. 1 am staying here, he told the jury in so many words, and you can do with me as you wish. He dared the state to live up to its side of the contract, and what else could the state tragically do but comply? As we have just seen, the argument from destruction is so undeveloped that little can be said either for or against it in its present form. Yet it contains a truth, and if modified and expanded, something indeed can be said for its validity. But the first argument, the one from the analogy Socrates sees between the parent and the state, is logically flawed and is profoundly disturbing as well. It contradicts a fundamental principle of Plato's own philosophy.

According to Plato, a proper definition expresses in words the common essence which is to be found in a possibly infinite series of individual instances. It is of what stays the same in the examples, objectively present in them and that which enables the mind to know and to recognize them. It enjoys, therefore, unity, self-identity, and universality. As Socrates states the matter in the *Euthyphro*, an early dialogue concerned with the definition of the holy, "Is not the holy always one and the same thing in every action?" He presses the question again later on when he reminds Euthyphro, "Well, bear in mind that what I asked of you was not to tell me one or two out of all the numerous actions that are holy; I wanted you to tell me what is the essential form of holiness which makes all holy actions holy. I believe you held that there is one ideal form by which unholy things are all unholy, and by which all holy things are holy." And so in the *Republic* Plato insists on the identity of justice in the state and justice in the individual. They are essentially the same, though appearing in different aspects and relations. If they were not equivalent then justice would be one thing here and another thing there. It would contradict itself and lose its identity in the differing.

Justice is precisely the virtue the *Crito* deals with. But is its justice one and the same in the state and in the individual? The Laws themselves say it is not:

> Then since you have been born and brought up and educated, can you deny, in the first place, that you were our child and servant, both you and your ancestors? And if this is so, do you imagine that what is right for us is equally right for you, and that whatever we try to do for you, you are justified in retaliating?

Of course, no one is going to assert that the justice of the state and that of the individual are so alike that there *really* exists no difference between the state and the individual. The state has power which the individual can never have. As we saw earlier, the claims of the whole state take precedence over the claims of the partial citizen when a conflict occurs. But the end of both state and individual is the same, which is the good. As one of the means to this end, the state then is just as accountable to reason as the individual. It must justify itself by saying how it too realizes the good. And there should be a reciprocal relationship between the two—the whole seeking the good of the part and the part seeking the good of the whole. Any power or authority either a parent or the state possesses must be redeemed by the vision of the whole good, or else it becomes a tyranny. But we find none of this reciprocity in the *Crito*. Plato so emphasizes the obligations of the citizen to the state that he completely ignores the obligations of the state to the citizen; he also forgets, or doesn't here believe, that the state after all is a human creation. The impression the *Crito* leaves of the state is that of a tyrant whose essence is found in power, not in reason. It doesn't have to give a rational account of itself to anyone; precisely like a god, it answers only to itself. I can do to you what I want to, the State tells Socrates in so many words, but you cannot do the same to me. My justice isn't the same as your justice. It is different. Thus, through the analogy of the parent and the state in the extreme version Plato gives to it, the virtue of justice loses its logical unity, and Plato has Socrates sacrifice himself to an irrational power.

The second principle relates to what we may call the validation of a moral concept. According to the principle, a virtue isn't such just because some extraneous authority says it is, but rather because of the essence of the virtue itself and the actual productions that essence effects in a given person. For example, an act of bravery performed by a soldier isn't courageous because some commander orders it to be so designated. It is courageous because the virtue in the soldier enabled him to maintain a cohesion of soul in the presence of destructive or dissolving forces. And in the *Euthyphro* Socrates says something isn't holy because the gods love it, but, on the other hand, the gods love it because it is holy. Piety and the other virtues have an objective content independent of the approval or disapproval of anyone or anything other than themselves. The morality of Plato, then, is non-authoritarian. It is natural in that it derives its principles not from an unrelated authority, but from human nature itself. It seeks to discover what makes or doesn't make for the good of the whole nature so that it can rationally justify its laws. But the analogy of the parent and the state deviates from this principle. It is legitimate for a parent frequently to insist on obedience on the part of a child and not to give any reason for the obedience but its own authority. Do this, the parent orders, because I tell you to do it. The *Crito's* analogy delivers to the state this prerogative of the parent. A moral concept then becomes validated not by its own essence, but by the approval of an extraneous authority, which is arbitrary and unbound by reason.

Elizabeth Daryush[1]
(5 December 1887–7 April 1977)

Charitessi 1911 (Cambridge, U.K.: Bowes & Bowes, 1912)
Verses by Elizabeth Bridges (Oxford: Blackwell, 1916)
Verses (London: Oxford University Press, 1930)
Verses: Second Book (London: Oxford University Press, 1932)
Verses: Third Book (London: Oxford University Press, 1933)
Verses: Fourth Book (London: Oxford University Press, 1934)
The Last Man and Other Verses (London: Oxford University Press, 1936)
Verses: Sixth Book (Oxford: Privately printed, 1938)
Selected Poems, edited by Yvor Winters (New York: Swallow/Morrow, 1948)
Verses: Seventh Book (South Hinksey, U.K.: Carcanet Press, 1971)
Selected Poems (South Hinksey, U.K.: Carcanet Press, 1972)
Collected Poems (Manchester: Carcanet New Press, 1976)

Elizabeth Daryush has been one of the most neglected poets writing in English in this century. She stubbornly held on to certain traditional poetic procedures and maintained a diction that frequently was criticized as archaic. The literary revolutions effected by Ezra Pound and T. S. Eliot never touched the somewhat insular attitude she had toward poetry. Consequently, she has been dismissed as belonging more to the discredited world of the late Victorians than to the poetically more authentic movements of the twentieth century. Yet such an assessment is slowly being recognized as both unjust and inaccurate. American poet-critic Yvor Winters championed her from the beginning of her career; Donald E. Stanford sought her out in her old age and published several of her last poems in the influential *Southern Review*. In her native England, such important poets as Roy Fuller and Donald Davie have recently "discovered" her and commented on the power and integrity of her best poems, and Michael Schmidt, the director of the Carcanet Press, has brought most of her work back into print. The writer of Daryush's obituary in the London *Times* speaks of Schmidt's having become "devoted to the Edwardian formality of the Daryushes—their 'magnificent humanity and dignity and ready complex of humour and wit.'" The emerging picture is that of an isolated figure who does not repeat tradition in an artificial manner but who uses traditional forms to create a vision of her own. Ironically, in view of her reputation as an extreme traditionalist, her future reputation might well rest on the experiments she conducted, following the lead of her father, Robert Bridges, in syllabic meter. Roy Fuller, for instance, penetrated behind the standard estimation of her work to see her as the forerunner in syllabic experimentation in this century, anticipating Marianne Moore and W. H. Auden, and he paid generous homage to her in the 1969 lecture he gave as Oxford Professor of Poetry.

She was born on 5 December 1887 to Robert Seymour Bridges, the poet laureate, and Mary Monica Waterhouse Bridges, the daughter of the famous nineteenth-century architect Alfred Waterhouse. There is a story that she was seen in her cradle by her father's friend Gerard Manley Hopkins, and if true it would imply a kind of continuity in English poetry. She lived much of her childhood at Chilswell, the house on Boar's Hill, overlooking Oxford, where the family moved in 1907, and was acquainted with John Masefield and Robert Graves when they lived on Boar's Hill. She also met Thomas Hardy. Her background was that of the privileged upper classes of the Victorian and Edwardian eras, a background she later criticized in her poetry and against which she rebelled. In the early 1920s she met Ali Akbar Daryush, who was introduced to her by Margery Fry, the sister of the Bloomsbury painter Roger Fry. She married Daryush on 29 December 1923. The couple went to Persia and lived there until 1927, when they returned to England. For the rest of her life she and her husband lived alone in their house Stockwell on Boar's Hill, close to Chilswell. She died on 7 April 1977, a few months before her ninetieth birthday. Those who visited her in her last years remember her as a strong, compelling figure with an acerbic streak to her conversation and a devotion to poetry undisturbed by the neglect and isolation she suffered all her life. She was almost totally blind during her last years and wore dark glasses even inside the house; yet one felt nothing went by her unobserved.

Her first book, *Charitessi 1911* (1912), and her second, *Verses by Elizabeth Bridges* (1916), are unobtainable today, but judging from *Verses* (1930) to the final poems, there is little dramatic development as such in her poetry; those conversions and often violent upheavals so frequently found in the lives and work of other twentieth-century poets are absent from her career. Instead, there is a deepening and surer investigation of a reality she never beguiled herself into thinking was other than it was. She thought the supposed powers of the romantic imagination hopelessly exaggerated. There are two exceptions to this generalization, one concerning subject matter, the other technique. Her early poetry is preoccupied with rather conventional subject matter and owes a great deal to the Edwardians, but *The Last Man* (1936) suggests a new awareness on her part of the anguish and pain caused by the profound changes that transformed English social life during the 1930s. Yvor Winters, writing in a 1936-1937 issue of the *American Review*, commented that "she appears to be increasingly conscious . . . of social injustice, of the mass of human suffering." This consciousness is presented ironically and indirectly in two of her best poems, "Still-Life" (*The Last Man*) and the conventional sonnet beginning "Children of wealth . . ." (*Verses: Sixth Book*, 1938). The focus in both these poems is on the privileged and the advantaged, whose wealth and social position protect them from and keep them ignorant of the knowledge of "elemental wrong" existing outside their narrow world. There is an unmistakable note of protest and outrage beneath each of these poems' polished and apparently undisturbed surfaces.

The other quite noticeable development she underwent concerns the experiment in syllabic meter which she inherited from her father. She once quoted him as saying that the traditional accentual-syllabic meter of English poetry had been almost exhausted, that a limited number of things could be said in such a meter and most of them had already been said. Consequently, a new meter, but one not formless and indeterminate like free verse, was needed to effect a new music in verse and to accommodate subject matter generally considered inappropriate in the conventional meter. Both Daryush and her father saw syllabics based on just the number of syllables in a line and leaving accent out of account as the solution to this problem. Daryush improved on her father's experiments by correcting their one error: he often gave syllabic identity to written but unpronounced clusters of letters in a line of verse. She gives such identity only to those syllables that are actually pronounced. And by always employing tight rhyme schemes she saved such a meter from the prosiness to which it is liable in the absence of an accentual regularity. "Still-Life" is one of the best examples of the subtle kind of music she was able to achieve in syllabic meter. It ends:

> she comes over the lawn, the young heiress,
> from her early walk in her garden-wood,
> feeling that life's a table set to bless
> her delicate desires with all that's good,
>
> that even the unopened future lies
> like a love-letter, full of sweet surprise.

But by and large her poetry pursues a steady course with no deviations or conversions invalidating what has gone before. The one theme that emerges most prominently in her work is the danger that imagination might beguile one into disregarding those tragic facts she considered inevitable and unavoidable in human life. She possessed a mind that insisted, almost at times to the point of bitterness, on disillusioning truth. For her, as for Thomas Hardy, poetry dealt with the "stubborn fact" of life as it is, and the only consolations it offered were those of understanding and a kind of half-Christian, half-stoical acceptance of the inevitable. Neither for her could poetry ever become merely an aesthetic experience centered around the cult of the beautiful that was so widespread and influential during the first decades of the twentieth century, the time she first began writing poetry. The flowers she alludes to in "Song: Throw Away the Flowers," published in *Verses: Fourth Book* (1934), are surely the rhetorical ones of such an aestheticism—they are found to be inadequate in an age preparing for war:

> Throw away the flowers,
> fetch stubborn rock;
> build for the hours
> Of terror and shock;
> go to timeless fact
> for what beauty lacked.

But her subject matter is not always so tragic. Scattered throughout all her books are the poems Yvor Winters and others consider her best work, poems dealing with the moral resources found in one's own being, a quiet stoicism mitigated by the Christian conception of charity, and a recognition of the beauties in the immediate, ordinary world around us. They are classical in the best sense of the word in that they possess "the sanity of self-restraint," to use Matthew Arnold's phrase, and they have the moral dignity of a person in conscious command of his life. One of the best examples of this type of poetry is "Faithless Familiars" (*Verses: Second Book*, 1932), which ends:

> Now the still hearth-fire
> intently gloweth,
> now weary desire
> her dwelling knoweth,
>
> now a newly-lit
> lamp afar shall burn,
> the roving spirit
> stay her, and return.

The language is seemingly bare and straightforward, with little or no ambiguous or connotative overtones to it, and its thematic content, the rejection of fulfillment through change and emotional abandonment, is counter to contemporary preoccupations. Donald Davie, in his introduction to the 1976 *Collected Poems*, suggests as a "useful starting point" for an appreciation of Daryush's poetry Yvor Winters' "confession" concerning the merits of such poetry: "The quality which I personally admire most profoundly . . . is the ability to imbue a simple expository statement of a complex theme with a rich association of feeling, yet with an utterly pure and unmannered style."

The defects of her poetry are a diction often unnecessarily archaic and a frequently melodramatic use of personified abstractions. But these defects will irritate only those readers so committed to the Pound-Eliot revolution in poetic style that they refuse to see virtue in any other poetry than that modern and imagistic. For readers who wish to explore the full range of English poetry, such defects should not blind them to the obvious excellencies of the poetry of Elizabeth Daryush, its thematic sturdiness and the subtle kind of music she was able to achieve in syllabic meter. Minor poets who stay at home and do solid good work often have a greater chance for survival of their work than those whose poems are flashier and more pretentious. One can well conceive of Elizabeth Daryush's surviving for this very reason.

References:

Donald Davie, "The Poetry of Elizabeth Daryush," introduction to *Collected Poems* (Manchester: Carcanet New Press, 1976), pp. 13-23;

Roy Fuller, Preface to *Verses: Seventh Book* (South Hinksey, U.K.: Carcanet Press, 1971);

Yvor Winters, Foreword to *Selected Poems* (New York: Swallow / Morrow, 1948);

Winters, *Forms of Discovery* (Denver: Swallow, 1967), pp. 347-348;

Winters, *In Defense of Reason* (Denver: Swallow, 1947, pp. 148-149;

Winters, "Robert Bridges and Elizabeth Daryush," *American Review*, 8, no. 3 (1936-1937): 363-367.

BOOK REVIEWS[1]

Review of *Angle of Geese* by N. Scott Momaday

N. Scott Momaday's reputation, before *Angle of Geese*, rested upon two works of prose, *House Made of Dawn*, a novel concerned with the dislocation and eventual disintegration of an Indian youth in urban America (parts of which were first published in *The Southern Review*), and *The Way to Rainy Mountain*, a half-mythical, half-historical account of Momaday's Kiowa ancestors, beautifully illustrated by the poet's father. These two books are considerable achievements, especially *The Way to Rainy Mountain*, which contains some of the most powerful prose written in recent years, or any year, for that matter. Yet *Angle of Geese*, made up of eighteen poems, three of which are in prose, is by far the greatest thing Momaday has done and should, by itself, earn for him a permanent place in our literature. Considering, though, the general insistence upon the loose and the anecdotal in contemporary poetry, I should realistically add that Momaday's poetic reputation will probably be quiet and underground.

Nearly all of his poems are concerned with what Yvor Winters, in his discussion of Momaday in *Forms of Discovery*, calls "the essential wilderness," the post-Romantic landscape of modern, secular thought, inscrutable and divested of ethical values, against which the human act takes place. More often than not, this act is personified by an animal, but one that has become, in the poem, emblematic and applicable to human terms. Because Momaday realizes the ultimately philosophical implications of this wilderness, his poems end up as serious meditations on the absolute distinction between what he calls in the title poem "the pale angle of time," the informed world of identity and purpose, and the state of death and nonbeing, "the essential wilderness" that finally destroys that world. Like [Edgar] Bowers and the other post-Symbolist poets, his approach is through description permeated with philosophic awareness:

> . . . this
> cold, bright body
> of the fish
> upon the planks,
> the coil and
> crescent of flesh
> extending
> just into death.

This theme is most perfectly realized in his greatest poem, "Before an Old Painting of the Crucifixion." On the one hand, there is the "critical expanse," operating in time and motivated by the human desire for "utterance" in art and religious thought; on the other, the nonhuman vacancy of a universe that completely frustrates that desire:

> These centuries removed from either fact
> Have lain upon the critical expanse
> And been of little consequence. The void
> Is calendared in stone; the human act,
> Outrageous, is in vain. The hours advance
> Like flecks of foam borne landward and destroyed.

The emotional control he is able to maintain in the face of this tragic perception, and with no religious belief to support him, is a measure of his greatness. The quietness and the concentration of the style reveal a mind that is as humanly fortified as it can be against the despair necessarily inherent in the subject.

In other poems this perception is less extreme. They are more concerned with the conditions of survival than with the inevitability of extinction. "The Bear," along with "Pit Viper," is an excellent example. The identity of the creature, worn down to the mere "fact of courage," holds itself together in the wilderness through an attitude of self-sufficient stoicism, a sort of expert indifference to the dangers always lurking behind the "countless surfaces" of the leaves. And in "Walk on the Moon," an epigram inspired by the Apollo mission, the emphasis is on the tentative human extension into and appropriation of the essentially non-human:

> Extend, there where you venture and come back,
> The edge of time. Be it your furthest track.
> Time in that distance wanes. What is *to be*,
> That present verb, there in Tranquility?

And other times he is capable, after the fact of annihilation, of a beautiful evocation of what he most loved in the past, the laughter and the old stories of his race, which is the subject of "Earth and I Gave You Turquoise," one of the most moving elegies in modern poetry:

> Tonight they dance near Chinle
>   by the seven elms
> There your loom whispered beauty
>   They will eat mutton
> and drink coffee till morning
>   You and I will not be there

Finally, to give one an idea of the stylistic achievement evident throughout all of *Angle of Geese*, I should like to quote entire a poem entitled "Buteo Regalis":

> His frailty discrete, the rodent turns, looks.
> What sense first warns? The winging is unheard,
> Unseen but as distant motion made whole,
> Singular, slow, unbroken in its glide.
> It veers, and veering, tilts broadsurfaced wings.
> Aligned, the span bends to begin the dive
> And falls, alternately white and russet,
> Angle and curve, gathering momentum.

What we have in this brief poem is a concise descriptive statement of a creature that knows its aim and lets nothing interfere with itself as it goes straight to the object. The intense concentration and power of the bird as it swoops down, "gathering momentum," upon the unprotected rodent, is unforgettable. The style also has the same concentration and singleness of purpose. The meter is syllabic, with no rhyme or rhetorical embellishments to enliven its "dryness," as J. V. Cunningham characterizes syllabic verse; the diction and word order as close to prose as is possible; and the tone of the poem is objective and matter-of-fact, each quietly insistent upon its denotative value. Nothing stands out of the evenly controlled context. And the movement of the poem is lean and muscular. If for no other reason than for its style, *Angle of Geese* would be an important book for anyone seriously interested in what American poetry is still capable of.

Angle of Geese by N. Scott Momaday, Boston: David R. Godine, 1974.

Review of *Collected Poems* by Elizabeth Daryush

After one finishes reading Elizabeth Dayrush's last book of verse, the *Collected Poems* (which is by no means complete—she was a severe self-critic and selected for this volume, published the year before her death in 1977, only her more successful poems, rejecting, in the process, over half of her previous work), one is struck above all by a sense of personal anguish underlying these hard poems that give so little comfort, and yet still are so intellectually and emotionally strengthening for the reader. The overwhelming majority of them are concerned with what she describes in one poem as the "stubborn fact" of tragedy, and she writes so effectively about it that the reader becomes aware at last of what she herself must have experienced to have done so. I do not mean to suggest she was confessional or autobiographical. Mrs. Daryush was both private and isolated, and had a sort of aristocratic disdain for the modern practice of revealing one's personal life in a medium she considered public and general. Her poetic method relied almost exclusively on traditional imagery and the dramatic use of personified abstractions, a method by and large in total disrepute among twentieth-century readers of poetry, the one fact, I think, which explains the neglect she suffered throughout all of her career. Yet the imagery and the abstractions never seem airtight or theoretical, nor does the emotional life they generate in the poems ever come off as pretentious or superficial. Before the writing of the poem she knew her subject thoroughly in terms of actual experience, experience that then was disciplined and made deeper by the limitations of form and meter. The poems themselves are evidence of this fact.

That she held on to that subject and never compromised it is remarkable in an age noted for the proliferation of so many beguiling alternatives. She had no understanding, for instance, of poetry as some nonreferential act of the imagination, a supreme fiction, in Wallace Stevens' sense of the term, that attempts to create in language another world, out of a failure to perceive this existing one and understand it rationally. For her, as for Thomas Hardy whom she resembles in more ways than one, poetry always dealt with the "stubborn fact" of life as it is, and the only consolations it offered were those of understanding and a kind of half-Christian, half-stoical acceptance of the inevitable. She had a mind that insisted, almost at times to the point of bitterness, on disillusioning truth. Neither for her could poetry ever become merely an aesthetic experience centered around the cult of the beautiful that was so widespread and influential during the first decades of this century, the time she first began writing poetry. The flowers she mentions in

"Song: Throw Away the Flowers" are surely the "rhetorical" ones of such an aestheticism—they are found to be inadequate in an age preparing for a world war:

Throw away the flowers,
 fetch stubborn rock;
  build for the hours
Of terror and shock;
  go to timeless fact
  for what beauty lacked.

Also she never fell victim to that last alternative of modern thought, a solipsism verging on a Gnostic abandonment of the social, political, and moral realities of twentieth-century life, a philosophy that restricts the poet to his own ego and denies him the possibility of any contact with someone outside himself. Consequently the sense of anguish mentioned earlier is never just personal or purely psychological in her poetry; it extends outward and responds to, as Donald Davie says in his excellent introduction to the *Collected Poems*, the profound changes that transformed, often painfully and tragically, English life in the first three decades of this century. "She appears to be," Yvor Winters wrote as far back as 1936 in the *American Review*, "increasingly conscious . . . of social injustice, of the mass of human suffering." We find this consciousness, presented ironically and indirectly, in two of her best poems, "Still-Life" and the sonnet beginning "Children of wealth." The focus in both these poems is upon the privileged and the advantaged whose wealth and social position protect them from and keep them ignorant of the knowledge of "elemental wrong" existing outside their narrow world. Yet the awareness of that wrong on the part of the poet is everywhere evident, through irony and indirection, in the context of the poems. (One of her most persistent themes, and one related to the foregoing, is the pity, which actually sometimes is scorn, she feels for innocence and inexperience, and the awareness of how they not only keep one from intellectual growth but also from feeling and emotional commitment. Eden is always a symbol for her of a stunted, desiccated state of being.)

Yet to emphasize those subjects relating to the tragic and deficient would be doing an injustice to her full thematic range. Besides the elegies she wrote on the death of her father, Robert Bridges, the most beautiful of which is "Fresh Spring in whose deep woods I sought," there is a series of poems on strictly philosophical topics; these have to do with a sort of homespun religious, metaphysical system she half-borrowed, half-made-up for herself, and with which she increasingly became preoccupied in the later part of her life. These are, it seems to me, her least successful work, partly because the language is not clear, partly because in them she is too thematically ambitious to relax with her subject and let it have its own way. Yet one of these, "Air and Variations", deserves special mention because of its metrical experimentation—in it she duplicates, with very minor changes, the meter Gerard Manley Hopkins used in *The Wreck of the Deutschland,* an astounding metrical feat interesting in and of itself. In other poems, and they are earlier ones, written in the 1930s, which make up as a group her greatest work, she is less idiosyncratic and more certain of herself, primarily because of the traditional values which she appropriates in them and uses to her own advantage. They deal with the moral resources found within one's own being, a quiet stoicism mitigated by the Christian concept of charity, and a recognition of the beauties in the immediate, ordinary world around us. They are "classical" in the best sense of the word in that they possess "the sanity of self-restraint," to use Matthew Arnold's beautiful phrase, and they have the moral dignity of a person in conscious command of his own life. One of the best examples of this type of poetry is "Faithless familiars":

> Faithless familiars,
> summer friends untrue,
> once-dear beguilers,
> > now wave ye adieu:
>
> swift warmth and beauty
> who awhile had won
> > my glad company
> I watch you pass on.
>
> Now the still hearth-fire
> > intently gloweth,
> now weary desire
> her dwelling knoweth,
>
> now a newly-lit
> > lamp afar shall burn,
> the roving spirit
> stay her, and return.

The language is seemingly so bare and straightforward, with little or no ambiguous or connotative overtones to it, and its thematic content, the rejection of fulfillment through change and emotional abandonment, so counter to contemporary poetic preoccupations, that it is little wonder the poem has found such a small audience. Davie admits this difficulty and suggests as a "useful starting point" Yvor Winters' "confession" concerning the merits of such poetry: "The quality which I personally admire most profoundly . . . is the ability to imbue a simple expository statement of a complex theme with a rich association of feeling, yet with an utterly pure and unmannered style."

It is true that at times her style loses its unmannered purity and becomes too compact and strained, just as her diction often becomes stereotyped and unnecessarily archaic. These are her chief faults, along with a frequently melodramatic use of personification, but they should not blind us to her excellence, her sturdy thematic seriousness, the subtle rhythms she achieves in syllabic meter. In a certain sense she is the last of the Victorians who lingered on into a century unsympathetic to her aims and concerns. (According to her obituary in the London *Times* she was seen by Gerard Manley Hopkins in her cradle, and among her acquaintances later in life was that other Janus-figure, Thomas Hardy.) The stylistic revolution of Pound and Eliot went unremarked by her; she kept away from it as she did from other modern currents and fashions, maintaining that there was something essentially conventional, in the best sense of the word, about poetry, and that style was subordinate to subject. She stayed home, was deliberately insular in that inimitable English way, and wrote poems about some very ancient issues that are to this day inescapable. Speaking of those poems in the introductory piece, she says, "I found them, and beside the worn road."

Collected Poems by Elizabeth Daryush. Manchester: Carcanet New Press, 1976.

Review of *In the Classic Mode: The Achievement of Robert Bridges* by Donald E. Stanford

The "case" of Robert Bridges at the present time is rather problematical. Most contemporary English poets who in the least feel inclined to connect themselves with a tradition have gone to Thomas Hardy as the more authentic voice to imitate. In the process they have either ignored or rejected Bridges as artificial and too aristocratically aloof from the "common life" that in one way or another provides the subject matter of most contemporary poems. (At first it was Hopkins, but now it seems increasingly to be Hardy whom he is unfavorably linked with.) In the minds of most of them Bridges is seen, if seen at all, as a sort of "imperialist," as, finally, an apologist for his own social class, those men of the late nineteenth century who, Susan Sontag informs us, "founded industrial empires, wrote hundreds of novels, made wars, and plundered continents." This, I think, is unfair to the man, but there is the question, closely related to class, of a self-sufficiency that often borders on smugness. That he could and did read Homer effortlessly, but wouldn't, for instance, Baudelaire, indicates not only, I suspect, a social inflexibility—he was a gentleman in life and literature—but also a certain intellectual, artistic insularity that is too comfortable with itself for our more catholic tastes and our greater, though sometimes questionable, talents for assimilation. There are times when he reminds one of nobody more readily than, say, a Shelley who played football at Oxford instead of writing "The Necessity of Atheism." He often spoke of metrical ruts that English poetry had got itself stuck in (ruts from which he quite successfully, during the later part of his career, extricated himself), but he was insufficiently aware of its intellectual ones. Too much of his poetry is merely a repetition of certain Romantic themes, all of which center around a semi-pantheistic Nature and the possibility found within it of what is always a *transcendent* Beauty. Yet his "case" is much more complex than these remarks by themselves would indicate. There are times when he breaks out of his immediate Romantic tradition and writes poems that in their plainness, their perfectly modulated cadences, their passionate intellectuality, to use Yvor Winters's phrase, remind one of the Renaissance masters, in particular Jonson and Campion, with Fulke Greville somewhere in the background. Consider these lines from "Low Barometer":

On such a night, when Air has loosed
Its guardian grasp on blood and brain,
Old terrors then of god or ghost
Creep from their caves to life again.

Late Victorian Darwinianism reverses itself in these lines and becomes charged with the moral and theological severities of Fulke Greville.

What Bridges obviously needs in this situation is a critic and anthologist who can distinguish wheat from chaff. He has found them both in two Americans, Yvor Winters and Donald E. Stanford. Winters is, of course, the earlier of the two. His *Forms of Discovery* and the posthumous *Uncollected Essays* contain brief but invaluable critical discussions, and his *Quest for Reality*, coedited with Kenneth Fields, perhaps the most severe anthology ever compiled, has the very best of the poems, which Winters had narrowed down at the end of his life to only five. Stanford works out of this base, but his recently published *In the Classic Mode: The Achievement of Robert Bridges* is more detailed in its critical and biographical treatment of individual poems (he makes extensive use of hitherto unpublished letters), and more thorough in that he considers the whole body of Bridges' work, not only the long and short poems, but the dramas and masques, as well as the criticism. His book is admirable. It is completely free of the jargon of scholarly specialization; he invariably chooses the right lines from the right poems, and his actual delight in the poetry is contagious, quite different from the grim neutrality of most academic writing. While admitting the greatness of Winters' pioneer work, one immediately sees that with Stanford's book, along with his own anthology of Bridges' poems, one gets a fuller, more rounded view of Bridges. What emerges from both men is the unavoidable fact that the "classical" Bridges, the Bridges, above all, of such poems as "Eros" and "Low Barometer," has to be taken seriously indeed.

Stanford is at his best in discussing the different metrical systems which Bridges adopted at various points in his career to meet the *vers libre* movement's objection that traditional English meter, accentual-syllabic as Stanford designates it, had become exhausted and monotonous. What Bridges did in the interest of novelty and vitality was to break up the formal combination of accent and syllabic count and to pursue one in isolation, so to speak, from the other. The result is either a meter governed exclusively by the number of syllables in a line, the meter, for instance, of *The Testament of Beauty,* or one governed just by the number of accents, the position of which is free and indeterminate. Being a poet himself, Stanford is quite aware of the fact that meter is far more than a technical matter (contrary to contemporary thinking, it is the one property of poetry that is not intellectual—the tribal bard knows this, if his New York and London brothers don't), and in his discussions of these metrical systems he points out the different sorts of emotional life they generate in a poem, as well as the subtle thematic nuances they necessarily bring about. Textures of poems are changed; new perceptions and feelings open up and become available to the poet. Consider the concluding lines of a late poem, "The College Garden," written in syllabics. The poet is describing a moment of rest in his old age when he feels like one who

> hath stripp'd his body naked to lie down and taste
> the play of the cool water on all his limbs and flesh
> and lying in a pebbly shallow beneath the sky
> supine and motionless feeleth each ripple pass
> until his thought is merged in the flow of the stream
> as it cometh upon him and lappeth him there
> stark as a white corpse that stranded upon the stones
> blocketh and for a moment delayeth the current
> ere it can pass to pay its thin tribute of salt
> into the choking storage of the quenchless sea.

The subject matter of these lines is the abandonment of the finite self to infinitude, symbolized here by the sea. A typical Romantic subject that had been dealt with countless times before, yet what is new in Bridges' treatment of it is the tone of stark realism which the syllabic dryness brings about. The meter prevents the poet from being merely literary; it forces him, as it were, to consider the abandonment as an actual possibility in the ordinary world, and one involving death itself. The allusion to Dante in the seventh line reinforces this tone.

All in all, what Stanford is asking us to do in this lucidly written book is to look more carefully at such lines and to consider the possibility that a poet like Bridges, archaic and "traditional" as we might judge him, can nevertheless write poems, valuable in themselves, that point the way to further experimentation.

In the Classic Mode: The Achievement of Robert Bridges by Donald E. Stanford. University of Delaware Press, Newark/Associated University Presses, London, 1978.

Review of *Seeing the World* by Dick Davis

As the title of his second book of poems indicates, an objective vision of things collected together in a meaningful whole, not fragmented in particularity, is the aim Dick Davis is working toward, and realizing, I might add, in various ways in all his poems. We should not confuse Davis' objectivity with a clinical, amoral dissection of reality; it is rather a clarity of sight, informed by human values, which seeks to free itself from subjective distortions so that its object of vision can be seen on its own luminous terms, in the spirit, as it were, of intellectual charity. In embracing such an aim, Davis separates himself from those destructive tendencies of modern thought which deny objective reality to the world, even destroy it in what Flaubert once called "feasts of holocausts," in order that the private vision of the autonomous and isolated ego can be preserved at all costs. In fact there is no destruction on the poet's part, or Flaubertian sacrificing, going on in Dick Davis' poetry. Style and content are compatible in his mind; aesthetics and moral wisdom mutually enrich each other, as do the personal and the traditional. And the objectivity of his vision always presupposes the presence of the discrete human being, with his own complicating and peculiar history to be reckoned with, without whom such an objectivity would be impossible.

A number of poems in Davis' book are concerned precisely with what interferes with "seeing the world" and living whole lives in it. They center around that same autonomous ego which has cut itself off from the moral and intellectual benefits of a viable tradition and retreated into itself to pursue there a life of pure desire. The figure of Don Giovanni, that protean personality of such apparent energy, haunts Davis, and in his treatment of the subject he realizes, as Mozart did before him, the self-destructive element in Don Giovanni's great cry for *liberta*. Davis adds a psychological dimension to the subject, specifically the idea that the human being is so constituted that desire pursued as desire can never be achieved, and that anyone who attempts such an impossibility will inevitably experience what Davis calls "a ghastly hydra of unconquered forms." The love affair, disowned in the public world but temporarily embraced in the private because of its compulsiveness, is another instance for Davis of the formlessness of desire. Using a dichotomy that owes something to J. V. Cunningham, Davis sets up the woman in the affair as a kind of betrayed, and betrayable, subjectivity, and the man as a detached intelligence, disillusioned and resigned to the impermanence of human passion, who renounces the affair because of his commitment to matters of art and intellect.

But in one of Davis' best poems, "Memories of Cochin," a poem celebrating the poet's own marriage to a woman of a different race from his own, such a destructive dichotomy is overcome and a synthesis is achieved which fuses the man and the woman, the objective and the subjective, into a whole. Marriage, not the affair, is the meeting-place where the abstract and the concrete, as he designates the opposites in another poem, can each discipline the excessive, even totalitarian, tendencies of the other, and make human growth possible. Davis enlarges the specific marriage theme in "Memories of Cochin" by setting the poem in a place noted for the extraordinary diversity of its races and historical influences, one in which Romans, Moslems, Christians, and Jews have mingled to form certain cultural densities that are impossible in other places isolated in provincial purity. Against such a background, we see the poet's marriage as a part of an ancient tradition of assimilation, of "seeing the world"; it then becomes an instance of that cosmopolitanism which someone has defined as the ability to move without fear in diversity and to enrich oneself spiritually and intellectually in the process.

But the one subject which engages Davis at the deepest level and which generates his best poems is one different from what we have been discussing. Most simply put, that subject is courage, the adhesive virtue, as Plato calls it, essential to the other virtues since it enables the human being to hold onto himself and to maintain those other virtues in the presence of disintegrating forces. These forces come from both the outside and the inside. "The Messenger" speaks of them as belonging to the poet's own past and his experience there of an "intolerable woe" that exerts its disturbing influence on him. In "Withernsea" they reside in the winter surf which tears "the cliff's vermilion mud into the sea." And in "Night on the Long-Distance Coach," a poem whose quiet tone is finally terrifying, they glitter inhumanly in the "wastes of lunar permanence" which the poet watches, almost against his will, from the window of his passing train, and which momently derange human definition. In the presence of such waste, the poet realizes that he is isolated in a world indifferent to his existence. Like Wittgenstein in "Wittgenstein in Galway," he is "locked out of that vast privacy / Of stone and sand, wild gulls and sea." The courage which Davis celebrates indirectly, never directly, resides in the human act, usually an artistic one, performed in opposition to these wastes. We see it most clearly realized in Davis' best poem, "Rembrandt Dying," and to an only somewhat lesser degree in such poems as "A Recording of Giuseppa de Luca," "St. Christopher," and the epigram on Maximilian Kolbe, the Polish priest at Auschwitz "who took upon himself," as Davis informs us in a footnote, "the death sentence passed on another prisoner."

Davis is a relatively young English poet, one almost unknown in this country, except to the readers of *The Southern Review*, in whose pages some of his poems have appeared. It would be of some benefit to American poetry if he were more widely known and read here. Apart from the importance of his subject matter, he is a master of style, which in his hands becomes a transparent medium through which depths are revealed. His style is often so unobtrusive and "plain" that readers more accustomed to murkier stuff might not immediately detect its nuances and subtle music. His meters and rhymes tighten without constricting, and they produce that poetic finality which is always a sign of great poetry. His handling of his influences, which include equally American and British poets, has resulted not in repetition but in his own voice. In short, Davis affords us an example of form and intelligence giving life in a poem, not stifling it.

Another reason exists for an American audience for Davis. If he can be of benefit to us, it is because we have already been of some benefit to him. Davis has read and studied American poetry as few other English poets have done, that is, without a trace of condescension or distancing politeness in his attitude. Consequently, the symbolic landscape of some of his poems shows a striking similarity to the landscape of such American poets as Tuckerman, Stevens, Frost, Winters, and Bowers. The last line of "Metaphor," for instance, in which he speaks of "sharp signs" which "glitter in the sky's immense grey waste," has a remote American ring to it. It provides an ahistorical vision of the pure wilderness, something slightly foreign to the historical preoccupations of most English poets today, and one an American should readily respond to.

Seeing the World by Dick Davis. London: Anvil Press Poetry, 1980.

Review of *Language as Being in the Poetry of Yvor Winters*
by Grosvenor Powell

In contrast to his poetry, the criticism of Yvor Winters has always received attention, even if the attention has been hostile and prejudiced. In fact, the intensity of the hostile reaction often simply indicated the impact the criticism actually made and the degree of seriousness with which it was taken by nearly every one of his more important literary contemporaries. If some of them hated him, they never took him lightly. But the truth of the matter is that his greatest achievement is his poetry, not his criticism. Winters himself thought of criticism as performing the ancillary role of clearing the intellectual air and dispersing its fog so that the poem could be written in the ensuing clarity. Some of his readers, aware of the poetry's superiority, have even used the criticism as just one more means of understanding the poetry, even as they concede the importance of the criticism as a thing in itself. Grosvenor Powell is among such readers, and his *Language as Being in the Poetry of Yvor Winters* is the first full-length study of Winters that puts the poetry at the center of attention and relegates the criticism to the subordinate position mentioned above. His book then is a corrective. In its comprehensive grasp of all the factors working in Winters' poetry and in the intelligent economy with which it is written, it performs its function admirably well.

In the first part of his study Powell discusses the philosophical background of Winters' mature poetry. He demonstrates the crucial importance that a poet's ideas have in determining the extent of reality he is able to incorporate in his poetry. In contrast to the Romantics and the imagists, whose principles isolated them to a narrow range of experience and then gave them no means of understanding that range so that they became victimized by it, Winters acquired certain ideas, according to Powell, by which he broke out of the solipsistic impasse of his youth and made contact with a reality outside his mind. These ideas not only extended and enriched his *being*, but they gave him the sense of it for the first time. The ideas all center around the powers of the mind, its ability to know the good, the connectedness of its conceptualizing activity with external reality, and the moral freedom with which it performs its operations. But Powell realizes that Winters is a poet, not a philosopher, and that the importance of ideas resides in the degree to which they are allowed to penetrate the texture of a poem and render its language a living instrument for saying something that only a poem can say about human experience. So his discussion of the philosophical extends to and includes the literary, artistic aspects of Winters' poetry, its metrics, its conventions and norms of feeling, and he shows how these technical aspects, none of which were accidents for Winters, augment the *being* of the poem, and that of its poet and its reader.

The second part consists of a chronological study of Winters' poetry, beginning with the early imagistic free verse and concluding with a poem as philosophically dense as "To the Holy Spirit." This section contains the best part of Powell's book, a study of the group of Winters' poems which Powell calls "Greek allegories." His explication of "Theseus" in particular is incisive and illuminating.

At two or three crucial points in the book Powell designates Winters' conception of *being* as Thomistic. For reasons which I hope I make clear in another essay in this issue, I do not think he is justified in doing so. Winters was very much influenced by Aquinas, especially in ethics and epistemology; he was convinced by and used the Fourth proof for the existence of God in the Introduction to *In Defense of Reason*; he *would* have been attracted by Thomistic intellectualism, its uncompromising separation of faith and reason, and the powers it gives the unaided human intellect. But the decisive difference from which everything else follows is that Aquinas defines ultimate being as pure existence and Winters defines it as pure mind. Aquinas follows what Gilson calls the metaphysics of *Exodus*; Winters, on the other hand, turns away from the datum of the Christian revelation back to a more classical view of being, one static and nonprovidential in nature. His philosophical ancestors on this score are Aristotle and Averroës, not any of the Schoolmen.

On the other hand, Powell recognizes and does ample justice to the tensions and the complications in Winters' thought. The persistence of the romantic attitudes of his youth, his prolonged preoccupation with the romantic obsession, the lifelong need he felt of protecting himself from the subhuman trance to which he saw the natural world tempting him—all this exists in Winters notwithstanding the theoretical solution to these problems which he had worked out along the lines of Aristotle and Aquinas. His best poems always exist in that "limber margin" between land and sea, between the demands of the intellect and the allurements of the wilderness. Powell points out an even deeper strain. "Although Winters believed in a unified universe," Powell says, "he also held a Manichaean position with regard to the influence of the supernatural on human experience. He felt that we are beleaguered in some undefined way by evil." His theism and Aristotelianism, in other words, never digested and got rid of the insoluble fear that ultimate reality might not be "pure mind" but something demonic and deliberately hostile as far as the human world is concerned.

Perhaps one of the reasons for this is the almost automatic

disinclination on his part to see the Absolute as anything other than something inimical to reason and inevitably and necessarily involving an irrational mysticism, a position which Aristotle and Aquinas would have found all but incomprehensible. "The Absolute is inscrutable," Winters states categorically in *In Defense of Reason*. But how can the Absolute be inscrutable in so far, and only that far, as it is admitted to be the creative cause of reason itself, as Winters' theism would necessarily have it? No cause can be less than any effect it produces. The Absolute, which in this case is God, then has to be scrutable to the bare extent that we know He is at least as good as the reason He created. Winters knew this on one level, but on another he was still worked upon by primitive and prerational influences, which, as Powell demonstrates, he never entirely overcame.

All of which proves that Winters is not the tightly wound clock of rationalism, ticking away with brutal regularity, which some of his critics would have him be. He was a poet working in the human stuff that does not easily fall into order at the behest of the theoretical intellect. To use Allen Tate's phrase, Winters was concerned with "knowledge carried to the heart," not left in the head. It also proves that his poetry is intellectually substantial, that it is embedded in intellectual history as much as it is saturated in the natural world it is always guarding itself against. Powell's book is an excellent and useful introduction to both these aspects of Winters' poetry.

Language as Being in the Poetry of Yvor Winters by Grosvenor Powell. Baton Rouge: Louisiana State University Press, 1980.

Review of *Entries* and *To Be Plain* by Raymond Oliver

Nietzsche said a corrosive skepticism infected all modern philosophy. The ancients and the medievals stood before the spectacle of being and wondered at it, wonder being, according to Aristotle, the origin of philosophy. The bane of the moderns beginning with Descartes is that they can never take anything for granted, not even their own bodies and the world around them. Everything must be subjected to an authenticating process that grimly assumes nothing is real until the method says it is. Moderns despise gifts and prize above all things self-originating invention. In literature this skepticism expresses itself in the enormous value now placed on imagination and originality. It is a commonplace in literary history that modern poets must make up their worlds and that they do so inside the unchartable currents of their own unique personalities, or other realities equally immediate and unquestionable. It is also a commonplace that they must be different from their predecessors. Their maturity is often, in fact, measured by their nerve for parricide, as well as by the violations they do to the language of their fathers.

We have in Raymond Oliver a poet and translator who is not animated by such Faustian ambitions as I have been describing. In both *Entries* and *To Be Plain: Translations* one is continually faced with both the actual, unimagined world and the poet's unembarassed delight in rendering its stuff and texture. He is an avowed enemy of all Gnostic and puritanical schemes that out of spiritual pride cut off the human being from devotion to the common earth and ordinary reality. The steam of frying garlic, the smell of coming snow, the way smoke hangs in the southern air—such incidentals, which possess a palpable reality in his transparent verse, are important for Oliver not because they *symbolize* spiritual reality but because they *embody* it in the flesh of the here and now. Such a vision of things explains his preoccupations with the themes of marriage and place. The wife breaks apart the solipsistic icons that exist only in the mind of the husband and brings him back to the reality of her own personhood, and the sensuous, tangible South over and over in Oliver corrects the excessively abstract and denatured modern mind that too often belongs nowhere.

As an example of Oliver at his very best I should like to quote entire "Adam to Eve" from *Entries*. The frank sensualism of the poem must be understood as existing in the Christian doctrine that Word became flesh, the subject, in fact, of the last poem of the book.

> Your strength and beauty flare out at your hips,
> Which stretch your contoured belly wide, convex

Yet firm. I know your breasts, your eyes, your lips;
But these are not the substance of your sex.

Making my hand a compass, I can trace
A semicircle from your navel down:
Here is your womanhood, the holy place,
Whose central triangle of solid brown

Shockingly swells above surrounding skin,
More prominent than hips, and purposive:
From here you take, to cherish deep within,
The touch of life that I, your husband, give.

I have been speaking so far primarily about Oliver's own poems in *Entries*, but what I have said applies also to the translations of *To Be Plain*, the two books being, in fact, of one piece. Of all styles available, the plain style, which *To Be Plain* exclusively concerns itself with, does the most justice to Oliver's vision of things. It can deal with the highest and lowest of subjects, with the exalted and the vulgar, to use J. V. Cunningham's terms. As Oliver's book also demonstrates, it is the most persistently useful of styles, ranging in time as it does from the archaic Greeks to the French seventeenth century, and surviving in our day in the poetry of Oliver and Cunningham. Such a style more than any other provides the fullest expression of psychological realism, of intellectual humility, of moral objectivity, traits which we see in Oliver's work. It views rhetorical fretting and Petrarchan ornamentation as evidence of an almost immoral pretentiousness, and it resists all attempts at human deification undertaken either through sex or religion. In a frequently brutal and insensitive manner, it insists on the limits placed on human nature. We are not gods, we are only men, as Greek choruses continually say.

Oliver's translations are excellent. He is most at home, it seems, with the French and the Germans, those, that is, slightly more expansive and interior than the clipped Greeks and Romans. The very best of them in my opinion is the epitaph on his brother's daughter by Andreas Gryphius, an unforgettable poem. Most rarely are the required talents for such a book to be found in a single person, for it combines the scholarly, the critical, and the creative, and in his mastery of all three Oliver recalls, strangely enough for his classicism, the achievement of Ezra Pound.

Entries by Raymond Oliver. Boston: David R. Godine, 1982.
To Be Plain: Translations from Greek, Latin, French, and German by Raymond Oliver. Florence, Kentucky: Robert L. Barth, 1981.

Review of *Witnesses* by Edgar Bowers;
The Birthday of the Infanta by Janet Lewis; and
Many Houses by Charles Gullans

Whatever Edgar Bowers writes is of utmost importance. Of all contemporary poets, he is most committed to making of his poems as definitive and unanswerable a statement on a particlar human situation as he can. He is never frivolous or pretentious and he always chooses the most serious subjects and uses the totality of his intellect on their execution. His latest work is a sequence of five poems written in blank verse and entitled *Witnesses*. Each poem is a dramatic monologue spoken by one of the earliest and most mythical characters of the Old Testament. But the poet has isolated these characters from their religious and archaeological contexts and transformed them into occasions for a meditative exploration of his own life. Their tense is present, their scene contemporary, and the consciousness informing them is very modern indeed. The overall theme of the sequence is so elusively stated, or suggested, that I for one would hesitate to make any confident statement as to its meaning. Certain motifs can be made out: the naming word in Adam, the human origin of the gods in Eve, and the mysterious relation between knowledge and death in Cain. The last two on Noah and Jacob present the least difficulties, and the very conclusion of the sequence gives us its best lines:

> Years up the ladder of the sky, beyond
> Air, fire, and water, a jet-plane barely moved,
> Marked on the blue as on the final stone—
> Feather, leaf, shell, fish-print or whitened bone.

But beyond this much one encounters the conditional and a proliferation of either-or's. I do not intend exactly to criticize Bowers for this ambiguity. It has been my own experience with an initially ambiguous poem by Bowers that years must sometimes pass before suddenly its meaning becomes clear and all its parts fall into place. Perhaps years are necessary for *Witnesses*. In any case, the poem is available, beautifully printed, and anyone interested in poetry should buy it and read it.

The second book under review here is Janet Lewis' libretto *The Birthday of the Infanta*, written for the composer Malcolm Seagrave and based on the short story of Oscar Wilde. An opera libretto published apart from its music is a rather risky business, primarily because a good libretto so subserviently exists for the music that completes it that a certain mediocrity seems to be built into its very nature. It has to be a kind of plain John the Baptist for the coming musical Messiah. What would happen, for instance, if Mozart had something like the last lines of *The Divine Comedy* instead of Da Ponte's unpretentious *Tutti contenti* for the concluding chorus of *The Marriage of Figaro*, surely as sublime as anything in Dante? And Lewis' work is no exception to this general rule. She is too good a craftsman in her own way not to have known what was called for and to have done the job as competently and self-effacingly as she could. But there are moments here and there when the old Lewis magic comes through, particularly during the soliloquy for the Dwarf. Any readers, though, meeting Janet Lewis for the first time here should go immediately after *The Birthday of the Infanta* to the recently published *Collected Poems*, then to the magnificent four novels, all published by the Swallow Press.

Of the three books under review it is Charles Gullans' *Many Houses* which is the most powerful and substantial. I say this in spite of the long and tiresome title poem, which takes up nearly half of the book and which presents us with the spectacle of an impressive poet trying to do what he can with urban and domestic California. The quotidian pastlessness and transient humanity of it all are too much for him, and at their greatest pitch they plunge him into unintentional pathos and sentimentality, such as we see in the party scene at the end of the poem. The host just too desperately praises his own party. The other half of the book is a different matter. There one finds a series of poems as solid as anything written in the last two or three decades. Gullans has resisted an untested classicism which merely pretends the irrational does not exist. He has gone down into and faced the chthonian regions of psychological, moral, and literary absurdity, where accidents gnaw at substance and where the unreal possesses more compulsion than the real. For this descent he armed himself with abstract plainness, and has come back with poems like "The Other Room," "Labuntur Anni," "The Parachutes," "Research," and "Cocktails." "Labuntur Anni" is the most moving. It reveals a tragic openness to experience, a desire still to learn even from utter loss. He is speaking of estranging, dividing years:

> And blessings issue from their stony faces.
> The gift of pain precedes humility,
> The gift of loss unburdens of possession:
> Malice, deceit, betrayal—each displaces
> Ignorance, pride, and brute naivete:
> And death, the welcome gift of intercession.

A great deal of experience lies behind these abstractions, and the power of the poem resides in Gullans' having stuck to them in the face of all the prevailing dogmas about the *image*. Of course, there are bad abstractions, slippery ones, evasive, simple-mindedly neat, and facile. There are others politically and scientifically motivated that are dehumanizing and abusive. We have been educated for two centuries or more about their misuse and should by now know the lesson well. But a good abstraction is good because of the extent of human experience it illuminates and the amount of reality it includes and conserves in language, the only possible reason for its existence. If one wants to understand, there is no way out of using some form of abstraction. Even the very attack against abstractions depends upon and uses abstraction. But Charles Gullans in *Many Houses* is beyond these polemics. There he quietly assumes the validity of abstraction and goes on with his own poetic business.

Witnesses by Edgar Bowers. Los Angeles: Symposium Press, 1981.
The Birthday of the Infanta by Janet Lewis. Los Angeles: Symposium Press, 1979.
Many Houses by Charles Gullans. Los Angeles: Symposium Press, 1981.

SHORT STORY

The Up-There[1]

The moonlight covered everything. The night was still and cold, as if life were suspended for a time being and God were thinking over the whole earth. Now and then an owl could be heard off in the distant woods, not disturbing the chilled silence, only conspiring with it.

Inside the wooden shack, the secret shuffling of mice could be heard on the broken glass which lay scattered on the kitchen floor. This had been the work of the winter wind. The ashes of the fire lay smouldering in the fireplace, while straying gusts of wind stirred them apathetically. The clock on the mantel ticked away determinedly in the darkness.

The sound of rat's feet, the death throes of the fire and the wheezing of the wind—an old woman's night.

Verdie lay in her bed, with a pile of multi-colored quilts over her small body. She was not asleep. Her eyes were wide-open, staring absentmindedly at the window, through which the moonlight was pouring.

"Now I am alone," she said aloud. "Nobody but me and the Up-there. I can hardly bear it at times. And I can't understand it neither. I knows that the Up-there ain't a-meaning for our life to be easy. I knows that we are just travelling through a big, black woods we ain't made a map of yet. And I knows it's thriving with snakes. I knows it. But I just can't understand it. And I don't like it."

Her voice now mounted and cracked with bitterness. Its dissonance seemed to shatter the cold stillness, as if it were begging for something to come to life in the barren winter.

"Yes sir, I guess the Up-there gonna snatch all dem sly, slimpy old snakes out of deir holes and swamps by deir tails and pop deir conniving heads off and then he's gonna throw them in the hell-pit and let them burn in the fires—deir scales flaking like burnt leaves. But why ain't he done it before? Why ain't he done it before?" she added, tears rolling down her cheeks. "And saved my boy."

Her heart beat rapidly. The white of her eyes widened in fury. She stirred herself and pulled her gaunt hand out of the covers and shook it in the cold air, like an angry ghost clamouring for vengeance.

"Just wait for the Spring. And, Up-there, I'm gonna search the woods and do your work. I'll kill the snakes and burn them at the foot of my boy's grave. I'll stamp out the Devil-Moccasin. And I won't give mind to Preacher or to You. I'll stand by myself."

Verdie slowly tucked her hand under the covers. She sighed heavily and turned over.

"I misses my boy. Lord, how he could keep me company in the winter-time with his whistling."

Her sleep came hard. Before the moon had fallen, she woke at intervals and clutched the quilts frantically.

"I'm gonna kill you—Devil." And then she sank back into her fitful sleep.

The sound of rat's feet, the death-throes of the fire and the wheezing of the wind—an old woman's night.

Winter passed. The hard earth seemed to dissolve as Spring came with its indiscriminate confusion of growth.

Verdie would rise every morning before the sun. She would bring in the kindling from the back porch and build herself a small fire in the kitchen stove. After her breakfast was cooked, she would sit down at the table and eat, while outside the soft, pearly light of pre-dawn slowly shifted into more positive colors. By the time Verdie finished her egg and hoecake, the sun had risen.

"Boy, I's given up a lot for you. I let my house and I ain't planted the cotton yet. But I's worked for pride—killing the snakes. And I ain't going to rest till I's killed all I can in Goodman Swamp. I loves you, boy."

Then she looked at the kitchen table where last evening's biscuit crumb lay scattered in a thin layer of dust. The cow out in the barn lowed forlornly as if in pain.

"Hush up, cow, I'll milk you when I gets back!"

She slowly got up from the chair and walked to the clothes rack where she took down her frayed army coat and put it on. It had been her son's and she regarded it as a sacred relic, although she knew she would have to take it off up in the day, she wore the coat anyway. As she passed the stove, her dress raised the fine particles of black ashes which floated up brilliantly in the crimson of the early morning sun. Her turbaned head was cocked defiantly to one side as she walked out of the house.

When she got to the back porch, she stopped for a minute, inhaling the fresh air of the morning. Then she thought of her work,

"I's tired and I's old but I's . . ."

She didn't get to finish her thought because she then caught the sight of a moving figure which at that moment had appeared out of the shadows of the pine trees. Verdie could tell at once that he was a man from the firmness and resolution with which he swung a long stick in front of him. He had his head pointed up at the sky, staring into the brightened clouds of the west.

Verdie looked at him for a long time, unable to move. She caught instantly the whole scene—the black figure emerging from the dark forest, while behind him the sky seemed to burst into an inferno of color. Terror sprang up within her.

"The devil," she whispered, as if trying to prevent even herself from hearing that word.

Swinging the stick, the man came closer and closer, heading straight towards Verdie. She could feel her heart thumping like a small ball in her throat.

Then the man started singing—a slow, plaintive song. Verdie caught the words.

> Were you there when they crucified my Jesus?
> Were you there when they nailed him to the cross?

Verdie sighed and sat down in relief on the sagging doorsteps. The man by now was in her yard.

"What you mean scaring a old woman like me fer? A Preacher ain't supposed to do that."

Preacher's face leaped into a smile—the kind of smile that at once reveals the man's nature as being kind and which even sets his eyes glittering.

"I sho didn't mean to."

"Well, you did. I thought for a minute you was . . . . No . . . I mean . . . Well—what you doing in these parts of the woods at this time of morning anyhow?"

"I just came back from the Britts'. Sister Britt died des morning in childbirth and I went over in the night to see if I could be of help. It was mighty sad her a-dying but the baby lived."

Verdie could tell from the way Preacher was looking at her that he was remembering that day seven months ago when he prayed over the dead body of her son, stretched out on the cooling board in the living room, with the two precise holes of the snake bite still visible on his right hand.

"Ain't it strange, Sister Verdie, life comes from a-dying just as death comes from living?"

Verdie stood silent.

"Well, I best move on. Sho appreciate the short cut through yo' woods. Coming to the All Day Service next first of April?"

Verdie still remained silent. The Preacher walked on. As she went over to the chinaberry tree, where she picked up her stick, momentarily she felt ashamed of herself for mistaking the Preacher as she did. Then she started for the woods.

Every day now for the past month, Verdie would journey out into the woods that ran only a short distance from her backdoor steps. She only carried the cane stick but she could bend and lash it like a buggy whip. By now Verde had killed around fifty snakes, each day burning them in her wash-pot and burying them at the foot of her son's grave which was under the fig tree. Her vengeance was still unquenchable and avid of more.

She walked along the worn path and looked up at the sun rising above the tall pine trees that stood like patient guards. Her steps this morning were slower and her face looked haggard.

"I's tired."

But she walked on, crossing a small cotton field, the ground full of bitter weeds, iron weeds and rank Bermuda grass.

"I ought to o' had that cotton planted."

Then she caught herself and waved her hand over her head, as if she were brushing that thought away from her mind.

"I remember my boy. And I's got other work to do," she said.

Now Verdie was deep in the woods, the shadows of the tall trees nearly obliterating her bent body.

She poked around the blackberry bushes and the pokeberry bushes and looked under logs. She waded out in the little creeks and thrust her cane-stick into the marshes and ferns.

"Come out, I says."

Her only answer was the birds, chattering in a disorganized chorus everywhere. It seemed as if the woods were vibrant and quivering with their shrill songs.

On she walked into the woods—the live oaks part where the grey moss hung down from the trees.

The sun by now had mounted the sky and cast its long shafts of light through trees. Verdie stopped and took off her coat. Her face was moist and hot. But she continued on, stopping here and there to inspect the hidden areas, hoping to discover her prey. But this morning she had had no luck. By now she had only found possum, wild squirrel and one baby alligator basking in the warm sun on the creek bank. Not her devil-moccasin.

Quite unexpected, Verdie came upon a thicket of wild dogwood which was full of white blossoms. As she intruded into their silence, the movements of her arms and legs shook down a few of the blooms. One lodged in the cup of her hand, quite as if it were sent there. She held the flower and looked at it intently. Verdie thought of Christ writhing in pain on that ancient tree and God shaking the whole earth in anger. A sudden thought darted through her mind.

"The Up-there had a son just like me and look what happened to . . ."

After leaving the dogwood thicket, she came to a marshy area covered with rank, bushy ferns. A little ways beyond flowed a very small creek, on whose opposite banks stood a wild apple tree. Verdie walked on, her feet splashing into the mud. Just as she reached the creek-bank, her foot slipped into the watery muck. She stood still for a moment and dropped the army coat. Then she strained hard to pull her stuck foot from the mud. In her awkwardness, she slipped and fell. The mud smacked her face and her eyes stung and hurt with the marsh water in them. She could not see anything but could only hear the thump-thump of her own heart. For a moment she absurdly remembered what her mother had once told her—that your heartbeat is the first and last thing you know in this life. Now Verdie slowly started sinking in the quagmire. She blindly reached out for the creek-bank. Verdie frantically clutched the firmer ground and dug her fingers deep into it. Then she strained hard and tried to pull herself over towards the bank. She only got a little ways—enough so that her chest lay partly bent over the bank. Uncertainly she raised one hand from her side and rubbed her eyes, still throbbing with pain. In a blurred vision she saw little splotches of vivid yellow sand bubbling up among the black mud. "Quicksand!" she said.

With a supreme effort of will and energy, she again tried to pull her body above the quicksand onto the bank. But the sand and mud held her and would not let go. Only her shaky hold of the creek-bank prevented the quicksand from sucking her deeper and deeper into the pit.

All around her the birds flew in and out of the trees, singing in the casual, carefree way of noon.

Fear clutched at Verdie's heart and her brain was agitated with visions of her death. They would never find her—out here in the depths of the woods, at the bottom of a muddy quicksand bed. No decent dry burial under the fig tree by the side of her son.

"Lord God, please help me. Lord, please help yo' poor child," she cried out. Her voice was piercing. It seemed to rend the very air of the woods, putting the birds to obedient silence.

Once again she tried to pull herself to the bank. Verdie closed her eyes and slightly raised her head. Then she pulled with all her strength.

Slowly she raised her stomach onto the bank, her hands trembling uncontrollably. Her body now seemed possessed of new strength and confidence and her hold onto the creek-bank was sure. Her breathing, though, was rasping and panting.

The mud clung to the top of her dress while big drops of water dripped from her.

Now all she had to do was to get her legs out. Again she strained, pulling fiercely against the bank. The expression on her face was blank and her eyes were extended wide in terror. Her dress was heavy and weighted with the cakes of mud. At last she raised her feet from the quicksand, their muscles jumping from the exertion.

Now Verdie lay on the creek-bank in the sunlight. After a few moments of heavy breathing, she broke down and cried. The tears came freely, mingling with the caked mud on her face. It made her happy—the happiness that only such tears can bring. Verdie thought of all that had happened this morning—her mistaking the Preacher for the devil—the brown, pierced dogwood reminding her of God's son on the cross and her escape from the quicksand pit. Then the tears came more abundantly.

"I ain't God. I can't do His work. You can't understand the purposes of God. And I's just a weak human being. I ought to have patience."

Then she looked up and saw the wild apple tree. The sun bore down upon it with the white-heat intensity of noon. Its green leaves bristled and shimmered in the sunlight. At its base stretched lazily was Verdie's devil-moccasin. The whole scene was like a Bible illustration to Verdie—the wild apple tree and the snake basking in the sunlight. Only this time it was the snake instead of a red apple. But Verdie did not give it a second thought. She only looked at the snake as it slid away through the grass and laughed. Her laughter seemed to mount the sky so free and joyous was it.

"I'll let you do the work, Up-there, you got all eternity do it in and all the fires, stars, sticks and stones to do it with."

She got up and walked back home to the un-milked cow and unplanted cotton field.

Ozark, our porch with some one holding John, "a wide porch!"

The house of Finlay's maternal grandmother, Toxey Ard Sorrell, in Ozark, Alabama.

OTHER PROSE

Editors' Preface to An Interview with Eudora Welty[1]

Eudora Welty is recognized as one of the best short-story writers in English, not only in this country but also in Europe. She needs no introduction; however, in order that this interview may be read in the right perspective, some comments are called for.

Some readers perhaps will be disappointed with Miss Welty's unwillingness to talk dogmatically about her work and her tacit refusal to discuss her private life. Perhaps they have read too many interviews with other writers who not only "explain" their work in great detail, but also go into their private lives, sometimes with rather embarrassing results. (And this type of thinking has become so dominant in the United States that many people read novels and poems and short stories not for their intrinsic artistic merit, but because they are interesting commentaries on their authors' private lives.)

Miss Welty does not do this. And we think the chief value of this interview is that in it she very gently forces us to question this confusion of "public" art with "private" life, and to make us distrust those writers who all too readily "explain" their work. After all, if a writer has to explain a work of art in terms of his private life, then something is wrong or missing in the work itself. For a writer to do such explaining is an admission of failure.

Also to be noted is her humility. How many times in this interview does she say, "I don't know," or, "I tried to do this or that"! One is reminded of that sentence in Henry James's short story "The Middle Years": "We work in the dark—we do what we can—we give what we have. Our doubt is our passion and our passion is our task. . . . The rest is the madness of art." "The madness of art" is something about which one cannot talk in neat, sure terms. There is a certain element of mystery in it which will always defy complete explication, and Miss Welty remains humble in the presence of it. She never violates this fundamental mystery.

The interview took place in Miss Welty's home in Jackson, Mississippi, on October 16, 1965. Nearly all of the stories discussed in it are found in the Modern Library edition of her short stories.

THE EDITORS

Concerning the Project For Which Assistance Is Requested from the Mary Roberts Rinehart Foundation[1]

The project I have in mind is a book of poems. Half of it will be made up of short poems, more than half of which have already been completed. The other will be a long poem, half-narrative, half-meditative, on the life of the artist-naturalist John James Audubon, limited to the Southern phase of his career. The rest of the short poems I can finish on my own, what with various part-time jobs I hold to. It is on account of the long poem that I am asking for your assistance. It will require two or three months of sustained work, including extensive readings in the literature on Audubon beyond what I have already done, some limited travel in Louisiana, particularly Baton Rouge, where a great number of the original prints are located, and St. Francisville, where he lived and worked during most of his stay in Louisiana, and, finally, the actual composition itself. I do not see at present how it will be possible for me even to begin it without a period of financial independence.

Before I give a synopsis of the project, let me make one or two general comments on the poem. First of all, I do not intend for it to be a loose, vaguely subjective account of this cunning, single-minded Frenchman. I hope that it will be rooted in history and fact, and evolve from actual observation of Audubon's wilderness, or the little that is left of it today. This does not mean that it will be unpoetic. For me the greatest poetry comes, not from fantasy, but from intense, realistic perceptions of the natural and human worlds. Secondly, the form will be that of traditional blank verse, but with enough variations to keep it from predictability.

The theme is the immersion of Audubon's mind and art in the American wilderness of the 19th century, his recovery from, and then the discipline and passion necessary to understand the experience and translate its beauty into art. Audubon is the prototype of the artist, who has to shift back and forth between two sometimes conflicting worlds: the experience of the wilderness, immediate, sensual, nonintellectual, and the mental state of detachment from that experience, in which the mind works through the wilderness into art. This often results in irony, and the central one in Audubon's life is that he has to kill the bird first before he can give it life in art. Apart from this, I hope to get across in the poem the simple fact of the American landscape, its vastness and compelling beauty

The poem will be in three parts. The first section is the "night journey," the artist leaving the security of a protected life to go on a journey, the end of which is the realization of his art. On the narrative level, this first part is concerned with the boat trip down the Mississippi, which Audubon took at the beginning of his career, in 1820, after having left his family behind, who planned to join him later. His destination is first New Orleans, and, afterwards, St. Francisville, where the vision of his life's work really began to come into focus: *The Birds of America*, the monumental work later published in London. I hope to get across the whole sense of the river and the frontier life along its banks, which Audubon observes and applies to himself:

> . . . through fog
> He saw against the open fires at dusk
> The narrow settlements from which he knows
> Himself estranged . . .

The boat is comprised of the kind of motley group that usually made up frontier boats of the time: ruffians, drifters, and con men, all of whom are contrasted with Audubon, a figure held together by will and purpose.

The second part will deal with his experiences in New Orleans. On the symbolic level, we have, in this section, the various kinds of temptations which the artist must first overcome before he can seriously begin his work. As in mythical contexts, the artist must first strip and cleanse himself before he can enter the sacred grove. In Audubon's case, this involves freeing himself from distractions, extricating himself from a confusing social scene, and clearing his mind of anything that would interfere with his art and his work in the wilderness. In my poem, this is what Audubon does in New Orleans. Against the background of a varied, colorful, but often violent swarm of life, which the port city was, Audubon attempts to make a living as a portrait painter. He gives it up, finally, after having decided that it is a compromise and an irrelevance to the main purpose of his life. The central figure of this part of the poem is the mysterious "nude" lady, whose portrait Audubon painted. He tells us in his *Journals* that his hands trembled as he held the brush, and he had to force himself to concentrate on the canvas. He interprets her as a kind of temptation, a Southern Circe, a beguiling gaze animated by secret beauty. But to give in to her would also be surrendering to a society decadent and artificial. He then leaves for St. Francisville and the woods around it, all swarming with life.

The last part will be much the longest and broadest in scope. It takes place primarily at Oakley Plantation, near St. Francisville, though it will cover other areas of the South that Audubon lived and worked in. Here he realizes his art and makes his first really significant breakthrough. I

plan to incorporate the many fascinating details, found in the *Journals*, concerned with the Louisiana wildlife and landscape. We see him in his semi-intuitive, semi-intellectual contact with the raw, even primitive, aspects of the wilderness, and observe the cunning and craft he used to get his prey and then to reproduce the almost inexplicable mystery of its livingness, the actual look in the mockingbird's eye as it hovers in the air, poised, its wings outspread, ready to fight the rattlesnake coiled tightly around its nest.

Finally, it is very difficult to talk about a poem that one wants to write, but which exists in the necessarily vague state it has before actual composition. This is true even if one knows exactly what one wants to say, as I do. Often the process of writing clarifies and reveals possibilities of development and amplification that were not apparent in the outline. And, hopefully, the poetry itself, once it gets written, will have transformed the stiff, even pompous-sounding, formulas of the outline into the moving, living thing that we all want.

Audubon at Oakley[2]

My Gallic cunning poured sweet wine into
The calyxes of trumpet-vines and caught
Small drunken birds a bullet blows apart.
Others I shot, pinned them to a board
To draw the fresh-killed life. Elusively,
The *is* that quickens in the living eye
Escaped the sweat of art, drying ink.
I tore blind pages till I reached the one
That pleased my avid mind. The wilderness
There teems with birds I never saw before:
White and wood ibises, the sparrow hawk,
The redcock woodpecker, and painted finch.
I hunted them for days and nights until
I throve in timelessness. One day stood out.
I heard below all things the river sough;
The fall was blazing in the silent trees.
I saw my book, taut wings of mockingbirds
In combat with the snake knotted beneath
The nest, its open mouth close to the eggs,
Now held forever in the lean, hard line.
And underneath, defining them, combined:
The clean abstraction of their Latin names,
The vulgate richness of this Saxon salt.

Questions for An Interview with Edgar Bowers[1]

1. Judging from the tone and some of the details of "The Prince" and "The Stoic" it seems that you were working less out of imagination than from actual historical sources. If so, would you care to elaborate on these sources? Did you encounter them in your intelligence work in World War II?

2. The European background figures so vividly in your poetry, especially in *The Form of Loss*, that it seems to have activated you more than the American background as such. I am wondering if you see any special reason for your response? Did your Southern background in any way prepare you for it or hinder you as the case might be?

3. What influence, if any, do you see Yvor Winters as having exerted on your poetry? If there is such an influence, is it Winters's poetry or criticism or both?

4. Your poetry employs so many of the techniques and thematic preoccupations of what Winters in the Johns Hopkins lectures and later in *Forms of Discovery* called "post-symbolism." Since a great deal of your poetry was already written by the time Yvor Winters made the critical formulation, I am wondering if you or your poetry in any way helped to clarify the concept for Winters? Did you arrive at it on your own apart from Winters?

5. What elements, if any, in your poetry do you see as peculiarly "Southern"? Was there any influence by Allen Tate? Which of your poems do you see as having specifically Georgian landscapes?

6. Helen [Pinkerton] Trimpi sees your poetry, except for some of *Autumn Shade*, as more essentialist than existentialist in the Thomist sense. Do you think this an accurate philosophical depiction?

7. Your background is Presbyterian, yet Catholic imagery figures prominently in your poetry, especially in *The Form of Loss*. Is there a poetic reason or any other that explains this?

8. Valéry seems a profound influence, as well as other 19th and 20th century French poets. Do you see yourself as more at home in the French than in the English tradition of the last two centuries?

9. What particular etching do you allude to in "Of An Etching"?

10. You have written two or three fine, beautiful poems on Mozart. What pieces of his do you especially admire? Do you see him as the emblematic classical artist? How would you define such classicism and how may one see it as different from post-symbolism?

Dust Jacket Comment for
The Burning Fields (1991) by David Middleton[1]

I have known and admired the poetry of David Middleton for close to fifteen years. His theme is the recovery from the subjective mind. The recovery takes the form of orthodoxy in religion and traditional forms in literature, but these forms are not mere repetitions of the past. They are means by which Middleton can sharpen and illuminate his experience. Middleton does not believe in formalism for the sake of formalism. He adds a new edge to the leaf. He is one of the most important poets to come out of the South, or anywhere else for that matter.

—John Finlay

Selections from Miscellaneous Writings, the Letters, and the Diaries

Editors' Note

The three sections above containing the essays, the reviews, and the one short story gather together all of the work, at least so far as is currently known, that Finlay did in these literary forms. But Finlay wrote other kinds of prose as well. These include his diaries and letters as well as notes, lists, fragments of various kinds, the book-length Ph.D. dissertation, and an unsuccessful grant application that reveals much concerning Finlay's poetics. In addition, although not written by Finlay, a number of stories about Finlay are remembered or have been recorded in prose by his family and friends. A few of these stories appear in Appendix C.

The following is a selection—what might be called a representative sampling or sampler—of these other kinds of prose. The principles of selection are the significance of these pieces in providing a better understanding of Finlay's life and works or the importance of the pieces as general comments on the human condition and on human experience. The principles of organization are chronological, when possible, as with the letters and most of the entries from the diaries. Otherwise, undated or isolated pieces are clustered into groups by thematic similarity, whenever that can be done, or aesthetically, like flowers in a bouquet. Some few pieces will simply have to stand on their own. To aid the reader, brief subsection headings and endnotes are also provided.

Comprehensive editions of all of the diaries and all of the letters are projects beyond the scope and intention of this volume, but such editions are worthy projects for future scholars. Finlay's diaries are all in The John Finlay Papers at Louisiana State University, as noted below in the bibliography and in "A Note on the John Finlay Papers."

The Finlay Papers mainly contain letters to Finlay. Finlay's letters to others remain mostly in private hands, although some few are housed in various university archival collections among the works of the recipients of the letters. The letters included in this volume are selections from those complete collections of letters between Finlay and a recipient that are in The Finlay Papers and available to the editors of this volume. Editions of the complete correspondence between Finlay and others as well as an edition of the Ph.D. dissertation on Yvor Winters are to be hoped for, as is a full-length biography. Most of Finlay's remaining immediate family members and longtime friends are now well into old age. Much about Finlay will be irretrievably lost when these persons pass away.

The editors trust that the selected works in this section of *"With Constant Light"* will demonstrate that some of Finlay's most moving and beautiful prose is contained in forms other than the essays, the reviews, and the single known short story. John Finlay was truly a man of letters, writing well in a wide variety of poetic forms and in several kinds of prose.

Selections from Miscellaneous Writings

That Scarlett! J.M.F.[1]

Scarlett represents the South and Rhett what the South had lost in the bellum. She lost Rhett, but she could not think of getting him back in such a time as it is but "tomorrow is another day." In my thinking we are still thinking and tomorrow is another day. You can't kill what is in a true Southerner. Do you suppose this time and day would kill the spirit of Scarlett? I hope not. But it has killed the spirit of many Southerners. I am not dead, yet.

***

Good evening, ladies and gentlemen.[2] I have the pleasure this evening of introducing Allen Tate to you. The details of Mr. Tate's public life you are familiar with: the famous Fugitive group of which he was a member when he was a student at Vanderbilt University, the Agrarian manifesto, *I'll Take My Stand*, to which he contributed an essay, and the later distinguished career as critic, novelist, biographer and, most importantly, as a poet. In fact they are so familiar that some graduate students have gotten ahold of him and written dissertations about him. So, I suppose we may safely pass all that by!

First of all, we must acknowledge debt as best we can. If the poets and critics help us to see our world and to "know the time" (to borrow from one of Mr. Tate's poems), then I am sure that many of us here tonight have a special debt to pay Allen Tate. I am thinking of all those whose reading of a short story by Henry James or a poem by John Donne has become more exact and perceptive because of a knowledge of Mr. Tate's criticism, as well as of the apprentice poets who have learned to use their language more effectively after carefully studying the technique of his own verse. Of course, we can never fully pay this kind of debt. But we can humbly and gratefully acknowledge it, which we now do.

The voices in which Mr. Tate has spoken are indeed wonderfully many; yet there is a thematic unity in all he has written. As Mr. Andrew Lytle has said: Mr. Tate's theme is nothing more or less than what is left of Christendom. . . .

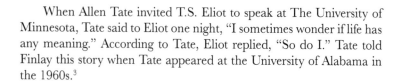

When Allen Tate invited T.S. Eliot to speak at The University of Minnesota, Tate said to Eliot one night, "I sometimes wonder if life has any meaning." According to Tate, Eliot replied, "So do I." Tate told Finlay this story when Tate appeared at the University of Alabama in the 1960s.[3]

August 25-28, 1966, I was the houseguest of Mr. Andrew Lytle at Monteagle, Tennessee. On August 27, 1966, Mr. Allen Tate who was staying at a nearby cottage (with his new bride) read two of my poems, the Sonnet + the moon piece, and said that they were "remarkable & excellent." (*I say this so that it will spur me on to more work, not to flatter my vanity.*) Mr. Lytle expressed similar views. Of course, I got some criticism too![4]

[Mr. Lytle] Speaking of the Agrarians: "We were modest prophets. We didn't know it was going to be as bad as it is." He said it was a mistake to call it an Agrarian defense; it should have been called a defense of Christian society.

Mr. Tate: "Literary fashions are like the reputations of Victorian ladies: they fall overnight."

March 11, 12, 1967, I visited Mr. Lytle in Monteagle. A good story about R.P. Warren—both he and Tate his roommate were studying— intense silence—all of a sudden Tate looked up and saw Warren over him with a paper knife in his hand—[5]

Aug. 20, 1969 (a black day but I suppose I should know something about this devil)[6]

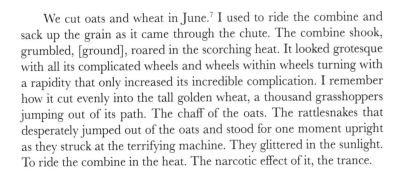

We cut oats and wheat in June.[7] I used to ride the combine and sack up the grain as it came through the chute. The combine shook, grumbled, [ground], roared in the scorching heat. It looked grotesque with all its complicated wheels and wheels within wheels turning with a rapidity that only increased its incredible complication. I remember how it cut evenly into the tall golden wheat, a thousand grasshoppers jumping out of its path. The chaff of the oats. The rattlesnakes that desperately jumped out of the oats and stood for one moment upright as they struck at the terrifying machine. They glittered in the sunlight. To ride the combine in the heat. The narcotic effect of it, the trance.

. . .

Her name was Red[8] and of the many animals I knew in my childhood on the farm it is she that I still remember most vividly. We kept her for over ten years, during which time my brother and I took turns milking and feeding her in a barn my father had built especially for her. She had good blood in her and at the height of summer could give up to three or four gallons of milk a day. I can still feel the weight of the milk pail between my knees and see the thick foam of her milk falling sluggishly in the early morning light over its brim. But her most impressive feature was her horns. They were long and magnificent and the upward thrust of their sharp points made her majestic, primitive, and unapproachable, especially after she had sleeked and honed them on the bark of pine trees.

The London churches—pushed, shoved, obscured, overshadowed by modern buildings which don't disdainfully look down upon them because they give the appearance of not even knowing of their existence.[9]

Notes on a Visit with English Poet
Elizabeth (Bridges) Daryush (1887–1977)

September 7, 1969

From London to Oxford by train today. Visited Elizabeth Daryush in her home outside Oxford. A fine rather strange house (few windows on the front) but comfortable and beautiful—Oriental rugs & Botticelli in the living room.

Mrs. Daryush is almost blind, wears sunglasses. She didn't like *Forms of Discovery*—"too dogmatic." [B]ut admires his earlier works. "Poetry is not a fact but an activity."

Her father's syllabic verse is wrong. She quoted him as saying that the old accentual-syllabic [line] had been worn out by him. There were a limited number of things to be done with it and he had done them.

"The English countryside was once beautiful." . . . She said I looked Scotch!

She said that Winters' interpretation of "Persian Dawn" & "Still-Life" was wrong. No metaphysical ideas & threats intended.

She arranges her poems (in her books) in such a way that the whole book itself becomes a poem.

Selections from the Letters

From Letters to David Middleton

24 April 1979 [10]

> Everything was exactly as it should be—good food, good friends, and good conversation

Dec. 15, 1981[11]

> . . . I myself despair of getting published, my experience so little furnishing any grounds for hope. We should really give it up and write for the dead, both of the past and the future. I really feel as if I live more with the dead than with the living. . . .

> I started back going to mass regularly, and, though the poor priest tries my patience during his sermons with what seems to me nothing but slack psychologism and the whole service appears so loose that I'm sure Aquinas is cringing in heaven over it, yet I tell myself something else is more important finally and use my discomfort as a purgatory . . .

30 January 1982 [12]

> Now I work in the mornings with the cows for my keep. The Ovid poem sounds very promising. Your phrase about drinking water from the wooden pail haunts me. I keep it these days in the back of my mind. The true classicism. . . . My recent immersion in Flaubert makes me acutely sensitive to the value of such luminous, specific details, which really do the work for you if you let them alone and give them their own area of resonance and breathing room.

9 March 1982

> Like you, I have no one to talk to, that is, about matters
> that really count, and sometimes I find myself wandering
> off into the pastures and talking to the cows! What
> pastorals!

4 October 1983 [13]

> Yes, I believe that poetry gives us knowledge, and of a
> kind found only in poetry. . . . The greatest poetry in
> tragedy and epic deals finally with those perceptions of
> intellectual truths often no more than the simplicity of
> human mortality, that are there whether or not the human
> performs an action or not—they cannot be other than
> they are. (All this is Aristotle, of course, but still useful.)
> The moral enters in when the human reacts to those
> truths. But the only reaction has to be either resignation
> or rebellion, neither of which affects the truths. The "iron
> sky" of Homer again.

17 January 1984 [14]

> What is it about the Greeks that so attracts us? I shall
> never forget the experience of sunlight when I lived on
> Corfu—the clarity, the brilliance of objects defined in
> unambiguous light. I could cry thinking about it. Will
> I ever get back there? Are we entering our prolonged
> American period, when Europe for all sorts of reasons
> has receded out of the picture?

From Letters to bookmaker Harry Duncan

Jan. 4, 1987 [15]

> Don't you think that both the printer and the poet are
> joint creators of a book? That appeals very much to my
> own medieval idea of craft, in all the senses of the word,
> which, as you know, includes the idea of mystery. In fact,
> the printer and the poet are indeed joint creators. And
> when you think about it, it seems silly to think otherwise.

June 12, 1987 [16]

I did have Dryden in mind, by the way, as I wrote the poem; in fact, the poem is a kind of hommage to him. I love Dryden who sometimes is, I think, my favorite poet, the one I would have liked to have known and been friends with. Of course I don't mean by this sentiment that I think he's the greatest poet in our language, but frequently he does come close. Hopkins says somewhere that he got at the bones and muscles of the English language—a wonderful insight!

From Letters to Donald E. Stanford[17]

Nov. 19, 1969

Dear Mr. Stanford,

For some time I have been reading the poetry and criticism of Yvor Winters as well as a good number of the American and English poets he recommends. I have decided that they are the ones I would really like to master, if that is possible. But I need help. Consequently I have applied for admission to the LSU Graduate School so that I would be able to study under you. I came to this decision after reading your very fine essay, "Classicism and the Modern Poet," in the Spring [1969] issue of the SOUTHERN REVIEW.

I would like to talk with you sometime soon, but only if it will be convenient with you. I will be free every weekend in December. Any Friday or Saturday that would suit you will also suit me. But if you have other plans or would be inconvenienced in any way I quite understand. I have enclosed a self-addressed envelope for your reply. I thank you very much for any time you might spend on this matter.

Yours truly,

[signed] John M. Finlay

Corfu continues to hold me. As the season changes it becomes beautiful in different ways. I'm living in a small fishing village at the extreme northern end of the island. The only way to get to town is by caique. Think of it! To get up before dawn and ride across the blue Mediterranean in a small Homeric boat! . . .

From a letter to Janet Lewis Winters[19]

Aug. 5, 1987

. . . It is the archaic Greek mind which particularly holds my attention. Why did the philosophical mind arise when and where it did—some such question I have been trying to get a hold on. The fact that the mind itself proves the existence of God has always struck me as true too. As long as you have an immaterial element in the mind— and memory proves such an element there—and believe that the mind did not create itself, then you have to posit as its cause an immaterial agent higher than the human being. . . .

We are having a good summer. We got the rains when we had to have them, and the fig tree right now is getting ready to produce its second crop.

From Letters to Stephen Utz[20]

Jan. 8, 1974 [Paris]

I feel rotten about our not having gotten together before I left. But things became very hectic, as they always do before departure, and I failed to get in touch with you. Which can be remedied, beautiful thought, by your coming over here next summer. Paris is beautiful, as you know. I live very close to St. Julian le Pauvre, the church where Dante prayed and meditated when the street arguments got too violent. Just across the way is Nôtre-Dame. The whole Latin Quarter fits me. Steve, the bookstores! *And one just for poetry.* I found Rimbaud, his ghost in . . . puppet shows, dimly lit bars, circus posters, open markets for flowers and fish. And impudent beggar-women who demand charity. . . .

Feb. 26, 1982 [21]

. . . I'm getting along quite well. A life of poverty out in the country seems to have been just what I needed, and drinking water out of a wooden bowl what my spirit needed. . . .

. . . Thanks very much for the Hill book. It was almost as if you were reading my mind—I had wanted it and had come close to buying it but always put it off. What do you think of his poetry? I myself have rather ambivalent feelings about it; it's so frequently alive and exciting and then it sinks into a labored and pedantic melodrama that, it seems to me, seeks to disguise itself by all the linguistic fireworks. But he is a remarkable poet and I'm pleased to have a copy of the poems sent by you.

Jan. 14, 1985[22]

. . . Thanks indeed for the Elizabeth Daryush book. Where in the hell did you find it? Like the T. Sturge Moore it must be the most difficult book in the world to locate and be able to buy. I shall prize it a great deal. Did you know I met her once when I was in England? In fact, I spent an afternoon with her. She was a marvelous lady, quite formidable, a sort of Edwardian Medea with a caustic tongue but an apparent tenderness that really took to the fact that I had actually read her. She knew Hardy and had been seen by Hopkins when he was visiting her father once and she was a babe in the cradle. I felt as if I were in the presence of the last relic of a lost age, an England that would never be again. . . .

Nov. 15, 1985

. . . It was the concept of *total war* that seems to have first originated among the Northern generals. Churchill once said the Civil War was the last war fought by gentlemen, but I'm afraid the actually few gentlemen were all on the

Southern side and it is one of our tragedies that they had such a sorry cause as slavery. . .

From Letters to Lewis P. Simpson[23]

Aug. 21, 1985

. . . But one can't help but guess at some sort of psychological compulsion in his [John Locke's] envy, some sort of nostalgia for happier philosophical times, some sort of quite profound dissatisfaction with the limitations of our ordinary minds. I might be reading too much in him, but the 3rd chapter of Bk. IV of the Essay strikes me as a kind of lament for our intellectual imperfection, with a muted anger underneath it that God has placed us in the middle position between omniscience and nescience, without our having the benefit either of knowledge or ignorance. . . [Locke's] standard of what constitutes knowledge is so damn exacting that the possibility of acquiring knowledge clean leaves the human world and flies off to other realms. It's tragic that none of the Enlightenment philosophers could have said and believed, for instance, what Aristotle said on the first page of the ETHICS: some subjects admit of absolute precision; others do not; those that don't, well, about them, let's be as precise as we can and leave the matter at that. But with the Enlightenment it seems to have been an all-or-nothing affair with no compromise allowed anywhere. And I don't think that it's any accident that the last achievement of the Enlightenment mind, the hydrogen bomb, can quite literally blow out of existence the whole imprecise and messy composition of biological and human life.

. . . I'm very happy that Sewanee had the sense to honor you as she is planning to do. Sewanee is the one place where so much of the best of the South has gone to recreate itself, to have fellowship with itself, and to honor itself, and you belong to the group more than anyone.

March 21, 1986

> . . . We still can't decide about selling the dairy. I really, after all, will miss the cows. They are like pets to us. I've even named some of my favorites after Greek gods and goddesses. The bulls are Zeus and Apollo, and a big white cow without one spot is Aphrodite. But farming as we know it is disappearing and we must face the reality. What else do you suppose will go as we keep plunging deeper and deeper into the corporate state? Are you now having a cold spell? I guess it's blackberry winter. I must stop and get this in the mail. Thanks again for what you sent, but above all, for your own work.

July 19, 1986

> No news here. The summer drones on in the great heated hum of things.

> What did you think of all that Hollywood stuff around the 4th of July? It seems to me that we have finally entered the Disneyland of the Mind under that actor and that we are now totally and shamelessly the most vulgar civilization that has ever been.[24] Pity poor Jefferson in his grave.

Aug. 14, 1986

> We are barely getting through this summer. The drought hasn't been so bad here, what for one or two thunderstorms the God of Job has sent us, but still it's been rough on the crops. Who knows yet if we will make anything? And the cows are being thinned out too by a strange disease the vet can't get his hands on. But farmers, as you know from experience, always live in the Book of Job, and we wouldn't know what to do if everything turned out smoothly and easily.

Nov. 28, 1986

> I hope you had a good Thanksgiving. I woke up this morning and heard the strangest sound coming from the woods in front of the house. I thought at first it was a dying man screaming for help. But then I realized what it

was—hound dogs treeing a coon. Remember that sound? Just one more step and dogs could talk.

From Jean Finlay, John Finlay's mother, to Lewis P. Simpson[25]

September 10, 1991

Dear Lewis Simpson,

I am at a loss for words to tell you how much your friendship and support of John during his terrible illness meant to John and us . . .

The nurses in the hospital all loved him so . . . and that helped. They said in all their profession . . . they had never seen anybody accept death so calmly and die with such dignity. I never heard him complain although I saw him very frustrated at times. We all miss him so much, and I know I always will but he lives in my heart.

Thank you so much for all you have written and done on behalf of John and the kind letter you wrote me after his death.

With best wishes and God Bless,

Jean Finlay

P.S. We are busy harvesting peanuts now and I am helping run errands for my son Billy. He is the farmer in the family as was his father. We hope to send you some in about 2 weeks.

God, you are the only thing I have.

⟪⟫

Keeping a journal is valuable. I'm beginning to understand why Johnson insisted upon it so.[26]

⟪⟫

From *The Blue Horse Composition Notebook,* 1961–1966
(opening entry, December 17, 1961)

Be patient. Don't try to move heaven and hell. . . . Be a craftsman. Be careful.[27]

⟪⟫

The little girl who gives things to people in order that they will like her. Her insecurity and need for love. Once at a Christmas party, she sat in a corner, a little apart from the main center of interest. She held a small bird in her hands—a pet with brilliant feathers of green and gold. No one was looking at her—paying her the attention she yearned for. Then she looked around the room furtively and then down at the bird. She raised the wings quickly and pinched the bewildered bird until all the girls looked her way and said, "What's the way with the bird?" "Nothing. She only wants love and company."[28]

⟪⟫

The Cuba crisis[29]—Jean + Neely and I riding out on the Tuscaloosa roads reciting poems and waiting for the end.

⟪⟫

1965. I had a dream about Heaven (not Heaven exactly, but that part of Purgatory which is nearest Heaven). At first I thought it was Claybank—but it changed—A garage in which there was a bottomless pit over which hung an apparatus like a crane—all the non-essential fell into it—The Space—green valley—tall, shady trees full of large flowers—azaleas, japonicas (big as the moon) invisible angels singing Alleluia; the sky that pale, gold blue before sunset; In the distance, banks & banks of marigolds; The Church; oil lamps instead of candles, girl acolytes; small church-light (circle) behind the altar came on when candles were lighted; Christ himself coming to church.[30]

A possible poem:[31]

Last Saturday night (Oct. 8, 1966, I think) went to a party given by Norman McMillan on some backwater of the Black Warrior outside Eutaw. Marvin, Minnie Bruce and Jeannie Robison + I went rowing in a boat (after we had all fallen into the river!) The night sky was clear—all the billion stars were shining in a perfect order. But what was amazing was that the water perfectly reflected the stars. Ain't there a poem somewhere here? I mean—water which is so unstable and formless and passive having superimposed upon it the eternity + fixity of the stars—those beautiful moments in our lives when time gracefully bears the burden of eternity or rather eternity is gracefully, yet momentarily realized eternity. All of which is nothing but a foreshadowing, a dim symbol of that great event—The Incarnation—the flesh and the Word one and the same.

The rats running behind the walls in Murray House:[32] the secret reality behind the appearance: the house slowly being eaten away while we think it is so permanent.

Words. Know them. Love them. A thousand possibilities of dress for the same manikin.[33]

~~~

What causes people to do evil?[34] Is it a hatred of themselves, a fear of death, an attempt to become a God (as in the instance of Satan, or for that matter, Adam and Eve?) All of these are really the same thing—But we must also remember that pure acts of evil are very rare . . . most of the time it is just an aimless drifting, a tepid state of indifference and fear of reality, neither cold or hot . . . . Evil does force a reality upon people . . . Satan is the last person who could be an atheist or even an agnostic, whereas Mrs. Smith on 7th St. is unthinkingly one or the other most of her life. (All of this is borrowed. There is so little originality in us. I can see why Eliot says that poets should not borrow but steal. Not that I am a poet!)

~~~

Jan. 5, 1965.

T.S. Eliot[35] died night before last. Funeral services tomorrow on Epiphany—

~~~

NOTHING LIKE ANYTHING BUT WHAT YOU HAVE SEEN, FELT, OR IMAGINED!![36]

~~~

Laurie's story[37]: A Southerner went to live in N.Y.—in an apartment house—a little white coffin in the hallway—"Who is in the little coffin?" he asked everybody—No one knew—apathy—"I'm going back down South to find out who is in the coffin."

~~~

Holy Saturday[38] Mama and I carried flowers out to Claybank to put on the graves. Wisteria, moss, honeysuckle, bridal wreath, japonicas—our remembrance of the dead only flowers that wilt in an hour or so—while Christ in the grave will make them good.

———

I would rise up in my dying hour to remind you of it.[39]

———

Met John Crowe Ransom[40] today in Columbus: a kind of southern gentleman, who sort of looked like a retired Baptist preacher—*but what a poet!*

———

Mama's fight [along] with all the other U. D. C. ladies over the Confederate soldier . . . in Miss Allie's house—she talked with Mayor Brown—They said they would hold hands and stand around the monument to keep them off of it . . .[41]

———

Dr. Fairchild's last comment to the class: "If there were any humanism in the system at all. But there isn't." It was one of the saddest statements I have ever heard said . . . completely pessimistic.[42]

———

On looking back over these notes, I am struck with the connection between a person's private life and his public art—I have been so thoroughly in agreement with Eliot, *et al* and their detachment, etc. until now . . .[43]

———

That peculiar color to the air after sunset during the last summer: gold, with a tinge of green to it: everything so *clear* and *distinct*. Is it the light in August? (!)[44]

⁘

"He was probably the only person I knew who never cheated at solitaire."[45]

⁘

December, 1970.[46] Ma and I saw the star that some think appeared at the birth of Christ. I had been unable to sleep and had gotten up to get some water. As soon as I had gotten to the sink, the star was the only thing I saw: tranquil, strong, intense and white. Ma said that it was "sincere" and went on to describe Judgment Day when those unfortunate ones who will be damned will "stay on this old earth and burn." She also said that the star made her feel as if the Nativity scene were a present reality.

—Enterprise, Alabama

From *The Blue Record Diary*, 1967–1972

After the fall art becomes necessary.[47] And art exists in time (which is merely the awareness of death) but should always have somewhere its idea of eternity which in poetry is best realized in some technical property—say, meter or rime, for instance. (Not just in those things alone, idiot.)

All art is basically a conservative impulse—to recapture the past and fix its meaning in the total scheme of things.[48]

There is no art in hell—only newspapers and picture magazines.[49]

"When working under limitations the master really proves himself." Goethe.[50]

"But on the other hand, wouldn't you have a certain distrust of an artist, whatever his medium, who felt despair because his art was not what life is? That is another confusion, if you like. Art is not supposed to be life; art is not trying to be life. Art has its own intentions." Mark Van Doren, *Invitation to Learning*, 1942.[51]

Jim of life after death: "I'll be wherever Waldo is."[52]

[A journal entry on a visit to London[53]]

As if to estrange, the late August afternoon, a cool and yellowish air, makes darker and greener the grass on which children play even down to the river's edge. The Thames, the mythical, and historical and almost human river, that now seems a tired and old god ready to give up its name. The shadows of the Houses of Parliament, and all the trees and buildings from there to Charring Cross lengthen [across] it, obscuring by failing degrees the oil and trash that litter its quiet Sunday afternoon surface. One has the illusion of a widened space, just right as a medium for the children's shrill cries, that is a kind of tolerant indifference absorbs the children's shrill cries into a widened space that looses them where they are lost or blended irrevocably into something else.

June, 1972.

On Saturday afternoon towards sunset I was walking home from one of the backfields. It was winter and the wind had lain with that savage dampness to it that makes Southern winters different from others. Along the road the ditches were covered with dead weeds out of which here and there a few thin stalks of dog fennel stood motionless in the freezing air. Beyond the ditches, on both sides of the road, the fields stretched away empty and rust-colored in cold sunlight. In one of them a farmhouse stood by itself some distance from the road. A tenant family managed somehow to live there in its three or four rooms. As I approached it its front windowpanes caught the fire of the setting sun and reflected it so fiercely that the whole inside of the house seemed burning quietly away. The black roof was too tall for the house and under its weight the flames behind the closed door appeared buried but broken in. As I stood there one of the dogs that belonged to the family must have seen me for it started barking viciously and would not stop until I finally walked on.[55]

A walk down to Pamela's house a little before sundown.[56] She was sitting in her "living room" with no lights on. We drank half a bottle of wine and smoked cigarettes. There were moments of silence during which we could hear the insects outside and the farm family rounding up sheep, feeding the chickens, and talking among themselves. Slowly the room got darker and darker. I watched the reflection of passing cars on the walls and thought of those long ago nights in Mama's house in the back room . . . .

Easter, 1972. Corfu.[57]

Easter was beautiful. But Easter Eve was more beautiful still. . . . The whole town of Corfu darkened, millions of candles illuminating the night, the processionals, the hushed excitement just before the priest shouts CHRIST IS RISEN and then the shouts, screams, embracings and salutations with the whole island lit up with fireworks whose brief yet far-flung lights exhaust even all those candles. [A] ritual meal [follows] in each home. . . . This meal is eaten only after the midnight service and consists of the new wine, cheese and olives and a meat dish filled with the innards of a lamb slaughtered the day before—the lungs, brains, eyes, kidneys, liver—everything. It is a kind of sacrament. . . . the Greek religion is strangely both literal and mysterious at the same time.

———

July 2, 1972

Yesterday James . . . and I rented small, automatic scooters and rode to Kassiopi.[58] We walked up to the fortress and then down to the beach. The path was steep and led to the rocks that sometimes had backs to them sharp as knives. We sat and listened to the waves. Albania was only a short distance away. The sun was hot and in the brown grass produced a haze almost narcotic in its effect. The fortress is Byzantine but only the walls (or part of the walls) are standing now. Nero supposedly danced there on one of his visits to Corfu. To think of the soldiers and ships once there, to realize its military importance and at the same time to see it turned into sheep pasturage with wild vines climbing up its walls is all very strange. The view from there is beautiful. As we went back to Corfu, freewheeling on the scooters, we suddenly came into view of the northern mountains towering above us. I saw them briefly and I also saw, again briefly, James make the sign of the cross and I heard him shout something I couldn't hear.

———

July 10, 1972 [59]

James, Janique + I walked part ways up the mountain to see the stars. No moon, no clouds. Crickets and other insects. I've never seen the stars so clear and beautiful. Fields of deep silence and the stars like flowers.

In dreams I see a faded photograph
Wrinkled by many hands.

The wasp on a snake's head
That coiled within our skulls.

For James and Janique

Nothing in Pelekas
But a Mozart trio
On the transistor
And getting fired at Glyfada.

From *The Green Paris Diary*, 1973[60]

Dec. 14, 1973

I bought this notebook this morning at a shop on St. Germain.[61] Two others also. One is gold (for poetry); one is red (for French, symbolism not yet figured out); this one is green (for diary, the hopefully lush and growing abundance of my new Paris life which will, please God, be turned into poetry).

Yesterday, the Eiffel Tower.[62] What can one say of it? Repeat Gide's remark that he would walk half way around Paris to avoid it? An example of "purity." It says nothing to the mind, soul, and, damnably, the body. It's just there.

In St. Séverin,[63] there is a stained-glass window I particularly liked. Christ surrounded by children, all moving towards him as to their source and pleasure. At first His face put me off or rather surprised me. It isn't the usual abstract expressionless kind one expects but "modern" and "personal." But looked at long enough, it becomes itself.

Dec. 3, 1973 [64]

On the train ride from Luxembourg to Paris I shared an apartment with an American couple and a French girl who was returning from a year or so stay in the U.S. The cold was almost unbearable to my Southern blood. The snow covered the night. No sleep. Worn out, exhausted. One small French town after another, glimpsed at from the train. At one station I made out the letters of CHARLEVILLE and came to. Later the girl told me she didn't like Rimbaud. He was "too much," in the sense of "overwhelming." Once while in Florida she had to read *A Season in Hell* and couldn't take it. She herself was somewhat like Rimbaud ended up as: lonely, without settlement, irrational, child-like, open willingly to strange influence he couldn't control and didn't want to, even dirty. I liked her. When I told her good-bye at the Paris station, it seemed as if she were about to cry. (I might have imagined this.) Not for me, but because of something inherently and uncontrollably sad in herself that requires only the least provocation to surface and dominate. (Again, my imagination?) Why am I going on with this? I liked the details: my first train on French soil, the night, the snow, the girl, Rimbaud, Charleville accidentally, unexpectedly made out in the night, and, most importantly, Florida, which is almost my half-home. Rimbaud got a little closer to me. Through the girl, he had wandered through Florida.

I bought a copy of *Charmes*, the paper, Gallimard edition.[65] On one page, the poetry: facing it an equal page of commentary. (I've reached at last my intellectual home!) Walking down the Paris streets, St. Germain, St-Michel, rue St.-Jacques early in the morning after a coffee and a *Herald Tribune*, I get the sense of being in a place where I can work out my destiny. (I feel uneasy with saying this, for fear I exaggerate or it, the destiny, will go away.) The small part of it I want very much to realize and can: the poetry. The rest, let it take care of itself as it will. I'm not being cynical. I've just worried about it too much in the past and want to forget it for a while. Paris is a state of mind I feel stimulated and comfortable in. (Remember, this all might be due to the excitement of a first visit. But shouldn't this excitement be kept up? In other words, shouldn't the good life be the usual thing?) Fact: I've a small apartment on rue St. Jacques, No. 27. Nôtre-Dame is close by; every night I hear its bells. The back of St. Séverin faces me (down a little ways, really). James, Janick and I can talk to each other across the narrow courtyard. Sparrows fly in and out of it.

James and I walked down the rue Mouffetard late this afternoon in the drizzle that almost was rain. Markets of all sorts: flowers, vegetables, fish, meat, cheese, wine. Skinned baby goats, unskinned rabbits and pheasants. All the fish piled on top of each other in their boxes seemed the sea brought to land. The glittering skin, the inscrutable eyes, the ungraspably wet bodies. James says that this section was where many of the 19th century poets lived and worked. He mentioned Rimbaud and Verlaine. It still is the center of the counter-culture. Many small theaters and cinemas, art shops and ateliers. The street has the right kind of shabbiness to it. Some of the buildings are dilapidated. Scaffoldings here and there. Small bars dimly lit with their groups of bearded (or otherwise) men in their twenties carrying on animated conversations enclosed in bluish-grey cigarette smoke. One could imagine the candles (or gas?) of the 19th century. One of the bars was presided over by an old woman, who, as I passed by, was yawning, which made her face seem toothless and grotesque. I could well imagine this all as a part of 19th century French poetry. We met an old woman who was selling one or two lemons on a small plate in the street. James says she's been there for a long time and that sometimes she sleeps in the Metro. I bought one of her lemons for a franc, which really was worth two. She pointed this out to me and when I refused the other one, she shrugged and said something like: Well, that's your business to be foolish with money![66]

On the walk to Île St. Louis:[67] How beautiful Paris is in those minutes (many of them) just before and after the sunrise. And this morning. thank heavens, there was a sun. Then leafless winter trees, the stark black limbs, formed a quiet archway over the street (the upper one by the Seine); the orderly row of closed bookstores; the stillness in the air; the light crimson of the sun; the pale blue sky; the sense of a magnificent city once again emerging into transparency. Crossing the Pont de la Tournelle (which connects the Île to the Left Bank), I stopped and watched the ducks. (But were they ducks? Small, graceful birds that looked more like seagulls; white feathers and grey that seemed to have some brown and blue in it.) They glided with wide, outstretched wings down to the river and, just above it, there was the quick, backward flutter of the wings, perfectly timed, which landed them with their dry wings folded an inch above the cold water. But they wouldn't stay still long. Up and down they went.

Dec. 14, 1973

The small square in front of St. Sulpice[68] gives one the impression of being in a provincial town, not a city like Paris. Again the sense of space, of allowing the buildings a chance to assume their own undisturbed proportions. This pleasure is heightened by the initial frustration of it: as you approach it from the side, through the smaller streets leading off St. Germain, the church is hemmed in and crowded against by surrounding buildings. But as you walk to the square, it opens up and the relief of finding the unhoped for space is overwhelming. The bottom row of columns is Doric; the upper row Ionic. I think I prefer the simpler Doric. As you walk across the square to the church the façade is an invitation to and a promise of majesty. The organ inside is famous. In the gray vistas of the marble lengths and heights, old women were walking slowly to masses being celebrated here and there in its chapels. I said prayers in the Virgin chapel behind the main altar.

December 15, 1973.
An organ concert at St. Séverin, Paris.

We sat and then leaned on the marble floor, the steps going up to the chancel. People here and there were walking around and talking. They were mostly young, and, with their dates, couldn't be expected to pay much attention to the music. . . . But there were one or two serious, bearded boys sitting in isolation and being very intent on the music. It all seemed medieval to me. One of the side chapels was lit by several candles stuck in large red pots filled with sand. Above them was a painting of the Virgin that looked like a Greek icon. One or two old women, dressed in black, were leaning over the chairs in front of them and praying. From the dimly lit distance, they looked as if they had collapsed in the candlelight and had given themselves up to the Mother.[69]

Dec. 16, 1973 [70]

Sunday. A bitter cold. Something between sleet and rain. I "accidentally" found the church of St. Julien le Pauvre. As soon as I walked in I felt as if I had found something that suited me. It is almost like a village church and it has about it the air of something strong, simple, clean and filled with an uncomplicated, totally sincere, grace. Its proportions are "accessible" and humane without any sacrifice of the spiritual grandeur that is so overwhelmingly present in the tall windows above the altar, in the strong pillars along the nave, and in the magnificently simple "ribs" that hold up the roof.

A Greek service was being performed when I was there. The air was filled with incense, and, as the priest was chanting the mysterious prayers, high above him, I could see, through the windows, black limbs of the trees outside, swaying in the icy wind. There was such a sense of being inside. Two derelicts, appropriately enough (since it's le Pauvre's church), were sitting in the back, half-asleep and trying to get warmed up, a hard job since even the church itself was cold. It was begun in 1170 and finished in 1240. At one time it was the church of the University; in it the University first held its sittings. And so it played an important part in that great intellectual ferment which took place here in Paris and to which we owe so much. Outside the church is the Square Viviani. The oldest tree in Paris is there, a (false?) acacia brought back from Guinea in 1601. "Behind St. Julien is Rue du Fouarre, which may owe its name to the straw on which they [the medieval students] sat at their outdoor lectures. Dante, who studied here, refers to the street as 'vico degli strami' (Paradiso X, 137); he speaks of violent discussions in the street and adds that he took comfort in going to St. Julien to say his prayers"—Cronin.

———

Dec. 18, 1973 [71]

I walked all the way from 27 rue Chaptal back to my apartment, drifting and taking my time, which ended up something like two or three hours. I stopped and roamed around the Tuileries. It was a beautiful day, not really cold (how the weather varies so far), plenty of sunshine, and that soft, mellow transparency in the air. I watched three old women feeding the pigeons. Two of them stomped on the bread with their shoes, softening and crumbling it for the birds. There were hundreds of them swarming around their feet. The other one later threw some of the grain on the ground, which diverted a hundred or two of the pigeons from the bread, and they were thick in the air and on the ground after the seeds. Then the old women sat back on their bench and had a great time chatting and watching the birds. From my distance it looked as if they were knee-deep in the swarming life and eating of the pigeons.

Dec. 19, 1973 [72]

I walked and walked today. I spent some time in Jeu de
Paume, which houses the Impressionists. For so many of these
paintings, distance is necessary for whatever appreciation
you wish to give them; a close examination reveals the
indistinctness, the vagueness, even sometimes the distortion,
that I don't particularly admire. In some of them, one gets
the eerie impression that you are watching the material world,
reality itself, just at the point of evaporation and dissipation.
Or that it is about to be done away with by millions of small
concentrated dots and swarms, thick like glue, of warm,
sweeping colors. Of course, not true of all of them. Van Gogh's
self-portrait, though, is a good illustration of what I'm talking
about. The surrounding pattern of thick, bright blue-green
colors, that remind me of liquid flames (whatever they would
be), seems to be locking in and engulfing the face. A kind of
total subjectivity is being suggested. And the frightened, quietly
desperate quality in his eyes, the sense of neurotic inability to
grasp and feed on tangible reality, or to make contact with
another person, all this is a result of those thick swarms of paint
that enclose the head. One way to get at what these painters
were after is to notice what is not in any (or most) of their
work: religion, man as a social being with certain obligations
and responsibilities, human love, the human face, "normally"
represented and illuminated by character, knowledge, moral
virtues or vices. What is there, of course, is nature, the sense
of being uncomplicatedly and amorally lost in the dream of
sensualness. The trees, the herbs, the flowers, the weathers
of the seasons permeate totally the ambiance of so many of
these paintings. Before one of them, which one I've forgotten
now, that had a view of some distant village hovering in the
lush new growth of spring and the warm sunshine, I got a
kind of brief throbbing sense of nostalgia for childhood and
the life one leads during that period, along with a great desire
to live as intensely and as long as I can. And in this emotion,
it came to me (admittedly melodramatic) that Paris can stab
the heart. So these painters are like so many of the French,
English and American poets of the 19th and 20th centuries.
It would be interesting to delve a little more deeply into their

correspondences and likenesses.

Later on the way back to rue St. Jacques, I passed the "existentialist" cafe, Deux Magots. At the side of the cafe some students had a band going. They were playing circus-like, um-bah-bah music; others were dancing, some even in the street. One was so damn typically French: thin, short, and brought in the nose to a sharp, satirical point. His movements were like those of a puppet that knew the nonsense of it all and yet enjoyed showing off in it. By the way, the "existentialism" of these cafes along St. Germain, Deux Magots, Café de Flore, Brasserie Lipp, is very comfortable these days, well fed and full of affected, well-dressed people. Is this really where anxiety started?

~~~~~~

Dec. 21, 1973

James and I went shopping for Janick's Christmas presents. And over to the American Center[73] for wood. As soon as you walk in, the impression of something shabby and dirty. "The smudge of moral chaos." The library is upstairs: old fashioned, poorly lit. The books unarranged and casually thrown together. A great, great many of them ripped off. Met a friend of James: He had the grippe; his eyes were watery; his face slightly drawn. Sleeping, resting and reading under a blanket on one of the larger couches in the library. An interesting type, American. I thought he was in his late thirties or early forties and was later dumbfounded to learn from James that he was only twenty-three. Facts: left home at 13 or so, a broken family; bitter, filled with despair, depressions; has travelled extensively on next to nothing; always the worst luck; picked up by criminals in Spain and robbed; violent and vicious when drunk; has a wife and child back home in Arizona he refuses to go back to (after having promised her he would); lives here and there in Paris, sleeps on streets, in libraries, friends' apartments, anywhere. He doesn't particularly like Paris but stays here because he knows it. No formal education yet reads a great deal. Resents those who do have education. I talked with him about Watergate and American politics. He seems to me to be a sad example of the typical dispossessed American, modern and amoral, who drifts against the rich, complex and mostly ordered background of a European culture he doesn't understand. But in ten years he probably will be dead. Already he's washed out, exhausted, and has a face lined and wrinkled. But it's unfair to press too far the contrast between the European background and the drifting American. Paris itself has been filled with their own. And the philosophies, or many of them, that result in this spiritual dispossession, that make it a necessity, were begun right here in Paris.

―――

I walked back from CBS[74] tonight. Not such a good night; lots of low fog-like clouds in the distance. But some good views: the Arc de Triomphe from the Place de la Concorde; the whole of the Champs-Élysées with its twinkling, multi-colored Christmas lights, looked protected and presided over by the giant monument: the Eiffel Tower looking spectral and gaunt against the trapped, yellowish light of the low-hanging clouds: the Nôtre-Dame and the Île de la Cité from Port Royal, a small village [respectfully] and lovingly clambering up the sides of the giant house of God. . . .

―――

Dec. 25, 1973 [75]

Christmas. Dinner at James and Janick, along with two other couples, one of whom lives upstairs. Later in the afternoon, went up to their apartment for coffee and a chocolate cake (provided by Janick, of course). They are Communists, blindly and dogmatically so Janick says. (But I can't see them fighting in the streets. Yet must remember that they are French Communists.) Their theoretical love of the masses, though, doesn't prevent them from having a very stylish, modern apartment with I'm sure very expensive furniture. A stereo. Records such as Woodstock, Bob Dylan, Simon and Garfunkel, Mozart, Bach, Leonard Cohen, etc. The walls were white, and, on one of them there was a poster with a picture of a Palestinian terrorist with a lethal looking, precision-perfect rifle held out to his side. As the party went on, a quiet game of chess between the two men, soft, sentimental American music in the background (Simon and Garfunkel), coffee in fine cups on comfortable chairs, etc. I felt [like] glancing at the poster—The effect of it: did it point out the contradiction between their bourgeoisie condition and the political beliefs they entertained, the whole modern business of playing with what is considered fashionable politics, whatever they may be at any particular moment, without being really seriously engaged? Or did it say, on the other hand, that, playing or not, our political ideas do have consequences and that the gun, described casually above the mantel in the first act, will have to be fired in the last?

Dec. 26, 1973[76]

Nothing

December 27, 1973

Nothing

From *The Orange Journal*, 1970s–1980s,
back in America, but the journal itself—Vélin D'Angoulême—was purchased in Paris[77]

The one who said she was God and was creating the world with her hands. For hours she would sit in a chair placed out of the way, with this intent, trance-like expression on her face, and slowly and seriously move her hands in a determined pattern that for her resulted in creation.

The older woman who gave me the drawing. How easily she would break down and cry, with her face grimaced and ugly, if someone had slighted her. Then in the same moment, it was all changed to curses and screams. She was crippled in one leg and consequently had some difficulty in walking. But this didn't stop her at all. The corridors were paced and the desire to find somewhere, in some corner or cell, the attention and love and respect she wanted in her child-like way, this was unappeased.

The very old woman who long ago in her youth had hanged her father from the loft of a barn. And at sunset. Each day at that time, she would begin her moan and wouldn't stop until after nightfall.

———

Their minds are arrested, stopped, paralyzed by incidents in their past from which they are unable to free themselves. Their minds, memories forever possessed by cruelty done to them; of such a ferocious and explosive nature that they cannot free themselves of it.

Though their bodies are frail, old, falling apart, yet the cruelty of demons, of past deprivations, of their protest against demons, "the evil brutal men have done to them," [cruelty] or energy drives them still, like puppets.

For most of these old women, the present does not exist. If you ask them what year it is, the answer will probably [be] either that they don't know or that it is twenty or thirty years removed from the present.

They are locked in a time during which they experienced the shock that led to their mental breakdown. That time and the people who populated it are their realities. The present is for other people. For them it doesn't exist.

———

The House:[78] Even now it stays in my mind. It is Sunday morning, early spring. They are coming over from Enterprise. Sunlight is flooding the hall. The magnolias and live oaks are outside, present like deities. Perhaps a brief history of the people who lived in the house my Grandfather—mother

———

You must make a Paris in your own mind.[79]

From *The Baton Rouge Diary,* June–October 1980[80]

June 5, 1980.

We are created out of nothing. Loss is, as it were, part of our constitute being. (Just think of all we must continually put into our bodies to keep them alive, the slaughter of herds, whole acres of grains.) And in those moments of spiritual and intellectual fatigue, the temptation to fall back into that aboriginal nothingness can be strong indeed, though the nothingness can bafflingly disguise itself as intense activity, which deceptively promises us life.

June 5, 1980.

I can't sleep tonight. It's 2 in the morning. As soon as I turn the lights out, the demon (as I not too poetically call it) comes out. It's as if I am being watched and judged by some suspicious tyrant who thinks nothing of me; as if I am determined to do something which will merit his idle disgust. Locked inside his own perfection, he waits in grim satisfaction, knowing that any moment I will do something which will confirm his opinion of my sorriness. And how many times have I performed exactly to his bidding, how much of myself have I torn up and given this beast to eat! There are so many more fathers beside this one. St. Augustine has God the Father say to his creature, "*I want you to be.*" This is the perfect father to whom I must bow.

June 6, 1980:

Will we ever (will *I* ever) be freed of the bondage of the psychological? Will I spend my life asking these questions, making these statements? I wish so much for sleep now. Soundless, dreamless sleep, buried, quiet, all the tissues healing, the wounds closing up and flesh and mind becoming whole again. I fear this is going to be a rough night. God help me.

June 10, 1980

. . . The health of the body, or rather the acceptance of the body, is an essential part of the moral life. Soul, body, and mind have to be in harmony with each other and with themselves, apart from the others. Benediction after Mass moved me profoundly—the element of adoration, almost of an impersonal or supra-rational nature, is so absent today and yet still such a need of human nature, that when it does happen, such relief is experienced.

June 24, 1980.

After the twilight, the crepuscular sadness occurs. The fatalistic sadness. The grey, seething lake where all is nothing. and nothing is all. A cancerous white corrupts the green world of its possible life. . . . My mind is fragmented silently with conflicts and contradictions and its very texture is torn apart. But I must not despair. I must go on.

July, 1980

Physician of souls, heal my diseased mind, restore it to health, so that, in grace and with grace, I may accept thy Love of me and give in turn my love of Thee. Amen.

I might be unfair in this, but it seems to me that too many of the pagan and even the Christian mystics transform some sort of tyrannical father into the purity of a godhead which they then locate outside life, even outside "being" itself. They never question this god, never talk back to him, as so often happens in both the Old and New Testaments (Job, etc.), but rather systematically annihilate themselves into that inhuman purity.

Keeping a journal is valuable. I'm beginning to understand why Johnson insisted upon it so.

Perfect love: "I want you to be" of St. Augustine

From journal passages concerning Finlay's Reflections on the Good Life

Someone who does not lead a good life wants to learn how he can lead a good life. He himself is not good. If he is not good, he cannot teach himself. Therefore he must go outside himself in order to become good. To stay within the self is to continue and strengthen the sickness itself. But what man can teach him? If knowledge and virtue are the same, then he must not only know what the good life is, he must live it, so that there is no disagreement at all between what he knows and what he does. (Really, an impossible ideal, but one of absolute necessity.)

And when we are talking about the good life, we are not talking about some specific, isolatable thing such as good-at-being-healthy, good-at-making-money, good-at-writing-a-poem, good-at-making-love, etc. Instead we are talking about a life considered in its totality, the whole thing in which these specifics might or might not be necessary parts.

Who are these men who know what the good life is? The priests? The philosophers?

A week or so ago I read Flaubert's Letters. He is the father (all these fathers!) (Is he the father really? There might be other

Frenchmen whom you know nothing about) of modernity, as far, that is, as literature goes. These seem to be the salient principles:

1. Art is a religion. The artist must prepare himself for his vocation in much the same way as a monk or hermit by isolating himself from ordinary experience and normal habits of living, and by making inhuman sacrifices.

2. The public is stupid, tasteless. The artist must shock the public, ignore the public, frustrate the public by doing everything he can to dissatisfy its simpleminded, conventional notions of what art should be. Art is irritation and discomfort. It is destruction of all previous presuppositions. The idea of an audience is dangerous for an artist.

3. Consequently all morality is to be eliminated as an impurity.

4. Style divorced from content. "I want to write a book about nothing in which everything will be style and only style."

5. The drive for such purity is really nihilism. "Art is like the God of the Jews who feasts on holocausts."

6. The pure, unclouded perception of the image, the vivid, luminous, startling *thing* that means nothing.

7. Consequently reason, the operation and results of the intellect, is eliminated also as an impurity.

———

Flaubert's Letters is one of the most dangerous books I've ever read, and yet I read them avidly.[81]

———

Notes for the Perfect Poem[82]

1. It must be about the truth. It must give truth.

2. It must be literal, very literal.

3. It must be symbolic, very symbolic, but symbolic only in terms of its literal "base" or narrative, not in terms not growing out of this literal whatever you may call it.

4. It must be literal, very literal.

5. It must be clean and lean and have the supple, yet firm movement of pure muscle.

6. It must be of the physical world, have winter mornings, summer nights, stripped trees, creeks, smoke, smells, the reflection of a star in a bucket of water, etc. in it so that the reader will say, "Oh, yes, this is just the way it really is."

7. Yet it must also be abstract.

8. It must come from a man who is mature and has mastered himself so that he is calm in the good knowledge he has of our mystery, our language and history.

9. It must be rooted in a particular place.

10. It must be whole in its beautifully compelling demand that its reader engages his wholeness, both his intellect and his emotion.

11. It must be moral and cause the reader to make one of the three following statements: "I should and want to lead that kind of life." "I should not and do not want to lead that kind of life." "I should and want to have the patience to resign myself to these unavoidable facts about life."

12. It must have both the intensity of engagement and the detachment of judgment.

13. It must be fully realized in language.

14. It must be plain.

Passages from the Dissertation

For [Yvor] Winters, the relationship of man with nature is complex. It is true he saw dangers in the natural world, but it is equally true he saw intellectual and spiritual benefits from the poet's *temporarily* immersing himself in sensory experience" [and enjoying] "the beauties of the natural world . . . ."[83]

He [Winters] held on to his "real beliefs" to the end and never compromised them. After "To the Holy Spirit" was written, his poetic career was all but finished; he had only three more short poems to write. The real work which remained for him to do was two books of criticism, *The Function of Criticism* and *Forms of Discovery*, and the anthology of short poems which he co-edited with Kenneth Fields, *Quest for Reality*. A great deal of *Forms of Discovery* was written while he was suffering from terminal cancer; in fact, close to the very end, he postponed an operation in order to finish the book. Donald Stanford has the best epitaph for him, which succinctly captures his peculiar combination of dignity and stubbornness. In the obituary notice which Stanford wrote for Winters in *The Southern Review*, Stanford quotes from a letter from a friend who had known Winters since his youth: "There never was anyone like Arthur [his name among his friends]. He got his work done and he died."[84]

273

From *The Paris Diary* (1973)

Dec. 24, 1973. Christmas Eve . . . . On the Metro or rather in the stations underground, I got my first glimpse of Metro life. There were "hippies" singing and begging for money. One old woman who, I think, was drunk beyond consciousness, was pathetically trying to sleep on crumpled-up bags and old clothes which were piled up on the Metro bench. No position suited her. One hand was extended and it moved awfully here and there, making meaningless gestures. Her cold poverty and discomfort were overwhelming. Once she turned over and in the full glare of the electric light, with her eyes closed and her lips moving silently, she made or rather tried to make the sign of the cross. Later, after the party, a small group of us went to Midnight Mass at St. Germain l'Auxerrois[85], which featured Gregorian music. It was the bells of this church which gave the signal for the massacre of St. Bartholomew.[86] And on the second Sunday of every month, a mass is celebrated for the souls of departed poets.

APPENDICES

Appendix A

The Dark Rooms of John Finlay by Lewis P. Simpson[1]

In October 1981, John Finlay—who had recently rejected the academy for the family dairy farm in Enterprise, Alabama—sent me a manuscript copy of a remarkable essay entitled "Flaubert in Egypt." Like his essay on Yvor Winters' "intellectual theism" published that same month in *The Southern Review*, the study of Flaubert's "inhuman ideal of art" (*The Hudson Review*, 1983) suggested that Finlay the poet aspired to follow Winters—or another admired model, Allen Tate—by identifying himself with the tradition, going back at least to Ben Jonson, of joining the vocation of the poet to that of the critical essayist. Indeed, the Flaubert essay announced a series of essays that would constitute a "book on the gods in modern literature, the various kinds of divinity, etc."; or more specifically, on the human intellect's "Gnostic" desire to alienate mind from both God and nature, and so itself to become God.

Something less tangible than the demands of farm labor must, I suspect, explain why it was the fall of 1986 before John reached the last stage of the book he had projected five years earlier. He was "working like a fiend" on the sixth and concluding essay, he said in a letter, but finishing his book was slow and agonizing, "like a journey through hell." Although ostensibly this metaphor applied only to the essay he was then struggling to complete—an intricate analysis of the theme of parricide in Nietzsche, Freud, and Kafka—John by implication referred to the whole job of writing he had imposed on himself. After he had finally completed his book in January 1987, he asked me to look at a tentative preface, in which he pointed out that he had necessarily written a "bleak book." Detecting very little happiness in modern literature, he said that "those of us who read it and study it, and also love it, must do with what we have."

Finlay holds to a severe conception of "what we have." In addition to Flaubert, Winters, Nietzsche, Freud, and Kafka, he envisions as the chief figures of the last two centuries John Locke, David Hume, John Stuart Mill, Cardinal Newman, G.M. Hopkins, and Paul Valéry. Justifying a roster of moderns that seems strangely constricted, even eccentric—that rules out the "giants," Joyce, Pound, Yeats, and Eliot—he declares that he has lost interest in figures about whom there hovers the repellent aura of "that hot-house, museum culture that Nietzsche criticizes for its historical parasitism."

In the draft introduction to his book, Finlay, it seems to me, asserts two things. One is that the modern literary giants have ironically become cultural clichés. The other thing is that the comprehension of modern literature demands insights that are basically more philosophical, psychological, and theological than aesthetic. To be sure, Finlay saw the "giants" as having been incapable of truly understanding their own motives. They had failed to grasp the devastating consequences inherent in the overriding motive of modern history: the death of reason in the Thomistic-Aristotelian sense, and hence of God, that had occurred with the modern subjectification of being. The intellect's refusal of "the rational clarities of Aristotle and Aquinas" and the consequent alienation of God from the human mind underlie the famous Joycean metaphor for the modern poet's fate, that is, a perpetual and doomed attempt to escape from the nightmare of history—from the enclosure of his vision in a sterile "aesthetic isolationism," or "aesthetic Gnosticism."

But the perceptions in *Flaubert in Egypt* defy summary. At times they assume a penetrating and dramatic originality, most notably, I think, in "The Dark Rooms of the Enlightenment." In this brilliant meditation Finlay subtly and startlingly reverses the standard depiction of the eighteenth-century philosophical mind as an undoubting believer in its own capacities. Taking his text from Locke's description of the mind as a dark room that is dimly illuminated when the candle of the intellect enters it, he shows how the philosophers of the Enlightenment recognized the incapacity of the mind to transcend itself and how this recognition was accepted even as it was refuted by the nineteenth century's most famous and articulate opponent of the Enlightenment, Cardinal Newman. "And so," Finlay says, "we come to the last irony," which is that the mind of the major ecclesiastical opponent of the Enlightenment mind and the mind that he opposes are one and the same. They meet "in what the [eighteenth-century] philosophers themselves would surely consider as their darkest room, the secret link, that is, between the anti-intellectual epistemology of modern philosophy and the non-rational subjectivism in modern religion."

By the time he completed the essays in *Flaubert in Egypt*, John Finlay—in his compulsive fascination with the tension between the rational and irrational in Western thought and emotion—had effectively united the poet and the essayist. The richest, if potentially bitterest, fruits of this union, however, were just beginning to be realized when he was forced to quit writing. We may discern this possibility at least in the one essay John sent me from a new book he started in 1987. Entitled "The Socratics and the Flight from This World," this study thrusts a candle into the dark rooms of Socrates—and, especially, of his latter-day disciples, the Cynics and the Stoics—to reveal that basically the pathos of the modern intellectual and spiritual situation is at one with the pathos of the intellectual and spiritual situation in the later Grecian world. Living in a society that had abandoned the idea that mind has the capacity to transcend its inherence in history, "Diogenes and his followers," Finlay says, "express their desire never to be hurt again. Inside the shell of their philosophy they shrunk themselves out of the world." At the very time he was silenced, the joining of poet and critic in John Finlay promised darker discoveries than he had yet made in his notable efforts to make the modern darkness visible.

Appendix B[1]

"The Deathless Word": John Finlay and the Triumph over Gnosticism by David Middleton. Introduction—here revised—to *Flaubert in Egypt and Other Essays* as published in 1992 under the title *Hermetic Light: Essays on the Gnostic Spirit in Modern Literature and Thought.*

John Martin Finlay was born on 24 January 1941 in the house of his maternal grandmother in Ozark, Alabama. His parents, Tom Coston Finlay and Jean Sorrell Finlay, owned a peanut and dairy farm outside the nearby town of Enterprise, and there Finlay came to know intimately the rhythms of the agricultural year. Throughout his childhood and youth, Finlay showed clear signs of becoming a man of letters—reading intently during the bus ride to the public schools in Enterprise, reciting Shakespeare to the cows whom he named after Greek goddesses, losing himself in books while the combine he would drive made its own way across the peanut fields, and even shouting out once in class "This is such inferior writing!" when he could take no more of the poetry of Longfellow.

Finlay attended the University of Alabama in Tuscaloosa from 1959 until 1966 earning his B.A. (1964) and his M.A. (1966) in English. While in Tuscaloosa, Finlay edited the college literary magazine, *Comment,* which printed some of his early poems, a short story, and an interview he and others conducted in Jackson, Mississippi, with Eudora Welty. According to his diaries, either in Alabama, Mississippi, or Tennessee, Finlay met and discussed literature with several important writers of the Southern literary renascence. These writers included Andrew Lytle, Robert Penn Warren, Allen Tate, Katherine Anne Porter, John Crowe Ransom, and Eudora Welty. (Shortly after a visit to Mr. Lytle's home, The Log Cabin, in Monteagle, Tennessee, on March 11–12, 1967, Finlay recorded in his diary: "Later Mr. Lytle looked over at me and said that my face was old-fashioned, it was the first time he had noticed it and that I should have died in 1863."

Not only during his Tuscaloosa years, but also during the four years he taught not far away at the University of Montevallo (1966–70), Finlay became interested in the poetry and critical theories of Yvor Winters (1900–68), the most prominent American defender and a master practitioner of traditional measured verse during the height of the free-verse rebellion. In Yvor Winters and also in Allen Tate, Finlay found models of the poet-critic that he himself aspired to be—that is, a writer whose principles, both literary and philosophical, are vividly embodied in the poetry and expressly articulated in the prose. It was quite natural, then, that after reading Donald Stanford's "Classicism and the

Modern Poet" in the spring 1969 issue of *The Southern Review*, Finlay would write to Stanford—himself a poet-critic and a former student of Yvor Winters—about coming to Louisiana State University for the doctorate including a projected dissertation on Winters. Encouraged by Stanford, Finlay entered LSU in 1970 and discovered both in Stanford and in *The Southern Review*—whose original series, 1935–42, had been edited by Cleanth Brooks and Robert Penn Warren—an almost ideal combination of Wintersian poetics and the southern literary tradition.

During most of the 1970s, Finlay lived in Baton Rouge working on the doctorate. He did take off two years (1972–74) which he spent on the Greek island of Corfu (1972), in Paris (1973), and back home in Alabama (1974). Evocative diary entries in The John Finlay Papers at LSU— some of which are now included in this Wiseblood Books collection of Finlay's prose—record the deep impression made on Finlay by the Mediterranean world and by the Roman Catholic churches he visited in Paris. In 1974, Finlay returned to LSU and graduated in December of 1980 upon the completion of his dissertation: "'The Unfleshed Eye': A Study of Intellectual Theism in the Poetry and Criticism of Yvor Winters." Also, after nearly two decades as an Episcopalian, Finlay converted to Roman Catholicism and entered the church at Easter in 1980 in part due to his reading of Saint Thomas Aquinas, whose theology became the measure and the means by which to detect serious errors in the thought and art of the writers he would study deeply in *Flaubert in Egypt and Other Essays*.

Finlay left Baton Rouge in the summer of 1981, returning to the family farm in Enterprise to read and to write his essays and poems. As expressed to me, his original plan was to try to produce an important book of essays and a significant full-length collection of poetry within a decade and then, if possible, to join the graduate faculty of a major university. Even as early as 1981, however, when news of the terrible disease first became public, Finlay felt certain he had the virus which causes AIDS. Thus it was that from 1981 to the spring of 1990, when the effects of AIDS, including paralysis and blindness, ended his career, Finlay wrote his book of essays and enough poetry for three chapbooks and eventually a collected edition—all while under a death sentence. Finlay's persistence in writing prose and poetry of high quality under such bleak conditions is surely one of the most courageous acts in contemporary literary history.

Finlay labored for many years with little hope of an audience, yet he never lost faith. In the early 1980s, he wrote to me that "we are each other's best and frequently only audience . . . we really write only for God and for ourselves . . . we must bear our isolation . . . what are we to do but work and pray?" Yet Finlay would certainly have savored the overwhelmingly favorable reception of his poems. The distinguished poet, critic, and translator Guy Davenport, for instance, has said of *Mind and Blood: The Collected Poems of John Finlay* that Finlay's verse "is so well written, so firmly made of a literary English that eludes epoch and fashion, that we can predict a future for it . . . a deserved place in American letters."

Davenport's high estimation of Finlay's poetry is corroborated by Lewis P. Simpson's judgment in "The Dark Rooms of John Finlay" that in the prose of *Flaubert in Egypt and Other Essays* with its "penetrating and dramatic originality," Finlay "effectively united the poet and the essayist." In these powerful general essays, Finlay probes the minds of key thinkers and writers of the nineteenth and twentieth centuries, finding in them fallacies, deformations, and contradictions that, when examined in the light of the Aristotelian-Thomistic synthesis of Roman Catholic theology, are shown to be virulent strains of a pervasive Gnostic spirit in modern literature and thought. Many of Finlay's poems are also studies of this spirit, but other poems complement the essays in depicting the ordered cosmos of Thomism in which there is an honored place for the rational intellect, in which the objectively existing natural world and the human appetites—both essentially good—have their proper places, in which evil is seen as deprivation rather than a thing of essence all but equal to the good, and in which the Gnostic ideas about matter, creation, irrational "knowledge" (*gnosis*), and the *Deus absconditus* undefiled by physicality are shown to be gross errors. And Christ's incarnation as the divine Word is at the center of everything.

Finlay's disclosure of the pervasiveness of the Gnostic spirit in modernity and his corresponding affirmation against that spirit of a pre-modern (and universal) order of values are by no means the routine activities of the scholar. Though filtered through vivid meditations on the works of others, the problems addressed in Finlay's essays are ones that tormented Finlay himself. His essays are not merely secondary criticism, but press toward primary forms in which a psychodrama is being played out and in which a *theomachia* involving the ultimate things is being almost desperately waged below the cool surfaces of the prose. A diary entry of 1966 recording an exchange between Finlay and Robert Penn Warren on the works of Allen Tate casts light on Finlay's own procedures and compulsions in the essays: "Finlay: 'I sometimes think that in order to understand Tate's work, you have to know something about his personal life. It seems he is hiding something about himself.' RP. Warren: 'I think you are right, Mr. Finlay.'" What Finlay's essays hide is the deep anguish that he himself suffered as a result of the same doubleness and psychic "split" that he discovers in the lives and works of the writers he examines in his essays.

Finlay often remarked that he "craved thought" and during the weeks and months he spent writing each of these essays—a long dark night of the soul and an intense Jacob-like wrestling both with demons and with angels—Finlay sometimes, as he said, would get "my days and nights mixed up," would pile up coffee cups on his desk till the kitchen held no more, and would often stand entranced in his rose garden staring and thinking in silence as a cosmic battle between darkness and the light reached its crisis in essay after essay and in his own riven mind.

II.

In a letter to Donald Stanford sent on 27 October 1981, Finlay announced that he was planning "a book on the gods of modernity, with each chapter written as if it were a separate essay." In his "Introduction" to the book, Finlay calls this approach one of "deliberate randomness" by which, in every essay, he would bring together in his mind the works of the writer under examination and a keen alertness to signs of the presence of the Gnostic spirit and then would wait for that parasitical spirit to come forth, forced out of hiding by his fine dissection of the mind of its host. Almost a kind of conjuring of a demon horrifyingly shown to have spread its errors everywhere one might chance to look, such an approach was based on Finlay's habit of deeply reading and rereading primary texts as well as the most important secondary criticism. This habit led to an intense, total engagement—both a love- and a battle-embrace—between Finlay's mind and the mind of his subject. Thus, Finlay can write sentences that poetically evoke an idea or experience almost as if he had absorbed the mind and style of the writer being probed, a writer by whom Finlay himself also seems simultaneously to be possessed. Then, in other sentences, Finlay detaches himself from his subject and performs an almost chemically pure analysis and clinically thorough diagnosis of his subject's intellectual disease. This double approach of identification/detachment and fascination/revulsion was rooted deep in Finlay; and so, although the essays are certainly deeply penetrating critiques of particular modern writers, they also constitute a secret history of Finlay's own inner life, a history wholly displaced into the apparently disinterested mode of the general critical essay. As Finlay says of Hopkins, the "symptoms" of such a history are "often disguised as the most impersonal of facts."

Finlay, of course, was far too shrewd not to know that these two processes of objective analysis and subjective psychoanalysis were simultaneously present in his work. In a letter written to me on 15 December 1981, Finlay asked rhetorically: "Have you thought of how our criticism so seemingly 'objective' and disinterested turns out almost against our will to be a sort of spiritual autobiography in disguise?" Finlay was acutely aware that there existed within his own being a deep division between, on the one hand, a strong impulse toward the Gnostic view of matter as evil and of salvific *gnosis* as mystical, and, on the other hand, a hard-won conscious assent to the Thomistic view that matter (though fallen) is substantially good and essentially real and that reason is a necessary and dignified part of our human nature, the thing we share with angels and with God. In his diaries especially, Finlay confessed that his relentless self-analysis had become a torment: "Will . . . I never be freed of the bondage of the psychological? Will I spend my life asking these questions, making these statements?" (6 June 1980). And a little over two weeks later he added: "My mind is fragmented silently with conflicts and contradictions and its very texture is torn apart. But I must not despair. I must go on." (24 June 1980).

These, then, are John Finlay's essays of desolation. And just as Hopkins tried to do in his sonnets of desolation, so here Finlay strives to locate, define, and resolve a dark conflict at the core of his being and thus to emerge into the light. The extreme difficulty in achieving this resolution and the compelling force of the case of Hopkins come together in a letter to me of 18 November 1984 in which a remark about how hard he has been working on the Hopkins essay prefaces a comment on Martin Luther and the unknowable secrets and sins hidden in the depths of the self: "Did you know that Martin Luther started the Reformation not when he became disgusted with indulgences and the confessional as such but when he realized that he didn't and couldn't know the sins inside himself? He became a secret to himself and couldn't be sure about anything." This frustrated probing of a self too stained by sin to be known becomes demonic in an admission Finlay made in a letter written to me while he was struggling with his essay on Valéry: "It [the essay] has nearly driven me mad. It is finally a study of evil and I think my problem with it, strangely enough, has to do with the demons in us resisting the light of Christ—they love the enclosed womb of obscurity and inactivity and don't want the truth about anything." (27 June 1984).

Yet Finlay was committed to the truth: he believed that it existed and that we could know it and therefore that we must, all our lives, struggle to know it even though opposed by demons who would thwart or seduce the intellect at every turn. Indeed, beauty itself—if divorced from truth—was to be suspected because amoral beauty can be all too compatible with evil. Thus, Finlay wrote to me on 9 November 1981: "Valéry is beginning to irritate me. The whole aestheticism of the French is cloying after a while. And Valéry isn't interested in truth or goodness—his mind is kept pure of all *that* vague messy stuff. Well, so be it. The concentration [camps] were burning away while he perfected his stylistic late masterpiece." Such Satanic aestheticism terrified Finlay not only in Valéry but also in Flaubert. In his diary for 5 June 1980, Finlay admitted that *"Flaubert's Letters* is one of the most dangerous books I've ever read, and yet I read them avidly." Finlay's remark about Valéry's perfecting his style while the concentration camps were burning reinforces his judgment on Flaubert's stated desire to perfect a style devoid of content: "The drive for such purity is really nihilism. 'Art is like the God of the Jews who feasts on holocausts.'" This quotation from Flaubert, incidentally, yielded the early working title for Finlay's book—*The Feasts of Holocausts*—a title which later became one of its three epigraphs.

As he was nearing the end of the book and writing its final essay—an essay, which, as Lewis P. Simpson notes, Finlay described to him as "like a journey through hell"—he confessed to Harry Duncan that he was "very tired of all modernity" and intended after the book to read "Chaucer and Aquinas, or folk like them" (4 January 1987). In fact, during the last two years in which he was able to write essays (1987-88), Finlay turned his attention not to the Middle Ages but to the ancient Greeks. Some years earlier, in a letter of 6 October 1982, Finlay had written to me of his love of the Grecian world: "The Greeks satisfy me in the deepest possible way. We should never, never get very far away from them. Let's learn Greek in our old age and meet death in a clean room with only a few well-worn Greek texts in our hands." Finlay completed two essays and drafted part of a third (on Plato's *Crito*) for his book on the Greeks when blindness due to AIDS forced him to stop. The two completed essays—"The Socratics and the Flight from This World" and "The Night of Alcibiades"—are studies in moral and philosophical deformations of the position of Socrates parallel to the studies in *Flaubert in Egypt and Other Essays* of modern deformations of the position of Aquinas. These two essays, along with the unfinished essay on Plato's *Crito*, are included in this edition of Finlay's prose.

Whether basing his analysis on principles found in Socrates or Aquinas, Finlay located the origin of human evil in man's prideful desire to deny his dependent creatureliness and thus to become a god, in his refusal to accept the reality of an objective world independent of any human perception of it, and in all maneuvers by any thinker, poet, or novelist to detach a part from the whole and to idolize that part as the whole or to weigh and value improperly the discrete portions of the whole in a manner inconsistent with reason.

In a fascinating prose note for an unwritten poem to have been called "Adam's Soliloquy," Finlay, nearly a decade before he undertook the first essay in his book, recounted the tragic human choice, lost in pre-history, that caused the primal evil of the Fall and released the Gnostic spirit into the world:

> First of all—before the Fall—man through the gift of God came to the knowledge of his existence, of its goodness and of the fact that because of it, he is like God, realizing all the time though that it is borrowed from God and derived from Him, though in and of itself it is nothing. I sometimes wonder if the Fall did not occur when man deliberately cut himself off from God and fooled himself into attempting the self-sufficient existence which is God; that is he *totally* imitated the divine unity that has not [been] or will not be fragmented by the subject-object relationship that inheres in our minds. A kind of suicidal act, a violation of nature which results in the plunge in[to] a kind of animalistic instinctualism, a 'pure' quality and finally a death.
>
> (diary entry, 26 February 1971)

This description of the Fall and its consequences leads directly to Finlay's fierce intellectual battle against what may have been his most dangerous and alluring Gnostic antagonist in all the essays: the serpent (Satan) of Paul Valéry's *Ébauche d'un serpent*. Speaking of his attraction to the beauty of the poem and yet his fear of its theological position, Finlay wrote to Harry Duncan on 23 January 1987 of his "two-partedness," his "conflict between the aesthetic and the truthful": "I lovingly translated his [Valéry's] poem, but I criticize it in the essay." Such "two-partedness" Finlay would find, and find reflected, in one form or another in every writer he engaged with in his book.

III.

As Finlay states in the "Introduction," he believes that a Gnostic spirit pervades modern literature and thought quite apart from conscious adherence by any writer to historical Gnosticism. This spirit, Finlay says, is most obviously present in "an ontological alienation of God from both the natural and the human world." Consequently, certain beliefs of the ancient Gnostics must be kept in mind because they reappear, as Finlay demonstrates, in a shockingly wide range of modern writers. These beliefs include the following: (1) there is an unknown or absent god (the *Deus absconditus*) who remains forever in his Pleroma (fullness) wholly apart from the material cosmos that was created by a lesser deity (Sophia) or deities (the Archons); (2) thus, the world of matter, including the body, is irredeemably evil, a fact that leads the believer to either asceticism or promiscuity in his disdain for the flesh; (3) but man possesses a spark of divinity mysteriously descended from the unknown god; (4) as a result, those few select souls who know this truth must try to reascend to that god by *gnosis* ("knowledge"); (5) this *gnosis*, however, is not the knowledge accessible to the rational intellect but rather a mystical knowledge esoterically possessed by those initiated into the mysteries known only through secret rituals and magic formulae. One or another of these beliefs reappears in some fashion in every writer Finlay examines.

In "Flaubert in Egypt," Finlay demonstrates that for Flaubert, as for the Gnostics, "Egypt" is the world of death-infested matter from which Flaubert wished to escape by detaching himself from life and ascending to the unknown god—in his case, the god Art. Flaubert accepted the premises of nineteenth-century science which seemed to leave the universe empty of human meaning. Only an art that attained the *aseity* of the unknown god could protect Flaubert from the horrors of matter and emotion—horrors seen in the face of the blind beggar who terrifies Emma Bovary.

Even more shockingly, in "The Dark Rooms of the Enlightenment," Finlay finds a Gnostic distrust of the rational intellect as a means of bringing us towards God not only in Cardinal Newman's erroneous elevation of the scientific mind of the Enlightenment into an omnipotent, anti-religious power but also in the very history of that mind from Locke to Hume, a history in which "the scientific light of observation and experience . . . found itself retreating into the subjective interior of the mind, even descending into the underworld of the psyche." Thus, the Enlightenment philosophers came at last to the "dark room" (Locke) of a solipsistic mind removed from God in a subjective world of pure perceptions. And Newman himself, whether he knew it or not, was left with no other pathway to God than that of the Gnostics: a mysticism apart from the rational intellect that the Enlightenment philosophers had apparently destroyed as an instrument that could give us any real knowledge of the divine.

In "The Slaughter of the Innocents," Finlay sees the conflict within Hopkins between the elective will (rooted in conscience) and the affective will (rooted in impulse and appetite) as a variety of the Gnostic civil war between spirit and matter. Hopkins was unable, Finlay says, to accept the Thomistic idea of a "commonwealth" of the appetites seen as good in themselves, nor could he simply accept his human self, with all its faults, as what Aquinas called "the burden of nature." Hopkins' God, Finlay argues, either stayed apart like the Gnostics' unknown god or else came down to free the poet from his natural "Jackself" in a kind of lightning-quick rescue mission into the world of matter. The ultimate struggle within Hopkins between an absorbed Romanticism, an acquired Thomism, and his native Victorian Puritanism ended in the victory of Puritanism, itself another eruption of an ancient Gnostic strain: a hatred of the appetites grounded in the flesh.

The Gnostic error detected in "The *Otherness* of Paul Valéry," especially as brooded on by Satan in Valéry's chilling poem *Ébauche d'un serpent*, is the rejection of the created world (God's *otherness*) by a mind that would become a deity such as it conceives God must have been before He committed the primal sin of *making*, His act of suicide. This mind, needless to say, is not rational, for it does not wish to know that it too is a creature. As Finlay says of Valéry's Satan, "he is pure self-awareness, not self-knowledge." Such a mind will vacillate, as Valéry himself does, between "extreme intellectualism" and "ecstatic mindlessness." Thus, the Satanic intellect attempts not just to reach but to become the Gnostics' unknown god. Yet, in its inevitable and intolerable failure to do so—or to know itself outside the reflecting medium of the objective world—this intellect becomes insane and finally kills itself. Until that act, however, it remains the single greatest threat to human understanding of the true nature of things.

In "The Unfleshed Eye: A Reading of Yvor Winters' 'To the Holy Spirit,'" Finlay discovers that Winters, like Valéry, finds nothing of God's essence in the natural world's "immeasurable haze." But Winters does not try to elevate the human mind to godhead; rather, he sees God as just "pure mind." In doing so, Winters follows the Gnostic separation of the unknown god from the world of matter; yet he diverges from the Gnostics in his firm conviction that we can know at least something of this God-as-Mind because He is the primal cause of our own minds. In contrast, then, to Flaubert, Newman, Hopkins, and Valéry, Winters is for Finlay an intermediate case of one who discerned a part, though not enough, of the truth about the rational intellect, especially in his belief in absolutes and in his consequent though most reluctant theism. Nevertheless, Winters errs, Finlay believes, in defining God as only "pure mind" rather than, like Aquinas, in recognizing God as pure existence. Finlay notes crucial differences between Winters' position—one that has the human mind struggling to know the divine mind as best it can through kinship and causality but fearing that both it and God are unintelligibly related to nature—and Aquinas's more comprehensive position. Thus, Finlay says: "On account of his definition of God [as pure existence], everything in Aquinas' universe, because it exists, participates in its own way in the Pure Existence of God; the natural world then for Aquinas through its analogy to God is saturated with order and intelligibility. That same natural world for Winters, because in its mindlessness it cannot participate in Pure Mind, is tainted with a disorder and an irrationalism that at times actually assume demonic proportions."

In the bleak concluding essay, "Three Variations on the Killing of the Father: Nietzsche, Freud, and Kafka," Finlay explores crucial distinctions between the Gnostics' unknown god eternally removed from a creation made bunglingly by lesser deities and the Christian idea of God the Father who lovingly made the world and whose nature can thus to some extent be known by the human mind interpreting what the senses perceive of that world. Nietzsche simply replaced the God he supposedly killed with a pathetic substitute, the *Übermensch*, whose will-to-power—like the mind of Valéry's Satan—is the only law in a world beyond objective truth. In Freud, God the Father contracts into the superego, strangely rooted in the very Id whose impulses it wars against, just as Hopkins' elective and affective wills had warred; and so, in the psychoanalyst as in the poet, the human psyche is split apart beyond any dream of wholeness. Kafka's God the Father was, of course, his own father whom Kafka internalized and deified as an unappeasable authority condemnatory of the son's entire life. Like the Gnostics' *Deus absconditus*, Kakfa's father-god is unattainably remote; meanwhile, the son is trapped by another, lesser father, Jehovah the Creator, in a meaningless universe He made and from which the prisoner's only escape is passive suffering and ascetic denial leading to the ultimate extinction of the emaciated self in "the foreign god of nothingness."

Thus ends John Finlay's terrifying "journey through hell." And yet, like Dante, Finlay emerges from hell not only in the unwavering allegiance in the essays to Thomism but also in powerful poems which make up the other half of Finlay's career as a poet-critic. And on a few of these poems some comment must be made in order to present a just and comprehensive picture of Finlay's total achievement.

IV.

Many of Finlay's poems confront the problems of modernity that as critic Finlay addresses in the essays. Other poems, however, go further to depict in striking details and incisive conceptual statements a divinely created and rationally intelligible world that is both good and whole. Of those poems that vividly heighten the essays' critique of modernity, one of the most haunting is "The *Illumination* of Arthur Rimbaud." There, the "furnace noon" and its "hermetic light" seem equivalent to the unknown god and the mystical knowledge of the Gnostics: "African sunlight seared the grimy walls, / The windows opened to the furnace noon. / He gazed into its objectless pure style, / Hermetic light destroying common earth, / Until he saw the fated animal reach night, / This century of holocaust and suicide." The poem, which bears the same title as the essay "Flaubert in Egypt," shows Flaubert recoiling like a Gnostic from the horrors of the flesh—here, an Egyptian prostitute with the "gleaming black skin of her milkless breasts." Flaubert is drawn only to the perfect work of art as to the *Deus absconditus*: "He dreamed the poem, freed of human act, / A smooth blank thing that turns in nothingness."

This inhuman detachment of the mind from what Finlay has called "the common agony of history" is chillingly apparent in his poem "Descartes in Holland": "He did not care to understand one word / The burghers said, and let thick fog create / A whiteness rendering his eyes absurd— / He had his mind inside for purer fate." All those who reject the goodness and the objective reality of the external world find their minds enclosed in solipsistic madness as does Narcissus in "Narcissus in Fire": "He moved apart. For nights in solitude / He watched his mind, in anguish at itself, / Exhaust the will and, burning in its own / Locked speed, turn into itself, deprived / Of those objective forms sustaining life." Such collapse of the God-given subject-object relationship leads in the end to dissolution: "He saw the blackness breed another scheme, / Himself the landscape surfacing brute waste. / And stared into its moon until his eye, / An open pulse, beat in the rustic fire."

Most troubling, perhaps, of these poems that wrestle with modernity is "The Case of Holmes," a poem in which, as in Hopkins, Valéry, and Freud in the essays, we find a deep cleavage suggestive of the Gnostic division between spirit and the flesh, good and evil. Yet even the great detective Holmes ("[t]he *scientific searcher*"), though he is relentlessly opposed to his arch-enemy Moriarty ("[t]he great *malignant brain*"), is also irrationally drawn to the very criminal element he stalks "[a]s skulking in the fog, urban nightwood, / He feels compressed, erotic brotherhood / And for the hardest criminal." Holmes survives by a relentless, intense alertness to evil, an alertness Finlay himself brings to bear on the subjects of his essays: "He matches brain to brain in the extreme / Of hot collected nerves and cold reserve. / Fear also makes him whole; he must preserve / One being in the conflict with that brain / Or else, at one mistake, he will be slain."

In other poems, and among them some of his best, Finlay finds peace in the assent to principles traceable to the Greeks with their vision of the unity of the cosmos and of the dignity of the human mind, and, even more so, in the assent to the principles of Christian theology that culminate in the works of Aquinas. In "The Fourth Watch," Finlay declares his faith in an address to God:

> You made us out of nothing, primal Word.
> Not lost or spilt in uncreated waste,

My essence is not You by matter blurred.
But nothing leaves in me its mortal taste.
I am because of You. And in Your claim
I find my life and speak Your holy name.

Perhaps the most complete statement of Finlay's beliefs is the splendid monologue "The Autobiography of a Benedictine," a poem which corresponds in many ways to the happiest times in the poet's own life. The last three stanzas of the poem—in their acceptance of the beauty, orderliness, and meaningfulness of the world, in their interweaving of the Greco-Roman and the Judeo-Christian cultures, and in their rejection of any angelic or violently mystical *gnosis*—may stand as Finlay's ultimate testament of faith both in reason and in the God who made men rational creatures by means of His "deathless Word":

That sun-struck Porch of Solomon,
Those eunuchs of the maddening groan
Who insult reason, who would stun
Our souls with God, I leave alone.

Athena's grove, its tempered air,
The autumn sun on her olive trees—
I thrive and bead my thankful prayer
To reason's source for clarities.

Our mind is not some Virgil cursed
To go back down to painful shades.
Faith dies itself and is dispersed
In minds the deathless Word pervades.

This rational intellect, which had its birth on the islands of Ionia, reached its classical culmination under the plane trees on the banks of the Ilissus outside Athens, the scene of Plato's *Phaedrus*. In *"Origo mentis"* ("The Origin of the Mind"), Finlay has the Western philosophical mind speak of its apotheosis there in the years just before Athens fell in the Peloponnesian War:

It was dense poems and Socratic light,
My endless afternoon before the war.
Shade of the plane made water underneath
So cool at noon, and in the summer too.
We waded in the stream and then lay back
Upon the sloping bank. Cicadas sang
Those monotones of music made with fire.

In these evocative lines, Finlay's deep allegiance to the philosophical mind is joyfully apparent.

In the spring of 1990, when he knew the end was near, Finlay dictated from his bed the final poem, his death poem: "A Prayer to the Father." In twelve plain lines that hover close to prose, the poet joins the essayist in triumph over the Gnostic spirit with his affirmation here of the goodness of the union of body and soul and in his deathbed witness to the dignity of the rational intellect drawn by its own nature and the affections not toward an unknown god but to a caring Father who listens to our prayers and who waits in love to receive each human soul:

> Death is not far from me. At times I crave
> The peace I think that it will bring. Be brave,
> I tell myself, for soon your pain will cease.
> But terror still obtains when our long lease
> On life ends at last. Body and soul,
> Which fused together should make up one whole,
> Suffer deprived as they are wrenched apart.
> O God of love and power, hold still my heart
> When death, that ancient, awful fact appears;
> Preserve my mind from all deranging fears,
> And let me offer up my reason free
> And where I thought, there see Thee perfectly.

John Finlay died of AIDS on 17 February 1991, the first Sunday in Lent.

Appendix C[1]

Answers by David Middleton to Questions Posed by Jeffrey Goodman

5 September 1999

1. Meeting John Finlay

I first met John Finlay on Good Friday of 1971 in my hometown, Shreveport, Louisiana at the wedding of a friend . . . My poem "For John Finlay" in *A Garland for John Finlay* (Thibodaux, LA: Blue Heron Press, 1990) recalls my first impressions of John and our later time as poet-friends in Baton Rouge—Allen Hall (the English building), the sweet-olives, and the Spanish architecture of the campus, the "summertime" of our friendship and our lives. Mrs. Jean Sorrell Finlay, John's mother, said John cried from blinded eyes when she read the poems to him over and over, one per day, from the *Garland*, which arrived at the Finlay farm on November 9, 1990. John died on February 17, 1991, so he did live just long enough to know how many British and American poets admired him. Contributors to the *Garland* included R.L. Barth, Edgar Bowers, Turner Cassity, Dick Davis, John Doucet, Dana Gioia, W.S. Di Piero, Charles Gullans, Warren Hope, Janet Lewis [Winters], David Middleton, Raymond Oliver, Helen Pinkerton, Wyatt Prunty, Lewis P. Simpson, Lindon Stall, Don Stanford, Timothy Steele, John Hazard Wildman, and Clive Wilmer. My poem reads as follows:

> For John Finlay
>
> I met you on Good Friday at the wedding
> Of a friend, and struck by your strong voice, broad
> Forehead, wiry build, determined to know you better.
> Later,
> In Baton Rouge, we read each other's poems
> Testing the rhythms, images, and rhymes,
> Struggling to master this greatest of all crafts,
> Craving the grace of one perfected page.
> Truly a man of letters who could love
> Blunt Johnson and the nuances of James
> And ask how that which says "the mind is weak"
> Can state its law and yet transcend the same,
> You wrote clean abstract poems in plainest style
> And sensuous descriptions charged with thought,
> Probing toward the source and end of intellect

That marks our place in all the Maker wrought.
Both natives of the South trying to reclaim
Something of Greece and Christendom, we'd walk
To the Union from our desks in Allen Hall
Talking of Homer, Dante, Winters, Tate,
A "Stanford" or a "Simpson" *Southern Review*,
Finding ourselves as poets and as friends
There, at LSU, in those sweet-olive days,
Summer seeming endless in sunlit colonnades.

When I first met John, I was in my last quarter as a senior at Louisiana Tech University in Ruston, Louisiana. At LSU John and Lindon Stall had met and become friends during the fall semester of the 1970-71 academic year when both began graduate school in Baton Rouge while I was still in Ruston. Lin and I, both Shreveporters, had met in 1968 at Tech as undergraduate English majors and had become friends, especially as fellow poets. Born in 1948, Lin is a year older than I. Finlay was born in 1941.

2. Classes with Finlay at LSU.

I took no classes at LSU with John Finlay. I know that John's reputation was that he skipped many classes yet often turned in brilliant papers. I heard that sometimes professors would overlook the absences and he would get an A; other times, he had to settle for a B. As a graduate assistant teaching freshman English, John got in trouble with the director of graduate studies for letting stacks of themes pile up ungraded. Once I recall he "hid" from a student seeking an explanation for a grade (John would not answer the phone in his apartment). John's life was often divided between extremes. According to Jean Finlay, John Finlay's mother, Finlay scored the highest possible score in English and the lowest possible score in math on his college entrance exam to attend The University of Alabama in 1959.

3. The Group of Poets around Don Stanford.

This is a subject worth exploring and might be a suitable subject for an essay one day. The main poets in this group in the 1970s were John Finlay, Wyatt Prunty, Lindon Stall, and myself. John came to LSU specifically to study under Donald E. Stanford, who, along with Lewis P. Simpson, was editor of *The Southern Review*. Finlay had read Stanford's essay "Classicism and the Modern Poet" in a 1969 issue of *The Southern Review* while he was still teaching English at The University of Montevallo in Montevallo, Alabama, and he knew that Stanford had been a student of Yvor Winters. The Finlay/Stanford correspondence survives and is now in The John Finlay Papers at LSU. I came to LSU because Lin was there and because of the influence of a family friend, Charles C. "Charlie" Clark, who was working on his Ph.D. at LSU in southern literature and who recommended LSU over Arkansas, the other university to offer me an NDEA fellowship, as better for someone interested in writing and studying modern poetry. Also, *The Southern Review*, founded by Cleanth Brooks and Robert Penn Warren, was at LSU. The "group" was not all that cohesive though in the early days John, Lin, and I were, to one degree or another, "Wintersians." Don and Maryanna Stanford's sherry parties were famous. Of the four of us, Finlay remained closest to Wintersian principles throughout his life. Stanford was always proud that he had attracted a group of poets just as Winters had done before him. We admired Don as a poet as well as a critic, scholar, and editor. Don later dubbed us "The LSU Formalists" and, as such, we were a part of the wider New Formalist Movement of the 1970s and after.

4. Why Finlay left and then returned to graduate school.

I do not know the direct, specific answer to this question. He spent time on the Greek island of Corfu (1972-73) and in Paris (1973-74). He returned to LSU in 1974 and was awarded the Ph.D. in English in December of 1980. I became closer to John after he returned to Alabama in the summer of 1981. John could be impulsive and restless. He did once tell me after he got his Ph.D. and returned home that he planned to write a book of verse and a book of essays, get them into print, and then apply to teach graduate-level classes at a major university (no freshman courses). This seemed, to say the least, a rather unlikely plan—unless it was no more than something made up to justify his living at home for years—but it was typical of John. His illness and death put an end to these plans, but he did finish the two books that I then saw into print as *Mind and Blood: The Collected Poems of John Finlay* (1992) and *Hermetic Light: Essays on the Gnostic Spirit in Modern Literature and Thought* (1994). He taught English part-time off and on at a junior college in Enterprise, perhaps mainly for pocket money and book money, and was also to have taught Latin there, but his final illness prevented that. Incidentally, John's title for his book of essays was *Flaubert in Egypt and Other Essays*. John Daniel, of John Daniel and Company, could not use the title because another book was coming out with that very title, an edition of Flaubert's letters written in Egypt, not long after Daniel was to print John's book in 1994. I am responsible for the title *Hermetic Light*, which comes from John's poem on Rimbaud,

"The *Illumination* of Arthur Rimbaud." This title change explains my seemingly inconsistent reference in the 1992 Preface to *Mind and Blood* to the original title of the book of essays.

Two stories now come to mind, so I will record them here:

John loved Elizabeth Daryush's poem "Still-Life." According to Don Stanford, Finlay flew to London on an impulse, went out to her home on Boar's Hill, Oxford, told her it was a great poem, then flew straight back to the US. His own poem "A Room for a Still Life" is almost certainly indebted to Daryush's poem. (This lightning visit was later confirmed as true.)

Too poor to afford a hotel in Athens in either 1972 or 1973, John camped out on the Parthenon all night staring at it, he said, as a symbol of the Grecian mind he loved. (My January 1990 *Poetry Pilot* essay on John was slightly incorrect on this point. He did not stay in a hotel there as I thought he had told me by phone when I was writing this piece, one of the few he knew of before he died.)

5. My personal relationship with John Finlay

My personal relationship with John consisted almost entirely of our common interests as poets. We often spent a whole Saturday going to every bookstore in Baton Rouge—or New Orleans—buying 10–15 books each. In those days before Books a Million and Barnes and Noble, Baton Rouge and New Orleans had a number of pretty good locally owned bookshops and one could still find the odd gem of a rare or used book, and bookstores regularly carried books on philosophy, history, etc. I still have my copy of Aristotle's *Physics* (1961, a University of Nebraska Press reprint, 1974) that I bought on one of these jaunts to New Orleans. I remember turning to a chapter therein entitled "Place, the Void, and Time" and how John and I thought that would be a great phrase to steal for a line in one of our poems and recited it dramatically in the car over and over.

Lin Stall owned Taliessin's bookstore in Baton Rouge for a few years, so John and I would meet there at times. It is now called Cottonwood Books. John and I once indulged in a fantasy that we would one day enter a bookstore, find a new book of verse printed on the most exquisite paper, open it, and there would be one poem on a single page inside. The poem would simply read "It is" and this would somehow be the final poem and the final answer to everything. Though a joke, this fantasy now seems to me perhaps related to Finlay's important "Notes for the Perfect Poem" write at about this same time (1971 or so).

I knew nothing at all of John's private life. I remember his apartments on East State Street, Roosevelt, and South Foster Drive. Thieves broke into his apartment on Roosevelt, found on a manual typewriter, books, and cigarettes and left, taking nothing. John was elated that this proved he lived the life of the mind. He never cooked. He ran up thousands on a credit card eating out and his mother paid it off at the end of each semester. (I only found this out later). His apartments contained books, a typewriter, cigarettes, instant coffee, and a small pan to heat water for coffee on the stove.

I do remember visiting him once when I was depressed and saying, "Life is meaningless," etc. Instantly, John shot back, with great seriousness and animation, "then why don't you go get a pistol and blow your brains out?" When I hesitated to reply, he said, "Well, you see, you don't really believe life is meaningless after all." I have never forgotten that moment. Consider this story in relation to his poems "The Locked Wards," "The Blood of Shiloh," "I Will Not Let Thee Go," and "A Portrait of a Modern Artist" in which people, *in extremis*, are still somehow connected to the goodness of life. Yet John once said to Dave Moreland, another LSU friend, "Do you think about death? I think about it all the time."

After my wife, Fran, and I moved to Thibodaux in 1977, I visited John in Baton Rouge or he came here to visit us until 1981 when he returned to Alabama. He loved for me to fix him huge omelets in my omelet-making pan. He repaid hospitality with wonderful talk. He borrowed money a few times—just spot cash—but always paid me back. Once he needed underwear so we went to a department store nearby. He had not bought such stuff in years apparently, and he held out a three-pack of briefs in his hands saying over and over SEVEN DOLLARS! SEVEN DOLLARS! as if this was an outrageous price to pay for such mundane items. Once back home in Alabama in 1981, he'd call at night when he was engrossed in a new poem or essay or reading a book. Once he'd been reading Aquinas and was struck with terror that in the modern world, compared to St. Thomas, there was "no thought" or as his accent and animation had it "NO THAWT! NO THAWT!"

I remember his reciting his double-poem "Two Poems for Oedipus" in our first house in Thibodaux. One time he killed a rattlesnake with a stick or small board on the banks of Bayou Lafourche in Thibodaux because he simply hated such snakes. Walking through town with us, he once spied a green lizard crawling down the white brow of the statue of the Virgin in someone's yard. He had a sharp eye and was horrified by such seemingly symbolic things. He was also drawn to a sculpted adolescent female Victorian angel set off by light at sunset on a tomb in St. John's Episcopal Church cemetery, our church now, but not then. Once, returning from New Orleans to Thibodaux after a book-buying trip, John and I saw the sun seeming to set in an odd, angular, wavering manner and John became terrified that the cosmos was descending again into chaos. Once he came down to visit us the wrong weekend and we had to hurry to the bank drive-up window at 5:25 P.M. on a Friday to get money for the weekend before the bank closed at 5:30. He became aware of his error as we sat in the car at the bank and was overwhelmed with mortification. We insisted, of course, that he stay.

I considered John a mentor and a poetic model. I was always in awe of his wide and constant reading, memory, and commitment to the life of the mind. His poems have that combination of simplicity, depth, wisdom, and luminous detail with symbolic implications that I find most moving in great literature. Because of him, I gave up my earlier "complex" style (Eliot/Pound) for the simplicity we find in Finlay, Winters, and Frost at their best.

In April of 1985 John and I had a serious falling out. He came to Thibodaux from Alabama for a literary festival and volunteered to go to New Orleans to pick up Bob Barth, a participant, who had brought out Finlay's first chapbook in 1984. I think John came to Thibodaux mainly to meet Bob with whom he soon formed a close friendship. (The dedication of Finlay's *Between the Gulfs*, 1986, reads "for Bob.")

They did not get to my house till midnight (we had given up on them coming by and gone on to sleep, and we had a guest staying with us, another festival participant. John finally came by around midnight and relentlessly knocked on the door till I finally got up and let them in. They stayed till 4:00 AM, then left. Both were animated, eager to talk literature, glad to see me, etc., but I was trying to get a good night's sleep to make it through the Southern Literary Festival, which my university, Nicholls State University, was hosting and for which I bore some major responsibilities and for which we had been planning for a year or more.

John was staying at a friend's apartment in Thibodaux. I was so furious at John for having come by so late and then having stayed till 4:00 AM that I deliberately phoned John at 9:00 A.M., woke him up, and chastised him for keeping us up most of the night before. John soon returned to Alabama and I communicated very little with him until I heard in 1989 he had AIDS. In the summer of 1985, I had offered by letter a partial apology on condition he "meet me halfway" as I put it—and he wrote back briefly that he would. This was the only argument we ever had. It shows perhaps the difference between my own very regulated kind of life and his sometimes more unstructured one.

But otherwise I heard little to nothing from John from that spring of 1985 falling out in Thibodaux until 1989 when I learned that John had AIDS. I called John immediately and we resumed our literary friendship, by phone now, as if nothing had ever happened. We kept in touch by phone from 1989 until just before he died. Near the end, he was too weak to hold the receiver of the phone. His mother did that while I talked and he mainly listened. I volunteered to be his literary executor, and he consented, probably on the basis of my having put together the *Garland*. "You'll have to be Bridges to my Hopkins" he said in a voice now slow and slurred because of his disease. This is an intriguing, wry remark that probably cuts two ways. His entrusting me with the executorship, given his total commitment to literature, was something I took with the utmost seriousness. His mother, whom I had never met, trusted me from our initial meeting and let me take back to Thibodaux all of John's manuscripts, letters, etc. on our first visit to Enterprise in May of 1991. I later organized these literary remains and donated them to LSU as The John Finlay Papers, where they remain today.

6. John Finlay's strengths and weaknesses as a person and a writer.

As a person, John was great company. His sometime late and irregular hours and habits often conflicted with my own, but that is neither here nor there. Once, as Lindon Stall told me years ago, John, coming in late to church, was chided for his lateness by Lin to whom John replied something like, "Well, in the Bible it says the first shall be last and the last shall be first." Despite his eccentricities, John was a true southern gentleman, always well mannered. But he was a divided person as well. He seems sometimes to have kept his friends in separate, watertight compartments. He certainly said little about his Alabama life to me. I learned about all that only after he died and we began what is now an annual summer visit to the Finlay farm. Interestingly, when he was in Thibodaux for that fateful 1985 festival, he did all he could to avoid being seen by Andrew Lytle, whom he had known and visited in Monteagle, Tennessee, years before. Perhaps he did not want to be reminded of his earlier self. I don't know, but it seemed strange; he was just terrified of Lytle seeing him (which, in fact, he didn't).

Finlay was deeply committed to Roman Catholicism. John once told a friend that Thomas More came to him in a dream holding his (More's) own bloody head and told him he had to convert to Roman Catholicism. John's sister Betty recently said that when the 1979 Episcopal Book of Common Prayer (the modern, liberal post-Cranmerian one) changed "visible and invisible" to "seen and unseen" in the Nicene Creed, John said that that was it—he had to go—since a thing can be unseen yet not invisible, just out of sight. Yet John told me it was Aquinas and the Petrine argument ("upon this Rock" etc.) that sent him to Rome. He was mad at the elderly Catholic priest in Baton Rouge who instructed him because John wanted to talk Thomism and the old priest (wisely, of course) said that John also had to feel all this in his heart, not just be an intellectual convert. John didn't want to link emotion and conversion too deeply. I also remember telling John at a cocktail party at LSU in 1979 that a very elderly priest had recently replied to a scholarly inquiry by saying that in the final weeks of his life in 1955 the Pulitzer Prize winning modernist American poet Wallace Stevens (1879–1955) had asked to be received into the Roman Catholic Church by this priest. Stevens had not been a churchgoer since his youth. In his famous poem "Sunday Morning" are the lines "She hears, upon that water without sound, / A voice that cried, 'The tomb in Palestine / Is not the porch of spirits lingering. / It is the grave of Jesus, where he lay.'" When I told John of this newly revealed story about Stevens' conversion, his mouth and eyes went wide open in astonishment. Undoubtedly, John was already moving in 1979 toward his own conversation to Roman Catholicism in 1980.

As for John as a writer of verse and prose, I would stand by what I have already said in print. His critical prose—excluding perhaps the uncollected book reviews—is, on the deepest level, autobiographical. In probably his most brilliant essay, the uncollected "The Night of Alcibiades," John is both Socrates and Alcibiades. Also, his excellent dissertation on Yvor Winters could be printed as a book, just as it is. It remains largely untapped as a source for Finlay studies.

I agree with you about all the flaws you found in his poetry as stated in your own essay in *In Light Apart*. X.J. Kennedy and Clive Wilmer in their essays also point out flaws. The only reason I myself did not point out these flaws in print was that as his executor I was "in his corner" so to speak initially in getting the best and widest possible hearing for his work. John was sometimes sloppy with meter, rhyme, line length along with syllable counting, filler words such as "still" (used twice in the closing lines of "Ovid in Exile") and could even be obscure as in the first few lines at the beginning of "The Fourth Watch" which he could never explain to me when I inquired about them. His emotional range is somewhat narrow (like T.S. Eliot's). He was not good in verse with humor or writing the epigram. (In person, though, he could be very humorous.) His diction is also often repetitive. He favors words about violence, madness, slaughter, the primeval, the ancient, the bloody, etc., perhaps too much. He may even, on some level, have feared the non-rational elements in verse. He often told me that he wanted to write verse that was just barely above the level of prose. He certainly felt that poetry revealed and then conveyed truth, not just beauty. Subject matter was of utmost importance.

Yet Finlay's best poems are free from, or transcend, his flaws. All of his poems remain so memorable—a true test of greatness. They stay in the mind and, once read, are virtually impossible to forget. Which are his best in my opinion? At a minimum, these: "The Wide Porch," "In the Adriatic," "The Bog Sacrifice" (a masterpiece)," Narcissus in Fire" (one of several fine poems on narcissism), "Audubon at Oakley" (almost as good as "The Bog Sacrifice" and surely his poetic credo), "*Origo mentis*" (a tour de force), "The Case of Holmes" (superb, and, again, autobiographical, Finlay as both Holmes and Moriarty; Finlay loved the TV Holmes played in the 1980s by Jeremy Brett and supposedly quite true to the stories), "The Inferno of the Americas" (for which he told me he read some history book on early Spanish explorers), "A Room for a Still Life" (probably the best poem we have attacking extreme feminism, a devastating, subtle, sly critique), "Ovid in Exile" (flawed in spots but another poetic credo/autobiographical poem of note), "For Henry James" (the italicized line is from James's letters, the 1970s–80s Leon Edel edition, which John had, when James had his first stroke and said "So it has come at last, the *distinguished thing*," meaning death), "Descartes in Holland" (another chilling poem on narcissism, this time, philosophical narcissism),"To a Victim of AIDS" (on himself and his behavior), "At a Spanish Fort Near the Pensacola Naval Station" (superbly done technically, on modern war, based on a real fort), "On Rembrandt's Portrait of An Old Man Reading the Scriptures," "The Autobiography of a Benedictine," "A Pastoral of the Primitives," "Salt from the Winter Sea" (one of John's favorites of his own poems, he said), "A Prayer to the Father" (a plain-style masterpiece, written heroically under terrible circumstances), "Flaubert in Egypt," "The Locked Wards" (a strangely hopeful poem on the indestructible sanity of the soul), "Through a Glass Darkly," and "The Symposium for Socrates."

Would I go so far as to say Finlay was a "great" poet? Yes, at his very best, I would say that that term applies. In any case, his verse should one day find a permanent place in anthologies of the literature of America, the South, and Alabama.

I do hope that the efforts I made from 1990 through 1999 have been for the best. Certainly all of Finlay's works will one day need to be re-edited and also collected into a standard edition. In the case of several of his unpublished poems, I had to make editorial decisions about versions of lines, decisions a later editor may wish to re-consider. This was true of "Flaubert in Egypt," "I Will Not Let Thee Go," and

"At Kalamai." Long after I am gone, perhaps I will be remembered as one who tried to help bring the work of a deceased friend of genius to wide public notice. No one else in 1991 seemed ready to do it, and even though I had little experience as an editor, I simply did what had to be done. Otherwise, John Finlay's literary remains would probably still be in that small corner room of his in the family home on the farm in Enterprise, if not picked over, scattered, and, eventually, lost.

David Middleton
Thibodaux, Louisiana
Labor Day Weekend 1999

Postscript (2018): Finlay's devotion to poetry and his sense of humor are seen in two replies (undated) that he wrote for the NOTES ON CONTRIBUTORS FORM for *The Southern Review*:

Works in progress: POEMS AND ONLY POEMS

John Finlay has just returned from a rhinoceros-hunting expedition in Central Africa where Sophia Loren flew down to have an affair with him. Currently he's in Baton Rouge having his teeth pulled.

Appendix D

The Break-In, a poem on John Finlay by David Middleton

> How strange seeing your poems in a book. . . .
> I once could feel the pathos of those nights
> About them still in hottest Baton Rouge,
> Black coffee, poverty, the sweated line!
>
> —John Finlay (1941–91), "To a Friend on
> His First Book," *Between the Gulfs* (1986)

Some forty years ago . . . yet in my mind
From time to time I see those rooms again—
That spare unshared apartment where you lived,
Earning the PhD at LSU—
A bed half-made, a nightstand with its lamp,
Ashtray, and cigarettes, and on the floor
A stack of books you read, then underscored,
Engaging every text, intently fixed,
Your very being seemingly at stake,
Choragos in tense dialogue with kings,
From Holy Writ and Plato's Socrates
To Thomas, Dante, and the troubled reigns
Of Nietzsche, Freud, Tate, Kafka, Winters, James,
All actors in the drama of a soul
You strove to save from tragic turn and fall.

Your place had little more—a single pan
To heat up coffee-water on the stove,
A black typewriter with its sticky keys,
Long yellow pads for drafts of verse and prose,
Scenes from your struggles with the Gnostic gods
Then foreign to an Alabama farm
Whose seasons of the church and earth were one.

And there you'd dwelt among the things that tell—
Spring dogwoods, Easter lilies, hyacinths,
Late summer's morning glories, white and blue,
The fall's frost-aster petals on the ground,
And Christmas holly weaving winter peace

303

For mantel, yard, grave, chancel, garden, door,
Or pastures you would cross to reach a slope
With sisters watching as you called and traced
Between the primum mobile and pond
The northern constellations, name by name—
The Hunter and the Dragon and the Lyre—
Job's Coffin held aloft by dark and stars.

At times that realm could seem so far away
And yet be near "in hottest Baton Rouge"
Where you walked back one night to quiet rooms
From wine and conversation, new work shared
Through dinner with likeminded poet friends
To spy a door ajar, a window prized
By thieves who'd broken in but then had found
Nothing worth stealing—old clothes, older books,
A manual Underwood, fair copies typed,
Ashes of finished cigarettes and thoughts,
No TV, radio, hi-fi, or cash—
And so fled empty-handed, cursing God.

And when you saw that all you had was there—
The cinder-block bookshelves' unpainted boards
Still holding Shakespeare, Milton undisturbed—
A poor man dancing past the robber band,
You knew you had been faithful to a gift
The Holy Ghost as Muse bestowed at birth,
Plowing by mind and hand down lines and rows,
True to the ancient sanctions of the land.

And though in your own way you'd come to drink
Like Socrates the poison of the age—
Narcissus leaning breathless to the pool,
Sherlock aroused for Moriarty's kiss—
You wrote late poems and essays to be whole,
Returning to that place where you were born,
Full harvests of a Blood Moon in the fields
As you stayed up all night, suffering AIDS
A decade while completing those two books,
Your story left for others who would strive
For mind's integrity, which, years ago,
A break-in had confirmed, exemplified,
As did your final moment's final breath

When from your deathbed halfway rising up,
With blinded eyes you looked beyond and said
"Plato?" to one now sent to take you home
To that last, great symposium of Love
At which the conversation never ends.

NOTES

Epigraph

1. John Finlay typed out this quotation from American novelist Henry James (1843–1916) and tacked it to the side of the wooden bookcase in his room in the family home in Enterprise, Alabama. In that room, Finlay did much of his writing, especially during the years 1981–90. This passage is from one of James' *Notebooks* (1891).

Preface by David Middleton

1. The story of John Finlay's life and works is told in "'The Deathless Word': John Finlay and the Triumph over Gnosticism" (Appendix B) and in essays by David Middleton and Jeffrey Goodman that are listed in the bibliography.

2. *The Baton Rouge Diary*, entry for June 10, 1980. The John Finlay Papers, Louisiana State University. See page 269 of this volume.

3. "The Dark Rooms of the Enlightenment: The Case of Cardinal Newman." See page 67.

4. "Flaubert in Egypt." See pages 36-37.

5. "The *Otherness* of Paul Valéry." See page 98.

6. Letter to Lewis P. Simpson, January 23, 1987. The John Finlay Papers, Louisiana State University.

7. The Greek essays appear beginning on page 133 of this volume.

8. This comment was made to David Middleton in 1994.

9. This remark can be found in Finlay's Dick Davis review, page 197.

10. Jeffrey Goodman, "Mind and Blood: An Introduction to the Poetry of John Finlay." *In Light Apart: The Achievement of John Finlay*. Edited by David Middleton (Glenside, PA: The Aldine Press, 1999), 20.

11. This short story is found on pages 213-218.

12. See Selections from Miscellaneous Writings, the Letters, and the Diaries on pages 241-248.

13. See page 263.

14. See page 239.

15. See page 239.

16. See page 268.

17. Conversation between David Middleton and John Finlay's mother, Jean Sorrell Finlay, May 1991, in Enterprise, Alabama.

18. See pages 39-40 in this book's companion volume: *"Dense Poems and Socratic Light": The Poetry of John Martin Finlay (1941–1991)*. Edited by David Middleton and John P. Doucet. (Wiseblood Books, 2020).

19. Conversation between David Middleton and John Finlay's mother, Jean Sorrell Finlay, May 1991, in Enterprise, Alabama. See also David Middleton's poem "The Break-In" (Appendix D), pages 303-305.

20. Private collection of David Middleton. Used with permission.

21. See page 94 in this book's companion volume, *"Dense Poems and Socratic Light": The Poetry of John Martin Finlay (1941–1991)*. Edited by David Middleton and John P. Doucet. (Wiseblood Books, 2020).

22. See the Correspondence between Lewis P. Simpson and John Finlay, The John Finlay Papers, Louisiana State University.

Flaubert in Egypt and Other Essays

Introduction

1. Allen Tate, "Mere Literature and the Lost Traveller," *Poetry*, 135:2 (November 1979): 96-97.

2. Tate, 100.

3. Tate, 99-100.

4. Tate, 100.

5. "The Poet makes himself a *seer* by a long, gigantic and rational *derangement* of *all the senses*. All forms of love, suffering, and madness. He searches himself. He exhausts all poisons in himself and keeps only their quintessences. Unspeakable torture where he needs all his faith, all his superhuman strength, where he becomes among

all men the great patient, the great criminal, the one accursed—
and the supreme Scholar!—Because he reaches the *unknown!*
Since he cultivated his soul, rich already, more than any man! He
reaches the unknown, and when, bewildered, he ends by losing
the intelligence of his visions, he has seen them. Let him die as he
leaps through unheard of and unnamable things." Letter of May
15, 1871, from Rimbaud to his publisher Paul Demeny. Arthur
Rimbaud, *Complete Works, Selected Letters.* Translated by Wallace
Fowlie (Chicago: University of Chicago Press, 1966), 307.

6. *Deus absconditus* is the hidden god, who remains removed from and
is indifferent to, or ignores, the suffering of human beings and the
human condition.

7. Jansenists: "Technically, Jansenism is summed up in five
propositions . . . The sense of these propositions is (1) that without
a special grace from God, the performance of His commandments
is impossible to men; and (2) that the operation of grace is
irresistible; and, hence, that man is a victim of either a natural or
a supernatural determinism, limited only by being not violently
coercive. This theological pessimism was expressed in the general
harshness and moral rigorism of the movement." *The Oxford
Dictionary of the Christian Church.* Edited by F.L. Cross and E.A.
Livingstone (Oxford: Oxford University Press, 1983, 2nd edition),
727. See this source for historical details of the Jansenist movement.

Flaubert in Egypt

1. Gustave Flaubert (December 21, 1821–May 8, 1880) was a French
novelist highly regarded for his realism and his devotion to the life
of art and to every detail in the artistic process. He was most famous
for his novel *Madame Bovary* (1857). The reader should see Finlay's
comments on Flaubert's letters and aesthetics in extracts from
The Baton Rouge Diary, 1980, pages 270-271. Several of Finlay's
comments in this Flaubert essay appear in his letters. To Donald E.
Stanford, editor of *The Southern Review* and Finlay's major professor
for his doctoral studies at Louisiana State University, Finlay wrote:
"I'm almost finished with the Flaubert essay which right now I'm
tired of. What a sad man finally! And how different from the fully
enriched sensibilities of James and Proust!" Finlay also commented
on this essay in letters to Lewis P. Simpson, scholar of American
literature and editor of *The Southern Review.* On October 27, 1981

Finlay wrote to Simpson: "I would like to give you a copy of an essay I've just finished on Flaubert. It owes a deal to *The Brazen Face of History*, especially those parts in which you discuss 'the great critique' and its ending in a kind of closure in complete modernity."

2. For another use of these details about the diving pearl-fishers and the prostitutes and for Finlay's assessment of Flaubert's aesthetics the reader should see Finlay's poem—also entitled "Flaubert in Egypt"—in *"Dense Poems and Socratic Light": The Poetry of John Martin Finlay (1941–1991)* (Wiseblood Books, 2020), page 100. Finlay also refers to Flaubert in his poem "A Portrait of a Modern Artist" on page 101 of the same volume.

3. *Götterdämmerung* is the final destructions of the gods, of social order, and of all things in a last battle with evil powers.

4. See Note 6 above to Finlay's "Introduction" to *Flaubert in Egypt and Other Essays*. It may be noted here that Lewis P. Simpson, scholar of southern literature and editor of *The Southern Review*, said to Finlay concerning this Flaubert essay, "I really want it—bad. [for *The Southern Review*] Flaubert in Enterprise, Alabama is what you are truly writing about, I think, but we won't change the title." The essay, however, was already under consideration at *The Hudson Review*, where it was accepted.

The Dark Rooms of the Enlightenment:
The Case of Cardinal Newman

1. John Henry Newman (February 21, 1801–August 11, 1890) was a priest and leader in the Oxford Movement in the Church of England before converting to Roman Catholicism in 1845. In 1879, he was made a cardinal-deacon by Pope Leo XIII. In 2010, he was beatified by Pope Benedict XVI. His numerous major works include *Tracts for the Times* (1833–41), *The Idea of a University* (f.p. 1852), and his spiritual autobiography *Apologia Pro Vita Sua* (f.p. 1864). The Enlightenment: "A philosophical movement of the eighteenth century, particularly in France but effectively over much of Europe and America. The Enlightenment celebrated reason, the scientific method, and man's ability to perfect himself and his society" (*A Handbook to Literature*, C. Hugh Holman, New York: The Odyssey Press, 1972 edition), 192. Finlay discussed his Newman essay and the Enlightenment in some of his letters. In a

letter of November 12, 1986 to Lewis P. Simpson, Finlay wrote: "I have been rereading parts of *The Brazen Face [of History*—by Simpson], especially the early part. The chapter on the fiction of the Revolution gave me a start. You say the motive of the Revolution was an act of the rational mind. I agree completely with you but then I remembered my essay on the Enlightenment where I say in so many words that the Enlightenment got rid of reason. I was then afraid I had contradicted both you and myself. Yet the more I think about it all three of us are right. I meant the intellect which apprehends absolutes in a supernatural sense, which would rule out the kind of pragmatic, provisional mind which can easily be called rational and which of course we see in the Enlightenment. You say it all in that essay when you say the modern mind is one of ideology and analysis. That's exactly the kind of mind I was trying to say exists in the Enlightenment and so we are in agreement." (The John Finlay Papers, Louisiana State University.) In a letter to Simpson written on November 28, 1986 Finlay added: "I think the trouble is that we still see the Enlightenment, not on its own theoretical terms, but as the Romantics saw it, and I am afraid they paid more attention to tone, style, and manner than to actual content. And so the tone would suggest the cool presence of an active mind, but the reality is that one can find in their theories of the mind all sorts of anti-intellectualisms. So what you say about the subjectification that begins with the Enlightenment is also what I was trying to say in the essay and so we don't disagree at all." (The John Finlay Papers, Louisiana State University.) In a letter to David Middleton composed on May 8, 1982, Finlay commented on Newman: "Newman let the vision of a world gone godless and sapless carry him to some philosophical tenets which I think are almost just as dangerous as the godlessness he was fighting. Philosophically he simply did away with the world and declared romantic war on the intellect—'faith' finally nothing but an 'assemblage of probabilities.' That concedes far too much to the enemy I think. And besides we don't have a Littlemore and the English rain pouring down outside in the night and a Passionist Father at whose feet we can fall down and beg to be received into the Church of Rome. I know we still have a Passionist Father but ours more likely would tell us to get up and think a little bit more about ourselves." (Private collection of David Middleton.) Littlemore: "Blessed John Henry Newman lived at The College at Littlemore from 1842–1846, making it a place of quiet prayer and study for himself and some friends. It was at the College on 9th October, 1845 that Newman, the famous Anglican preacher, Fellow of Oriel College, and leading figure of the Oxford Movement was received into full communion with the Roman Catholic Church by Blessed Dominic Barberi, an Italian missionary priest." (The International Centre of Newman Friends at Littlemore, Oxford, online.) Newman began his service as priest (Anglican) at St. Mary the Virgin in Littlemore in 1828. He lived a quietly spiritual life in Littlemore from 1842 to 1846. The word "Case" in the subtitle of Finlay's essay implies that he is, at least in part, assuming the roles of psychoanalyst and detective. Also see Finlay's essay on the "case" of Gerard Manley Hopkins as well as the poem "The Case of Holmes" in *"Dense Poems and Socratic Light": The Poetry of John Martin Finlay (1941–1991)* (Wiseblood Books, 2020), page 54.

2. *Érasez l'infâme*: crush the infamous (Voltaire on religion, especially the Catholic Church).

3. On the retreat of the mind inside itself, the reader should see Finlay's poems "Narcissus in Fire," "Descartes in Holland," "If a Man Drive Out a Demon. . .," and "Aeneas in Modernity" in *"Dense Poems and Socratic Light": The Poetry of John Martin Finlay (1941–1991)* (Wiseblood Books, 2020), pages 38, 72, 103, and 129.

4. Finlay's poetry often addresses the related idea of a self-divided mind or mind versus body or two "selves" within one person in a kind of civil war. Such poems, in addition to those cited in Note 3 above, would include "Two Poems for Oedipus," "In Another Country," and "The Case of Holmes" in *"Dense Poems and Socratic Light": The Poetry of John Martin Finlay (1941–1991)* (Wiseblood Books, 2020), pages 52, 53, and 54. Finlay was intrigued with the statement "the mind is weak" because the "mind" making that statement must itself not be weak in order to discern the weakness of the "other" mind. (Recollection of David Middleton.)

5. The second poem in Finlay's "Two Poems for Oedipus" addresses some aspects of this kind of life. See *"Dense Poems and Socratic Light": The Poetry of John Martin Finlay (1941–1991)* (Wiseblood Books, 2020), page 52.

6. Finlay addresses the question of the mind as a dark room threatened by insanity in poems such as "The Blood of Shiloh," "A Portrait of a Modern Artist," and "The Locked Wards" in *"Dense Poems and Socratic Light": The Poetry of John Martin Finlay (1941–1991)* (Wiseblood Books, 2020), pages 80, 101, and 102.

7. I realize Berkeley also believed in an order of nature; his immaterialism, he thought, still allowed an object for scientific knowledge; his proof for the existence of God presupposes an order and harmony in those perceptions that constitute the natural world. But all the time he insisted that any similarity among the perceptions, which has to be for any natural order to exist, was strictly speaking only apparent and had no basis in reality. If he had gone ahead and consistently applied that merciless logic of his to the order of nature that he had already applied to the objective existence of matter, that order could not have survived the argument. (Note by John Finlay.)

8. See Note 4 above.

9. F.H. Bradley, in his *Ethical Studies*, would later dispose of the phenomenological doctrine of the mind with his famous joke. He refers in his quip to Alexander Bain, the Victorian philosopher to whose psychological work Mill was indebted for part of his own theory: "Mr. Bain collects that the mind is a collection. Has he ever thought who collects Mr. Bain?" About Mill's own philosophical evasion that we have just cited, Bradley says that when Mill had "the same fact before him which gave the lie to his whole psychological theory, he could not ignore it, he could not recognize it, he would not call it a fiction; so he put it aside as a 'final inexplicability,' and thought, I suppose, that by covering it with a phrase he got rid of its existence." (Note by John Finlay.)

10. There are some particular philosophical doctrines that Newman shares with the Enlightenment. Like Berkeley, Hume, and Mill, Newman did not believe in the objective existence of material phenomena. He thought that the content of our sensations, or sense data, was indeed an object of our consciousness—we *know* that—but that its reference to anything external to our minds was a matter of faith, not of knowledge. And Newman fell at times into states of what, I think, can be called dualistic solipsism. In a famous passage from the *Apologia*, he speaks of his childhood experience of being isolated "from the objects which surrounded me" and of resting "in the thought of two and only two absolute and luminously self-evident beings, myself and my Creator." As an adult, in one of the *Parochial and Plain Sermons*, he said, "To every one of us there are but two beings in the whole world, himself and God." (Then exactly whom was he speaking to in his sermon?) And the theory of probability that he worked out in *A Grammar of*

Assent owes much to Locke's *Essay Concerning Human Understanding.* I should also mention here that Newman believed, as he said in one of the *University Sermons,* that "since the inward law of Conscience brings with it no proof of its truth, and commands attention to it on its own authority, all obedience to it is of the nature of Faith." Morality for Newman, consequently, was more the sign of obedience than the ordering principle of the rational mind, of the being to whom obedience is to be paid. In so freeing itself from rational control, Newman's conscience then resembles the *moral sentiment* of David Hume. (Note by John Finlay.)

11. Some of Finlay's finest poems are based, in whole or in part, on his understanding of this synthesis. These poems include "The Fourth Watch," "A Prayer to the Paraclete," "The Autobiography of a Benedictine," and his final poem, "A Prayer to the Father." See *"Dense Poems and Socratic Light": The Poetry of John Martin Finlay (1941–1991)* (Wiseblood Books, 2020), pages 41, 84, 86, and 94.

The Slaughter of the Innocents:
The Case of Gerard Manley Hopkins

1. Gerard Manley Hopkins (1844–1889) was an English poet and a Jesuit priest. His poems celebrate the uniqueness of each thing in God's creation. His so-called "dark sonnets" of 1885–89 seem indicative of a personal crisis that was not only theological but also psychological, and perhaps sexual as well. The word "Case" in Finlay's subtitle, as in the subtitle of the essay on Newman, suggests that Hopkins is being subjected to a wide-ranging kind of analysis. (See the end of Note 1 above to the essay on Newman.) As with other of Finlay's essays, Finlay saw something of himself in Hopkins. But Finlay, especially in his poetry and his statements of poetics, found a way out of Hopkins' dilemma. Finlay's hard-won final victory is the subject of David Middleton's essay "'The Deathless Word': John Finlay and the Triumph over Gnosticism" (Appendix B to this volume, pages 280-292). See also Finlay's important statements on his poetics—poetics much different from those of Hopkins—in his "Concerning the Project For Which Assistance Is Requested from the Mary Roberts Rinehart Foundation" and "Notes for the Perfect Poem" found in this volume on pages 225-227 and 272. The phrase "the slaughter of the innocents" recalls King Herod's order that all young male Hebrew children in or near Bethlehem be killed so that the declaration of the Wise Men

that Herod's successor as king had just been born in Bethlehem would not come true. As Finlay notes in his essay, Hopkins applied this phrase "the slaughter of the innocents" to his burning of his earlier poetry manuscripts, which he thought it proper to do, upon his converting to Roman Catholicism and becoming a Jesuit priest. Finlay commented on his Hopkins essay in several letters. In a letter to David Middleton of November 18, 1984, Finlay stated: "I'm working through Hopkins . . . . I'm beginning to see my way to what I want to say in the essay. Did you know that Martin Luther started the Reformation not when he became disgusted with indulgences and the confessional as such but when he realized that he didn't and couldn't know the sins inside himself? He became a secret to himself and couldn't be sure about anything." (Private collection of David Middleton.) In a letter of November 18, 1985, Finlay wrote to Donald E. Stanford: "Would you do me a favor? Would you read this essay on Hopkins and see if I have made any mistakes as to his biography and poetry? I am very anxious to know what you think about the validity of my interpretation. If you can even somewhat approve or see the rough justice of what I say, I'll know I'm on safe ground." (The John Finlay Papers, Louisiana State University.) In a letter of January 14, 1985, Finlay wrote to Lewis P. Simpson: "I've decided Freud more than Scotus, not, of course, to say Aquinas, explains Hopkins. What pathological Catholics those Puritan and Platonist Englishmen make!" (The John Finlay Papers, Louisiana State University.) When Finlay was near death, he replied to David Middleton's offer to serve, if need be, as his literary executor, "You'll have to be Bridges to my Hopkins." English poet Robert Bridges, (1844–1930), close friend of Hopkins, served as Hopkins' literary executor.

2. Hopkins devised a detailed vocabulary for this new meter and its theological underpinnings. Among the most important of these terms are *sprung rhythm*, *inscape*, and *instress*. The term *sprung rhythm* refers to "the meter of poetry whose rhythm is based on the number of stressed syllables in a verse without regard to the number of unstressed syllables." The word *inscape* means "the individually-distinctive inner structure of the nature of a thing; hence, the essence of a natural object, which, being perceived through a moment of illumination—an epiphany—reveals the unity of all creation." *Inscape* is "the inward quality of objects and events, as they are perceived by the joined observation and introspection of a poet." The word *instress* indicates "the force, ultimately divine, which creates the inscape of an object or an event, and impresses

that distinctive inner structure of the object on the mind of the beholder, so that he can perceive it and embody it in a work of art." C. Hugh Holman, *A Handbook to Literature* (New York: The Odyssey Press, 1972), 507, 273.

3. Born in Scotland, Duns Scotus (ca. 1266–November 8, 1308) was an important Roman Catholic theologian. In his doctrine of *haecceitas* ("thisness") Scotus argued that each thing has particular distinguishing properties that make it what it is and nothing other— the "dogginess" of the dog that makes it a dog and not a cat, and what makes one dog different from all other dogs, etc.

4. By contrast with Hopkins, Finlay's poems concerning God the Father, God the Son, and God the Holy Spirit assume the traditional kinship and adoption metaphors for our relationship with God. Examples of such poems include "A Prayer to the Father," "The Fourth Watch," "A Prayer to the Paraclete," and "The Autobiography of a Benedictine" in *"Dense Poems and Socratic Light": The Poetry of John Martin Finlay (1941–1991)* (Wiseblood Books, 2020), pages 94, 41, 84, and 86.

5. This war between the elective will and the affective will can be seen in many of Finlay's poems, in his essays on Gnosticism, and in his own life. For further comment on this matter, see David Middleton's essay "'The Deathless Word': John Finlay and the Triumph over Gnosticism" (Appendix B to this volume, pages 287-288). Among Finlay's poems on varieties of this divided self and warring wills or mind versus blood are "Ash Wednesday," "Narcissus in Fire," "Two Poems for Oedipus," "In Another Country," "The Case of Holmes," "Descartes in Holland," "To a Victim of AIDS," and "Through a Glass Darkly," in *"Dense Poems and Socratic Light": The Poetry of John Martin Finlay (1941-1991)* (Wiseblood Books, 2020), pages 36, 38, 52, 53, 54, 72, 73, and 127.

6. I intend the word in the same broad sense in which, for instance, E.R. Dodds uses it with the ancient Greeks in his *The Greeks and the Irrational*. The idea of any conflict between soul and flesh or God and nature is the one here intended, not the specific historical tradition of puritanism in Hopkins's own England. (Note by John Finlay.)

7. *Deus absconditus*. See Note 6 above to Finlay's "Introduction."

8. Compare Finlay's poems on human dignity in extremis "The

Locked Wards" and "The Blood of Shiloh" in *"Dense Poems and Socratic Light": The Poetry of John Martin Finlay (1941–1991)* (Wiseblood Books, 2020), pages 102 and 80, as well as the entry in the Paris Diary for December 24, 1973, page 274.

9. *Deus absconditus.* See Note 6 above to Finlay's "Introduction." Compare this statement on worshipping God through "self-annihilation" to Finlay's poem "Death in Asia Minor" in *"Dense Poems and Socratic Light": The Poetry of John Martin Finlay (1941–1991)* (Wiseblood Books, 2020), pages 59-60.

10. Finlay addressed this general question of the poet writing privately and apart from an audience both in his diaries and in several poems. These poems include "Ovid in Exile," "The History of a Traditionalist," "Go Little Book," and "A Portrait of a Modern Artist." *"Dense Poems and Socratic Light": The Poetry of John Martin Finlay (1941–1991)* (Wiseblood Books, 2020), pages 70, 83, 93, and 101. In "The History of a Traditionalist," one line seems to reject Hopkins' poetics as Finlay argues of the traditional poet: "He never fetished tight control." What Finlay says in this paragraph about a public dimension and a totally hidden private dimension to a work of art applies to the essays in *Flaubert in Egypt and Other Essays.* For more on this matter, see Appendix B.

11. "Fascinated gaze." Hopkins' homosexual tendencies may be compared with Finlay's own tendencies and, in his case, practice. There is also his likely self-addressing poem "To a Victim of AIDS." Moreover, Finlay's comments here on the scene in Hopkins' "The Loss of the Eurydice" of the drowned sailor come strikingly close to the scene in Finlay's poem "The Bog Sacrifice" about the exhumation of a young man's body: "But even as a corpse his beauty reanimates the drowned man and brings him back to life for Hopkins's fascinated gaze."

12. Sprung meter. See Note 2, just above.

13. Compare Finlay's poem on patricide and guilt, "The Black Earth," in *"Dense Poems and Socratic Light": The Poetry of John Martin Finlay (1941–1991)* (Wiseblood Books, 2020), pages 39-40, as well as his essay "Three Variations on the Killing of the Father: Nietzsche, Freud, and Kafka," pages 113-130.

The *Otherness* of Paul Valéry

1. Paul Valéry (1871–1945) was a French poet and essayist who spent most of his life in Paris. He was a friend of French Symbolist poet Stéphane Mallarmé. In 1925, he was elected to the Académie français. He is buried in Sète, his hometown, in the graveyard of his poem *Le Cimetière marin*. In a letter to Donald E. Stanford (date uncertain, possibly December 1984), Finlay wrote: "I've been possessed by the Valéry essay and have literally gotten my days and nights mixed up over it." Finlay's sister JoAnn Finlay Hall, speaking for herself and her sister Betty Finlay Phillips, recalls: "Betty and I both have the vivid memory of John staying up late in the night, reading, smoking cigarettes and drinking coffee. His room was a mess!" On January 24, 1985 Finlay wrote to Lewis P. Simpson of the revision process he went through with the Valéry essay: "The demon of revision, as [Henry] James calls it got ahold of me recently and I rewrote the Valéry essay. I think I made a better version of it. What do you think? I seemed to me I needed a paragraph here and there, that a few longer quotes would help the matter, and give it more authority. I especially reworked the first and last parts, the first part being just too moralistic for the cool Frenchman and the last part too compact for comfort. And even as I just read it over I had to 'chicken-scratch' in a few more last minute revisions." (The John Finlay Papers, Louisiana State University.)

2. By contrast, Finlay, in his final poem, "A Prayer to the Father," affirms the divinely ordained union of body, mind, and soul in each human being. Cartesian dualism is subjected to analysis in Finlay's poem "Descartes in Holland." See *"Dense Poems and Socratic Light": The Poetry of John Martin Finlay (1941–1991)* (Wiseblood Books, 2020), pages 94 amd 72.

3. Jansenist. See Note 7 to Finlay's "Introduction" above.

4. On the idea of a purely self-reflecting symbolist poem of pure mind see Finlay's "Flaubert in Egypt" whose closing lines describe such a poem: "He dreamed the poem, freed of human act, / A smooth blank thing that turns in nothingness." *"Dense Poems and Socratic Light": The Poetry of John Martin Finlay (1941–1991)* (Wiseblood Books, 2020), page 100.

5. Finlay describes this kind of mind in his poem "Narcissus in Fire": "He watched his mind, in anguish at itself / Exhaust the will and

burning in its own / Locked speed, turn into itself, deprived / Of those objective forms sustaining life." Finlay's poem "The Faun" also meditates on this problem of the mind and its relation to itself and the world. What happens to a mind in rebellion against the God-given order of things (natural law) is vividly described in Finlay's poem "A Portrait of a Modern Artist." These three poems connect with many other statements in this essay. See *"Dense Poems and Socratic Light": The Poetry of John Martin Finlay (1941–1991)* (Wiseblood Books, 2020), pages 38, 95, and 101.

6. See Note 5 just above.

7. Compare Finlay's poem "For Henry James." American-born novelist Henry James (1843–1916) died in London during the height of the carnage of The Great War (1914–1918). James is addressed in Finlay's poem: "You stared at, as you died, / the warships on the Thames, / gigantic blank hulks / of steel bound to a war / blinded to your distinctions— / your last discovery of Europe." The "aerial bombers" Finlay refers to here in the essay may be compared to the modern warplanes in his poem "At a Spanish Fort Near the Pensacola Naval Station" and the "new minds" that made and fly them: "Our warriors are freed from earth, /Angelic, clean, new minds that hate / Those limits of our mundane birth, / Which soar outside the mesh of fate. // We hardly see the whitening jet / Straining toward the blinding sun. / Our mind can only sense its threat / In sound, its screaming loaded run." *"Dense Poems and Socratic Light": The Poetry of John Martin Finlay (1941–1991)* (Wiseblood Books, 2020), pages 71 and 75.

8. See Note 7 just above on the "Angelic, clean, new minds" of modernity.

9. See Finlay's final poem, deliberately written as his death poem, "A Prayer to the Father": ". . . Body and soul, / Which fused together should make up one whole, / Suffer deprived as they are wrenched apart." *"Dense Poems and Socratic Light": The Poetry of John Martin Finlay (1941–1991)* (Wiseblood Books, 2020), page 94.

10. Finlay's poem "The Autobiography of a Benedictine" shows the way out of this dilemma. As is so often the case, the diseases that Finlay diagnoses in the essays, and also in some of the poems, find their cures stated in other poems.

11. Finlay has a number of poems on being trapped in various kinds of terrifying rooms, both physical and metaphysical. These poems

include "A Room for a Still Life," "A Room in Hell," "The Locked Wards," and "The End of the Affair." *"Dense Poems and Socratic Light": The Poetry of John Martin Finlay (1941–1991)* (Wiseblood Books, 2020), pages 58, 74, 102, and 104.

12. Finlay's essays on Flaubert and Hopkins also address this subject of the self-divided mind, warring minds, or multiple minds.

13. Compare Finlay's poem "'If a Man Drive Out a Demon. . .'" in *"Dense Poems and Socratic Light": The Poetry of John Martin Finlay (1941–1991)* (Wiseblood Books, 2020), page 103.

14. John Finlay's full translation of *Le Cimetière marin* appears in *"Dense Poems and Socratic Light": The Poetry of John Martin Finlay (1941–1991)* (Wiseblood Books, 2020), pages 116-120.

15. In a letter to David Middleton of November 9, 1981, Finlay expressed his opinion of French literary aestheticism and the Nazis: "The whole aestheticism of the French is cloying after a while. And Valéry isn't interested in truth or goodness—*his* mind is kept pure of all *that* vague messy stuff. Well, so be it. The concentration [camps] were burning while he perfected his stylistic late masterpiece." (Private collection of David Middleton.) In his poem "The *Illumination* of Arthur Rimbaud," Finlay compresses much of the argument of his Flaubert and Valéry essays, including the horrors of two world wars and other occasions of mass slaughter and cultural self-destruction, into six lines: "African sunlight seared the grimy walls, / The windows opened to the furnace noon. / He gazed into its objectless pure style, / Hermetic light destroying common earth, / Until he saw the fated animal reach night, / This century of holocaust and suicide." *"Dense Poems and Socratic Light": The Poetry of John Martin Finlay (1941–1991)* (Wiseblood Books, 2020), page 97.

16. On such a mind see Finlay's poems "Narcissus in Fire," "The Faun," and "Descartes in Holland." *"Dense Poems and Socratic Light": The Poetry of John Martin Finlay (1941–1991)* (Wiseblood Books, 2020), pages 38, 95, and 72.

The Unfleshed Eye: A Reading of Yvor Winters' "To the Holy Spirit"

1. Yvor Winters (1900–1968) was an American poet and literary critic who had a profound influence on Finlay. Born in Chicago, Winters was a doctoral student and then a professor of English at Stanford

University from 1927 until his retirement in 1966. Winters' earlier poems are in free verse, but in the late 1920s he turned to traditional measured verse. Finlay's Ph.D. dissertation at Louisiana State University is entitled "'The Unfleshed Eye': A Study of Intellectual Theism in the Poetry and Criticism of Yvor Winters" (December 1980). Chapter 4 of the dissertation is an earlier version of Finlay's essay on Winters' poem "To the Holy Spirit." The dissertation's abstract provides a helpful background to Finlay's essay on that poem: "Yvor Winters' early poetry, from 1920 to 1928, was written in free verse; the aesthetic principle governing it centered on the image 'purified' of conceptual content and consisting of a 'fusion' between the natural object being described and the poet's own mind. The result is a kind of naturalist mysticism, destructive of judgments and evaluations of the conscious intellect. The early poetry also registers the effect of certain scientific theories on Winters' mind; these theories were mechanistic and deterministic in nature, and they turned Winters' world into one in which moral and intellectual values had no reality. Other themes that appear in the early poems are the absence, or non-existence of God, the fear of death, and the apprehension that the ultimate nature of the universe might be demonic.

"In the late twenties Winters underwent an artistic and intellectual reformation in reaction to the free-verse and the stylistic violence which that verse finally degenerated into. He embraced a classicism that respected and acted upon the powers of the conscious mind. Writing in conventional meter and employing a style both imagistic and abstract, he wrote poems dealing with the possibility, and the realization, of moral control and intellectual order. His new poetics rested on the philosophical assumption that absolute truth exists. In order to safeguard that truth and save himself from subjective relativism, he was driven by what he viewed as philosophical necessity to a theistic position. He was influenced in this process by Aristotle and Thomas Aquinas. Only the existence of God could guarantee and validate truth and assure its independence of the human mind.

"Winters most reluctantly admitted theism. He had an instinctive fear of the supernatural; he was afraid the supernatural, its ineffability and absolute foreignness, would generate intellectual confusion in the human realm, which he wanted protected at all cost. Consequently, he defined God in the most intellectually respectful terms at his disposal. God becomes Pure Mind or Perfect Concept, existentially neutral and non-providential as far as the human is concerned. Such a 'perfect mind' becomes the absolute standard by which everything is judged. We see the effects of this definition and the subsequent standard in Winters' view of the natural world, the body-soul composite in man, and the 'giant movements' working in society at large. Since the natural world, as well as man's own body, does not participate in the reality of the Pure Mind, it was viewed by Winters with some distrust as a possible impediment to man's realizing his moral and intellectual good. Since Winters believed so much of modern society was noted for thoughtlessness, he viewed it suspiciously and recommended detachment and isolation as the means of saving oneself from moral and intellectual contamination. 'To the Holy Spirit,' a poem written in his late forties, summarizes all themes related to theism and is his most complete statement on the subject" (iv–vi).

2. "The fourth way [to prove the existence of God] is based on the gradations observed in things. Some things are found to be more good, more noble, and so on, and other things less. But comparative terms describing varying degrees of approximation to a superlative; for example, things are hotter and hotter the nearer they approach what is hottest. Something therefore is the truest and best and most noble of things, and hence either most fully in being; for Aristotle says that the truest things are the things most fully in being. Now when many things possess some property in common, the one most fully possessing it causes it in the others: fire, to use Aristotle's example, the hottest of all things, causes all other things to be hot. There is something therefore which causes in all other things their being, their goodness, and whatever other perfections they have. And this we call God." Thomas Aquinas, *Summa Theologiae*, IA, 2, 3.

3. *humanitas*: the realm of all things human—human nature, human culture, the human condition and its problems; also, human kindness.

4. See Finlay's poems on this subject "Narcissus in Fire" and "Aeneas in Modernity" in *"Dense Poems and Socratic Light": The Poetry of John Martin Finlay (1941–1991)* (Wiseblood Books, 2020), pages 38 and 129. Also related is *"Origo mentis,"* Finlay's poem on the struggle of the western philosophical mind to free itself for objective meditation on and analysis of the true nature of things.

5. In the "Foreword" to *In Defense of Reason* (Chicago; Swallow Press, 1947, 10, 11, 14) Winters states: "The absolutist believes in the existence of absolute truths and values. Unless he is very

foolish, he does not believe that he personally has free access to these absolutes and that is own judgments are final; but he does believe that such absolutes exist and that it is the duty of every man and of every society to endeavor as far as may be to approximate them. . . . The theory of literature which I defend in these essays is absolutist. I believe that the work of literature, in so far as it is valuable, approximates a real apprehension and communication of a particular kind of truth. . . . Finally, I am aware that my absolutism implies a theistic position, unfortunate as this admission may be. If experience appears to indicate that absolute truths exist, that we are able to work toward an approximate apprehension of them, but that they are antecedent to our apprehension and that our apprehension is seldom and perhaps never perfect, then there is only one place in which these truths may be located, and I see no way to escape this conclusion."

6. On the analogy between God's "intellectual essence" and the human mind see Finlay's poems "After Samuel Johnson's *Summe Pater*" and "A Prayer to the Father." On God the Holy Spirit, see Finlay's "A Prayer to the Paraclete." *"Dense Poems and Socratic Light": The Poetry of John Martin Finlay (1941–1991)* (Wiseblood Books, 2020), pages 79, 94, and 84.

7. Compare Finlay's poem "A Prayer to The Paraclete," an orthodox Christian meditation, and "At Claybank," a poem set in Claybank Cemetery, near Ozark, Alabama. Some of Finlay's family members are buried at Claybank. See *"Dense Poems and Socratic Light": The Poetry of John Martin Finlay (1941–1991)* (Wiseblood Books, 2020), pages 84 and 32. Winters' poem "To the Holy Spirit" may be found in his *Collected Poems* (Chicago Swallow Press, 1960, 138-39). Other of Winters' poems cited by Finlay in his essay are also to be found in the *Collected Poems.*

8. Compare the first stanza of Finlay's poem "Dunescape with a Greek Shrine": "The further dunes receive the pounding sea. / They never stay the same— / Both wind and wave constrain / Their shapeless drifts so they can never be." But Finlay's poem closes in a more affirmative and Christian manner than its opening stanza might suggest: "We wait until winds clear the moon and see / The burning oil inside / A shrine above the tide, / Protected by these dunes out of this sea." This ever-changingness, even of hills or mountains, is a part of one of Finlay's finest poems, "In the Adriatic": "In translucent night, rising from the sea, / The coastal mountains ended in the moon. / Up to their heights, cultivated

groves / Held them in place. Under reflecting leaves, / The turning undersides of thin pale fish, / The twisted olive trunks were rooted deep. / Miles down, in isolated clefts of rock, / As in a well, black water sucked the base." *"Dense Poems and Socratic Light": The Poetry of John Martin Finlay (1941–1991)* (Wiseblood Books, 2020), pages 77 and 33.

9. Finlay discusses Valéry's views in "The *Otherness* of Paul Valéry."

10. Compare Finlay's poem "Ash Wednesday" on the tension between mind and heart (body/emotions). *"Dense Poems and Socratic Light": The Poetry of John Martin Finlay (1941–1991)* (Wiseblood Books, 2020), page 36.

11. See the insightful critique of Finlay's essay by poet, historian, and Thomistic thinker Helen Pinkerton Trimpi, including a helpful summation of the history of Gnosticism from ancient times to the modern age, Trimpi's own reading of Winters' "To the Holy Spirit," and a discussion of other poems by Winters such as "A Prayer for My Son" and "A Testament to One Now a Child," poems that may be not too far removed from Thomism. "Act of Resistance: Finlay on Winters' 'To the Holy Spirit,'" by Helen Pinkerton Trimpi, *In Light Apart: The Achievement of John Finlay.* Edited by David Middleton. (Glenside, PA: The Aldine Press, 1999), 136-51.

12. Compare Finlay's poem "Odysseus" first published along with "Audubon at Oakley" under the overall title "Two Poems in Memory of Yvor Winters," *The Southern Review*, 18.2, Spring 1982, 356-57. (See pages 42 and 44 above.)

13. Two poems by Finlay, "At Some Bar on Laguna Beach, Florida," and "A Room in Hell"—which is a revised version of "At Some Bar on Laguna Beach"—put the obscuring of moral distinctions in terms of an encounter in a bar: "Inside a tinted half-light / Blurred the scars of error. / Careful, suspicious insight / Lost its edginess" ("At Some Bar on Laguna Beach") and "The surf of phantasies, / Drenching deathless mind, / Dissolves rigidities, / The little we had been" ("A Room in Hell"). Also relevant to this question is Finlay's almost certainly self-directed poem "To a Victim of AIDS." *"Dense Poems and Socratic Light": The Poetry of John Martin Finlay (1941–1991)* (Wiseblood Books, 2020), pages 115, 74 and 73.

14. See Finlay's review of Powell's book *Language as Being in the Poetry*

of Yvor Winters, a review included in the present edition of Finlay's prose on pages 201-203. Finlay said of his review that "its last four paragraphs are related in subject to my [essay] 'The Unfleshed Eye.'"

15. On evil as a deprivation of the good, see Finlay's poem "'If a Man Drive Out a Demon. . .,'" *"Dense Poems and Socratic Light": The Poetry of John Martin Finlay (1941–1991)* (Wiseblood Books, 2020), page 103.

16. See Finlay's translations of two Latin poems by Samuel Johnson, "After Samuel Johnson's Latin Poem to Thomas Lawrence, M.D." and "After Samuel Johnson's *Summe Pater*." *"Dense Poems and Socratic Light": The Poetry of John Martin Finlay (1941–1991)* (Wiseblood Books, 2020), pages 78 and 79.

Three Variations on the Killing of the Father: Nietzsche, Freud, and Kafka

1. Frederick Nietzsche (1844–1900) was a German philosopher among whose most important ideas are the Apollonian-Dionysian polarities in human experience and art, the will to power, the eternal return, and the *Übermensch* or Overman. See the article on Nietzsche by Walter Kauffman in *The Encyclopedia of Philosophy*. Edited by Paul Edwards. (New York: Macmillan: 1967): 5.504–14. Sigmund Freud (1856–1939), an Austrian, was the founder of modern psychoanalysis. See the article on Freud by Alasdair MacIntye in *The Encyclopedia of Philosophy*, 3.249-253. Franz Kafka (1883–1924) was the Czech (Bohemian) author of novels and short stories in German that expressed the anxiety and alienation of modern man caught up in situations he cannot understand or control. His works include the novels *The Trial* (1925) and *The Castle* (1926). On the importance to Finlay of this idea of the killing of the father, see Finlay's poem "The Black Earth" in *"Dense Poems and Socratic Light": The Poetry of John Martin Finlay (1941–1991)* (Wiseblood Books, 2020), page 39, as well as an entry in The Baton Rouge Diary (page 268 in this volume). Finlay commented on his progress on this essay in several letters. In a letter to David Middleton of June 15, 1981, Finlay wrote: "I'm still reading Freud and Nietzsche all the way through. You must pray for me, they so fascinate me, especially Nietzsche who has passages that actually move and snap on the page with a kind of intellectual electricity."

(Private collection of David Middleton.) Finlay also discussed this essay in a letter of October 24, 1986 to Lewis P. Simpson: "I'm working like a fiend these days, trying to finish the book [*Flaubert in Egypt and Other Essays*] by Christmas. The last chapter is on Nietzsche, Freud, and Kafka, and I feel as if the whole thing were a journey through hell or rather that *cloaca* St. Peter talks about in Dante. What do you think about Kafka? Can anybody really make anything of him? It seems to me that his art got sucked back into the primitive determinism of dreams and who the hell knows anything about what goes on in a dream? In other words, there's no way to interpret him and know you are even halfway right. But there's a power, isn't there, in the stories." After finishing the last part of the essay—on Kafka—Finlay sent that section to Simpson, along with a letter, on January 23, 1987. Finlay comments on being finished with the essay: "I am enclosing the last part of the essay, the part on Kafka. If you have the time and only if you have the time, I would appreciate to learn what you think of it. Right now I don't know. And I'm tired of it. I feel as if I have been on some journey to hell and plan to read from now on only such writers like Chaucer and Aquinas!"

2. See Finlay's essay above on Paul Valéry.

3. Finlay was so impressed with *The Fate of the Earth* (1982) by Jonathan Schell that Finlay wrote Schell a letter expressing his admiration for the book, which deals with the possibility and consequences of nuclear holocaust. Recollection by David Middleton.

4. For a contrasting view, see Finlay's poem "The Autobiography of a Benedictine" in *"Dense Poems and Socratic Light": The Poetry of John Martin Finlay (1941–1991)* (Wiseblood Books, 2020), page 86.

5. Again, see Finlay's own view on this matter as expressed in "The Autobiography of a Benedictine."

6. Compare other examples of self-division, doubleness, or warring opposites in the essays in *Flaubert in Egypt and Other Essays*.

7. This feeling of being alienated from the divine is the subject of Finlay's poem "The Last Act." *"Dense Poems and Socratic Light": The Poetry of John Martin Finlay (1941–1991)* (Wiseblood Books, 2020), page 35.

The Night of Alcibiades

1. After completing *Flaubert in Egypt and Other Essays*, a book which documents the deficiencies of certain seminal modern thinkers in relation to the Aristotelian-Thomistic tradition and the prevalence of Gnosticism in modern literature and thought, Finlay began a second book of essays in which Greek thinkers after Socrates were seen in light of Socrates' philosophical position and personal life. Illness and death prevented Finlay from completing this book, but three essays survive: "The Night of Alcibiades," "The Socratics and the Flight from This World," and a partial draft of an untitled essay on Plato's *Crito*. In one way or another, these essays detect in human nature, history, and philosophical thought a dangerous tendency toward the subjective, the mystical, the irrational, and a counterbalancing tendency toward the objective, the logical, and the rational. On a deep level, all of these studies in prose, as well as his poems, demonstrate that Finlay himself felt this potentially tragic division at the core of his own being. Finlay's whole life can be seen as a heroic attempt to affirm what may generally be called the Socratic, the Aristotelian, and the Thomistic traditions in these matters. Also see Appendix B, "'The Deathless Word': John Finlay and the Triumph over Gnosticism" by David Middleton, for comments on Finlay's projected book of essays on the Greeks. Given the circumstances of his final illness only a few late letters contain comments on this unfinished book or on one of the two finished essays: "The Night of Alcibiades" and "The Socratics and the Flight from This World." In a letter of October 28, 1987 to Lewis P. Simpson, Finlay said, "I'm starting something about the Greeks. I have just finished the part on Socrates and Alcibiades which when I've xeroxed I'll send it to you. I enjoyed the hell out of writing it. I think we writers are all puritans when it comes to the pleasure of writing—if it comes easily and happily, it must then be worthless—that is of course [is why] I am now suspicious of the thing. But who knows?" In a brief handwritten note of January 20, 1988 to Simpson Finlay wrote: "Here is the essay ["The Socratics and the Flight from This World"]. I hope you like it but please don't feel the need to reply to it. You are a busy man with your own work. I just want you to have a copy of it. It's part of a book on the Greeks and follows another essay on Socrates and Alcibiades. Thanks for the card and all the news. A longer letter later." The

dramatic tension between Finlay's Alcibiades and his Socrates recalls similar divisions in the essays in *Flaubert Egypt and Other Essays* and in some of Finlay's poems already noted above. With this essay in particular, the reader may wish to keep in mind a comment Finlay made in a letter to David Middleton written on December 15, 1981 in which Finlay asked rhetorically, "Have you thought of how our criticism so seemingly 'objective' and disinterested turns out almost against our will to be a sort of spiritual autobiography in disguise?" Finlay's knowledge and love of the Greeks is expressed not only in these essays but also in many of his finest poems. These poems include "In the Adriatic," "The Last Act," "Narcissus in Fire," "Odysseus," "The Archaic Athena," "Three Voices After the Greek," *"Origio mentis,"* "Two Poems for Oedipus," "The Defense of Solon," "Death in Asia Minor," "At Kerkera," "Ovid in Exile," "Dunescape with a Greek Shrine," "The Faun," "At Kalámai," "Aeneas in Modernity," and "The Symposium for Socrates." *"Dense Poems and Socratic Light": The Poetry of John Martin Finlay (1941–1991)* (Wiseblood Books, 2020). When "The Night of Alcibiades" appeared posthumously in *The Hudson Review*, 47:1, Spring 1994, 57-79, Frederick Morgan, founding editor of *The Hudson Review* (1948–), said to David Middleton that in all his years as editor he had never had such a strong positive reaction "coast to coast" to an essay as he did to Finlay's essay.

2. For more information on Alcibiades and on other people, places, schools of thought, and historical events in this essay and the two Greek essays that follow the reader should see such works as *The Oxford Companion to Classical Literature*, edited by Sir Paul Harvey (Oxford: The Clarendon Press, 1969), *The Oxford Classical Dictionary*, edited by N.G.L. Hammond and H.H. Scullard (Oxford: The Clarendon Press, 1970), *The Encyclopedia of Philosophy*, edited by Paul Edwards (New York, Macmillan, 1967, 8 vols.), and online sites such as the *Encyclopedia Britannica, Ancient History Encyclopedia*, and similar sources. It is important to note that Finlay wrote his essays to be read not as heavily end-noted, purely scholarly essays but as self-contained literary-quarterly style essays wherein Finlay provides the reader with what information he wants the reader to have in mind in order to experience the essay as a form of literary art: the quarterly essay. Finlay's essays have very few, if any, endnotes by Finlay himself. Thus, in keeping with Finlay's intentions and with the nature of the quarterly essay, purely scholarly notes to this and the other two Greek essays, as with the essays in *Flaubert in Egypt and Other Essays*, have been

kept to as few as possible. Other notes will emphasize connections between Finlay's essays and his poetry.

3. Some might argue that instead of being fragmented by democracy the interiors of Alcibiades' soul were firmed up enough by the Greek aristocratic concept of honor. They would see him, like Achilles of the epic, as being part of that "shame-culture" which E. R. Dodds discusses in *The Greeks and the Irrational*. For someone in such a culture, the most important thing, what gives meaning to his life, is the respect, honor, and glory he obtains from his fellows for performing noteworthy deeds. This is doubtlessly true to a great extent with Alcibiades. But two considerations immediately intrude themselves and undermine the "honor" thus attributed to him. First of all, his egotism existed, unlike Achilles', in a philosophical and religious vacuum. If we can say that Achilles believed in himself and in the gods, we must say that Alcibiades believed solely in himself. The difference between the two positions is great indeed. In the older culture, for instance, there was an objective standard provided by the divinity and the society protected by that divinity by which one could determine exactly what "honor" was and on whom and why it should be conferred. But in the newer culture honor was determined by the discrete individual, and there was always the possibility that the private determination might not agree with that of one's fellows. Since honor presupposes some public agreement in fact as to what is honorable and what is not, such relativism undermines its very existence. With Alcibiades it lost its public sanctions and became outrage. The second consideration is concerned with what-gets-done. Shame-cultures will tolerate only successes and care nothing for unrealized interior intention, whether good or bad. Judged by such an uncompromising and severe standard, we are forced to see Alcibiades' life as a failure. He never finished anything. He never was long enough at any one place for him to acquire and keep consolidated political or military power. He showed indeed at all times brilliant promise and actually achieved some considerable military successes at the end, but they were not sustained. Whether this was his fault or not, shame-culture would have dismissed him as unentitled to its honors. (Note by John Finlay.)

4. Compare Finlay's late poem "The Symposium for Socrates": "No flute girls shall seduce us at this feast / And make us stupid in their music's power. / We will not bloat our minds on wildest myths / Concerned with early thugs of made-up gods, / Their brutal loves

and broils with savages. / The sometimes bitter, sometimes tragic lore / Of these our human lives, wisdom like salt / Which our own minds can gather from the sea, / Shall be tonight the substance of our talk." This poem embodies the joys of the philosophical life that Finlay led in writing his essays on the Greeks, as well as the essays in *Flaubert in Egypt and Other Essays*, and also in his poetry and in his conversations and correspondence with friends.

5. "Socrates (it would appear from Plato) inferred from the harmony of the universe that it is organized and vivified by the Divine Spirit. He inclined to the view that the soul is immortal and will meet with judgment and retribution hereafter. There was a mystical side to his teaching later developed by Plato and the Neo-Platonists. He believed that he was himself the recipient of warnings addressed to him on occasion by the Divine Voice [*daemon*]." *The Oxford Companion to Classical Literature*. Edited by Sir Paul Harvey (Oxford: The Clarendon Press, 1969), 400.

6. "The war dragged on" . . . F.E. Adcock. Frank Ezra Adcock (1886–1968) was Professor of Ancient History at Cambridge University (1925–1951) and the author of many books in the field of classical studies.

7. *Elenchus* is otherwise known as the Socratic method as practiced by Socrates in Plato's dialogues. The method uses question and answer to elicit a universal truth, especially by proving the opposite of an assertion made by another participant in the conversation.

8. Compare Finlay's poem "The Wide Porch" in which, after helping his uncle clean family graves, Finlay prepares to leave the farm in Enterprise: "I swept away the clotted leaves and dirt / From graves my uncle took me out to clean. / The massive autumns drunk in the own seed, / Staining the chill slabs, nothing underneath— / I then moved outward to become myself." (*"Dense Poems and Socratic Light": The Poetry of John Martin Finlay (1941-1991)* (Wiseblood Books, 2020), page 31.

9. Finlay's original title for this essay was "A Cock for Asclepius." Asclepius was the Greek god of healing. It was customary to sacrifice a rooster to Asclepius after being cured of a disease. Asclepius was the son of Apollo and Coronis, daughter of Phlegyas, King of the Lapiths. Finlay's pun on "cock" will be lost on few readers of this essay.

10. Samuel Johnson (1709–1784) ("Dr. Johnson") was the famous English man of letters known for his essays, poetry, and biographies and for being the author of *A Dictionary of the English Language* (1755). Finlay wrote two poems after Johnson's Latin verse: "After Samuel Johnson's Latin Poem on Thomas Lawrence, M.D." and "After Johnson's *Summe Pater*." *"Dense Poems and Socratic Light": The Poetry of John Martin Finlay (1941–1991)* (Wiseblood Books, 2020), pages 78 and 79. Johnson, both as a prose stylist and as a thinker and moralist, had a profound influence on Finlay.

11. See *Early Greek Philosophy* by Jonathan Barnes (New York: Penguin, 1987) for the surviving fragments by the Pre-Socratic Greek philosophers along with scholarly commentary on these fragments.

12. Compare this statement to lines from Finlay's poem "'If a Man Drive Out a Demon. . .'": "I know that evil is the absence of a good, / A mind deprived, a truth misunderstood." *"Dense Poems and Socratic Light": The Poetry of John Martin Finlay (1941–1991)* (Wiseblood Books, 2020), page 103.

13. See Finlay's poem "Autobiography of a Benedictine" whose third stanza reads: "I feel at ease here on this earth / And love the dogma of God's flesh. / Why should we see a poisonous dearth / In what God still creates afresh?" *"Dense Poems and Socratic Light": The Poetry of John Martin Finlay (1941–1991)* (Wiseblood Books, 2020), page 86.

14. In her balanced and tactful critique of Finlay's essay printed above, "The Unfleshed Eye: A Reading of Yvor Winters' 'To the Holy Spirit,'" poet and Thomistic thinker Helen Pinkerton Trimpi observes that Winters' reluctant intellectual theism and Stoic acceptance of human fate are offset somewhat by another poem, one that points, as does Finlay's statement here, to Jesus and Socrates. Trimpi writes: "Winters' other important treatment of Socrates [in addition to his poems 'Socrates' and 'A Prayer for My Son'] is called 'A Testament to One Now a Child.' . . . In this poem, again his interest is in Socrates as a heroic model, but, significantly for interpreting what the 'Holy Spirit' connotes, Socrates is linked with Jesus of Nazareth. And both are presented as heroic models of action and thought and as evidence of a kind of divine revelation, or at least the experience of an 'absolute' source of truth. He writes in stanzas 2 and 3: 'God is revealed in this: / That some go not amiss, / But through hard labor teach / What we may reach. // These gave us life through death: / Jesus of Nazareth, / Archaic

Socrates / And such as these.' Evidently Winters links Socrates with Jesus as revelatory of God or the divine, in their action. Socrates' 'daemonic' promptings and Jesus's promptings by the Holy Spirit or by the Father are conflated in Winters' interpretation into similarly effective revelations of 'God.'" "Acts of Resistance: Finlay on Winters' 'To the Holy Spirit.'" *In Light Apart: The Achievement of John Finlay.* Edited by David Middleton. (Glenside, PA: The Aldine Press, 1991), 150-151.

15. See the definitions and etymologies of "Idiotic" and "idiot" in the *Online Etymology Dictionary.* These words can refer to or characterize someone who is unskilled or unlearned or who lives in the private sphere and does not take part in matters in the public sphere.

16. G.C. Field: British philosopher Guy Cromwell Field (1887–1955). His *Plato and His Contemporaries* appeared in 1930.

17. Yearly ritual initiations into cults honoring Demeter and Persephone. Eleusis, a village near, Athens, was the center of this cult. See "Eleusinian Mysteries." *Encyclopedia Britannica* online. Alcibiades reportedly conducted a mocking celebration of the Mysteries in one of his carousals.

18. See Note 9 above.

19. Compare Finlay's praise of American-born novelist Henry James (1843–1916), who spent most of his adult life in Europe and who became a British citizen in 1915. James died at the height of the carnage of The Great War (1914–18), which threatened European civilization with destruction. As Finlay says to James in the poem "For Henry James": "How private you became . . . / with nothing left in the end—no Europe or America— / but stoic courtesy, / death a *distinguished thing.*" *"Dense Poems and Socratic Light": The Poetry of John Martin Finlay (1941–1991)* (Wiseblood Books, 2020), page 71; note to the poem, page 241.

20. This statement may be compared to two of Finlay's poems. In "After Samuel Johnson's *Summe Pater,*" Finlay translates Johnson's Latin verses in which Johnson prays to the Father that a stroke has not affected Johnson's mind: "Father most strong, whatever you intend / As to my body's fate—but Jesus, plead— / Do not destroy my mind. Can I offend / In begging life in me for Your own seed?" And in "A Prayer to the Father" Finlay, as his own death nears, pleads with God to spare his mind: "O God of love and power,

hold still my heart / When death, that ancient, awful fact appears; / Preserve my mind from all deranging fears, / And let me offer up my reason free / And where I thought, there see Thee perfectly." *"Dense Poems and Socratic Light": The Poetry of John Martin Finlay (1941–1991)* (Wiseblood Books, 2020), pages 79 and 94; notes to the poems, pages 242-243 and 247.

The Socratics and the Flight from This World

1. See Finlay's poem "The Defense of Solon" in *"Dense Poems and Socratic Light": The Poetry of John Martin Finlay (1941–1991)* (Wiseblood Books, 2020), page 55; note to the poem, page 237.

2. Finlay refers here not to Christian mystics but to the Socratics, those philosophers and schools of philosophy that came after Socrates, Plato, and Aristotle. Finlay discusses these philosophers and schools and the tendency in some of them to see ultimate reality as wholly beyond the material world, the "this world" of the title of the essay.

3. Or *daimon, daemon*. See Note 5 above to "The Night of Alcibiades."

4. This "special knowledge" is that of Gnosticism, whose modern manifestations are the subject of the essays in *Flaubert in Egypt and Other Essays*. Finlay sees a connection between modern Gnosticism and the beliefs of some of the Socratics.

5. Born in Germany, Eric Voegelin (1901–1985) lived in America where he became known for his studies in the field of political philosophy. His many books include *The New Science of Politics* (1952), *Politics and Gnosticism* (1968), and the magisterial multi-volume *Order and History* (1956–death), which, among many other subjects, addresses the question of the influence of Gnosticism on western culture. Volume 3 is entitled *Plato and Aristotle* (1957).

6. See the section on Nietzsche in Finlay's essay "Three Variations on the Killing of the Father: Nietzsche, Freud and Kafka," along with Note 1 to that essay, printed above.

7. It is true that at one point in Book 1 of *De Anima* Aristotle states emphatically that "it is surely better not to say that the soul pities, learns, or thinks, but that the man does these with his soul." But as D. W. Hamlyn informs us in his Introduction to *De Anima* in

the *Clarendon Aristotle Series*, the philosopher "rarely lives up to his dictum." And in his commentary on the passage in Aristotle referred to, Mr. Hamlyn explains further the failure by noting that "the concept of person or subject is . . . missing from Aristotle's discussion of problems in the philosophy of mind." (Note by John Finlay.) D.W. Hamlyn: David Walter Hamlyn (1924–2012), professor of philosophy at Birkbeck College, London.

8. On this sense of "agony" compare lines from Finlay's poem "The Defense of Solon": "I never was afraid of power. I fused / It with strict justice, disregarding blood, / And made a rod I used to rule the state. / Justice bade me pay homage to the whole. / The sun-struck body gleaming in its sweat, / Its health confirmed agony of games, / But body lit with light of ruling mind— / That image formed my model for the laws." *"Dense Poems and Socratic Light": The Poetry of John Martin Finlay (1941–1991)* (Wiseblood Books, 2020), page 55.

9. See Note 15 above to "The Night of Alcibiades."

10. *agora*: a place of assembly for a public meeting.

11. Eduard Zeller (1814–1908) was a German philosopher who specialized in Greek philosophy, especially pre-Socratic philosophy.

12. The Porch: a place in Athens where Zeno and the Stoics taught. The Garden: the place where Epicurus taught in Athens.

13. Compare lines from Finlay's poem "Narcissus in Fire": "He moved apart. For nights in solitude / He watched his mind, in anguish at itself, / Exhaust the will and, burning in its own / Locked speed, turn into itself, deprived / Of those objective forms sustaining life." *"Dense Poems and Socratic Light": The Poetry of John Martin Finlay (1941–1991)* (Wiseblood Books, 2018), page 38.

[On Plato's *Crito*]

1. John Finlay died before he could finish this essay or provide a title. The editors have added a title in brackets.

2. The *Crito* takes place in the prison where Socrates is awaiting the day and time of his execution, when he is to drink the hemlock. Socrates explains why he does not try to escape and why as a

citizen he is compelled to uphold the laws of the state, including the decision of the jury to condemn him to death.

Elizabeth Daryush

1. This essay appeared in *The Dictionary of Literary Biography: British Poets, 1914–45*. Edited by Donald E. Stanford. (Detroit, MI: Gale Research: 1983), 20, 109-112. The standard format for a DLB essay—including the title, birth and death dates, and the placement of primary works and secondary references—has here been maintained. See also the notes Finlay made just after his September 1969 visit with Daryush in England (page 240 in the Other Prose section). Finlay greatly admired Daryush's poem "Still-Life," which was an influence on his own poem "A Room for a Still Life." The note for Finlay's poem in *"Dense Poems and Socratic Light": The Poetry of John Martin Finlay (1941–1991)* (Wiseblood Books, 2020), poem page 58; note, page 238, the companion volume to this volume of his prose, reads as follows: Finlay loved the poem "Still-Life" by English poet Elizabeth Bridges Daryush (1887–1977), daughter of English poet laureate Robert Bridges (1844–1930). In September of 1969, Finlay flew to England in order to meet Daryush at her home outside Oxford and express his admiration for her poetry. A fine essay on the relationship between Daryush's poem "Still-Life" and Finlay's "A Room for a Still Life" is Glenn Bergeron's "John Finlay's 'A Room for a Still Life' and Elizabeth Daryush's 'Still-Life'" in *In Light Apart: The Achievement of John Finlay*. Edited by David Middleton (Glenside, PA: The Aldine Press, 1999), 178-83. These two poems are in the tradition of the ekphrastic poem, a poem based on a work of art (such as a "still life"), though in both cases here the antecedent "still life" picture or picture-like scene seems to have been invented by the poet.

Book Reviews

1. For reasons of clarity and consistency, the titles of these seven reviews have been standardized in the text. The original titles of the reviews as well as their dates and places of publication may be found in the bibliography at the end of this volume. Bibliographical information on the book or books under review appears at the end of each review.

Short Story

The Up-There

1. From *Comment*, Winter 1962, 37-44. Finlay's early journals are filled with ideas for, and scenes from, possible short stories. So far as is presently known, "The Up-There" is the only short story that Finlay completed and published. See also the "Editors' Preface" to "An Interview with Eudora Welty," printed above. The views expressed in the Preface are probably close to Finlay's own views on the writing of fiction.

Other Prose

Editors' Preface to An Interview with Eudora Welty

1. "Editors' Preface to 'An Interview with Eudora Welty,'" *Comment*, Winter 1965, page 11. Finlay was one of three interviewers, and, based on style and content, appears to be the main or sole author of this preface. The interviewers' questions and Miss Welty's answers follow the preface. Eudora Welty (1909–2001) was a southern novelist and short story writer. She lived her whole life in her family's house in Jackson, Mississippi. Her novel *The Optimist's Daughter* (1972) won the 1973 Pulitzer Prize for Fiction. The interview took place in Welty's Jackson, Mississippi home. Finlay's one known short story, "The Up-There," printed above, was written in accordance with the principles of fiction writing as stated in this "Editors' Preface."

Concerning the Project For Which Assistance Is Requested from The Mary Roberts Rinehart Foundation

1. Finlay was not awarded a Rinehart grant nor did he write the long poem on Audubon's years in Louisiana, but he did write a short poem, "Audubon at Oakley," that appears in the *Mind and Blood* section of *"Dense Poems and Socratic Light": The Poetry of John Martin Finlay (1941–1991)* (Wiseblood Books, 2020), page 44 and is printed just after this proposal in this volume. This Rinehart proposal may be read as a major statement of Finlay's poetics.

2. Oakley was a plantation outside St. Francisville, Louisiana, where Audubon lived and worked during the summer and fall of 1821. (Note by John Finlay.) For more on Finlay and Audubon see Note 15 to *The Wide Porch and Other Poems* section of *"Dense Poems and Socratic Light": The Poetry of John Martin Finlay (1941–1991)* (Wiseblood Books, 2020), page 233.

Questions for an Interview with Edgar Bowers

1. This interview never took place. Edgar Bowers had agreed to be interviewed by David Middleton, who solicited questions for Bowers from Finlay and others, but in the end Bowers decided against being interviewed. Finlay was a great admirer of Bowers, whom he met sometime during the 1987–88 academic year when Finlay flew to California to do a poetry reading at the University of California at Santa Barbara. Born in Rome, Georgia, Edgar Bowers (1924–2000) taught English for most of his life at UC Santa Barbara. He is considered by many to be one of the most outstanding formalist poets of the twentieth century. He won the Bollingen Prize for poetry in 1989. Finlay deeply admired Bowers' poetry. Finlay's carefully considered questions for the Bowers interview provide insight into Finlay's own poetics and other concerns. Bowers' poem "John" appears in *In Light Apart: The Achievement of John Finlay*. Edited by David Middleton (Glenside, PA: The Aldine Press, 1999), 13-14.

Dust Jacket Comment for
The Burning Fields (1991) by David Middleton

1. This comment appeared on the back cover of the paper edition of *The Burning Fields*, by David Middleton, LSU Press, 1991. Composed and dictated in August of 1990, this was John Finlay's very last writing. His final poem, "A Prayer to the Father," was dictated to his sister Betty in the spring of 1990.

Selections from Miscellaneous Writings,
the Letters, and the Diaries

1. This statement was written on the flyleaf of a 1954 edition of Margaret Mitchell's novel *Gone with the Wind* (1936). Finlay wrote these words at age 15. He expresses a view commonly held

by southerners, both then—and, to some degree, and in some cases—now. In his later years, Finlay composed a series of poems entitled *The American Tragedies*. The poems in this sequence show a maturing of Finlay's views on American history as he examines the fate, in the nineteenth and twentieth centuries, of Native Americans, African Americans, southerners and northerners, and Roman Catholic immigrants in the South. *The American Tragedies* can be found in *"Dense Poems and Socratic Light": The Poetry of John Martin Finlay (1941–1991)* (Wiseblood Books, 2020), pages 167-177. Finlay's sisters JoAnn Finlay Hall and Betty Finlay Phillips write concerning their brother's love of the South and of books: "John's love of the South and his attitude of southerners probably was influenced a lot by Annie Laurie Cullens. She was a great historian of the South, writing poems and also chapters for a history book for elementary school. Also, our grandmother, Toxey Ard Sorrell, [and] Annie Laurie were devoted members of the UDC [United Daughters of the Confederacy]. We grew up with black families who worked for Daddy on the farm and much respect and companionship was shared. I do not remember any discussions of racial hatred." For the influence on John Finlay of two University Alabama professors with deep southern roots— Hudson Strode and August Mason—see Jeffrey Goodman's essay "The Romance of Modern Classicism: Remarks on the Life and Work of John Finlay, 1941–1991," *The Alabama Literary Review*, 14:2, Fall 2000, 28-29. In the Acknowledgments for his edition of *Jefferson Davis: Private Letters, 1823–1889* (New York: Harcourt, Brace, and World, 1966), 566, Strode wrote, "I am indebted to John M. Finlay, Instructor of English at Alabama College for valuable assistance in selecting and discarding of letters." Alabama College later become the University of Alabama at Montevallo.

2.   These paragraphs are what have survived of Finlay's introduction of Allen Tate at the University of Alabama, Tuscaloosa, sometime in mid-1960s. Compare Finlay's poem "For Allen Tate" in the *Mind and Blood* section of *"Dense Poems and Socratic Light": The Poetry of John Martin Finlay (1941–1991)* (Wiseblood Books, 2020), page 105. Finlay inscribed this poem in his copy of Tate's *Collected Essays*, 1959. Also see Finlay's "Introduction" to his book *Flaubert in Egypt and Other Essays*, printed above as well as Lewis P. Simpson's discussion of Tate and Finlay in his essay "John Finlay and the Situation of the Southern Writer" and Appendices C and D in *"Dense Poems and Socratic Light": The Poetry of John Martin Finlay (1941–1991)* (Wiseblood Books, 2020), pages 31-34, 199-213, 186-

189, and 190-193. Allen Tate (1899–1979) was a major influence on Finlay both as a poet and as an essayist.

3. Finlay repeated this anecdote from Allen Tate of an exchange between Tate and Eliot in a conversation with David Middleton. Finlay met Tate on at least two occasions and corresponded with Tate in the 1960s and 1970s. The Finlay/Tate letters are at Princeton.

4. The two poems referred to are probably "Out In the Country, Late At Night" and "Sonnet," both collected in *"Dense Poems and Socratic Light": The Poetry of John Martin Finlay (1941–1991)* (Wiseblood Books, 2020), pages 137-138 and 141.

5. Andrew Lytle (1902–1995) was a southern Agrarian novelist, scholar, and editor of *The Sewanee Review* (1961–1973). R.P. Warren is Robert Penn Warren (1905–1989), the internationally recognized southern poet, novelist, editor, and scholar. Tate and Warren were roommates at Vanderbilt University as undergraduates.

6. This comment was written by Finlay on the inside title page of his copy of *The Portable Emerson*, edited by Mark Van Doren (1946, 1968 printing). Finlay would have seen as horrifying certain aspects of Emerson's philosophy of life, especially his understanding of the nature of good and evil and his belief in the human progress toward perfection. Yvor Winters, on whose works Finlay wrote his Ph.D. dissertation, said of Emerson "the ignorance of both philosophy and theology exhibited in such ideas as these is sufficient to strike one with terror." Yvor Winters, *In Defense of Reason* (Chicago: Swallow Press, 1947), 588.

7. This brief sketch of farm life is from *The Red 3-in-1 Notebook* kept in the 1980s.

8. Finlay's sisters JoAnn Finlay Hall and Betty Finlay Phillips write that "Red was the family milk cow and almost a pet to us. John walked Red up the lane and recited Shakespeare. He also named a beautiful bull we had Prince Valiant." This brief sketch of Red is also from *The Red 3-in-1 Notebook*.

9. These comments on London architecture are handwritten on stationery from the Royal Hotel, London. The remarks are undated, but the stationery is the same as that used to make notes on the following entry concerning his September 7, 1969 visit to

the home, outside Oxford, of English poet Elizabeth Daryush. Daryush's home was on Boar's Hill. *Forms of Discovery: Critical and Historical Essays on the Forms of the Short Poem in English*, 1967: a book by Yvor Winters (1900–68). Her father: Robert Seymour Bridges (1844–1930), poet laureate of England, 1913–30. Her father's syllabic verse: a system of verse called "Neo-Miltonic syllabics" or "loose alexandrines" in which the numerical norm of each line is twelve syllables but occurring in no regular, repeated rhythmical pattern. "Persian Dawn" and "Still-Life": poems by Daryush. Winters' interpretation: "Robert Bridges and Elizabeth Daryush" in *The Uncollected Essays and Reviews of Yvor Winters*, 1973, 271-83.

10. This note was written after Finlay accidentally came down from Baton Rouge to Thibodaux, Louisiana the wrong weekend to stay with David and Francine Middleton. All extracts from the Finlay-Middleton correspondence are from copies in the private collection of David Middleton.

11. Finlay's first chapbook of verse, *The Wide Porch and Other Poems*, was not published until 1984, when Finlay was forty-three. Finlay converted to Roman Catholicism at Easter 1980 in Baton Rouge. Thomas Aquinas (1225–1274) was a Catholic priest, Dominican friar, and theologian. He has been designated as a Doctor of the Catholic Church. His *Summa Theologiae* (1265–74) had a profound impact on Finlay and influenced his decision to convert to Roman Catholicism. Once, after reading Aquinas on the family farm in Alabama, Finlay called David Middleton and exclaimed in his Alabama accent that compared to the thought in Aquinas' works there is "NO THAWT! NO THAWT!" in the modern world.

12. Middleton's Ovid poem was never written, but Finlay composed a poem entitled "Ovid in Exile." See *"Dense Poems and Socratic Light": The Poetry of John Martin Finlay (1941–1991)* (Wiseblood Books, 2020), page 70. According to classical tradition, the lyric poet drinks wine from a cup for inspiration, but the epic poet drinks water from a wooden bowl. Flaubert: See Finlay's essay "Flaubert in Egypt" and the notes thereto, printed above (pages 35-46 and 311-312), as well as Finlay's distillation above (pages 270-271) of Flaubert's aesthetics as derived from Flaubert's letters. Finlay's comment on "luminous detail" is in harmony with his writing the post-symbolist poem, a poem whose argument proceeds mainly, if not entirely, by way of precise descriptive details charged with definite meaning.

13. The phrase "the iron sky" appears in Finlay's poem "The Dead and the Season," line 10. See also "The Wide Porch," line 1. *"Dense Poems and Socratic Light": The Poetry of John Martin Finlay (1941–1991)* (Wiseblood Books, 2020), pages 64 and 31.

14. See *The Green Corfu Diary* entries (pages 255-257).

15. Harry Duncan (1916–1997) was one of America's most distinguished makers of hand-printed books. Duncan published Finlay's chapbook *The Salt of Exposure* in 1988 on The Cummington Press. Over the years Duncan also published books of poems by Wallace Stevens, Yvor Winters, Robert Lowell, and Allen Tate. On the poet and the printer as "joint creators" of a book, see Finlay's poem "Of Harry Duncan, Bookmaker," in *"Dense Poems and Socratic Light": The Poetry of John Martin Finlay (1941–1991)* (Wiseblood Books, 2020), page 130.

16. By "the poem" Finlay meant his poem "Ovid in Exile." *"Dense Poems and Socratic Light": The Poetry of John Martin Finlay (1941–1991)* (Wiseblood Books, 2020), page 70. Dryden is John Dryden (1631–1700), the English neoclassical poet who often wrote rhyming couplets. Hopkins is Gerard Manley Hopkins (1844–1889), Jesuit priest and experimentalist English poet.

17. Donald E. Stanford (1913–1998) was editor of *The Southern Review* at Louisiana State University and Finlay's major professor for his doctoral studies at LSU. Stanford, a former student of Yvor Winters (1900–1968), was also a formalist poet and a scholar of modern poetry—especially of Robert Bridges (1844–1930), who was poet laureate of England and the father of poet Elizabeth Daryush (1887–1977). All extracts from the Finlay-Stanford correspondence are from The John Finlay Papers, Louisiana State University.

18. Finlay sent Stanford this note on a postcard from the Greek island of Corfu, 1972. See selected entries above from Finlay's *The Green Corfu Diary*.

19. Janet Lewis [Winters] (1899–1998), poet and novelist, was married to Yvor Winters (1900–1968) whose poems and critical prose had a profound impact on Finlay. Lewis's poems on American Indians influenced some of Finlay's poems in the late sequence *The American Tragedies*. A letter from Finlay to Lewis about this sequence appears as Appendix E in *"Dense Poems and Socratic Light": The Poetry of John*

Martin Finlay (1941–1991) (Wiseblood Books, 2020), page 194. For a meditation on both the birth and the development of "the archaic Greek mind," see Finlay's poem *"Origo mentis"* in the *Mind and Blood* section of *"Dense Poems and Socratic Light,"* pages 50-51. Janet Lewis Winters sent David Middleton a copy of this letter to her from Finlay after Finlay's death in 1991.

20. Stephen (Steve) Utz was a longtime friend of Finlay's from his Baton Rouge days and is a professor in the School of Law at the University of Connecticut. See selected entries below from Finlay's *The Green Paris Diary*. Finlay left Corfu in 1973 and spent part of 1973 and 1974 in Paris. All extracts from the Finlay-Utz correspondence are from The John Finlay Papers, Louisiana State University.

21. This letter was written from the Finlay farm in Enterprise. Geoffrey Hill (1932–2016) was a highly regarded English poet.

22. Elizabeth Daryush (1887–1977) was an English poet and daughter of English poet laureate Robert Bridges (1844–1930). Thomas Hardy (1840–1928) was an English novelist and poet (1840–1928). Gerard Manley Hopkins (1844–1889) was an English poet, Jesuit priest, and friend of Robert Bridges. Finlay refers in this letter to his meeting with Daryush on September 7, 1969. Notes Finlay recorded about this meeting are printed above. page 240.

23. Lewis P. Simpson (1916–2005) was an editor of *The Southern Review* and a renowned scholar of American and Southern literature. The Finlay-Simpson correspondence is especially notable for discussions of Finlay's essays that appear in *Flaubert in Egypt and Other Essays*. All extracts from the Finlay-Simpson correspondence are from The John Finlay Papers, Louisiana State University. John Locke (1632–1704) was an English philosopher. The *Essay* referred to is Locke's *Essay Concerning Human Understanding* (1689). The ideas in this letter became a part of Finlay's essay on John Henry Newman. Sewanee is The University of the South located in Sewanee, Tennessee.

24. See Finlay's poem "Under the Reign of the Actor," *"Dense Poems and Socratic Light": The Poetry of John Martin Finlay (1941–1991)* (Wiseblood Books, 2020), page 69. By "that actor" Finlay means President Ronald Reagan (1991–2004; president, 1981–1989). Finlay's sister JoAnn Finlay recalls concerning their brother John's political views, "We all talked politics with conservative views

. . . I believe John was a conservative but not die-hard." It may be noted here that Simpson said of Finlay's essay "Flaubert in Egypt" "I really want it—bad. [for *The Southern Review*] Flaubert in Enterprise, Alabama is what you are truly writing about, I think, but we won't change the title." The essay, however, was already under consideration at *The Hudson Review*, whose editor, Frederick Morgan, accepted it.

25. Jean Finlay, Letter to Lewis P. Simpson: Though not a letter by Finlay himself, this letter from Finlay's mother to Simpson, written some months after her son's death on February 17, 1991, seems an appropriate way to end this section of extracts from John Finlay's letters.

26. This entry is from *The Baton Rouge Diary*, 1980 and may serve as an introduction to Finlay's diary keeping. See Finlay's two translations from the Latin verse of Samuel Johnson (1709–1794) in *Mind and Blood* (1992), "After Samuel Johnson's Latin Poem to Thomas Lawrence, M.D." and "After Samuel Johnson's *Summe Pater*.") in *"Dense Poems and Socratic Light": The Poetry of John Martin Finlay (1941–1991)* (Wiseblood Books, 2020), pages 78 and 79.

27. Be patient . . . : This is the opening entry in Finlay's earliest surviving diary (and perhaps his first such diary) *The Blue Horse Composition Notebook* (1961–1966). December 17, 1961.

28. The little girl: This is probably an idea for a short story, or perhaps a story told to Finlay.

29. The Cuban Missile Crisis, October 1962, when the United States and the Soviet Union seemed to be on the verge of nuclear war. Jean Orr and Neely Bruce were friends of John Finlay.

30. I had a dream about Heaven . . . . Claybank is the cemetery near Ozark, Alabama, in which members of the Finlay family are buried. See Finlay's poem "At Claybank" and the note to the poem in *"Dense Poems and Socratic Light": The Poetry of John Martin Finlay (1941–1991)* (Wiseblood Books, 2020), page 32; note, pages 227-228.

31. A possible poem . . . : This entry for a "possible poem" recalls a scene similar to that of Finlay's early poem "A Voyage," in *"Dense Poems and Socratic Light": The Poetry of John Martin Finlay (1941–1991)* (Wiseblood Books, 2020), pages 138-139. Norman

McMillan is Professor Emeritus of English at the University of Montevallo in Montevallo, Alabama, and an Alabama writer.

32. Murray House was a residence provided by the Episcopal Church for Episcopal students at the University of Alabama, Tuscaloosa. Finlay, who converted from Methodism to the Episcopal Church at Easter of 1962, stayed in Murray House 1964–1966 while a student at Alabama.

33. Compare comments by English poet W.H. Auden (1907–1973): ". . . a poet is, before anything else, a person who is passionately in love with language. . . . [this] is certainly the sign by which one recognizes whether a young man is potentially a poet or not. 'Why do you want to write poetry?' If the young man answers, 'I have important things to say,' then he is not a poet. If he answers, 'I like hanging around words listening to what they say,' then maybe he is going to be a poet." W.H. Auden, "Squares and Oblongs," in *Poets at Work*. Edited by C.D. Abbott. (New York: Harcourt, Brace, & Co., 1948), 171.

34. This entry is an early example of the kind of philosophical thinking that Finlay, in later years, would develop in his essays. On the nature of evil, see Finlay's poem "'If a Man Drive Out a Demon. . .,'" in *"Dense Poems and Socratic Light": The Poetry of John Martin Finlay (1941–1991)* (Wiseblood Books, 2020), page 103.

35. T.S. Eliot (1888–1965) is the American-born modern poet famous for poems such as *The Love Song of J. Alfred Prufrock* (1915), *The Waste Land* (1922), *Ash Wednesday* (1930), and *The Four Quartets* (1943). In 1927, Eliot became a British citizen and joined the Church of England. In 1948, he was awarded the Noble Prize in Literature. He died in London.

36. This is Finlay's emphatic note to himself as a young writer to devote himself to his craft. Compare his later list (ca. 1970) of the qualities of a good poem, "Notes for the Perfect Poem," page 272.

37. Laurie is probably Annie Laurie Cullens. See Note 1 on pages 338-339. As in the works of William Faulkner, this idea for a story shows the complexities of southern history and a southerner's consciousness of such history. See Finlay's early poem "In Memory of William Faulkner" in *"Dense Poems and Socratic Light": The Poetry of John Martin Finlay (1941–1991)* (Wiseblood Books, 2020), page 152.

38. Holy Saturday is the day between Good Friday and Easter Sunday. Claybank, near Ozark, Alabama, is the final resting-place of members of the extended Finlay family. On tending to these family graves, see Finlay's poem "At Claybank" in *"Dense Poems and Socratic Light": The Poetry of John Martin Finlay (1941–1991)* (Wiseblood Books, 2020), page 32.

39. Finlay's diaries record such statements either as being interesting in themselves or in some cases as possible seeds for stories or poems.

40. John Crowe Ransom (1888–1974) was a member of The Fugitive Poets and the Southern Agrarians, two important groups of twentieth-century southern writers. He was a contributor to *I'll Take My Stand* (1930), a defense of the agrarian way of life against industrialism. Ransom taught English at Vanderbilt, then became founding editor of *The Kenyon Review* at Kenyon College in Gambier, Ohio. Finlay also met other important southern writers including Andrew Lytle, Allen Tate, Robert Penn Warren, Eudora Welty, and Edgar Bowers.

41. Finlay's sister JoAnn Finlay Hall says, "I believe he was referring to MaMa, our [maternal] grandmother. There was a Confederate statue monument in the town square by the courthouse in Ozark. Miss Allie was Allie Garner, MaMa's friend and the mayor was Douglas Brown. Mother never joined the UDC and the statue, I believe, is still there today. I do not recall this incident happening, but the UDC in Ozark was very much alive with the ladies. John spoke to one of their meetings and was in the Ozark paper. Ozark was an older town and had many families with ties to the Confederacy." U. D. C. is United Daughters of the Confederacy. "The General Organization of the United Daughters of the Confederacy was founded in Nashville, Tennessee, on September 10, 1894, by Mrs. Caroline Meriwether Goodlett of Tennessee as Founder and Mrs. Lucian H. (Anna Davenport) Raines of Georgia as Co- Founder. The UDC is the outgrowth of numerous ladies' hospital associations, sewing societies and knitting circles that worked throughout the South during the War Between the States to supply the needs of the soldiers. After the War, these organizations kept pace with the changing times and evolved into cemetery, memorial, monument and Confederate Home Associations and Auxiliaries to Camps of Confederate Veterans. Out of these many local groups, which for nearly 30 years rendered untold service to the South and her people, two statewide organizations came

into existence as early as 1890: the Daughters of the Confederacy in Missouri and the Ladies Auxiliary of the Confederate Soldier's Home in Tennessee. The association with these two organizations makes the UDC the oldest patriotic lineage organization in the country." (From "History of the UDC," United Daughters of the Confederacy, online website.)

42. Dr. Fairchild. Not yet identified.

43. Compare Finlay's "Editors' Preface" to the interview with Eudora Welty, page 223, and the notes from *The Baton Rouge Diary* (1980), pages 270-271, on Flaubert's aesthetics. Also of interest are comments Finlay made on the autobiographical nature of seemingly objective critical prose, for which see David Middleton's "'The Deathless Word': John Finlay and the Triumph Over Gnosticism," Appendix B. T.S. Eliot's doctrine of the non-personal "objective correlative": "The only way of expressing emotion in the form of art is by finding an 'objective correlative'; in other words, a situation, a chain of events which shall be the form of that particular emotion; such that when the external facts, which must terminate in sensory experience, are given, the emotion is immediately evoked." T.S. Eliot, "Hamlet and His Problems." *The Sacred Wood* (London: Methuen, 1920), 100.

44. *Light in August* (1932) is a novel by southern writer William Faulkner (1897–1962).

45. Another remark probably recorded as an aphorism worth remembering.

46. December 1970. Ma and I. Ma was Finlay's paternal grandmother, Mattie Coston Finlay (1887–1976). Of this journal entry, JoAnn Finlay Hall has stated, "I remember John saying at one time poets or writers could embellish on experiences or happenings or something like that. Unless he saw the star twice, this was my recollection. I think it was at Christmas or in the winter. We all ran into the dining room and looking out the window saw this gigantic white star very low in the sky. We were stunned by its brightness. I think I remember hearing it was the North Star and comes only once in someone's lifetime. I'm sure Ma was there as I think it was Christmas as we related it to the star the Wise Men saw. It was something we were all spellbound at seeing. I remember the excitement we all had."

47. After the fall . . . .: For another statement by Finlay on the Christian doctrine of the Fall of Man see comments by Finlay recorded in David Middleton's "'The Deathless Word': John Finlay and the Triumph Over Gnosticism," Appendix B, page 286. This diary entry affirms Finlay's commitment to writing traditional metrical (measured) verse a well as his belief in the Christian doctrine of the Fall of Man.

48. All art is basically conservative: This statement provides evidence as to why Finlay was committed to traditionalist verse.

49. There is no art in hell: This humorous remark is further confirmation of the seriousness of Finlay's commitment to the literary art.

50. "When working under limitations": Like the two immediately previous entries, this entry demonstrates Finlay's commitment to writing metrical poetry on important human experiences and concerns. Goethe is the German writer Johann Wolfgang von Goethe (1749–1832).

51. "But on the other hand": Like the three entries just above, this recorded quotation from his reading (Finlay was an avid and constant reader all of his life) shows Finlay in these early years developing the poetics that would inform his mature poems. Mark Van Doren (1894–1972) was a longtime professor of English at Columbia University.

52. Jim of life after death: Jim is not yet identified. Waldo is probably Finlay's Uncle Waldo Ard. This entry is another example of Finlay recording a casually made remark that had philosophical implications. Finlay once asked a friend of his, David Moreland, whether he thought much about death. Moreland replied, "Well, once in a while." Finlay said, "I think about it all the time."

53. A journal entry on a visit to London: The complete journal has not survived. These reflections on the spiritual implications of London architecture—modern and pre-modern—were probably made in September of 1969 when Finlay flew to England to meet poet Elizabeth Daryush.

54. *The Green Corfu Diary*: Finlay lived on the Greek island of Corfu during parts of 1972 and 1973. Finlay's sisters, JoAnn Finlay Hall and Betty Finlay Phillips, recall the reason for their brother's going

to Corfu: "We believe John went to Corfu because he wanted to see the history of the [Greek] philosophers. He did not work for anyone from Alabama. He may have done construction, but we know he worked in the olive tree orchards. He spoke of how the workers and he took a nap at noon in the orchard." Jeffrey Goodman writes of Finlay's time on Corfu and Finlay's poem "Odysseus": "Corfu was purported to be the mythic island of Phaeacia where Odysseus visited King Alcinous. There he listened with high wonder as the rhapsode sang of the hero's past adventures. This no doubt attracted Finlay strongly. Apropos, he began the brief persona poem 'Odysseus' (in honor of Yvor Winters) by saying 'I could not know the meaning of that time / . . . Until I heard the voyage beat out in words.'" On working in "olive tree orchards" see Finlay's evocation of such orchards in his poem "In the Adriatic." Both "In the Adriatic" and "Odysseus" appear in *"Dense Poems and Socratic Light": The Poetry of John Martin Finlay (1941–1991)* (Wiseblood Books, 2020), pages 33 and 42.

55. On Saturday afternoon: Compare similar imagery in Finlay's poem "Off Highway 27," set in rural south Alabama. *"Dense Poems and Socratic Light": The Poetry of John Martin Finlay (1941–1991)* (Wiseblood Books, 2020), page 108. This entry, and others, especially in *The Green Paris Diary*, seem to have been written as finished works of literary art meant for eventual sharing with other people.

56. A walk down to Pamela's house: Pamela is not yet identified. This is another entry that finds parallels between life on Corfu and life back home in Alabama on the family farm.

57. Easter on Corfu: This would be Easter as celebrated by the Greek Orthodox Church. In 1972, Easter fell on April 2 in accordance with Orthodox calculation using the Julian calendar.

58. Yesterday James and I . . . : Kassiopi was, traditionally, a small fishing village but is now also a tourist resort. It is located on the northeast coast of Corfu. Pelekas is a hillside town on Corfu with beautiful beaches nearby. Glyfada is a suburb of Athens.

59. James, Janique, and I: James and Janique are not yet identified. Both moved on to Paris where Finlay writes of them in his Paris diary. Finlay records several times in this diary his being moved by the mountains on Corfu and the stars seen above at night.

60. Finlay spent time in Paris in 1973 and 1974. This diary expresses Finlay's hope that he had at last found an intellectual home where he could best write poetry. Many of his most evocative entries are from this diary.

61. I bought this notebook. See Note 60 above.

62. Yesterday the Eiffel Tower: Gide is Parisian-born French author André Gide (1869-1951). Gide won the Nobel Prize in Literature in 1947.

63. In St. Séverin . . .: Located on the Left Bank, St. Séverin is a Roman Catholic church rebuilt in the Gothic style in the fifteenth and sixteenth centuries. Its history can be traced back to Séverin of Paris, a hermit of the fourth and fifth centuries, who lived by the river Seine.

64. On the train: Charleville is the hometown of French poet Arthur Rimbaud (1854–1891). *A Season in Hell* is the English translation of Rimbaud's *Une Saison en Enfer* (1873). See Finlay's poem "The *Illumination* of Arthur Rimbaud" and the accompanying note in *"Dense Poems and Socratic Light": The Poetry of John Martin Finlay (1941–1991)* (Wiseblood Books, 2020), poem, page 97; note, pages 247-248. Meeting a French girl on the train who had read Rimbaud in Florida, not far from Finlay's home, in south Alabama, matches similar correspondences in the Corfu diary. Back home in Alabama in 1974, Finlay wrote in a diary entry addressed to himself: "You must make a Paris in your own mind." See also the poem "Ovid in Exile" and the note to that poem in *"Dense Poems and Socratic Light": The Poetry of John Martin Finlay (1941–1991)* (Wiseblood Books, 2020), poem, page 70; note, page 240.

65. I bought a copy . . . : *Charmes* (1922) is a book of poems by French writer Paul Valéry (1871–1945). See Finlay's essay on Valéry, printed above, as well as Finlay's poem, "The Graves by the Sea," his translation of Valéry's "Le Cimetière marin," which is included in *"Dense Poems and Socratic Light": The Poetry of John Martin Finlay (1941–1991)* (Wiseblood Books, 2020), pages 116-120. *The [International] Herald Tribune* was one of many names given over the years to an international English-language newspaper read all over the world, especially by expatriates from English-speaking countries.

66. James and I . . .: This is another example of a well-crafted diary

entry, almost like a miniature short story or prose poem. The same could be said of most of the entries from the Paris diary that follow. The Metro is the subway system in Paris.

67. On the walk to . . .: The Île St.-Louis is an island in the river Seine in Paris. La Pont de la Tournelle is an arch bridge over the river Seine.

68. The small square in front of St. Sulpice . . .: St. Sulpice is the second largest church in Paris, after Notre-Dame. It is named after St. Sulpitious the Pious (d. 644)

69. We sat and then leaned . . .: See Note 68 immediately above.

70. Sunday. A bitter cold . . .: St. Julien Le Pauvre is a thirteenth-century church built in the Romanesque style. It is a Melkite Greek Rite Catholic church. The word *fouarre* is French for *thatching* or *straw*. Dante: "That's the eternal light of Sigier, who, / Lecturing down Straw Street, hammered home / Invidious truths, as logic taught him so." *Paradiso*, Canto X, lines 136-138. Trans. Dorothy Sayers and Barbara Reynolds (New York: Penguin, 1962), 139. Cronin: Vincent Cronin, author of *The Companion Guide to Paris* (1963).

71. Dec. 18, 1973: I walked all the way . . .: The Tuileries is a public park and garden between the Louvre Museum and the Place de la Concorde.

72. Dec. 19, 1973: I walked and walked today. Jeu de Paume: an arts center in the Tuleries Gardens. Existentialism ". . . emphasizes existence rather than essence and sees the inadequacy of the human reason to explain the enigma of the universe as the basic philosophical question. . . . the existentialist assumes . . . that the significant fact is that we and things in general exist but that these things have no meaning for us except as we through acting upon them can create meaning. . . . [The existentialist tends to] distrust concepts and to emphasize experiential concreteness. . . . A part of [the existentialist's] awareness is the sense man has of meaninglessness in the outer world; this meaninglessness produces in him a discomfort, an anxiety, a loneliness in the face of man's limitations and a desire to invest experience with meaning by acting upon the world, although efforts to act in a meaningless 'absurd' world would lead to anguish, greater loneliness, and despair. Man is totally free, but he is also wholly responsible for what he makes

of himself. This freedom and responsibility are the sources for his most intense anxiety." From "Existentialism" in *A Handbook to Literature* by C. Hugh Holman (New York: The Odyssey Press, 1972), 212-13.

73. James and I went shopping . . .: The American Center: "Founded in 1931, the center was a frequent gathering point for American expatriate artists and writers before World War II and even more so in the late 1940's and 50's. It also organized classes in English and in modern American dance that were very popular with young French people." "American Center in Paris Must Sell Its Home." Alan Riding, January 25, 1996, online.

74. I walked back to CBS tonight: Finlay worked at CBS in Paris, most likely as a janitor.

75. Dec. 25, 1973: Christmas dinner . . .: Compare this entry to the entry for December 19, 1973.

76. Dec. 26 and 27, 1973 diary "entries": Finlay's initial elation about living in Paris ended with these final entries. A final date, "Dec. 28," does not even have the word "Nothing" written down. Later, back in America, Finlay would write down a reminder to himself: "You must make a Paris in your own mind." (See Note 64 above.)

77. The following passages are selected from detailed notes in *The Orange Journal* (1970s–80s) on psychiatric patients in Bryce Hospital, Tuscaloosa, Alabama, where Finlay briefly worked, answering the telephone, in 1974. Compare his poem on some of these patients, "The Locked Wards" and draft lines for this poem in *"Dense Poems and Socratic Light": The Poetry of John Martin Finlay (1941–1991)* (Wiseblood Books, 2020), pages 102 and 159-161. The note to "The Locked Wards" in that poetry volume reads as follows: Finlay worked at Bryce Hospital in Tuscaloosa, Alabama in 1974. "The Locked Wards" is based on Finlay's observations of mental patients in Bryce, whose original name, when founded in 1861, was the Alabama State Hospital for the Insane. Finlay kept a journal (*The Orange Journal*) in which he made many notes about these patients. JoAnn Finlay Hall writes the following concerning "The Locked Wards": "Bryce was the state mental institution located in Tuscaloosa. Our grandmother's husband, Warren Martin Sorrell, went there in his 30's and died there. It was always very hushed about as my grandmother never talked about him. They had four small children and she went home to

live with her mother in Ozark [Alabama] in the house of the poem 'The Wide Porch.' I remember John looking his records up at the hospital. . . . Betty [Finlay Phillips] recalls John answering a suicide hot line while working at Bryce Hospital." *The Orange Journal* was kept after Finlay was back in America, but the journal itself—Vélin D'Angoulême—was purchased in Paris.

78. "The House . . .": Compare these notes to Finlay's poem "The Wide Porch," in *"Dense Poems and Socratic Light": The Poetry of John Martin Finlay (1941–1991)* (Wiseblood Books, 2020), page 31.

79. "You must make a Paris in your own mind": Compare this entry to the whole sequence of entries above from *The Green Paris Diary*. Also see Note 64 above.

80. From *The Baton Rouge Diary*: This journal was kept during the year Finlay finished writing his Ph.D. dissertation on Yvor Winters at Louisiana State University. Finlay was awarded the Ph.D. in December of 1980 and in the summer of 1981 returned for good to his family's farm in Alabama. *The Baton Rouge Diary* is the darkest of Finlay's diaries. Its entries indicate deep spiritual, psychological, and sexual conflicts in his thoughts and actions.

81. Compare Finlay's essay "Flaubert in Egypt" as well as his poem by the same title in *Mind and Blood* (1992).

82. This important statement of Finlay's poetics is from what survives of a journal kept in the 1970s. Note 2 is almost certainly repeated as Note 4 for emphasis.

83. This passage is from Finlay's Ph.D. dissertation, "'The Unfleshed Eye': A Study of Intellectual Theism in the Poetry and Criticism of Yvor Winters." Directed by Donald E. Stanford. Louisiana State University, Baton Rouge, Louisiana, 1980, page 145. Compare the poem "Salt from the Winter Sea" in *"Dense Poems and Socratic Light": The Poetry of John Martin Finlay (1941–1991)* (Wiseblood Books, 2020), page 88.

84. This passage is from the closing paragraph of Finlay's Ph.D. dissertation, 194-195. Yvor Winters' completion of his literary work just before his death may be compared to Finlay's life and work.

85. St. Germain l'Auxerrois. This church's bell was rung on the night of August 23, 1572 to signal the beginning of the St. Bartholomew's

Day Massacre.

86. The Massacre of St. Bartholomew's Day occurred in Paris on August 24 and 25, 1572. Thousands of Huguenot Protestants were slain, first in Paris and later in other parts of France.

APPENDICES

Appendix A

1. This essay by Lewis P. Simpson originally appeared as the foreword to Finlay's book *Hermetic Light: Essays on the Gnostic Spirit in Modern Literature and Thought* (Santa Barbara, CA: John Daniel and Company, 1994), 9-12.

Appendix B

1. This essay by David Middleton originally appeared as the afterword to Finlay's book *Hermetic Light: Essays on the Gnostic Spirit in Modern Literature and Thought* (Santa Barbara, CA: John Daniel and Company, 1994), 141-57.

Appendix C

1. This is a revised and corrected version of answers sent by David Middleton in 1999 in response to questions posed by Jeffrey Goodman. Goodman's essay "The Romance of Modern Classicism: Remarks on the Life and Work of John Finlay, 1941–1991," *The Alabama Literary Review,* 14:2, Fall 2000, 25-49, remains the best bio-critical introduction so far published on Finlay's life and works.

Appendix D

1. "The Break-In" appeared in *The Southern Review,* Autumn 2016, 52.4, 650-52. The poem by John Finlay quoted from as an epigraph was written for his friend and fellow poet Lindon Stall (b. 1948) whose chapbook of verse, *Responsoria,* appeared in 1983 on R. L. Barth Press. I am indebted to Mr. Stall for his memory of the cinder-block bookshelves in Finlay's Baton Rouge apartment. It has been suggested that Finlay's dying query—"Plato?"— was addressed to some guiding figure whom Finlay in his mind

surely saw and thought to be the spirit of Plato coming to receive him. It may have been uttered in response to his perception of one greater than Plato, a divine being whom Finlay would have fully recognized only in passing through and beyond death. John Finlay's two major books of verse and prose, referred to in the poem, are *Mind and Blood: The Collected Poems of John Finlay* (1992) and *Hermetic Light: Essays on the Gnostic Spirit in Modern Literature and Thought* (1994). Works by Finlay alluded to in "The Break-In" include the poems "Narcissus in Fire," "The Case of Holmes," and "The Symposium for Socrates." Finlay's essay on Socrates and Alcibiades—"The Night of Alcibiades"—is also relevant. The names in stanza one are those of writers who deeply influenced Finlay. Finlay wrote essays about some of them. The break-in as described in the poem happened in Baton Rouge, Louisiana in the 1970s. Finlay grew up on his family's farm in Alabama. There he spent the last ten years of his life (1981–1991) reading and writing as his health slowly failed.

A Recollection

A Recollection of John Finlay, the Man and Storyteller

1. Cathy Edmonston was an administrative assistant in the Department of English at LSU in the 1970s–80s. Tom Watson: Dr. Thomas Watson was a professor of English. Faye Rifkin was the longtime secretary of the Department of English at LSU. This recollection is on page 365.

John Finlay: A Bibliography (1962–2020)

Books, Chapbooks, Cards

The Wide Porch and Other Poems. 18 poems. Florence, Kentucky: Robert L. Barth, 1984.

Between the Gulfs. 17 poems. Notes by Finlay on the poems *"Origo mentis"* and "Death in Asia Minor." Florence, Kentucky: Robert L. Barth, 1986.

The Salt of Exposure. 19 poems. Omaha, Nebraska: Printed by Harry Duncan on The Cummington Press, 1988.

A Prayer to the Father: Poetry and Prose by John Finlay. Selected and edited from The John Finlay Papers by David Middleton. 25 poems. 9 excerpts from Finlay's diaries. Thibodaux, Louisiana: Blue Heron Press, 1992.

Mind and Blood: The Collected Poems of John Finlay. Edited and with a Preface by David Middleton. Santa Barbara, California: John Daniel and Company, 1992. This edition assembles the four earlier collections (with important late authorial emendations of several poems in the two Barth chapbooks) as well as 10 uncollected poems published in literary journals.

Hermetic Light: Essays on the Gnostic Spirit in Modern Literature and Thought. Introduction and six essays. Foreword by Lewis P. Simpson. Edited and with an Afterword by David Middleton. Santa Barbara, California: John Daniel and Company, 1994. Main title chosen by the editor from a line of one of Finlay's poems, "The *Illumination* of Arthur Rimbaud." Finlay's title for this book, *Flaubert in Egypt and Other Essays,* could not be used for this edition.

Notes for the Perfect Poem. Four-page, one-fold card. 14 prose statements. Excerpt from Finlay's poem *"Origo mentis"* along with a brief historical comment on the background of poem by David Middleton. Thibodaux, Louisiana: Blue Heron Press, 1994.

The Deathless Word: Christian Meditations from the Diaries and Poetry of John Finlay. Four-page, one-fold card. 4 journal entries. Excerpt from Finlay's poem "The Autobiography of a Benedictine." Thibodaux, Louisiana: Blue Heron Press, 1994.

The American Tragedies: A Chronology of Six Poems. Edited and with an Afterword by David Middleton. Robert L. Barth, 1997.

John Finlay: A Commemoration Upon the Occasion of the Twenty-Fifth Anniversary of His Death on February 17, 1991. Edited by David Middleton and John P. Doucet. Privately printed in a limited edition, 2016. Previously unpublished and uncollected poems, letters, diary entries, and other prose from The John Finlay Papers at Louisiana State University and other sources.

Dissertation

"'The Unfleshed Eye': A Study of Intellectual Theism in the Poetry and Criticism of Yvor Winters." Directed by Donald E. Stanford. Louisiana State University, Baton Rouge, Louisiana, 1980. Now available on-line.

Previously Uncollected Essays

"Elizabeth Daryush." *The Dictionary of Literary Biography: British Poets, 1914–45.* Vol. 20. Edited by Donald E. Stanford. Detroit: Gale Research Company, 1983.109-12.

"The Night of Alcibiades." *The Hudson Review.* 47.1 (Spring 1994). 57-79.

"The Socratics and the Flight from This World." *Hellas.* 8.2 (Fall/Winter 1997). 63-80.

A Statement on Poetics. *Louisiana English Journal.* 32 (new series). 1996. 14-15. Three photographs of John Finlay. 12, 17, 18. The Mary Roberts Rinehart Foundation Proposal.

Uncollected Poems

"The Return." *The Epigrammatist.* 6.1 (April, 1995). 20.

"Told from the Nineteenth Century." Revised version superseding the version available for publication in *Mind and Blood. Louisiana English Journal* 3.2 (new series). 1996. 16.

Book Reviews

"N. Scott Momaday's *Angle of Geese.*" Review of *Angle of Geese* by N. Scott Momaday. *The Southern Review* 11.3 (Summer 1975). 658-61.

"Elizabeth Daryush." Review of *Collected Poems* by Elizabeth Daryush. *The Southern Review* 14.2 (Spring 1978). 404-08.

"Robert Bridges." Review of *In the Classic Mode: The Achievement of Robert Bridges* by Donald E. Stanford. *PN Review* (Manchester, England) 6.6 (1979). 78-79.

"Dick Davis' *Seeing the World*." Review of *Seeing the World* by Dick Davis. *The Southern Review* 17.3 (Summer 1981). 654-56.

"Grosvenor Powell's *Language as Being*." Review of *Language as Being in the Poetry of Yvor Winters* by Grosvenor Powell. *The Southern Review* 17.4 (Autumn 1981). 1001-03.

"The Poetry of Raymond Oliver." Review of *Entries* and *To Be Plain* by Raymond Oliver. *The Southern Review* 19.1 (Winter 1983). 178-80.

"Three from the Symposium." Review of *Witnesses* by Edgar Bowers, *The Birthday of the Infanta* by Janet Lewis, and *Many Houses* by Charles Gullans. *The Southern Review* 19.1 (Winter 1983). 181-83.

Other

Strode, Hudson. *Jefferson Davis: Private Letters, 1823–1889*. New York: Harcourt, Brace and World, 1966. "I am indebted to John M. Finlay, Instructor in English at Alabama College, for valuable assistance in the selecting and discarding of letters." Comment by Strode on page 566 (Acknowledgments).

The Cartesian Lawnmower and Other Poems by Don Stanford. Florence, Kentucky: Robert L. Barth, 1984. Chosen, edited, and arranged by John Finlay. [unattributed].

"Of Harry Duncan" in *A Garland for Harry Duncan* (Austin, Texas: W. Thomas Taylor, 1989). 25.

Untitled jacket comment for the paperback edition of *The Burning Fields* [poetry] by David Middleton. Baton Rouge, Louisiana: LSU Press, 1991. Finlay's last writing, dictated from his sickbed in August of 1990.

"After Samuel Johnson's Latin Poem to Thomas Lawrence, M.D." and "After Johnson's *Summe Pater*." Translations from the Latin. *Samuel Johnson: Selected Latin Poems Translated by Various Hands*. Edited by Bob Barth. Edgewood, Kentucky: Robert L. Barth, 1987; 1995. 11, 13 in 1995 edition.

Manuscripts, Papers, Library, Future Projects

The John Finlay Papers. LSU Libraries, Lower Mississippi Valley Special Collections, Louisiana State University, Baton Rouge, Louisiana. These papers contain Finlay's published books, his journals, copies of *Comment* (the University of Alabama [Tuscaloosa] literary journal Finlay edited and contributed to in the years 1962–67, including an interview with Eudora Welty), miscellaneous items, letters to Finlay from poets such as Robert L. Barth, Edgar Bowers, and Janet Lewis, and letters from Finlay to Janet Lewis, David Middleton, Helen Pinkerton, Donald E. Stanford, and others. Letters from Finlay to Lewis P. Simpson are in *The Southern Review* files and the Simpson Papers at LSU. Books from John Finlay's library containing significant marginalia are in the possession of David Middleton (Finlay's literary executor). See fuller note below on The John Finlay Papers.

Works About John Finlay

Barbarese, J. T. "Modernity and the Divided Intellect." Review-essay on *Hermetic Light: Essays on the Gnostic Spirit in Modern Literature and Thought* by John Finlay. *The Sewanee Review* 102.3 (Summer 1994). 486-92.

Barth, R. L. "'Plainest Naked Truth': John Finlay's *The Salt of Exposure.*" Review of *The Salt of Exposure* by John Finlay. *The Southern Review* 25.1 (Winter 1989). 255-58.

Barth, R. L. Review of *Mind and Blood: The Collected Poems of John Finlay. The Classical Outlook* 70.4 (Summer 1993). 148-49.

Clark, William Bedford. "Testament of a Traditionalist." Review of *Mind and Blood: The Collected Poems of John Finlay. The Sewanee Review* 101.2 (Spring 1993). lxix–lxx.

Clark, William Bedford. "'The Sweated Line': The Unclaimed Legacy of John Finlay." A review-essay on *Mind and Blood: The Collected Poems of John Finlay. Explorations: The Levy Humanities Series, University of Southwestern Louisiana* VII (1993). 53-61.

Davenport, Guy. Review of *Mind and Blood: The Collected Poems of John Finlay. Louisiana Literature 101* (Spring 1993). 70-72.

Goodman, Jeffrey. "Heroic and Tragic Story: Spotlight Shines on Poet's Work Several Years after His Death." *The Mobile Register.* 25 January 1998. 5D.

Goodman, Jeffrey. "The Romance of Modern Classicism: Remarks on the Life and Work of John Finlay, 1941–1991." *Alabama Literary Review.* 14.2, Fall 2000, 25-49. A major essay on Finlay.

Hammond, Ralph. [Poet Laureate of Alabama]. "John Finlay's Flowering of Poetry." Review of *Mind and Blood: The Collected Poems of John Finlay. Alabama Arts* 11.1 (Spring 1993). 36.

Jacket comments by Donald E. Stanford, Janet Lewis, Dick Davis, and R. L. Barth for *Mind and Blood: The Collected Poems of John Finlay.* Santa Barbara, California: John Daniel and Company, 1992. Back of dust jacket.

Jacket comments by Helen Pinkerton Trimpi, Guy Davenport, W.S. Di Piero, and William Bedford Clark for *Hermetic Light: Essays on the Gnostic Spirit in Modern Literature and Thought*. Santa Barbara, California: John Daniel and Company, 1994. Back of dust jacket.

Middleton, David. "With Constant Light: The Poetry of John Finlay." Review of *The Wide Porch and Other Poems* by John Finlay. *The Southern Review* 21.2 (Spring 1985). 558-63.

Middleton, David. "Featured Poet: John Finlay." *Poetry Pilot*. The Academy of American Poets. (January 1990). 3-9.

Middleton, David, editor. *A Garland for John Finlay*. Thibodaux, Louisiana: Blue Heron Press, 1990. Poems by 20 American and British poets; comments on Finlay's poetry by Janet Lewis and Donald E. Stanford; an essay on Finlay's prose by Lewis P. Simpson; and "John Finlay: A Bibliography (1971–1991)."

Middleton, David. Review of *The Salt of Exposure* by John Finlay. *The Classical Outlook* 68.3 (Spring 1991). 106, 108.

Middleton, David. "Blood and Mind: John Finlay (1941–1991)." *The Southern Review* 27.3 (Summer 1991). 723-26.

Middleton, David. "Preface" to *Mind and Blood: The Collected Poems of John Finlay*. Santa Barbara, California: John Daniel and Company, 1992. 15–18.

Middleton, David. "'The Deathless Word': John Finlay and the Triumph over Gnosticism." Afterword to *Hermetic Light: Essays on the Gnostic Spirit in Modern Literature and Thought*. Santa Barbara, California: John Daniel and Company, 1994. 141-57.

Middleton, David, editor. *In Light Apart: The Achievement of John Finlay*. Glenside, PA: The Aldine Press, 1999. Essays and poems by Finlay and by various hands and with a descriptive bibliography of works by and about Finlay.

Middleton, David. "John Finlay." Entry on Finlay in the *Encyclopedia of Alabama*, 2009. Online.

Middleton, David. "John: An Anglican Meditation on Literary Gifts and Giving." *The Anglican*. 41.3 Pentecost 2013. 36-40. The story of *A Garland for John Finlay*.

Middleton, David. "In Allen Hall: LSU, *The Southern Review*, and Baton Rouge." *The Southern Review*. 52.4, 2016. 645-49. Includes reminiscences of Finlay at LSU in the 1970s–80s.

Middleton, David. "The Break-In." *The Southern Review*. 52.4, 2016. 650–52. Poem on Finlay and a story about him from his years at LSU as a graduate student in the 1970s.

Oliver, Judy. "Alabama Poet Expresses Creative Vision, Originality." Review of *Mind and Blood: The Collected Poems of John Finlay. The Montgomery Advertiser* 13 December 1992. 6F.

Simpson, Lewis P. "The Dark Rooms of John Finlay." *The Southern Review* 27.3 (Summer 1991). 727-29. Also printed in *A Garland for John Finlay* and as "Foreword" to *Hermetic Light: Essays on the Gnostic Spirit in Modern Literature and Thought* by John Finlay.

Stanford, Donald E. "Dense Poems and Socratic Light." Review of *Mind and Blood: The Collected Poems of John Finlay*. *The Southern Review* 29.1 (Winter 1993). 186–91.

Stanford, Donald E. "The Poetry of John Finlay." *The Southern Review* 27.3 (Summer 1991). 730-32.

Stanford, Donald E. "The Poetry of David Middleton and John Finlay." *Hellas: A Journal of Poetry and the Humanities* 7.1 (1996). 10-11.

Stefanescu, Alina. "Lyrics and Life of Alabama Poet, John Finlay." September 19, 2012. Online.

Wildman, John Hazard. Review of *The Wide Porch and Other Poems* by John Finlay. *South Central Review* 1.4 (Winter 1984). 106-07.

Wilmer, Clive. Obituary for John Finlay. *PN Review* (Manchester, England) 17 (July/August 1994). 3-4.

Wilmer, Clive. "Darkness Visible." Review of *Mind and Blood: The Collected Poems of John Finlay*. *PN Review* 95 (January/February 1994). 60-61.

The John Finlay Papers

The works in this edition of Finlay's prose are to be found in The John Finlay Papers, Mss. 4415, Louisiana and Lower Mississippi Valley Collections, Hill Memorial Library, LSU Libraries, Baton Rouge, Louisiana 70803. Telephone: 1-225-578-6544. Anyone possessing poems, letters, or other writings by, about, or related to John Finlay, as well as photographs or recordings or other materials, is invited to consider placing them in The John Finlay Papers. A detailed catalogue of items already in The John Finlay Papers may be obtained from Archives at Louisiana State University.

These papers contain the diaries, essays, poems, published books and chapbooks (including copies with late authorial corrections), notes and drafts, book reviews both by and about Finlay, secondary criticism, miscellaneous items, Finlay family letters, and correspondence between John Finlay and a number of literary figures including Robert L. Barth, Edgar Bowers, Dick Davis, Andrew Lytle, David Middleton, Lindon Stall, Donald E. Stanford, Lewis P. Simpson, Clive Wilmer, Janet Lewis Winters, and others.

We are ready to assist any scholar who is interested in the life and works of John Finlay.

David Middleton,
Literary executor for John Finlay
Poet in Residence Emeritus
Nicholls State University
Thibodaux, Louisiana

davidmiddleton@charter.net
david.middleton@nicholls.edu

(985) 448–4456

John P. Doucet, Ph.D.
Dean, College of Sciences and Technology
Nicholls State University
Thibodaux, Louisiana

john.doucet@nicholls.edu

(985) 448–4385

A Recollection of John Finlay,
the Man and Storyteller by Cathy Edmonston[1]

David,

. . . I am finally able to sit down and send this fond memory of John. There are many but this one is one of my favorites.

Each morning a group of us, John, Faye, Tom Watson, and myself would gather together and have coffee in Faye's office. We sat around discussing all manner of things—the department, politics, classes, our families, etc. Most often there was much humor involved in these conversations.

On one occasion, I remember telling them something humorous my son had said about the Goodyear blimp that was flying around the campus the weekend of a nationally televised football game. John proceeded to tell us about an incident that involved his elderly aunt and uncle who lived in rural Alabama. He said it was nighttime and for some reason a blimp was flying over their area. It was lit up and flying low. John's uncle woke up, saw it, and said to his wife, "Wake up, momma, the Lord is here and you are not ready." We laughed until I thought we would cry. While the story was hilarious, John's delivery was priceless.

What a wonderful and special human being who was a friend to many of us and who is sorely missed. Whenever I think of him it always brings a smile to my face. So many of the dear people who made the English Department the unique place it was [are] gone, but they will always hold a very special place in my heart and memory.

—Cathy

DAVID MIDDLETON

Until his retirement in June of 2010, David Middleton served for thirty-three years as Professor of English, Poet-in-Residence, Distinguished Service Professor, Alcee Fortier Distinguished Professor, and Head of the Department of Languages and Literature at Nicholls State University in Thibodaux, Louisiana. He was made Professor Emeritus at Nicholls in January of 2011. In August of 2014, Middleton was named the first Poet in Residence Emeritus at Nicholls.

Middleton has served as John Finlay's literary executor since Finlay's death in 1991. Works by Finlay that Middleton has edited and seen into print as well as Middleton's own publications on Finlay are listed in the bibliography of this volume.

Middleton's books of verse include *The Burning Fields* (LSU Press, 1991), *As Far as Light Remains* (The Cummington Press [Harry Duncan], 1993), *Beyond the Chandeleurs* (LSU Press, 1999), *The Habitual Peacefulness of Gruchy: Poems After Pictures by Jean-François Millet* (LSU Press, 2005), *The Fiddler of Driskill Hill: Poems* (LSU Press, 2013), and *Outside the Gates of Eden* (Measure Press, 2020). Middleton has also published several chapbooks of verse including *The Language of the Heart,* (Louisiana Literature Press, 2003), which won an award from *The Advocate* (Baton Rouge) as the best book of verse by a Louisianian for 2003. In March of 2014, *The Fiddler of Driskill Hill* won Second Honorable Mention from the Louisiana Library Association as Best Book of the Year for 2013 by a Louisianian or about Louisiana.

In April of 2006 Middleton won The Allen Tate Award for best verse published in *The Sewanee Review* for 2005. In November of 2006 Middleton won the State of Louisiana Governor's Award for Outstanding Professional Artist for 2006.

Middleton's verse has appeared in *The Alabama Literary Review, The Anglican, The Anglican Theological Review, The Classical Outlook, Chronicles: A Magazine of American Culture, Critical Quarterly, Europe, The Formalist, Louisiana Literature, The Louisiana Review, The Lyric, Measure: A Review of Formal Poetry, Modern Age, The North American Anglican, POEM, The Sewanee Review, The Sewanee Theological Review, The South Carolina Review, The Southern Review, Xavier Review,* and elsewhere.

Middleton has served as poetry editor for *The Classical Outlook, The Anglican Theological Review, The Louisiana English Journal,* and *Modern Age.* Middleton also served as Advisory editor at *Measure: A Review of Formal Poetry.*

JOHN P. DOUCET

Then in his twenties, John Doucet became the youngest poetry contributor to *A Garland for John Finlay* (Blue Heron Press, 1990). Prior to that time, Doucet studied poetry under David Middleton as a undergraduate student at Nicholls State University. Doucet is now Distinguished Service Professor, Alcee Fortier Distinguished Professor, McIlhenny Professor of Human and Environmental Genetics, and Dean of the College of Science and Technology at Nicholls State.

Doucet's poetry has appeared in *Drastic Measures*, *The Epigrammatist*, and *Louisiana English Journal*, as well as other journals. He is author of the chapbooks, *A Local Habitation* and a *Name: Poems from the Lafourche Country* (Blue Heron Press, 1995) and the forthcoming *A Grumble of Pugs*. Since 2016, he has developed a series of lecture-readings from his portfolio of formalist poetry on scientific topics. The lectures, entitled "Motion of the Outer Rime," "A Night or Two in Neander," and "Lincoln's Thalamus and other Gray Matters," have been features of successive annual meetings of the Louisiana Academy of Sciences. A selection of these poems will appear later in 2020 in *Chronicles: A Magazine of American Culture.*

In the decade between 1993 and 2003, Doucet wrote and produced 13 plays immersed in Louisiana Cajun history and culture and enjoyed a four-year residency at the Oak Alley Outdoor Dinner Theater in Vacherie, Louisiana. His first play, *"Tant que Durera la Terre,"* which chronicled survival of his great-great grandfather's family during the Great Cheniere Hurricane of 1893, was awarded the Louisiana Native Voices and Visions Playwriting Award. He is past recipient of the Louisiana Division of the Arts Fellowship in Playwriting.

Doucet is also contributing editor of the history anthologies, *Lafourche Country II: The Heritage and Its Keepers* and *Lafourche Country III: Annals and Onwardness*, as well as senior editor of the *Proceedings of the Louisiana Academy of Sciences* and columnist for *Point of Vue* magazine (Houma, Louisiana).

Made in the USA
Columbia, SC
24 June 2020